Contemporary Challenges for Cyber Security and Data Privacy

Nuno Mateus-Coelho
Lusófona University, Portugal

Maria Manuela Cruz-Cunha
Polytechnic Institute of Cávado and Ave, Portugal

A volume in the Advances in Information Security,
Privacy, and Ethics (AISPE) Book Series

Published in the United States of America by
>   IGI Global
>   Information Science Reference (an imprint of IGI Global)
>   701 E. Chocolate Avenue
>   Hershey PA, USA 17033
>   Tel: 717-533-8845
>   Fax: 717-533-8661
>   E-mail: cust@igi-global.com
>   Web site: http://www.igi-global.com

Library of Congress Cataloging-in-Publication Data

Names: Mateus-Coelho, Nuno Ricardo, 1981- editor. | Cruz-Cunha, Maria
   Manuela, 1964- editor.
Title: Contemporary challenges for cyber security and data privacy / edited
   by Nuno Mateus-Coelho and Manuela Cruz-Cunha.
Description: Hershey, PA : Information Science Reference, [2023] | Includes
   bibliographical references and index. | Summary: "This book explores
   modern challenges for cyber security and information protection"--
   Provided by publisher.
Identifiers: LCCN 2023040145 (print) | LCCN 2023040146 (ebook) | ISBN
   9798369315286 (h/c) | ISBN 9798369315293 (ebook)
Subjects: LCSH: Computer security. | Data privacy. | Computer
   crimes--Prevention. | Computer networks--Security measures.
Classification: LCC QA76.9.A25 .C66779 2023 (print) | LCC QA76.9.A25
   (ebook) | DDC 005.8--dc23/eng/20231012
LC record available at https://lccn.loc.gov/2023040145
LC ebook record available at https://lccn.loc.gov/2023040146

This book is published in the IGI Global book series Advances in Information Security, Privacy, and Ethics (AISPE) (ISSN: 1948-9730; eISSN: 1948-9749)

British Cataloguing in Publication Data
A Cataloguing in Publication record for this book is available from the British Library.

All work contributed to this book is new, previously-unpublished material. The views expressed in this book are those of the authors, but not necessarily of the publisher.

For electronic access to this publication, please contact: eresources@igi-global.com.

Advances in Information Security, Privacy, and Ethics (AISPE) Book Series

Manish Gupta
State University of New York, USA

ISSN:1948-9730
EISSN:1948-9749

MISSION

As digital technologies become more pervasive in everyday life and the Internet is utilized in ever increasing ways by both private and public entities, concern over digital threats becomes more prevalent.

The **Advances in Information Security, Privacy, & Ethics (AISPE) Book Series** provides cutting-edge research on the protection and misuse of information and technology across various industries and settings. Comprised of scholarly research on topics such as identity management, cryptography, system security, authentication, and data protection, this book series is ideal for reference by IT professionals, academicians, and upper-level students.

COVERAGE

- Telecommunications Regulations
- Device Fingerprinting
- Data Storage of Minors
- IT Risk
- Security Classifications
- Network Security Services
- Cookies
- Technoethics
- Cyberethics
- Access Control

IGI Global is currently accepting manuscripts for publication within this series. To submit a proposal for a volume in this series, please contact our Acquisition Editors at Acquisitions@igi-global.com or visit: http://www.igi-global.com/publish/.

Titles in this Series

For a list of additional titles in this series, please visit:
http://www.igi-global.com/book-series/advances-information-security-privacy-ethics/37157

AI Tools for Protecting and Preventing Sophisticated Cyber Attacks
Eduard Babulak (National Science Foundation, USA)
Information Science Reference • © 2023 • 233pp • H/C (ISBN: 9781668471104) • US $250.00

Cyber Trafficking, Threat Behavior, and Malicious Activity Monitoring for Healthcare Organizations
Dinesh C. Dobhal (Graphic Era University (Deemed), India) Sachin Sharma (Graphic Era University (Deemed), India) Kamlesh C. Purohit (Graphic Era University (Deemed), India) Lata Nautiyal (University of Bristol, UK) and Karan Singh (Jawaharlal Nehru University, India)
Medical Information Science Reference • © 2023 • 206pp • H/C (ISBN: 9781668466469) • US $315.00

Emerging Perspectives in Systems Security Engineering, Data Science, and Artificial Intelligence
Maurice Dawson (Illinois Institute of Technology, USA)
Information Science Reference • © 2023 • 315pp • H/C (ISBN: 9781668463253) • US $250.00

Global Perspectives on the Applications of Computer Vision in Cybersecurity
Franklin Tchakounte (University of Ngaoundere, Cameroon) and Marcellin Atemkeng (University of Rhodes, South Africa)
Engineering Science Reference • © 2023 • 300pp • H/C (ISBN: 9781668481271) • US $250.00

Handbook of Research on Data Science and Cybersecurity Innovations in Industry 4.0 Technologies
Thangavel Murugan (United Arab Emirates University, Al Ain, UAE) and Nirmala E. (VIT Bhopal University, India)
Information Science Reference • © 2023 • 600pp • H/C (ISBN: 9781668481455) • US $325.00

Perspectives on Ethical Hacking and Penetration Testing
Keshav Kaushik (University of Petroleum and Energy Studies, India) and Akashdeep Bhardwaj (University of Petroleum and Energy Studies, India)
Information Science Reference • © 2023 • 300pp • H/C (ISBN: 9781668482186) • US $225.00

Malware Analysis and Intrusion Detection in Cyber-Physical Systems
S.L. Shiva Darshan (Department of Information and Communication Technology, Manipal Institute of Technology, India) M.V. Manoj Kumar (Department of Information Science and Engineering, Nitte Meenakshi Institute of Technology, India) B.S. Prashanth (Department of Information Science and Engineering, Nitte Meenakshi Institute of Technology, India) and Y. Vishnu Srinivasa Murthy (Department of Computational Intelligence, Vellore Institute of Technology, India)
Information Science Reference • © 2023 • 310pp • H/C (ISBN: 9781668486665) • US $225.00

701 East Chocolate Avenue, Hershey, PA 17033, USA
Tel: 717-533-8845 x100 • Fax: 717-533-8661
E-Mail: cust@igi-global.com • www.igi-global.com

Table of Contents

Preface.. xiv

Chapter 1
Cloud Computing: A Security and Defense Proposal... 1
    Michele Livio Perilli, University of Foggia, Italy
    Michelangelo De Bonis, University of Foggia, Italy
    Crescenzio Gallo, University of Foggia, Italy

Chapter 2
Sophisticated-Sinister-Stealth Attacks 17
    Akashdeep Bhardwaj, University of Petroleum and Energy Studies, India

Chapter 3
Risk Management in the Current Digital Reality of Organizations... 31
    Daniel Jorge Ferreira, University of Trás-os-Montes and Alto Douro, Portugal
    Henrique S. Mamede, INESC-TEC, University of Porto, Portugal
    Nuno Mateus-Coelho, COPELABS - Lusófona University, Portugal

Chapter 4
The Role of Blockchain Technology in Organizational Cyber Security.................................. 51
    Dauda Sule, Air Force Institute of Technology, Kaduna, Nigeria
    Jude Enenche Ameh, Sheffield Hallam University, UK
    Suleiman Abu Usman, Air Force Institute of Technology, Kaduna, Nigeria

Chapter 5
The Dilemmas of Criminal Liability Regarding Cybercrimes on Wireless Sensor Networks (WSNs) 70
    Joshua Ojo Nehinbe, Edo State University, Uzairue, Nigeria

Chapter 6

Hacking: Evolution, Conceptualization, and the Perpetrators 83

Carolina Roque, Faculty of Law, University of Porto, Portugal
Maria Canudo, Faculty of Law, University of Porto, Portugal
Samuel Moreira, Faculty of Law, University of Porto, Portugal & Faculty of Law, University
*   Lusíada, Portugal*
Inês Sousa Guedes, Faculty of Law, University of Porto, Portugal

Chapter 7
Methodologies Based on Hardware Performance Counters for Supporting Cybersecurity 108
Pablo Philipe Pessoa, Federal University of Pernambuco, Brazil
Aline do Monte, Federal University of Pernambuco, Brazil
Camila Dantas, Federal University of Pernambuco, Brazil
Paulo Maciel, Federal University of Pernambuco, Brazil

Chapter 8
How Can Cyberhate Victimization and Perpetration Be Understood? Towards a Psychological
Approach 130
Maria Vale, Psychology Research Centre (CIPsi), School of Psychology, University of
*   Minho, Braga, Portugal*
Marlene Matos, Psychology Research Centre (CIPsi), School of Psychology, University of
*   Minho, Braga, Portugal*

Chapter 9
A Black Hole Attack Protection Approach in IoT-Based Applications Using RLNC 151
Abidhusain Syed, VTU Belagavi Karnataka, India
Baswaraj Gadgay, VTU Kalburgi, India

Chapter 10
Exploratory Research of Cyber Security Dimensions: Selected Use Cases Analysis 166
Abhishek Vaish, Indian Institute of Information Technology, Prayagraj, India
Vatsala Upadhyay, Indian Institute of Information Technology, Prayagraj, India
Samo Bobek, Faculty of Economics and Business, University of Maribor, Slovenia
Simona Sternad Zabukovsek, Faculty of Economics and Business, University of Maribor,
*   Slovenia*

Chapter 11
Cyber Criminals and Data Privacy Measures 198
Karima Belmabrouk, Université des Sciences et de la Technologie d'Oran Mohamed
*   Boudiaf, Algeria*

Chapter 12
Privacy Protection Challenges in Statistical Disclosure Control 227
Poonam Samir Jadhav, Department of Computer Engineering, SIES Graduate School of
Technology, Nerul, India
Gautam M. Borkar, Department of Information Technology, Ramrao Adik Institute of
Technology, D Y Patil (Deemed) University, Nerul, India

Chapter 13
Ransomware-as-a-Weapon (RaaW): A Futuristic Approach for Understanding Malware as a
Social Weapon 247
Kuldeep Mohanty, KIIT University, India
Ghanshyam S. Bopche, National Institute of Technology, India
Sheryl Brahnam, Missouri State University, USA
Satya Ranjan Dash, KIIT University, India

Compilation of References 267

About the Contributors 302

Index 307

Detailed Table of Contents

Preface xiv

Chapter 1
Cloud Computing: A Security and Defense Proposal 1
Michele Livio Perilli, University of Foggia, Italy
Michelangelo De Bonis, University of Foggia, Italy
Crescenzio Gallo, University of Foggia, Italy

Cloud computing involves large numbers of computers connected through a network that can be physically located anywhere. Providers rely heavily on virtualization to deliver their cloud computing services. Cloud computing can reduce operational costs by using resources more efficiently. Starting with a look at cloud types, such as software as a service (SaaS), platform as a service (PaaS), infrastructure as a service (IaaS), and cloud models such as public clouds, private clouds, hybrid clouds, community clouds, difference between a data center and cloud computing with relative advantages are explained, and finally why most of companies are migrating to this kind of technology. In the second part of chapter, the focus is on the risks and security of cloud computing. These complex architectures are highly vulnerable; therefore, it is proposed artificial intelligence (AI) models to protect them. Many system protection techniques have been realized to defend cloud-computing systems, but many works are in progress. The authors analyze the state of art on this subject.

Chapter 2
Sophisticated-Sinister-Stealth Attacks 17
Akashdeep Bhardwaj, University of Petroleum and Energy Studies, India

APTs typically involve a series of carefully planned and coordinated steps, including reconnaissance, initial compromise, establishment of a foothold, and lateral movement to other systems. To carry out their objectives, APT actors may use various techniques, including social engineering, spear-phishing, and exploitation of software vulnerabilities. APTs are often launched by nation-state actors or well-funded criminal organizations, who have the resources and expertise to carry out complex attacks. Detecting and responding to APTs requires a multi-layered approach that includes robust cybersecurity measures, such as network segmentation, intrusion detection and prevention systems, and endpoint protection. Additionally, organizations must have a strong incident response plan in place to quickly identify and contain APT attacks before they cause significant damage. These aspects are discussed in detail in this chapter.

Chapter 3

Risk Management in the Current Digital Reality of Organizations...31

    Daniel Jorge Ferreira, University of Trás-os-Montes and Alto Douro, Portugal

    Henrique S. Mamede, INESC-TEC, University of Porto, Portugal

    Nuno Mateus-Coelho, COPELABS - Lusófona University, Portugal

The global overview of the challenges faced in trying to minimise the risks of organisations in the face of cyber-attacks is arduous for any organisation. Defining an appropriate risk management model that proactively minimises cybersecurity incidents is a critical challenge. Many malicious attacks occur daily, and there is only sometimes an adequate response. There is a significant investment in research to identify the main factors that may cause such incidents, always trying to have the most appropriate response and, consequently, potentiating the response capacity and success. At the same time, several different methodologies evaluate risk management and the maturity level of organisations. Due to the lack of predictive models based on data (evidence), there is a significant investment in research to identify the main factors that may cause such incidents, starting to design models based on AI - Artificial Intelligence. This research will go in the direction of developing a user-friendly model supporting the assessment of the methodological aspects of an organisation.

Chapter 4

The Role of Blockchain Technology in Organizational Cyber Security..51

    Dauda Sule, Air Force Institute of Technology, Kaduna, Nigeria

    Jude Enenche Ameh, Sheffield Hallam University, UK

    Suleiman Abu Usman, Air Force Institute of Technology, Kaduna, Nigeria

Distributed ledger technology (DLT), decentralized finance (DeFi), blockchain – these are terms that have been trending especially in technology circles. Today, blockchain has gained more acceptance, but sceptics continue to raise concerns about the technology's scalability, security, and long-term viability. There are also concerns regarding its being associated with crime and the dark web, which might imply it will have negative consequences if adopted. It has its own peculiar cyber security loopholes, but these can be addressed. That notwithstanding, organizations stand to gain from the blockchain in terms of cyber security; especially its qualities of decentralization and immutability. It has been successfully implemented in some sectors with positive results. This chapter seeks to illustrate how the blockchain can be used to boost and optimize cyber security for organizations.

Chapter 5

The Dilemmas of Criminal Liability Regarding Cybercrimes on Wireless Sensor Networks (WSNs)70

    Joshua Ojo Nehinbe, Edo State University, Uzairue, Nigeria

New studies have revealed serious dilemmas that can confront investigators in the arrest and investigations of suspects of complex cybercrimes on wireless sensor networks (WSNs) and whenever they must subsequently institute criminal liability against agents of the crime. Accordingly, some investigators continue to face challenges to criminalize proven suspects and allocate compensations for negligence to lawless complainants. This chapter used mixed methods and different datasets to critically examine and explain the above issues. Datasets that were qualitatively and quantitatively analyzed with Snort IDS suggest that criminal liabilities on WSNs may be settled with concurrent negligence in the ratio of 0.27, comparative negligence in the ratio of 0.32; contributory negligence in the ratio of 0.18 and vicarious negligence in the ratio of 0.23. Similarly, employer may be criminalized for cybercrimes committed by his employee, employee can be criminalized for cybercrimes committed by his employer, and employer with his employee can be criminalized jointly for their negligence to stop cybercrimes on WSNs.

Chapter 6

Hacking: Evolution, Conceptualization, and the Perpetrators 83

Carolina Roque, Faculty of Law, University of Porto, Portugal
Maria Canudo, Faculty of Law, University of Porto, Portugal
Samuel Moreira, Faculty of Law, University of Porto, Portugal & Faculty of Law, University Lusíada, Portugal
Inês Sousa Guedes, Faculty of Law, University of Porto, Portugal

This chapter aims to present a theoretical foundation on hacking, focusing on the perpetrator's profile, his modus operandi, and typologies. First, a conceptualization and characterization of the phenomenon's key terms is presented. Next, the chapter addresses the historical evolution of the perception of the phenomenon, from the moment of its emergence to the current understanding. The most prominent typologies in the scientific literature will be described, which seek to distinguish the perpetrators of the behaviors according to criteria related to their practice. While focusing on the cybercriminals, the chapter emphasizes the hacker's figure, directing the review on their sociodemographic profile and contextual aspects. Finally, the personality factors prevalent in hackers are characterized, namely according to the big five model and the dark triad model. This chapter, using criminological lens, will increase the knowledge of the hackers and its modus operandi. The implications of this knowledge will be outlined.

Chapter 7

Methodologies Based on Hardware Performance Counters for Supporting Cybersecurity 108

Pablo Philipe Pessoa, Federal University of Pernambuco, Brazil
Aline do Monte, Federal University of Pernambuco, Brazil
Camila Dantas, Federal University of Pernambuco, Brazil
Paulo Maciel, Federal University of Pernambuco, Brazil

Cybersecurity is a critical area of information technology, where prevention, detection, and mitigation of cyberattacks are crucial to ensure system and data integrity. This chapter presents several methods and strategies that adopt hardware performance counters (HPCs) as the paramount protection utility, with the aid of analysis and advanced techniques from several areas of statistics and computing, to support cybersecurity. Furthermore, the chapter discusses the need for broader approaches, including preventive and protective measures, regular penetration testing, user awareness, implementation of robust security policies, and advanced threat detection techniques. While traditional security tools such as implementing IDSs, IPSs, firewalls, antivirus, and other solutions are critical, they must be complemented with more comprehensive approaches to deal with the increasing sophistication of cyberattacks, and HPCs provide this support with efficiency.

Chapter 8
How Can Cyberhate Victimization and Perpetration Be Understood? Towards a Psychological
Approach 130
  *Maria Vale, Psychology Research Centre (CIPsi), School of Psychology, University of
      Minho, Braga, Portugal*
  *Marlene Matos, Psychology Research Centre (CIPsi), School of Psychology, University of
      Minho, Braga, Portugal*

The freedom of expression enabled through information and communication technologies (ICT) has been misused to create, (re)produce, and distribute cyberhate. Otherwise known as online hate speech, it refers to all forms of ICT-mediated expression that incites, justifies, or propagates hatred or violence against specific individuals or groups based on their gender, race, ethnicity, religion, sexual orientation, or other collective characteristics. This chapter aims to contribute to a comprehensive analysis of cyberhate among adolescents and adults. It is structured into three main sections. The first operationalizes the key conceptual characteristics, disentangles the similarities and differences between cyberhate and other forms of violence, and presents the known prevalence of victimization and perpetration. The second identifies the main sociodemographic correlates and discriminates the risk and protective factors with theoretical frameworks. The chapter concludes with recommendations for prevention and intervention strategies that demand a multi-stakeholder approach.

Chapter 9
A Black Hole Attack Protection Approach in IoT-Based Applications Using RLNC 151
  Abidhusain Syed, VTU Belagavi Karnataka, India
  Baswaraj Gadgay, VTU Kalburgi, India

Smart environments have recently transformed the standard of human existence by increasing comfort and efficiency. IoT, or the internet of things, has become an instrument for developing intelligent environments. But because of security vulnerabilities in IoT-based systems, applications for smart environments are in danger. Harmful items have a significant effect on cyber defence mechanisms. In order to stop security attacks against IoT that exploit some of these security vulnerabilities, IoT-specific intrusion detection systems (IDSs) are crucial. Due to the limited computing and storage capacities of IoT devices and the specific protocols used, it's conceivable that conventional IDSs are not an option for IoT environments.

Chapter 10
Exploratory Research of Cyber Security Dimensions: Selected Use Cases Analysis 166
  Abhishek Vaish, Indian Institute of Information Technology, Prayagraj, India
  Vatsala Upadhyay, Indian Institute of Information Technology, Prayagraj, India
  Samo Bobek, Faculty of Economics and Business, University of Maribor, Slovenia
  *Simona Sternad Zabukovsek, Faculty of Economics and Business, University of Maribor,
      Slovenia*

Cybersecurity research is gaining a lot of importance in recent times. Bibliometric analysis of cyber security research showed major areas and their overlapping. Due to overlapping research areas with allied areas like system engineering, networking, computer science, information technology, management science, etc., the impact of cyber security research is often hard to gauge. This chapter aims to present the research dimension of cyber security as a number of use cases and an attempt to connect the researcher to understand research areas of cyber security and its complexities through use cases to make them visualize the problem better. In this chapter, the following use cases are presented and analyzed: the role of social media in cyber security issues, how traditional network-based attacks influence the IoT environment, the dynamics of malware and its impact on AI-based detection systems, and security in embedded systems.

Chapter 11

Cyber Criminals and Data Privacy Measures 198

    Karima Belmabrouk, Université des Sciences et de la Technologie d'Oran Mohamed
        Boudiaf, Algeria

Cyber criminals pose a significant threat to data privacy, seeking to exploit weaknesses in digital security systems to gain access to sensitive information. Data privacy measures, such as antivirus software, firewalls, and employee training, are implemented to protect against unauthorized access and theft of personal and sensitive data. However, cyber criminals continue to find ways to circumvent these measures, leading to an ongoing arms race in the world of cybersecurity. To stay ahead of evolving threats, ongoing investments in research and development, as well as partnerships between government agencies, private sector organizations, and cybersecurity experts, are crucial in strengthening data privacy measures and protecting against cyber criminals.

Chapter 12

Privacy Protection Challenges in Statistical Disclosure Control 227

    Poonam Samir Jadhav, Department of Computer Engineering, SIES Graduate School of
        Technology, Nerul, India
    Gautam M. Borkar, Department of Information Technology, Ramrao Adik Institute of
        Technology, D Y Patil (Deemed) University, Nerul, India

Due to privacy and confidentiality issues, a significant portion of the data collected by statistics agencies cannot be directly published. These issues span the legal and ethical spectrums. Statistical disclosure control (SDC) is an important tool to protect the privacy of individuals when releasing sensitive data for statistical analysis. However, there are several challenges that need to be addressed to ensure effective privacy preservation while also allowing for accurate statistical analysis. This chapter discusses the challenges faced by SDC in preserving privacy from a privacy preservation perspective. The challenges include the trade-off between privacy and data quality, increasing complexity of data, new data collection methods, and legal and ethical considerations. The rise of machine learning and artificial intelligence presents additional challenges. The chapter emphasizes the need for ongoing research and collaboration between statisticians, computer scientists, and policymakers to develop effective SDC techniques that balance privacy and data utility.

Chapter 13

Ransomware-as-a-Weapon (RaaW): A Futuristic Approach for Understanding Malware as a
Social Weapon 247

    Kuldeep Mohanty, KIIT University, India
    Ghanshyam S. Bopche, National Institute of Technology, India
    Sheryl Brahnam, Missouri State University, USA
    Satya Ranjan Dash, KIIT University, India

The use of information technology has widened in the past few years. With the evolving IT industries and infrastructure comes an ocean of development and opportunities and a series of new cyber threats. Ransomware is an inevitable threat that brings inconceivable devastation that one could hardly imagine.

Essentially, ransomware is not a new threat. But it is evolving into a new and massive cyber threat that not only extorts money and sells user data into the darknet but has also started targeting users, forcing them to contribute to any existing social problems, for instance, poverty. Ransomware has mapped its journey from a weaker failure model to a highly evolving business model called ransomware-as-a-service (RaaS) model. This chapter discusses ransomware from its origin to an evolved cybercriminal business model. It also reveals all those hidden and unexplored consequences and threats that ransomware can bring with it, focusing on future technologies. Apart from looking into the future, the implications of ransomware as a weapon for social problems have been well discussed.

Compilation of References 267

About the Contributors 302

Index 307

Preface

In an age characterized by relentless technological advancement, our world has become intricately intertwined with the digital realm, offering unprecedented convenience, connectivity, and innovation. Yet, this rapid evolution has brought forth an equally rapid proliferation of cyber threats and security challenges that permeate every facet of our lives. The fabric of our societies, economies, and personal interactions has been woven together with intricate digital threads, making the preservation of cyber security and data privacy paramount to our collective well-being.

This book, *Contemporary Challenges for Cyber Security and Data Privacy*, embarks on a profound exploration of the intricate tapestry of cyber security and data privacy challenges in the modern landscape. In collaboration with a distinguished group of contributors, we delve into the multifaceted dimensions of these challenges, dissecting their complexities and offering insights that are essential for organizations, professionals, and individuals to navigate this intricate domain.

The digital ecosystem we inhabit is marked by unprecedented interconnectedness, driven by technologies that have transcended the confines of traditional boundaries. In Chapter 1, "Risk Management in the Current Digital Reality of Organizations," authored by Daniel Ferreira, Henrique Mamede, and Nuno Mateus-Coelho, we confront the formidable task of managing risks in a world where cyber-attacks loom as constant threats. This chapter underscores the urgency of adopting proactive risk management models that can shield organizations from the ever-evolving cyber threat landscape.

The pervasive influence of Cloud Computing takes center stage in Chapter 2, "Cloud Computing: A Security and Defense Proposal," as Michele Perilli, Michelangelo De Bonis, and Crescenzio Gallo navigate the nuances of this transformative technology. This chapter provides a comprehensive analysis of cloud models, types, and their security implications, advocating for the integration of Artificial Intelligence as a safeguard against vulnerabilities.

In Chapter 3, "Sophisticated-Sinister-Stealth Attacks," authored by Akashdeep Bhardwaj, we delve into the realm of Advanced Persistent Threats (APTs), exposing their intricate orchestration and the multi-layered defense mechanisms required to thwart them. This chapter offers a detailed understanding of the techniques employed by nation-state actors and well-funded organizations, underscoring the importance of a robust response strategy.

The transformative potential of Blockchain Technology is laid bare in Chapter 4, "The Role of Blockchain Technology in Organizational Cyber Security," authored by Dauda Sule, Jude Ameh, and Suleiman Usman. In this chapter, we embark on a journey to explore the revolutionary impact of blockchain in fortifying cyber security and data integrity, while addressing concerns and heralding its potential for organizational enhancement.

Moving from technology to legal and ethical dimensions, Chapter 5, "The Dilemmas of Criminal Liability on Cybercrimes on Wireless Sensor Networks (WSNs)," authored by Joshua Nehinbe, navigates the complex terrain of criminal liabilities in cybercrimes. This chapter confronts the intricate legal conundrums presented by cybercrimes on wireless sensor networks, shedding light on the nuances of attributing liability in these scenarios.

In Chapter 6, "Hacking: Evolution, Conceptualization, and the Perpetrators," co-authored by Carolina Roque, Maria Canudo, Samuel Moreira, and Inês Guedes, we traverse the evolution of hacking from its historical roots to its present manifestations. This chapter delves into the psychology of hackers, revealing their sociodemographic profiles and personality traits, offering a criminological lens into this complex world.

Chapter 7, "Methodologies Based on Hardware Performance Counters for Supporting Cybersecurity," authored by Pablo Pessoa, Aline do Monte, Camila Dantas, and Paulo Maciel, introduces an innovative approach to cyber security. This chapter advocates for the integration of hardware performance counters in bolstering cyber defenses, highlighting the indispensability of a multi-faceted approach.

The psychological underpinnings of cyberhate are scrutinized in Chapter 8, "How Can Cyberhate Victimization and Perpetration Be Understood? Towards a Psychological Approach," authored by Maria Vale and Marlene Matos. This chapter delves into the complexities of cyberhate, shedding light on its prevalence, risk factors, and implications, while offering insights into potential prevention and intervention strategies.

Continuing the exploration of technology's impact, Chapter 9, "A Black Hole Attack Protection Approach in IoT-Based Applications Using RLNC," co-authored by Abidhusain Syed and Baswaraj Gadgay, navigates the intricacies of safeguarding Internet of Things (IoT) applications from cyber threats. This chapter delves into the vulnerabilities of smart environments, offering innovative approaches to protect these systems.

In Chapter 10, "Exploratory Research of Cyber Security Dimensions: Selected Use Cases Analysis," Abhishek Vaish, Vatsala Upadhyay, Samo Bobek, and Simona Sternad Zabukovsek bridge the gap between research and practice in cyber security. By dissecting select use cases, this chapter unveils the intricate dimensions of cyber security, providing a deeper understanding of the evolving landscape.

Karima Belmabrouk takes us into the realm of cyber criminals and data privacy measures in Chapter 11, "Cyber Criminals and Data Privacy Measures." This chapter scrutinizes the evolving landscape of cyber criminality, emphasizing the importance of continually innovating data privacy measures to counter malicious intent.

In Chapter 12, "Privacy Protection Challenges in Statistical Disclosure Control," co-authored by Poonam Jadhav and Gautam Borkar, we embark on a journey into the challenges of preserving data privacy in statistics. This chapter unveils the complexities of preserving data privacy in statistical analysis, and underscores the importance of holistic approaches.

Finally, Chapter 13, "Ransomware-as-a-Weapon (RaaW): A Futuristic Approach for Understanding Malwares as a Social Weapon," authored by Kuldeep Mohanty, Ghanshyam Bopche, Sheryl Brahnam, and Satya Dash, sheds light on the ominous potential of ransomware. The chapter delves into the potential societal consequences of ransomware attacks, offering a futuristic perspective on their disruptive implications.

The chapters within this book collectively form an intricate mosaic that paints a vivid picture of the contemporary challenges that cyber security and data privacy pose in our digitally interconnected world. The insights presented here aim to empower readers with the knowledge and tools to navigate this dynamic landscape, to fortify defenses against emerging threats, and to ensure a safer and more secure digital future. As we delve into the rich tapestry of this book, may we gain a deeper understanding of the challenges at hand and forge a path towards resilience in the face of a rapidly evolving digital frontier.

Nuno Mateus-Coelho
COPELABS - Lusófona University, Portugal

Maria Manuela Cruz-Cunha
Polytechnic Institute of Cávado and Ave, Portugal

Chapter 1
Cloud Computing:
A Security and Defense Proposal

Michele Livio Perilli
University of Foggia, Italy

Michelangelo De Bonis
University of Foggia, Italy

Crescenzio Gallo
ⓘD https://orcid.org/0000-0002-3929-462X
University of Foggia, Italy

ABSTRACT

Cloud computing involves large numbers of computers connected through a network that can be physically located anywhere. Providers rely heavily on virtualization to deliver their cloud computing services. Cloud computing can reduce operational costs by using resources more efficiently. Starting with a look at cloud types, such as software as a service (SaaS), platform as a service (PaaS), infrastructure as a service (IaaS), and cloud models such as public clouds, private clouds, hybrid clouds, community clouds, difference between a data center and cloud computing with relative advantages are explained, and finally why most of companies are migrating to this kind of technology. In the second part of chapter, the focus is on the risks and security of cloud computing. These complex architectures are highly vulnerable; therefore, it is proposed artificial intelligence (AI) models to protect them. Many system protection techniques have been realized to defend cloud-computing systems, but many works are in progress. The authors analyze the state of art on this subject.

INTRODUCTION

The terms data center and cloud computing are often used incorrectly. Data Center is typically a data storage and processing facility run by an in-house IT department or leased offsite. From a business perspective, the data center is the pivot on which business processes, communications and services depend, both towards internal users and towards customers, suppliers, partners, etc. Today there is no type of

DOI: 10.4018/979-8-3693-1528-6.ch001

business that has not supported the management of its assets and resources on a Data Center, the beating heart of digital transformation and, more generally, of the digital economy.

Otherwise, Cloud Computing is an off-premise service that offers on-demand access to a shared pool of configurable computing resources. These resources can be rapidly provisioned and released with minimal management effort. Data centers are the physical facilities that provide the compute, network, and storage needs of cloud computing services. Cloud service providers use data centers to host their cloud services and cloud-based resources.

Data centers consist of buildings that contain infrastructures, systems, resources and technological assets that users access to storage data, to use applications and digital services. A data center can occupy one room of a building, one or more floors, or an entire building. Data centers are typically very expensive to build and maintain. For this reason, only large organizations use privately built data centers to house their data and provide services to users. Smaller organizations, that cannot afford to maintain their own private data center, can reduce the overall cost of ownership by leasing server and storage services from a larger data center organization in the cloud.

When we begin to implement analysis of a cloud-computing system, a series of problems arise to be addressed, such as:

- Organizational data accessing anywhere and anytime.
- Ease of subscribing only to the chosen services.
- Minimize the need for onsite IT equipment, maintenance, and management.
- Equipment, energy, physical reducing costs.
- Personnel training needs reducing.
- System resources quickly adapting to increasing data volume required.

Cloud Computing is today heavily applied in every field. About ten years ago one of the first application was in e-learning. In 2013 some researchers proposed an Architecture for Programming Education Environment as a Cloud Computing Service (Elamir *et al.*, 2013). A study found that cloud-computing adoption is well accepted in information technology sector (Hassan *et al.*, 2022).

In the first part this chapter shows different types of cloud-computing services: Software as a Service (SaaS), Platform as a Service (PaaS) and Infrastructure as a Service (IaaS). Subsequently, there is a description of cloud models such as Public Clouds, Private Clouds, Hybrid Clouds, Community Clouds. Then it deals with virtualization concept, difference between virtualization and dedicated server, the different architectures with Hypervisor layer (Cisco Networking Academy, 2020).

In second part this chapter shows the state of art on cyber security aspect in cloud-computing. We explain how Artificial Intelligence can help traditional security tecniques to improve and ensure data privacy in cloud systems.

SOFTWARE AS A SERVICE (SaaS)

In this service type the applications are on provider systems and are disposal to user profile. User logins on platform and uses applications configured in his profile. Applications are in cloud and user doesn't need to manage them. User's only concern is entering data for his application. Applications provided can be word processing, data base, email and so on. Here are some common characteristics of SaaS services:

- Multi-tenancy cloud architecture, so all users and applications share a common, centrally managed infrastructure.
- Easy access via any connected device, which simplifies access to data and information and keeps data in sync.
- Web-based interfaces, which are built on the same web that users already navigate and know on a daily basis (this can help increase adoption and usage rates).
- Collaborative and social features, which allow people in different geographical locations or teams to collaborate effectively.

The future of SaaS and cloud computing is likely to see increased adoption of specialist services, greater end-to-end integration, an increasing emphasis on relationships between customers and key suppliers, and even more sophisticated, data-backed intelligence. Software as a Service (SaaS) is increasingly used by firms for sourcing business application software. SaaS can enable a cost reduction and quality improvement of existing operations and provide rapid and low-cost innovation (Loukis *et al.*, 2019). Reducing the operation cost of cloud service providers while maintaining service efficiency has become an important topic. Some proposals we have in literature to suggest a resource provision strategy for SaaS in cloud computing (Liao *et al.*, 2017).

PLATFORM AS A SERVICE (PaaS)

This service is dedicated to software development, it's a specialized service in which cloud provider is responsible for providing users access to the development tools and services used to deliver the applications. These users are generally programmers and may have control over configuration setting. PaaS simplifies work for developers by enabling them to create and deploy their code on optimized environments. This service offers many advantages such as:

- Saving time in getting the cloud solutions you need quickly and easily.
- Choosing your application or software and distributing the user licences.
- Adding development capabilities without adding staff.
- More easily developing for multiple platforms, including mobile.
- Efficiently managing the application lifecycle. PaaS provides all of the capabilities to support the complete web application lifecycle: building, testing, deploying, managing, and updating within the same integrated environment.

Among implementation fields can be mentioned services about Security, data encryption software for transactions or to store company's passwords, CRM (Customer Relationship Management) to manage customer data, BPM (Business Process Management) to manage business processes. It can be used to centralize data and get a simplified overview.

INFRASTRUCTURE AS A SERVICE (IaaS)

The cloud provider is responsible for giving IT managers access to the network equipment, virtualized network services, and supporting network infrastructure. This cloud service allows IT managers to deploy and run software code, which can include operating systems and applications. IaaS represents scalability for complex projects, is a simple way for organizations to get additional resources that meet their needs.

This cloud service certainly provides scalability, it can rapidly increase system efficiency that is undergoing critical workload spikes; customization, the user can create a virtual infrastructure that adapts to his needs; cost saving, maintaining your own physical infrastructure and outsourcing this type of resource to a cloud service provider, the user can get the same services at a lower cost.

It is possible to list some examples of common services such as:

- Hosting services, complex website application developments, this model is suitable for a resource-intensive set of IT services (often is called ITaas, Information Technology as a service).
- Building a model for storing and recovering your data (backups) in the event of an incident. A disaster recovery plan (DRP) is an essential element for ensuring both business continuity and high availability for web applications.
- Developing artificial intelligence (AI). This technology uses a lot of resources (CPU, RAM, storage space, bandwidth) because it involves storing and analyzing high volumes of data (big data), as well as training machine learning algorithms.

PUBLIC CLOUD

Applications and services offered in a public cloud are made available to the general population (Cisco Networking Academy, 2020). IT infrastructure is shared with the other customers of the cloud service (home users or businesses). It is usually located off premises, not locally, within the data centers hosted by the cloud service provider (it can also be made available in the company's data centers). Services and applications are always part of an IT environment external to the service provider. Cloud services are usually offered with different subscriptions, plans or complete packages. Despite stringent security precautions and extremely secure data centers, the multi-user approach can pose too great a security risk for sensitive corporate data, where stringent regulations have to be met.

Advantages of this model are:

- Operational costs saving, thanks to outsourcing to the service provider and easy access to the cloud environment.
- Public cloud services reduce the effort required to administer servers and meet compliance and security standards.
- High security standards make things easier for small and medium-sized businesses with limited resources to devote to cybersecurity.
- Cloud software and applications are always updated and can be expanded or scaled as needed.

While disadvantages of this model are:

- Multi-user approach can mean an unacceptable security risk for enterprises with high security and compliance standards.
- The use of cloud services from external providers can lead to dependency on the provider's IT environment.
- Cloud infrastructure is not always located in the customer's country, which can lead to security gaps regarding data sovereignty in the case of different data legislation (e.g. between Europe and the USA).

PRIVATE CLOUD

Private Cloud consists of computing services and IT environments not made available to multiple users but hosted internally by the company in the form of an intranet or data center (Cisco Networking Academy, 2020). The cloud environment remains a prerogative of a single organization. A private cloud can be set up using the organization's private network, though this can be expensive to build and maintain. It can also be managed by an outside organization with strict access security. The services and applications always remain within the private network and are not included in networks shared with third parties. Cloud services and cloud computing can be tailored exactly to the needs of a company. Private Cloud offers increased security measures, especially for critical business processes or sensitive administrative operations. An analysis of the advantages and disadvantages is given below.

Advantages:

- The highest security standards thanks to an exclusive cloud infrastructure owned by the company.
- Possible both on premises, with your own IT resources, and off premises, with virtualized IT resources guaranteed through managed cloud hosting.
- Flexible and fast access to the company's internal IT environment for selected user groups.
- Tailor-made cloud services that can be expanded and adjusted according to organization needs.

Disadvantages:

- High investments for exclusive cloud services, IT resources, hardware and software licenses.
- Less flexibility when compared to public clouds.
- A private cloud and on premises without virtualization requires IT skills and more effort for administration and maintenance.
- Under certain circumstances, cloud servers on premises with poor IT security are more dangerous than servers secured by cloud service providers.

HYBRID CLOUD

A hybrid cloud is made up of two or more clouds (example: part private, part public), where each part remains a separate object, but both are connected using a single architecture (Cisco Networking Academy,

2020). In hybrid cloud companies have the ability to share services and applications between public and private clouds. Considering the high performance of public clouds, this system allows you to combine the high security of a private cloud with the performance of public clouds. Costs can also be adapted to needs thanks to the flexible distribution of workloads.

COMMUNITY CLOUD

The differences between public clouds and community clouds are the functional needs that have been customized for the community. In community cloud the infrastructure is provided for the exclusive use of a specific community by organizations that share concerns (Cisco Networking Academy, 2020). It could be owned, managed by one or more organizations in the community, or a third party, or some combination thereof. For example, healthcare organizations which must remain compliant with policies and laws that require special authentication and confidentiality, generally adopt a community cloud.

VIRTUALIZATION

Cloud computing and virtualization are often used interchangeably, but mean different things. Virtualization is the foundation of cloud computing. Without it, cloud computing would not be possible. Virtualization separates the operating system (OS) from the hardware. Various providers offer virtual cloud services that can dynamically provision servers as required. Virtualization is the technology that provides the opportunity to create virtual servers, storage, networks, and other physical machines. Virtual software mimics the functions of physical hardware to run multiple virtual machines simultaneously on a single physical machine. Companies use virtualization to use their hardware resources efficiently and get greater returns from their investment. It also powers cloud computing services that help organizations manage infrastructure more efficiently.

To fully understand meaning of virtualization, it is first necessary to know some of the history of server technology. Until a few years ago, enterprise servers consisted of a server OS only, such as Windows Server or Linux Server, installed on specific hardware. All of a server's RAM, processing power, and hard drive space were dedicated to the service provided (e.g., Web, email services, etc.). The first advantage of virtualization is efficient resource use. It improves hardware resources used in data center. For example, instead of running one server on one computer system, you can create a virtual server pool on the same computer system by using and returning servers to the pool as required. Another advantage results the automated IT management, indeed you can manage physical computers by using software tools. Administrators create deployment and configuration programs to define virtual machine templates. You can duplicate your infrastructure repeatedly and consistently and avoid error-prone manual configurations. Furthermore, an important support you have in disaster recovery. In a traditional environment, without virtualization, a cyberattack can negatively affect business operations, regaining access to IT infrastructure and replacing or fixing a physical server can take hours or even days. On contrary the process takes minutes with virtualized environments. This prompt response significantly improves resiliency and facilitates business continuity so that operations can continue as scheduled.

Now it is shown how virtualization architecture replaces traditional server architectures such as Web Server, E-mail Server, SQL Server, File Server, Radius Server, DHCP Server and so on. Virtualization uses specialized software, called "hypervisor", to create several cloud instances or virtual machines on one physical computer.

The hypervisor is a program, firmware or hardware, that adds an abstraction layer on top of the physical hardware. The abstraction layer is used to create virtual machines which have access to all the hardware of the physical machine such as CPUs, memory, disk controllers, and NICs. Each of these virtual machines runs a complete and separate operating system (see Figure 1).

Figure 1. Server one and server two

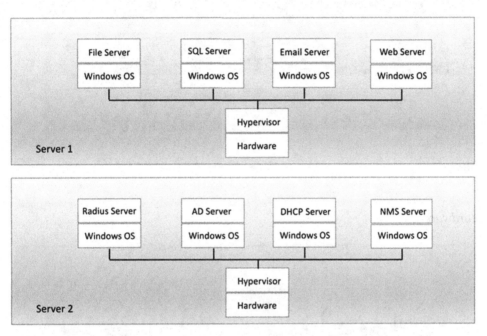

We have two main types of Hypervisor: type 1 and type 2. In the first type, called "bare-metal hypervisor", it runs directly on the computer hardware. It has some operating system capabilities and is highly efficient because it interacts directly with the physical resources (see Figure 2). In type 2, hypervisor runs as an application on computer hardware with an existing operating system. This type of hypervisor is implemented when running multiple operating systems on a single machine (see Figure 3). Type 2 hypervisors are also called hosted hypervisors. This is because the hypervisor is installed on top of the existing OS, such as macOS, Windows, or Linux.

NETWORK VIRTUALIZATION

Computer network elements such as switches, routers, and firewalls can be virtualized. An organization with offices in multiple geographic locations can have several different network technologies working together to create its enterprise network. Network virtualization is a process that combines all of these network resources to centralize administrative tasks. Administrators can adjust and control these elements virtually without touching the physical components, which greatly simplifies network management.

Figure 2. Hardware

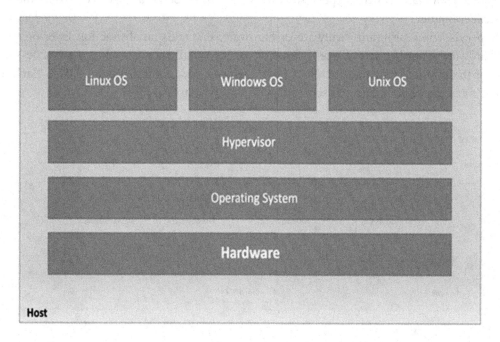

Figure 3. Hardware

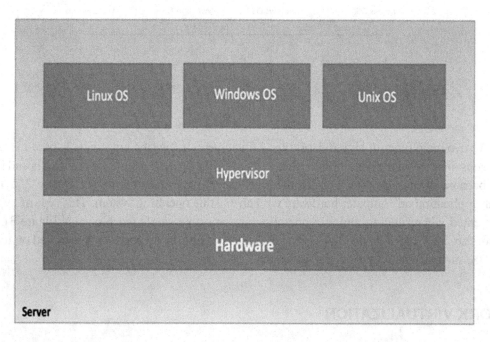

We mention two different approaches: Network Function Virtualization (NFV) and Software Defined Network (SDN). NFV is a way to reduce cost and accelerate service deployment for network operators by decoupling functions like a firewall or encryption from dedicated hardware and moving them to virtual servers. Instead of installing expensive proprietary hardware, service providers can purchase inexpensive switches, storage and servers to run virtual machines that perform network functions. This collapses multiple functions into a single physical server, reducing costs and minimizing truck rolls. We now focalize our attention on SDN. It controls traffic routing by taking over routing management from data routing in the physical environment.

A typical SDN architecture (see Figure 4) consists of three elements:

- Application layer, which communicates requests for resources or information about the network.
- Control Plane, which uses information from applications to decide how to route a data packet.
- Data Plane, which gets information from Control Plane about where to move data.

Figure 4. Cloud orchestration

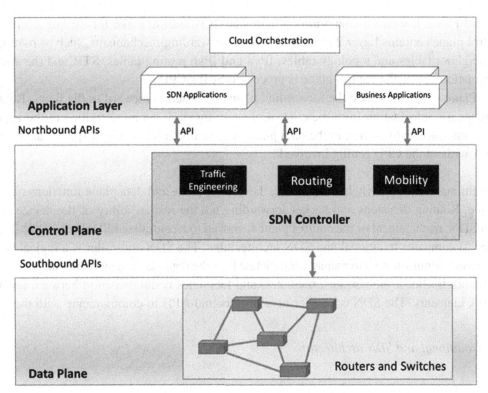

These three elements can be located in different physical locations.
SDN offers multiple benefits over traditional networking, such as:

- **Greater control with greater speed and flexibility:** Instead of manually programming multiple vendor-specific hardware devices, developers can control traffic flow on the network simply by programming a controller based on standard software. Network administrators also have more flexibility in choosing networking equipment, as they can choose an open source protocol to communicate with any number of hardware devices through a central controller.

- **Customizable Network Infrastructure:** Administrators can configure network services and allocate virtual resources to change network infrastructure in real time through a centralized location. Network administrators can thus optimize data flow on the network, prioritizing those that require greater availability.
- **Trusted security:** A software-defined network provides visibility into the entire network, for a more holistic view of security threats. With proliferation of smart devices connecting to the Internet, SDN offers clear advantages over traditional networking. Developers can create separate zones for devices that require different levels of security, or immediately quarantine corrupted devices so they don't infect the rest of network.

A network device contains the following planes:

- Control Plane, it works as the brains of a device. It is used to make forwarding decisions. The control plane contains Layer 2 and Layer 3 route forwarding mechanisms, such as routing protocol neighbor tables and topology tables, IPv4 and IPv6 routing tables, STP, and the ARP table. Information sent to the control plane is processed by the CPU.
- Data Plane, generally called the forwarding plane, it is used to forward traffic flows. Routers and switches use information from the control plane to forward incoming traffic out the appropriate egress interface. Information in the data plane is typically processed by a special data plane processor without the CPU getting involved.

In a traditional router or switch architecture, the control plane and data plane functions occur in the same device. Routing decisions and packet forwarding are the responsibility of the device operating system. In SDN, management of the control plane is moved to a centralized SDN controller. The figure (see Figure 5) compares traditional and SDN architectures. The SDN controller is a logical entity that enables network administrators to manage and dictate how the data plane of switches and routers should handle network traffic. It orchestrates, mediates, and facilitates communication between applications and network elements. The SDN controller uses northbound APIs to communicate with the upstream

Figure 5. Traditional and SDN architecture

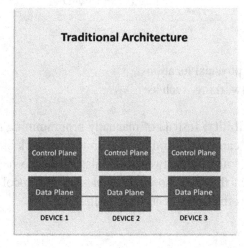
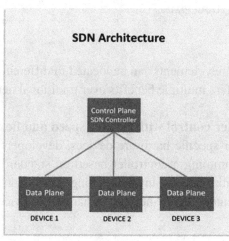

applications. These APIs help network administrators shape traffic and deploy services. The SDN controller also uses southbound APIs to define the behavior of the data planes on downstream switches and routers. It defines the data flows between the centralized control plane and the data planes on individual routers and switches. Each flow traveling through the network must first get permission from the SDN controller, which verifies that the communication is permissible according to the network policy. If the controller allows a flow, it computes a route for the flow to take and adds an entry for that flow in each of the switches along the path. All complex functions are performed by the controller.

QUALITY OF SERVICE (QoS) AND SECURITY ASPECTS IN SDN ARCHITECTURE

Nowdays many works are in progress on SDN architecture. Although there have been many valid proposals for the implementation of this architecture, in a recent study some researchers found a lack of systematic reviews on SDN data plane failure recovery techniques (Khan *et al.*, 2023). Starting from the root causes of failures in the traditional core network and their detection, they classify the current failure recovery techniques for SDN into two categories: traditional and artificial intelligence (AI) approaches. AI-based techniques enable efficient failure recovery and enhance the quality of service. They also consider performance measure metrics to evaluate and determine the limitations of existing solutions.

Other research is analyzing SDN-based Wireless Mobile Architecture to highlight the challenges to be overcome before applications and services that requires high capacity, low latency, and reliability (Do *et al.*, 2021).

Today focus is Quality of Service (QoS) in SDN, the real issue is determining how to efficiently maximize it to improve performance of network (Zhou *et al.*, 2022). Average latency, packet loss ratio and throughput are metrics considered. Researchers formulated dynamic routing in an SDN as a Markov decision process proposing a Deep Reinforcement Learning algorithm called the Asynchronous Advantage Actor-Critic QoS-aware Routing Optimization Mechanism (AQROM) to determine routing strategies that balance the traffic loads in the network. AQROM can improve the QoS of the network and reduce the training time via dynamic routing strategy updates; that is, the reward function can be dynamically and promptly altered based on the optimization objective regardless of the network topology and traffic pattern.

Other studies have been conducted in integration of SDN with Service Oriented Architecture (SOA) to maintain the QoS in these networks (Khan *et al.*, 2021). Researchers from both academia and industry have proposed and developed several resolutions for QoS management in SDNs. However, gaps still exist in developing and applying such resolutions for QoS management in SOA-based SDNs. Researchers categorize the relevant QoS management approaches into five main categories of *QoS based controller design*, *Resource allocation-based approach*, *Queue scheduling and management-based approach*, *QoS-driven optimal routing*, and *Service Level Agreement (SLA) based quality management in SDN*. They then compare the working of techniques in each category against the identified requirements for guaranteeing end-to-end QoS provisioning in SOA based SDN architecture.

In terms of security, the SDN architecture presents problems that still afflict the academic and industrial world.

For example, researchers studied how to solve ARP based attacks problem in ethernet protocol. This protocol suffers from scalability issues when the number of hosts grows up in a single broadcast domain, increasing broadcast traffic in the network. The existing SDN based solutions are lacking of security mechanism. A solution to fix the problem could be a multistage security algorithm (Munther *et al.*, 2022). It consists of three stages; each stage incorporates specific analysis to identify the packet status or behavior, and react accordingly based on its status. The first stage inspects the source MAC address, while the source IP address analysis occurs at the second stage. Finally, the third stage examines the destination IP address for incoming ARP packets.

Another field rapidly evolving is SDN architecture applied to Smart Industrial Internet of Things (IIoT). Confidential information is exchanged with cloud infrastructure to provide clients with access to distant resources, such as computing and storage activities in the IIoT. There are also significant security risks, concerns, and difficulties associated with cloud computing applied to IIot. Some researchers propose Blockchain (BC) and SDN into a cloud computing platform for the IIoT. "DistB-SDCloud" is an architecture for enhanced cloud security for smart IIoT applications (Rahman *et al.*, 2015). A distributed structure is implemented to improve the reliability and speed of physical and logical data on cloud infrastructure for smart IIoT applications. BC with the addition of secret sharing security enhancement is possible in cloud services with the improvement of data security. BC technology helps detect malicious use by enforcing in the detection of providers to detect suspicious suppliers. IIot is essentially a network-dependent application in which the majority of the work is done through the use of sensor devices, and the collected data is transferred from one sector of the business to another without the need for human intervention. This organization attracts intruders who wish to alter the data gathered for the processing of highly sensitive information. A hash value is generated in this architecture to secure the information transmitted through the BC structure, which stores the information in a public ledger where any changes can be detected by others connected to the ledger. As a result, no third party can interfere with the transaction.

NEW FRONTIER OF AI-BASED CYBERSECURITY

The integration of artificial intelligence (AI) into the field of cybersecurity has opened up new frontiers for developing more effective and automated solutions to prevent and mitigate security threats. AI has shown promising potential for network intrusion detection, user behavior monitoring, access management, and enhancing data and communication security in cloud computing.

AI can analyze large volumes of data quickly and efficiently, detecting patterns and anomalies that may indicate malicious activities. For example, machine learning algorithms trained using AI can detect anomalous user behaviors within a system, thereby identifying unauthorized access attempts or privacy violations. Moreover, AI can create more sophisticated authentication systems based on biometric recognition and other advanced identity verification methods.

Although AI represents a new frontier in cybersecurity, it is important to note that it cannot function as a magic solution. Rather, it must be integrated with other security technologies and strategies to achieve comprehensive and reliable protection.

In the cloud computing environment, numerous security threats need to be addressed, such as ensuring data confidentiality and integrity, proper authentication and authorization, and managing user access with certificates, licenses, and quarantine (Zhou *et al.*, 2021). The problem of data privacy is more significant than in traditional networks due to issues such as lack of authentication, authorization, account controllability, and poor key management maintenance.

One of the most significant threats in the cloud computing environment is the Distributed Denial of Service (DDoS) attack (Karuppiah *et al.*, 2019). These attacks can be effectively managed using intrusion prevention systems (IPS), although they remain vulnerable at the firewall level (Sabahi, 2011). DDoS attacks are considered both at the virtualization and network levels.

In the cloud environment, the concept of multitenancy poses a challenge since resources are shared among multiple servers. Data isolation can be performed through virtual machine (VM) isolation in Infrastructure-as-a-Service (IaaS) systems, memory processing and data isolation can be achieved by separating service execution from application programming interface (API) and operating system as in Platform-as-a-Service (PaaS) systems, and obtaining isolated data by running a transaction simultaneously from different servers as in Software-as-a-Service (SaaS) systems. (Beah *et al.*, 2012)

Cloud services are vulnerable to internet protocol vulnerabilities such as man-in-the-middle attacks and IP spoofing attacks, which can affect cloud performance. Additionally, malware injection attacks occur when malicious software, applications, and virtual machines are designed by hackers and injected into the cloud, affecting the normal execution of the program. Compliance with regulations to provide external audits is necessary in the cloud to maintain data segregation security.

One promising application of AI in cybersecurity is the development of new generation intrusion detection systems (IDS). IDS can be classified into signature-based and anomaly-based systems. Signature-based IDS compare incoming network traffic with known attacks in their database, while anomaly-based IDS model normal traffic through AI learning algorithms and detect deviations from the patterns. Implementing real-time anomaly-based IDS is a challenging task, given the rapid increase in network traffic and limited computational resources. (Kanimozhi *et al.*, 2019)

In conclusion, the integration of AI into cybersecurity is an exciting development that promises more effective and automated solutions to prevent and mitigate security threats in cloud computing and other contexts. However, it is crucial to recognize that AI is not a panacea and must be integrated with other security technologies and strategies to provide comprehensive and reliable protection.

REFERENCES

Behl, A., & Behl, K. (2012). *An analysis of cloud computing security issues. Information and Communication Technologies (WICT).* IEEE.

Cisco Networking Academy. (2020). *Enterprise Networking, Security, and Automation Companion Guide (CCNAv7)* (1st ed.). Cisco Press.

Do, H.M., Gregory, M.A., & Li, S. (September 2021). SDN-based wireless mobile backhaul architecture: Review and challenges. *Journal of Network and Computer Applications, 189.* doi:10.1016/j.jnca.2021.103138

Elamir, A. M., Jailani, N., & Bakar, M. A. (2013). Framework and Architecture for Programming Education Environment as a Cloud Computing Service. *ScienceDirect* [Elsevier.]. *Procedia Technology, 11*, 1299–1308. doi:10.1016/j.protcy.2013.12.328

Hassan, A., Bhatti, S. H., Shujaat, S., & Hwang, Y. (2022). To adopt or not to adopt? The determinants of cloud computing adoption in information technology sector. [Elsevier.]. *Decision Analytics Journal, 5*, 100138. doi:10.1016/j.dajour.2022.100138

Kanimozhi, V., & Prem Jacob, T. (2019). Artificial Intelligence based Network Intrusion Detection with hyper-parameter optimization tuning on the realistic cyber dataset CSE-CIC-IDS2018 using cloud computing. *ICT Express, 5*(3), 211–214. doi:10.1016/j.icte.2019.03.003

Karuppiah, M., Das, A. K., Li, X., Kumari, S., Wu, F., Chaudhry, S. A., & Niranchana, R. (2019). Secure remote user mutual authentication scheme with key agreement for cloud environment. *Mobile Networks and Applications, 24*(3), 1046–1062. doi:10.100711036-018-1061-8

Khan, N., Salleh, R. b., Koubaa, A., Khan., Z., Khan., M.K., & Ali, I. (2023). Data plane failure and its recovery techniques in SDN: A systematic literature review. *Journal of King Saud University - Computer and Information Sciences, 35,* 176-201.

Khan, S., Hussain, F.K., & Hussain, O.K. (2021). Guaranteeing end-to-end QoS provisioning in SOA based SDN architecture: A survey and Open Issues. *Future Generation Computer Systems, 119,* 176-187). doi:10.1016/j.future.2021.02.011

Liao, W., Chen, P., & Kuai, S. (2017). A Resource Provision Strategy for Software-as-a-Service in Cloud Computing. The 14th International Conference on Mobile Systems and Pervasive Computing (Mobisc 2017). *ScienceDirect* [Elsevier.]. *Procedia Computer Science, 110,* 94–101. doi:10.1016/j.procs.2017.06.123

Loukis, E., Janssen, M., & Mintchev, I. (February 2019). Determinants of software-as-a-service benefits and impact on firm performance. *Decision Support Systems, 117,* 38-47. doi:10.1016/j.dss.2018.12.005

Munther, M. N., Hashim, F., Latiff, N. A. A., Alezabi, K. A., & Liew, J. T. (2022). Scalable and secure SDN based ethernet architecture by suppressing broadcast traffic. *Egyptian Informatics Journal, 23*(1), 113–126. doi:10.1016/j.eij.2021.08.001

Rahman, A., Islam, M. J., Band, S. S., Muhammad, G., Hasan, K., & Tiwari, P. (2023, April). Rahman., A., Islam, Md.J., Band, S., Muhammad, G., Hasan, & K., Tiwari, P. (2015). Towards a blockchain SDN-based secure architecture for cloud computing in smart industrial IoT. *Digital Communications and Networks, 9*(2), 411–421. Advance online publication. doi:10.1016/j.dcan.2022.11.003

Sabahi, F. (2011) Cloud computing security threats and responses. *Communication Sofware and Networks (ICCSN), IEEE 3rd International Conference,* (pp. 245–249). IEEE.

Zhou, W., Jiang, X., Luo, Q., Guo, B., Sun, X., Sun, F., & Meng, L. (2022, December). AQROM: A quality of service aware routing optimization mechanism based on asynchronous advantage actor-critic in software-defined networks. *Digital Communications and Networks.* doi:10.1016/j.dcan.2022.11.016

Zhou, Y., Luo, Y., Obaidat, M. S., Vijayakumar, P., & Wang, X. (2021). PAMI-anonymous password authentication protocol for medical internet of things. *IEEE Global Communications Conference (GLOBECOM).* IEEE. 10.1109/GLOBECOM46510.2021.9685900

ADDITIONAL READING

Ahmad, A., Alzahrani, A. S., Ahmed, N., & Ahsan, T. (2020). A delegation model for SDN-driven federated cloud. [Elsevier.]. *Alexandria Engineering Journal*, *59*(5), 3653–3663. doi:10.1016/j.aej.2020.06.018

Del-Pozo-Puñal, E., García-Carballeira, F., & Camarmas-Alonso, D. (2023). A Scalable Simulator for Cloud, Fog and Edge Computing Platforms with Mobility Support. [ScienceDirect, Elsevier.]. *Future Generation Computer Systems*, *00*, 1–16. doi:10.1016/j.future.2023.02.010

Golightly, L., Modesti, P., Garcia, R., & Chang, V. (2023). *Securing Distributed Systems: A Survey on Access Control Techniques for Cloud*. Blockchain, IoT and SDN, Cyber Security and Applications. doi:10.1016/j.csa.2023.100015

Liao, Q., & Wang, Z. (2018). Energy consumption optimization Scheme od Cloud Data Center based on SDN. 8th International Congress of Information and Communication Technology (ICICT- 2018) [Elsevier.]. *Procedia Computer Science*, *131*, 1318–1327. doi:10.1016/j.procs.2018.04.327

Núñez-Gómez, C., Carrión, C., Caminero, B., & Delicado, F.M. (2023) S-HIDRA: A blockchain and SDN domain-based architecture to orchestrate fog computing environments. *Computer Networks 221 (109512)*. ScinceDirect, Elsevier.

Oguchi, M., & Hara, R. (2016). A Speculative Control Mechanism of Cloud Computing Systems based on Emergency Disaster Information using SDN. The 3rd International Symposium on Emerging Information, Communication and Networks (EICN 2016). [Elsevier.]. *Procedia Computer Science*, *98*, 515–521. doi:10.1016/j.procs.2016.09.065

Ronaghi, M. H., & Ronaghi, M. (2022). A contextualized study of the usage of the augmented reality technology in the tourism industry. [Elsevier.]. *Decision Analytics Journal*, *5*, 100136. doi:10.1016/j.dajour.2022.100136

Xiang, F., Zhou, P., Zuo, Y., Tao, F., & Zhang, D. (2022). Manufacturing Service Network of Digital Twin Systems Under Cloud Computing Environment. 32nd CIRP Design Conference. *ScienceDirect, Procedia Cirp*. Elsevier.

Yang, C., Liao, F., Lan, S., Wang, L., Shen, W., & Huang, G. Q. (2021). *Flexible Resource Scheduling for Software-Defined Cloud Manufacturing with Edge Computing. Engineering, ScienceDirect*. Elsevier.

KEY TERMS AND DEFINITIONS

Application Programming Interface (API): A software intermediary that allows two applications to talk to each other.

Artificial Intelligence (AI): The ability of a digital computer to perform tasks commonly associated with intelligent beings.

Cloud Computing: The on-demand availability of computer system resources accessed by Internet.

Community Cloud: Applications and services offered by one or more organizations.

Distributed Denial of Service (DDoS) Attacks: Distributed Network Attacks. This type of attack takes advantage of the specific capacity limits that apply to any network resources, such as the infrastructure that enables a company's website.

Hybrid Cloud: This is made up of public and private cloud connected using a single architecture.

Infrastructure as a Service (IaaS): A network virtualized equipment and services offered in cloud.

Intrusion Detection System (IDS): A monitoring system that detects suspicious activities and generates alerts when they are detected.

Intrusion Prevention System (IPS): A network security tool (which can be a hardware device or software) that continuously monitors a network for malicious activity and takes action to prevent it, including reporting, blocking, or dropping it, when it does occur.

Network Function Virtualization (NFV): An approach decoupling functions like a firewall or encryption from dedicated hardware and moving them to virtual servers in cloud.

Network Virtualization: Computer network elements such as switches, routers, and firewalls virtualized in cloud.

Platform as a Service (PaaS): It's a specialized service in which cloud provider is responsible for providing users access to the development tools and services used to build the applications.

Private Cloud: Consists of computing services and IT environments not made available to multiple users but hosted internally by the company.

Public Cloud: Applications and services offered to the general population.

Quality of Service (QoS): Quality of service (QoS) is the description or measurement of the overall performance of a service, such as a telephony or computer network, or a cloud computing service.

Software as a Service (SaaS): The applications are on provider systems and are disposal to user profile in cloud.

Software Defined Network (SDN): Network virtualization approach controlling traffic routing by taking over routing management from data routing in the physical environment.

Virtual Machine (VM): A computer resource that uses software instead of a physical computer to run programs and deploy apps.

Virtualization: The act of creating virtual computer hardware, storage devices, and/or computer network devices.

Chapter 2
Sophisticated–Sinister–Stealth Attacks

Akashdeep Bhardwaj

https://orcid.org/0000-0001-7361-0465

University of Petroleum and Energy Studies, India

ABSTRACT

APTs typically involve a series of carefully planned and coordinated steps, including reconnaissance, initial compromise, establishment of a foothold, and lateral movement to other systems. To carry out their objectives, APT actors may use various techniques, including social engineering, spear-phishing, and exploitation of software vulnerabilities. APTs are often launched by nation-state actors or well-funded criminal organizations, who have the resources and expertise to carry out complex attacks. Detecting and responding to APTs requires a multi-layered approach that includes robust cybersecurity measures, such as network segmentation, intrusion detection and prevention systems, and endpoint protection. Additionally, organizations must have a strong incident response plan in place to quickly identify and contain APT attacks before they cause significant damage. These aspects are discussed in detail in this chapter.

1. INTRODUCTION

Advanced persistent threats (APTs) are sophisticated, targeted attacks aimed at stealing sensitive information or disrupting critical systems. These attacks are often silent, meaning they can go undetected for long periods of time, making them particularly dangerous. APT (What is Advance Persistent Threat, IGI-Global, n.d.) is a sophisticated, targeted attack that is designed to gain unauthorized access to a specific network or system for the purpose of stealing sensitive information, disrupting operations, or both. APTs are often carried out by well-funded and highly skilled threat actors, such as nation-state actors, cybercriminals, or hacktivists. Unlike traditional cyber-attacks, which are typically opportunistic and automated, APTs are carefully planned and executed over a period, often using a variety of tactics to evade detection. These attacks are also persistent, meaning that the attackers may remain undetected within the target network for weeks, months, or even years, allowing them to carry out their objectives without being detected.

DOI: 10.4018/979-8-3693-1528-6.ch002

APTs are a growing concern for organizations of all sizes and across all industries, as they can result in significant financial losses, damage to reputation, and legal liability. To defend against APTs, organizations must employ a multi-layered security approach, including network segmentation, intrusion detection and prevention, and endpoint protection. Additionally, organizations must have a strong incident response plan in place to quickly identify and contain APT attacks before they can cause significant damage. APTs are considered sophisticated attacks because they are highly targeted and designed to evade traditional security measures. APT actors are often well-funded and highly skilled, using a variety of techniques to gain access to a target network or system and remain undetected for extended periods of time.

Unlike traditional cyber-attacks, which are often automated and indiscriminate, APTs are carefully planned and executed over a period of weeks, months, or even years. This requires a significant level of expertise and resources, as well as the ability to adapt and evolve as security measures are improved. APTs also involve a series of carefully planned and coordinated steps, such as reconnaissance, initial compromise, establishment of a foothold, and lateral movement to other systems. APT actors may use various techniques, including social engineering, spear-phishing, and exploitation of software vulnerabilities, to achieve their objectives. Because APTs are designed to remain undetected, they can be challenging to detect and mitigate. This is why they are often considered among the most sophisticated cyber-attacks, requiring organizations to employ a multi-layered security approach and have a strong incident response plan in place to quickly identify and contain APT attacks before they can cause significant damage.

Here are brief descriptions of the top APT attacks that have occurred in the past few years:

- **SolarWinds Attack (Krener, 2023):** In December 2020, it was discovered that Russian state-sponsored hackers had compromised SolarWinds, a popular IT management software, and inserted a malicious code that gave them access to thousands of organizations, including multiple US government agencies.
- **Hafnium Attack (Deuby, 2023):** In early 2021, a Chinese state-sponsored group known as Hafnium targeted on-premises Microsoft Exchange servers, exploiting several zero-day vulnerabilities to gain access to email accounts and sensitive data of thousands of organizations worldwide.
- **REvil Ransomware Attack (Constantin, 2021):** In July 2021, the REvil ransomware group, believed to be based in Russia, targeted Kaseya, a US-based software provider, and exploited a vulnerability to deploy ransomware to over 1,500 businesses worldwide, demanding a $70 million ransom payment.

2. APTS ARE SOPHISTICATED

APTs are sophisticated attacks (*Advanced Persistent Threats and Nation-State Actors | Cybersecurity and Infrastructure Security Agency CISA*, n.d.) because they are highly targeted and tailored to a specific organization, which requires a significant amount of research and reconnaissance to carry out. This often involves studying the target's infrastructure, business operations, and employees to gain insight into the organization's vulnerabilities and potential attack vectors. Once the attacker has a clear understanding of the target's infrastructure and weaknesses, they can use various methods to gain initial access, such as social engineering, spear-phishing, or exploiting software vulnerabilities. APT actors often use custom malware or other techniques that can evade traditional security measures, making them difficult to detect.

After gaining a foothold in the target network, the attacker will often move laterally to other systems, seeking out valuable data and credentials that can be used to achieve their objectives. They may also employ techniques like steganography or encryption to conceal their activities and evade detection. Another factor that makes APTs sophisticated is their persistence. Unlike traditional attacks that are often quick and disruptive, APTs are designed to remain undetected for long periods of time. This requires the attacker to be patient, and to continually adapt their tactics and techniques as security measures are improved or changed. Overall, APTs are considered among the most sophisticated cyber-attacks due to their highly targeted nature, tailored approach, use of advanced techniques, and persistence. To defend against APTs, organizations must employ a multi-layered security approach and continually improve their security posture to stay ahead of evolving threats.

Here are some examples of how APTs can be sophisticated attacks:

- **Targeted Approach:** APTs are highly targeted and tailored to a specific organization, which requires extensive research and reconnaissance. For example, in the 2017 Equifax breach (Fruhlinger, 2023), APT actors targeted a vulnerability in an unpatched web application framework that was specific to Equifax's systems. This allowed the attackers to bypass the company's security measures and gain access to sensitive data.
- **Stealthy Techniques:** APT actors often use stealthy techniques that can evade traditional security measures, making them difficult to detect. For example, in the 2020 SolarWinds supply chain attack, (Wolfe, 2023) APT actors inserted malware into SolarWinds' Orion software updates, which were then distributed to the company's customers. The malware remained undetected for several months, allowing the attackers to steal data and credentials.
- **Persistence:** APTs are designed to remain undetected for long periods of time, which requires attackers to be patient and continually adapt their tactics and techniques. For example, in the 2018 Marriott breach (*TechCrunch Is Part of the Yahoo Family of Brands*, 2022), APT actors had access to the company's systems for four years before being discovered. During that time, the attackers were able to steal data on millions of customers, while remaining undetected.
- **Advanced Tools:** APT actors often use advanced tools and techniques that can bypass traditional security measures. For example, in the 2016 Bangladesh Bank heist (Zetter, 2016), APT actors used custom malware to infiltrate the bank's systems and steal $81 million. The attackers used sophisticated techniques, including social engineering and the creation of fake accounts, to carry out the attack.

Overall, APTs are considered sophisticated attacks due to their targeted approach, use of stealthy techniques, persistence, and advanced tools. To defend against APTs, organizations must employ a multi-layered security approach and continually improve their security posture to stay ahead of evolving threats. APTs are a highly targeted approach to cyber-attacks, meaning that they are specifically designed to infiltrate and compromise a specific target organization. APT actors carry out extensive research and reconnaissance on their target to gain insight into their infrastructure, business operations, and employees. This allows the attackers to identify vulnerabilities and potential attack vectors that can be used to gain access to the target's network. Once the attackers have a clear understanding of their target, they use various methods to gain initial access, such as social engineering, spear-phishing, or exploiting software vulnerabilities. The goal is to achieve a foothold in the target's network that can be used to launch more sophisticated attacks.

The targeted approach of APTs is what sets them apart from other types of cyber-attacks. Unlike traditional attacks that are often automated and indiscriminate, APTs are designed to achieve a specific objective, such as stealing sensitive data or disrupting critical infrastructure. This requires a significant amount of expertise and resources, as well as the ability to adapt and evolve as security measures are improved. Overall, APTs are a highly targeted approach to cyber-attacks, requiring extensive research and reconnaissance to carry out. To defend against APTs, organizations must be vigilant and adopt a multi-layered security approach that includes threat intelligence, user education, and advanced security tools.

3. OPERATION AURORA

In 2009, APT actors carried out a highly sophisticated attack against Google and other high-profile companies. The attack used a combination of spear-phishing and malware to gain access to the targets' systems. The attackers were able to evade detection for months and steal sensitive data, including source code and intellectual property. Operation Aurora (Cohen, 2022) was a highly sophisticated and well-known Advanced Persistent Threat (APT) attack that occurred in 2009. The attack was launched against several high-profile technology companies, including Google, Adobe, and Yahoo. The primary objective of the attack was to steal sensitive intellectual property and source code from these companies.

The attackers used a combination of social engineering and zero-day exploits to gain initial access to the target's systems. They then used custom malware to infiltrate and exfiltrate data from the target's networks. The attackers were highly skilled and used advanced techniques to evade detection, including encrypting their communications and using a variety of command-and-control servers. The attack was discovered in January 2010 when Google publicly announced that it had been the victim of a cyber-attack. The attack had been ongoing for several months before it was detected. Google stated that the attack had originated from China, and it was believed to be state sponsored.

The attack had a significant impact on the technology industry, as it highlighted the increasing threat posed by APTs and the need for improved security measures. The attack also led to increased scrutiny of the Chinese government's cyber activities and strained diplomatic relations between the US and China. Operation Aurora is still considered to be one of the most sophisticated APT attacks to date. It demonstrated the level of skill and sophistication that APT actors are capable of, as well as the importance of adopting a multi-layered security approach to defend against these types of threats. Operation Aurora was a highly coordinated and sophisticated cyber-attack that targeted several high-profile technology companies, including Google, Adobe, and Yahoo. The attack is believed to have been launched by a state-sponsored Chinese hacking group, although the Chinese government denied any involvement.

Figure 1 illustrates the source code folder for the operations Aurora attack for reference. The attack was initiated through a spear-phishing campaign, where the attackers sent targeted emails to employees of the targeted companies, with links to a malicious website or a malicious file attachment. When the employee clicked on the link or opened the attachment, it installed a backdoor on the computer that gave the attackers access to the company's network. The attackers used custom malware and advanced techniques to evade detection and move laterally through the network to locate and exfiltrate sensitive data. The attackers were highly skilled and used encryption to communicate with their command-and-control servers, making it difficult for security teams to detect their presence.

The attack was discovered by Google in December 2009, who noticed unusual network activity that was traced back to a zero-day vulnerability in Internet Explorer. The investigation uncovered a widespread

Figure 1. Screenshot displaying source code folder named Aurora

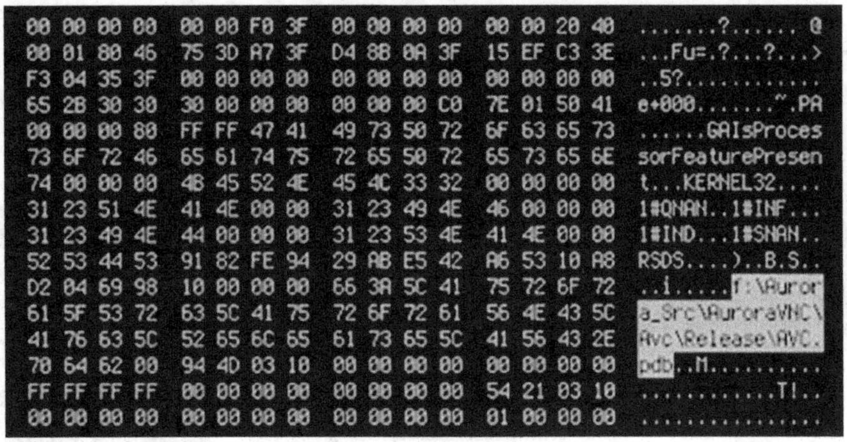

and coordinated cyber-attack against Google and other technology companies. The attackers had been active for several months and had stolen intellectual property, source code, and other sensitive data. The attack had a significant impact on the technology industry and raised concerns about the threat posed by state-sponsored APT groups. It also highlighted the importance of adopting a multi-layered security approach, including employee education, vulnerability management, and advanced threat detection and response capabilities.

Operation Aurora remains a significant milestone in the evolution of APT attacks and serves as a reminder of the need for constant vigilance and improved security measures.

4. CARBANAK

In 2014, APT actors launched a sophisticated campaign against banks (Vijayan, 2019) in over 30 countries, using custom malware to infiltrate their systems. The attackers were able to steal millions of dollars by gaining access to ATMs and making fraudulent transactions. The attack was highly targeted and persistent, allowing the attackers to remain undetected for a long time. Carbanak was the name given to a highly sophisticated Advanced Persistent Threat (APT) group that carried out a large-scale cyber-attack on financial institutions in over 30 countries between 2013 and 2016. The group was responsible for stealing millions of dollars from banks and financial institutions by compromising their internal networks and systems, Figure 2 presents the steps and process followed by Carbanak.

Carbanak used a range of sophisticated techniques to gain access to their targets, including spear-phishing attacks and the use of remote access trojans (RATs). The group also leveraged custom malware to gain persistent access to their targets and evade detection by security software. Once inside a target network, Carbanak used advanced techniques to move laterally through the network, steal credentials, and gain access to critical financial systems. The group used a combination of social engineering, surveillance, and lateral movement to gain access to the most valuable data and systems. The group was able to carry out a range of fraudulent activities, including unauthorized transfers, ATM cashouts, and falsifying account balances. The group was able to steal millions of dollars from financial institutions and evade detection by disguising their activities as normal bank transactions.

Figure 2. Carbanak theft process

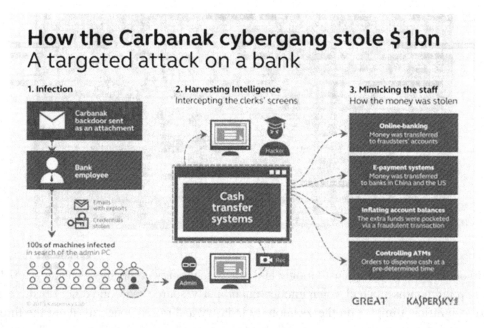

The Carbanak group was eventually identified and disrupted by a coalition of international law enforcement agencies and security firms in 2018. The group had been active for several years, and it is believed that the total amount stolen was in the hundreds of millions of dollars. Carbanak is considered one of the most significant APT groups to date due to the scale and sophistication of their operations. The group demonstrated the level of skill and resources available to APT actors and the need for financial institutions to adopt advanced security measures to defend against these types of threats. The Carbanak attack was one of the most sophisticated and well-organized cyber-attacks to date. The attack targeted over 100 financial institutions in 40 different countries and resulted in the theft of hundreds of millions of dollars. The group behind the attack was eventually identified as a Russian cybercrime gang.

The attack began with spear-phishing emails sent to bank employees, containing links or attachments that when clicked, installed a backdoor onto the victim's computer, which allowed the attackers to gain control of the system. The attackers then conducted reconnaissance to identify critical systems and moved laterally through the network to gain access to them. They also used advanced tactics, such as hijacking the bank's ATM network and initiating fraudulent transfers and withdrawals. The impact of the Carbanak attack was significant. In addition to the financial losses suffered by the targeted institutions, the attack also eroded public trust in the security of the global financial system. The attack highlighted the need for increased security measures, particularly in the financial sector, and led to the implementation of new regulations, such as the EU's Network and Information Security (NIS) directive. Mitigating the threat posed by advanced persistent threats like Carbanak requires a multi-layered security approach that combines people, process, and technology. This includes employee training to improve cybersecurity awareness, implementing best practices for securing networks and systems, and deploying advanced threat detection and response technologies. Other measures include regular vulnerability assessments, incident response planning, and collaboration with industry peers and law enforcement agencies.

Overall, the Carbanak attack served as a stark reminder of the ever-increasing threat posed by APTs and the need for financial institutions to remain vigilant and proactive in the face of these evolving threats.

5. APT10

APT10 (Sayegh, 2023) is a Chinese-based APT group that has been active since at least 2009. The group has been involved in a range of attacks against governments, technology companies, and defense contractors. Their attacks are highly sophisticated and involve the use of custom malware and techniques to evade detection. APT10 is a notorious Advanced Persistent Threat (APT) group that is believed to be operating out of China. Also known as "Red Apollo" and "Stone Panda," APT10 is known for carrying out highly sophisticated and targeted cyber-attacks against a wide range of industries, including government agencies, technology companies, and financial institutions.

APT10 is thought to have been active since at least 2009, and over the years, the group has developed a range of advanced tools and techniques to conduct its operations. These include spear-phishing attacks, zero-day exploits, and custom malware that is designed to evade detection by traditional security software. One of the most significant campaigns attributed to APT10 is the Cloud Hopper campaign, which was discovered in 2016. This campaign involved the group compromising managed service providers (MSPs) to gain access to the internal networks of their clients. This allowed the group to access highly sensitive data belonging to a wide range of organizations, including government agencies and large corporations. The impact of APT10's activities has been significant, with many organizations suffering financial losses and damage to their reputation as a result of their attacks. In response, many organizations have implemented new security measures to defend against the threat posed by APT10, including increased investment in threat detection and response technologies, and improved employee training and awareness programs. Figure 3 presents the APT10 attack methodology for reference.

Figure 3. APT10 attack methodology

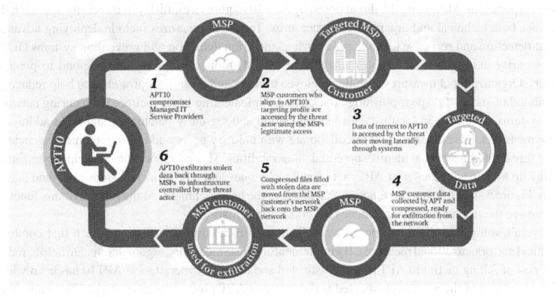

APT10, also known as Red Apollo or Stone Panda, is a sophisticated Chinese-based advanced persistent threat (APT) group that is known for conducting targeted cyberattacks against a wide range of industries, including government agencies, technology companies, and financial institutions. APT10 has been active since at least 2009 and has developed a range of advanced tools and techniques to conduct its operations. Figure 4 presents the hashes in MD5 algorithm of the documents stolen off the Japan banks.

Figure 4. Hash values of stolen documents by APT10 group

File Name	MD5	Size	C2
自民党海洋総合戦略小委員会が政府に提言申し入れ.doc Government Recommendations from the Liberal Democratic Party's Comprehensive Strategic Maritime Subcommittee	4f83c01e8f7507d23c67ab085bf79e97	843022	eservake.jetos[.]com 82.221.100.52 151.106.53.147
グテマラ大使講演会案内状.doc Invitation to Lecture by Guatemalan Ambassador	f188936d2c8423cf064d6b8160769f21	720384	eservake.jetos[.]com 151.106.53.147 153.92.210.208
米国接近に揺れる北朝鮮内部.doc North Korean interior swayed e approach of the United	cca227f70a64e1e7fcf5bccdc6cc25dd	733184	eservake.jetos[.]com 153.92.210.208 167.99.121.203

The impact of APT10's activities has been significant. The group has been linked to numerous high-profile cyberattacks, including the Cloud Hopper campaign, which compromised managed service providers to gain access to the internal networks of their clients. This campaign allowed APT10 to access highly sensitive data belonging to a wide range of organizations, including government agencies and large corporations. Mitigating the threat posed by APT10 requires a multi-layered security approach that includes both technical and organizational measures. Technical measures include deploying advanced threat detection and response technologies, such as intrusion detection and prevention systems (IDPS) and security information and event management (SIEM) tools, to identify and respond to potential threats. Organizational measures include employee training and awareness programs to help reduce the likelihood of successful spear-phishing attacks, and implementing best practices for securing networks and systems, such as using multi-factor authentication and regularly patching systems. In addition to these measures, it is also important to collaborate with industry peers and law enforcement agencies to share threat intelligence and identify potential vulnerabilities. This collaboration can help organizations to stay up to date with the latest APT tactics and techniques and take proactive steps to defend against them. Figure 5 shows the macro function that displays the lure document. At the bottom of this function, we can see the readable text that matches the contact information.

Overall, mitigating the threat posed by APT10 requires a comprehensive approach that combines technical and organizational measures. By implementing these measures, organizations can help to reduce their risk of falling victim to APT10's sophisticated and targeted cyberattacks. APT10 has been widely regarded as one of the most sophisticated and dangerous APT groups operating today. The group's ex-

Figure 5. Macro function displaying the lure document

```
Sub ShowMsg()
Dim msg As String
msg =
    "Œ̄'J•ů•F '"ƒOƒeƒ}ƒ†"ú-{'åŽgu††hi" _
    & "u't•ÄƒOƒAƒeƒ}ƒ†,Ì—»óA†Û'è,Æ"W-]v" _
    & "y"úžžz 2018"N 8—Ž9"úi-Øj1†F00'16:30@" _
    & "y†ìèz "ú"å'J'Ûƒrƒ<B1 †ì<cŽ°ì"ú"å'J'ÛƒNƒŠƒ}ƒbƒN—Ÿ†ƒZƒ"ƒ^[†E-×j" _
    & "@@@@ "—<ž"sç'å"c<æ"åK'¬2-2-3@Tel.: 03-3591-3831" _
    & "yŽåÅz `è"ÊŽÐ'c-@lƒ†ƒeƒ"ƒAƒƒŠƒJ<¦†ì" _
    & "yu††'èzuƒOƒAƒeƒ}ƒ†,Ì—»óA†Û'è,Æ"W-]v" _
    & "yuŽtz Œ̄'J'•ů•F '"ƒOƒeƒ}ƒ†"Á-†'S— 'åŽg" _
    & "yŽQ†Á"ìz †ì`ð 2,000 †~Á"ñ†ì`ð 3,000 †~ / 'åŠw†@E'åŠw‡@-'-¿" _
    & "y"ðlz" _
    & "‡@\ž,Ý̄Ž̄•tƒæ'…‡ 50-†,Ü,Å,Å,·B,"',ß,É`È†°,®,ç,"\ž,Ý†°,',cB" _
    & "‡A\ž'÷,ßØ,èF•†¬2018"N8—Ž6"úì—Žj" _
    & "¨`È†°WEBƒTƒCƒƒg,®,ç,"\,už,Ý,-,¾,³,cB" _
    & "URL: https://latin-america.jp/seminar-entry" _
    & "yÛ×ƒ`ƒ†ƒVz(PDF) ,±,¿,ç,ðƒNƒŠƒbƒN" _
    & "yƒ†ƒeƒ"ƒAƒƒŠƒJ<¦†ìz" _
    & "§100-0011"—<ž"sç'å"c<æ"åK'¬2-2-3"ú"å'J'Ûƒrƒ<120Ž" _
    & "Tel: 03-3591-3831 Fax: 03-6205-4262 E-mail: info@latin-america.jp"
ActiveDocument.Content.Text = msg
ActiveDocument.Save
End Sub
```

tensive resources, advanced tools and techniques, and highly targeted approach make them a significant threat to organizations in a wide range of industries.

6. SOLARWINDS

In late 2020, APT actors carried out a highly sophisticated supply chain attack against SolarWinds (Zetter, 2023), a software company that provides IT management tools to numerous organizations. The attackers inserted a backdoor into SolarWinds' Orion software updates, which were then distributed to the company's customers. The attack was highly targeted and stealthy, allowing the attackers to remain undetected for several months while stealing sensitive data. The SolarWinds attack, also known as the Sunburst attack or the Solorigate attack, was a highly sophisticated supply chain attack that was discovered in December 2020. The attack is believed to have begun as early as March 2020 and went undetected for several months. Figure 6 presents the Solar Winds attack timeline.

The attack targeted the Orion network management software from SolarWinds, a popular tool used by many large organizations and government agencies to manage their networks. The attackers compromised SolarWinds' software development environment and inserted a malicious backdoor into the Orion software updates. This allowed the attackers to gain access to the networks of SolarWinds' customers who had installed the compromised software. The attack was attributed to a group of state-sponsored Russian hackers known as APT29, also known as Cozy Bear. APT29 has been linked to a few other high-profile cyber-attacks, including the hack of the Democratic National Committee in 2016.

The impact of the SolarWinds attack was significant, with numerous high-profile organizations and government agencies affected. It is estimated that up to 18,000 organizations may have been impacted by the attack, including the US Treasury Department, the Department of Homeland Security, and several

Figure 6. Solar winds attack timeline

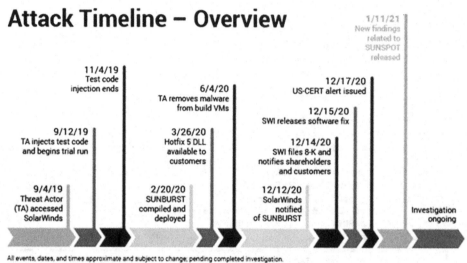

Attack Timeline – Overview

Fortune 500 companies. The attackers were able to access sensitive data and communications, including email correspondence and intellectual property. The SolarWinds attack highlighted the potential vulnerability of software supply chains and the need for increased security measures to prevent such attacks. Following the attack, many organizations implemented new security measures, such as increased network monitoring, more frequent software updates, and the use of multifactor authentication. Figure 7 presents the attack methodology followed by Solar Winds attack.

Figure 7. Solar winds attack process

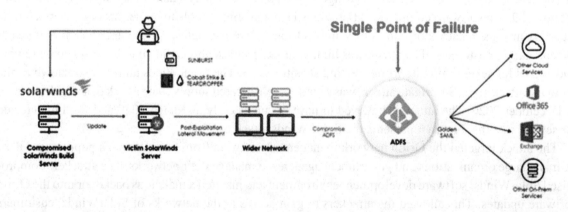

In addition, the US government has taken steps to increase cybersecurity measures, including the creation of a Cybersecurity and Infrastructure Security Agency (CISA) to coordinate the government's response to cyber threats, and the establishment of a task force to investigate the SolarWinds attack. SolarWinds attack was a wake-up call for organizations and governments worldwide, highlighting the need for increased vigilance and improved security measures to protect against advanced and persistent cyber threats.

These are just a few examples of how APTs can be sophisticated attacks. APT actors are constantly evolving their tactics and techniques, making it important for organizations to stay vigilant and continually improve their security measures to defend against these threats.

7. APTS ARE SINISTER

APTs are considered sinister because they are designed to infiltrate a specific target, such as a government agency or large corporation, and then operate in the background for an extended period of time, often years, without being detected. During this time, the attackers can steal sensitive data, spy on communications, and carry out other malicious activities, often with the goal of causing significant harm to the target organization. Unlike other types of cyberattacks, APTs are highly sophisticated and often use advanced techniques and tools to evade detection and maintain access to the target network. This makes APTs difficult to detect and even more challenging to defend against. Additionally, APTs are often carried out by nation-states or other highly organized groups, which have significant resources and capabilities at their disposal. The sinister nature of APTs is further compounded by the fact that they often target critical infrastructure and other high-value targets, which can have severe consequences if compromised. For example, an APT that successfully infiltrates a power grid or a water treatment plant could cause widespread disruption and potentially put human lives at risk. APTs are considered sinister because they are highly sophisticated and targeted cyberattacks that are designed to infiltrate a specific target and remain undetected for an extended period of time. These attacks are often carried out by nation-states or other highly organized groups, and they can have significant consequences for the target organization, including theft of sensitive information, disruption of critical infrastructure, and other malicious activities.

The impact of APT attacks can be severe and far-reaching, including:

- **Theft of sensitive information:** APT attackers are often looking to steal sensitive information, such as intellectual property, financial information, or personal data. This information can be used for a range of nefarious purposes, including identity theft, fraud, and espionage.
- **Disruption of critical infrastructure:** APT attackers may also seek to disrupt critical infrastructure, such as power grids, water treatment facilities, or transportation networks. This can cause significant harm to the target organization and even result in loss of life in some cases.
- **Reputational damage:** A successful APT attack can result in significant reputational damage for the target organization, leading to loss of customers, loss of revenue, and long-term harm to the organization's brand.
- **Financial loss:** APT attacks can also result in significant financial loss for the target organization, including costs associated with incident response, legal fees, and regulatory fines.

The impact of APT attacks can be severe and long-lasting. Organizations must remain vigilant and prepared to defend against these attacks by implementing strong security controls, regular security assessments, and having a robust incident response plan in place. Overall, the sinister nature of APTs underscores the importance of taking a proactive and comprehensive approach to cybersecurity. This includes implementing strong security controls and regular security assessments, as well as investing in employee training and incident response planning to be prepared for a potential APT attack.

8. APTS ARE STEALTHY

APT attacks are often designed to be stealthy and evade detection for an extended period of time. This is achieved through a combination of advanced techniques and tools that allow the attackers to blend in with normal network traffic and avoid detection by traditional security measures. For example, APT attackers may use sophisticated malware that is specifically designed to avoid detection by antivirus software and other security tools. They may also use encryption and other methods to hide their communications. APT attacks are often designed to be stealthy for a few reasons:

- **To evade detection:** APT attackers use advanced techniques and tools that allow them to blend in with normal network traffic and avoid detection by traditional security measures. By remaining undetected, the attackers can maintain their access to the target network and continue to carry out their malicious activities for an extended period of time. They use sophisticated techniques to evade detection: APT attackers use advanced techniques such as polymorphic malware, rootkits, and zero-day exploits to evade detection by traditional security measures. These techniques allow attackers to hide their activities and remain undetected for an extended period of time.
- **To remain persistent:** APT attacks are often carried out by nation-states or other highly organized groups with significant resources and capabilities. These attackers are willing to invest significant time and effort to achieve their objectives, and they may wait months or even years before taking action. By remaining stealthy, the attackers can maintain their access to the target network and continue to collect valuable information over an extended period of time. They remain hidden for an extended period of time: APT attacks are designed to remain hidden for an extended period of time, often months or even years. This allows attackers to gather as much information as possible and carry out their objectives without being detected.
- **To cause maximum damage:** APT attackers are often motivated by political, economic, or military objectives. By remaining undetected and operating in the background, the attackers can collect sensitive information, steal intellectual property, or disrupt critical infrastructure without being detected. This can cause significant harm to the target organization and achieve the attacker's objectives. They use targeted attacks: APT attackers use targeted attacks, such as spear-phishing emails, to gain access to the target's network. These attacks are designed to be highly convincing and often include personal information about the target to make them more believable. They use lateral movement: Once APT attackers gain access to a target's network, they use lateral movement to move laterally across the network, gathering information and maintaining access to the target's systems. This allows them to remain hidden and avoid detection by security measures that may be in place.

APT attacks are stealthy because they are designed to remain undetected for an extended period of time, using advanced techniques to evade detection and remain hidden. This makes them particularly challenging to defend against and requires a proactive and comprehensive approach to cybersecurity. The stealthy nature of APT attacks makes them difficult to detect and even more challenging to defend against. This underscores the importance of taking a proactive and comprehensive approach to cybersecurity, including implementing strong security controls, regular security assessments, and employee training.

9. CONCLUSION

APT attacks are highly sophisticated and targeted cyber-attacks that are designed to infiltrate a specific target and remain undetected for an extended period. These attacks are often carried out by nation-states or other highly organized groups, and they can have significant consequences for the target organization, including theft of sensitive information, disruption of critical infrastructure, and other malicious activities. APTs are stealthy and persistent, using advanced techniques and tools to evade detection and maintain access to the target network. This makes them difficult to detect and even more challenging to defend against. To mitigate the risk of APT attacks, it is essential to take a proactive and comprehensive approach to cybersecurity, including implementing strong security controls, regular security assessments, and employee training.

Overall, APT attacks are a serious and ongoing threat to organizations of all sizes and in all industries. It is essential to remain vigilant and prepared to defend against these attacks by staying up to date on the latest threat intelligence, implementing best practices for cybersecurity, and having a robust incident response plan in place.

REFERENCES

Advanced Persistent Threats and Nation-State Actors (n.d.). Cybersecurity and Infrastructure Security Agency CISA.https://www.cisa.gov/topics/cyber-threats-and-advisories/advanced-persistent-threats-and-nation-state-actors

Cohen, G. (2022). Throwback Attack: Operation Aurora signals a new era in industrial threat. *Industrial Cybersecurity Pulse*. https://www.industrialcybersecuritypulse.com/threats-vulnerabilities/throwback-attack-operation-aurora-signals-a-new-era-in-industrial-threat/

Constantin, L. (2021). REvil ransomware explained: A widespread extortion operation. *CSO Online*. https://www.csoonline.com/article/570101/revil-ransomware-explained-a-widespread-extortion-operation.html

Deuby, S. (2023). Timeline of a Hafnium attack. *Semperis*. https://www.semperis.com/blog/timeline-of-hafnium-attack/

Fruhlinger, J. (2023). Equifax data breach FAQ: What happened, who was affected, what was the impact? *CSO Online*. https://www.csoonline.com/article/567833/equifax-data-breach-faq-what-happened-who-was-affected-what-was-the-impact.html

Kerner, S. O. S. M. (2023). SolarWinds hack explained: Everything you need to know. *WhatIs.com*. https://www.techtarget.com/whatis/feature/SolarWinds-hack-explained-Everything-you-need-to-know

Sayegh, E. (2023, February 21). Spotlight On APT10. *Forbes*. https://www.forbes.com/sites/emilsayegh/2023/02/21/spotlight-on-apt10/?sh=29a3b73f491e

TechCrunch is part of the Yahoo family of brands. (2022). TechCrunch. https://techcrunch.com/2022/07/06/marriott-breach-again/

Vijayan, J. (2019, June 4). Carbanak attack: Two hours to total compromise. *Dark Reading*. https://www.darkreading.com/attacks-breaches/carbanak-attack-two-hours-to-total-compromise

What is Advanced Persistent Threat? (n.d.). IGI Global. https://www.igi-global.com/dictionary/advanced-persistent-threat/69860

Wolfe, T. (2023, August 9). *What You Need To Know About the SolarWinds Supply-Chain Attack.* SANS Institute. https://www.sans.org/blog/what-you-need-to-know-about-the-solarwinds-supply-chain-attack/

Zetter, K. (2016, May 17). That insane, $81M Bangladesh bank heist? Here's what we know. *WIRED.* https://www.wired.com/2016/05/insane-81m-bangladesh-bank-heist-heres-know/

Zetter, K. (2023, May 2). SolarWinds: The untold story of the boldest Supply-Chain hack. *WIRED.* https://www.wired.com/story/the-untold-story-of-solarwinds-the-boldest-supply-chain-hack-ever/

Chapter 3
Risk Management in the Current Digital Reality of Organizations

Daniel Jorge Ferreira
https://orcid.org/0000-0002-6155-5443
University of Trás-os-Montes and Alto Douro, Portugal

Henrique S. Mamede
https://orcid.org/0000-0002-5383-9884
INESC-TEC, University of Porto, Portugal

Nuno Mateus-Coelho
https://orcid.org/0000-0001-5517-9181
COPELABS - Lusófona University, Portugal

ABSTRACT

The global overview of the challenges faced in trying to minimise the risks of organisations in the face of cyber-attacks is arduous for any organisation. Defining an appropriate risk management model that proactively minimises cybersecurity incidents is a critical challenge. Many malicious attacks occur daily, and there is only sometimes an adequate response. There is a significant investment in research to identify the main factors that may cause such incidents, always trying to have the most appropriate response and, consequently, potentiating the response capacity and success. At the same time, several different methodologies evaluate risk management and the maturity level of organisations. Due to the lack of predictive models based on data (evidence), there is a significant investment in research to identify the main factors that may cause such incidents, starting to design models based on AI - Artificial Intelligence. This research will go in the direction of developing a user-friendly model supporting the assessment of the methodological aspects of an organisation.

DOI: 10.4018/979-8-3693-1528-6.ch003

1. INTRODUCTION

Due to the fact that this is the beginning stage of a PhD thesis in the challenging topic of information security, the work being done here is an exploration work of what has to be done.

All of the models are conceptual and have not been put through any kind of experimentation; rather, they serve as the framework and the product of one year's worth of study, so providing the basis for the work and artefact that are now in the process of being developed.

The subsequent step will consist of the investigation of the models that have been mentioned in this article and the resolution of the research queries.

The dilemma that arises from approaching danger while simultaneously failing to respond to security incidents is discussed in the book "Risk Assessment and Decision Analysis with Bayesian Networks" (Abu, 2018). It is indicated in that passage that common approaches like risk registers and heat maps are not sufficient to manage the risk assessment in an appropriate manner. On the other hand, the book titled "Visualisation Analysis" (Ahmad et al., 2020) discusses the "clear advantages of using data visualisation to understand better the connections between these data compared to using textual or numerical forms" (page).

When managers working in cybersecurity have access to this information, they are able to make decisions more rapidly, evaluate the investment and return, and decide the significance of a decision. The powers of visualisation and interpretation are extremely important for these managers (Atkins & Lawson, 2020).

In order for businesses to continue their operations in the market, they were had to go through a transition. This highlighted a cybersecurity risk that had been dormant up until that point and resulted in the creation of new organisational vulnerabilities (Yeoh et al., 2021).

The term "cybersecurity risk" has been used in a variety of ways, and only a handful of academics have developed definitive definitions for it. However, other researchers have investigated trends in these uses. For instance, Oltramari and Kott (2022) suggest that practitioners explain cyber risk in terms of a system's configuration rather than the possibility that damage would occur. This is in contrast to the common practise of focusing on the likelihood of damage occurring. Others describe risk assessment as the "general process of risk identification, risk analysis, and risk assessment," whereas risk management is described as "coordinated activities to direct and control an organisation regarding risks" Bowen et al., (2011).

Therefore, the visualisation and use of data are helpful in the process of decision-making, which is crucial for every organisation, regardless of size or nature, and has an effect on all of the system components Conti et al., (2018). When it comes to making sound decisions, having access to high-quality information is absolutely necessary Craigen et al., (2014).

1.1 Problem Identification and Research Question(s)

Cybersecurity risk management has found its way into many parts of modern life, including banking, finance, healthcare, life, business activities, and project management et al., (2022).

Despite the fact that various works on cybersecurity risk management are currently available Halima Ibrahim Kure (2022), Cuchta et al. (2019), the body of knowledge needs include works that take into account the aforementioned contextual information when performing risk management for critical infrastructures.

Conti et al. (2018) describes how the increasing number of attacks demands the need for forensic and cybersecurity professionals for real-time identification, investigation, and protection against cyber threats. These professionals are needed since the frequency of attacks is increasing.

Because neither the organisation nor the providers are entirely certain of the information that belongs to this category Abu (2018), further research is required to define CTI, which stands for "Cyber Threat Intelligence."

The utilisation of evidence-based information derived from cyber threat intelligence (CTI) enables the avoidance of potential dangers. Works that have been done and business rules that are currently in place underline the importance of CTI and propose solutions for exchanging threat intelligence. Even if a lot of work has been put into it, the organisation still has to pay greater attention to the ways in which CTI information might help CSRM actions so that it can pro-actively adopt the controls that are necessary to decrease risk.

Because of the rising sophistication, multi-vector nature, and unpredictability of these attacks, the function of Cybersecurity Risk Management (CSRM) has become increasingly problematic (Kure & Islam, 2019; Cruz-Cunha & Mateus-Coelho, 2021).

degree of comprehension, thesis for a doctoral programme The amount of project knowledge, the level of cybersecurity and threats, and the sensitivity levels of model parameters are all integrated into the model parameters in order to analyse cybersecurity and threats (Hakan, 2022; Alnatheer, 2015) through analysis in order to generate solutions that are more reliable and realistic.

We have established our two research problems after doing a literature review, which are as follows.

Even though some assessment models have been developed to evaluate how well an organisation can manage cybersecurity risks, there should be more assessment models available to evaluate organisations' readiness to successfully achieve and maximise the expected results of effective risk management in cybersecurity. RP1: There should be more assessment models available to evaluate organisations' readiness to successfully achieve and maximise the expected results of effective risk management in cybersecurity.

RP2: Organisations are at a major risk from new attack vectors because they lack the resources and the strategy essential to compete with new business models. In order to achieve the benefits associated with efficient cybersecurity risk management, organisations need support developing action plans to eliminate their readiness gaps (laid the groundwork), mature the organisation, respond efficiently and securely, and optimise their return on investment. This assistance is required in order to realise the full potential of effective cybersecurity risk management.

The following is a concise summary of our questions pertaining to the material.

Is there a benefit to making decisions using a visual depiction of the facts connected to risk?

- The identified problem 1 (RP1) is the primary concentration of this RQ1 investigation.

RQ2: Is it possible that the visualisation of risk information could help in the selection of an investment and make it easier to understand the return on investment in security?

- This question, RQ2, centres on the identified problem 2 (RFP2) as the primary topic of discussion.

2. RESEARCH METHODOLOGY

This essay provides a review of the research that has been conducted on the use of InfoVis and other methods of information visualisation to the decision-making process.

It was possible to identify, through an in-depth examination, that very few of the materials examined and analysed are related to this form of decision-making that is based on risk assessment and the utilisation of visualisation tools as the key outputs of the author's work. This was able to be determined because of the fact that the author's work was the primary focus of the investigation.

According to the findings of our study, there has been some research done on information visualisation to aid in decision-making; however, there has not been any research done on the assessment of security risks. We were not successful in locating a large study or InfoVis research in this field that might be useful to organisations in the decision-making process (there are just two, as was said).

The ability to make decisions more quickly through the use of information visualisation can be of significant support and value to enterprises who are experiencing problems in this area. This can both increase the value of the organisation and enable it to respond to the most difficult security risk in a proactive manner.

3. RESEARCH BACKGROUND

Because management is somewhat involved, as was said before, the numerous Standards and Frameworks that are currently in use can only rarely provide a brief solution, which necessitates the connection of two or more Frameworks.

These are based on controls that need to be put in place, and they occasionally need to provide the right visibility through signals that may be associated. This enables businesses to make the best choices possible in a preventative manner.

An example of this is the list of tools and frameworks related to risk management in security and cybersecurity that was published by ENISA (ENISA is the Agency for Cyber Security of the European Union), which will be explored further down.

According to the compilation, ENISA has identified a number of RM-related frameworks and procedures that are well-known and widely used. These frameworks and methods provide high-level guidance for risk management processes that may be applied by a wide variety of businesses.

3.1 Cybersecurity Risk Analysis

The process of risk assessment needs to be finished first, before any evaluation of an organisation can take place. In addition, it is and needs to be included in the process of proactive learning that an organisation utilises anytime it wants to anticipate the occurrence of such situations. To this end, it is essential to have analysis indicators, which will allow you to anticipate and forecast the situation and take appropriate action in a timely manner.

An essential component of cybersecurity risk assessment is the investigation and evaluation of the potential threats and openings that may exist inside the information systems, networks, and data of an organisation. This procedure is necessary for developing a cybersecurity strategy that is effective and for putting the appropriate protections in place to protect against attacks that are carried out online. There is nothing more important than determining the various stages of a cybersecurity risk management process in order to guarantee that our research and development strategy is suitable for the requirements really faced by companies.

Provide a description of the assets and the categories they fall under: The first thing that needs to be done is to identify and classify the most valuable assets that an organisation possesses, such as its data, systems, applications, and network infrastructures. Before determining the appropriate level of security, one must first determine the relevance and value of each item. Only then can the appropriate level of protection be determined.

Determine any possible dangers: Find the potential cyberthreats and attack pathways that could be exploited to steal or otherwise compromise the organization's assets. Weaknesses in the organization's systems or procedures, such as for instance malicious actors, malware, social engineering, insider threats, and other types of vulnerabilities, are some examples of what we may place here.

Vulnerabilities assessment Conduct a comprehensive analysis of the company's information technology (IT) infrastructure to identify and understand any potential flaws. Part of this procedure involves looking for vulnerabilities in programmes, devices, configurations, or even processes themselves, which would allow attackers to take advantage of the situation.

Conduct research into the following effects: Conduct an investigation into the consequences that could be had on the company's resources in the event of a successful attack using information technology. It is important to take into consideration, in terms of money, operations, reputation, and the law, the potential repercussions that could emerge from a breach of security.

In order to evaluate the likelihood that a cyberattack would occur, it is necessary to investigate past data and patterns, as well as market trends, threat intelligence, and any other applicable information. Because of this, you will then have the opportunity to successfully contribute to the allocation of resources and the establishing of risk priorities.

Putting the risk assessment higher up on the priority list: Combining the findings of the effect and probability studies is an effective way to arrive at an assessment of the overall risk posed by each potential danger. Rank the risks in order of priority, taking into account how serious they are and how much of an impact they could have on the organization's day-to-day activities.

Where can I find the adjustment options? Find out how effective the control measures are that can be used to cut down on the risks, and then evaluate their performance. It is possible that putting in place security measures such as firewalls, intrusion detection systems, access controls, encryption, security training and awareness initiatives, and incident response plans is required.

Find the controls: Once the hazards have been identified, find the controls that can reduce or eliminate as many of those risks as possible. It is possible that putting in place security measures such as firewalls, intrusion detection systems, access controls, encryption, security training and awareness initiatives, and incident response plans is required.

An examination of costs and benefits is performed. It is important to make a comparison between the potential consequences of the risks and the expenses and difficulties associated with putting control measures into action. The company will be able to more effectively allocate its resources if a cost-benefit analysis is conducted to determine which security solutions are both the most cost-effective and the most efficient.

Taking action to manage and cut down on potential dangers: Develop a risk treatment strategy, outlining in detail the actions that must be carried out in order to mitigate the dangers that have been pinpointed. Adopting technical controls, upgrading security policies and practises, doing routine vulnerability assessments and intrusion testing, and putting in place capabilities to respond to incidents are all examples of possible actions that fall under this category.

Conduct an investigation and keep an eye on: Always keep a close check on the cybersecurity posture of the organisation, perform risk assessments on a regular basis, and make any necessary adjustments in the event that new dangers or holes are discovered.

The process of doing a cybersecurity risk analysis should be an iterative one that is carried out on a regular basis. This is necessary so that a company can adapt to shifting business conditions and evolving threats. This strategy assists firms in making decisions, allocating resources, and developing a strong cybersecurity protection posture for their organisations.

3.1.1 Framing of Risk Analysis in Cybersecurity

In the document defined by the Cybersecurity Information Sharing Act of 2015, risk analysis cuts across all sectors of society. This act authorises and encourages private companies to take defensive measures to protect and mitigate cyber threats, as well as the sharing of information regarding indicators of cyber threats. Additionally, it mandates that private companies share information regarding cyber threat indicators. ##NO_NAME##, (2015).

3.1.2 The Way of Communicating and Interpreting

The disclosure of potential dangers is one of the most significant challenges. In spite of the fact that there are standards and rules, every organisation evaluates and interprets the same risks in their own unique way, which is frequently inconsistent because there are not enough facts. This empirical method will inevitably lead to deviations associated with biases, which will be made even more pronounced due to the absence of standardisation (Diesch et al., 2020). The value of a standardised approach to naming things has been demonstrated in a variety of contexts, including transdisciplinary research. For example, the lack of a uniform vocabulary was a barrier to the development of new research investigations. This was because the terminology utilised in these studies rendered it impossible to evaluate them in relation to previous research endeavours (Halima Ibrahim Kure, 2022). The standardising of a vocabulary is typically accomplished by adopting a formalised and systematic nomenclature (Hakan, 2022; Eigner, 2013). This is done with the intention of making communication amongst stakeholders hailing from a variety of fields easier. In order to increase cybersecurity communication, Ramirez recommends that practitioners initiate change by utilising technical language that is understandable by all disciplines. They also argue that the first step towards building a standardised cybersecurity language is to enhance research efforts geared at recognising terminology-related trends (Hevner et al., 2004). This is because, according to them, this is the best way to identify emerging terminology patterns. In addition to public policy, computer science, management, and social science, Hussain et al. (2020) suggests adding these four more sub-disciplines to the field of cybersecurity.

3.1.3 Use of Data, Visualization, and Interpretation

The analysis of data, as well as its usage and interpretation, as a means of providing a response in advance to a prospective incident, constitutes one of the key issues. The CIA pillars (Confidentiality, Integrity, and Availability) are the sole risk indicators that are taken into consideration by people responsible for risk management when conducting risk assessments and having risk-related conversations. Some people believe that a comprehensive model of cybersecurity risk should include variables other than the CIA, more specifically time and people, as key elements in determining the level of danger that a system, network, or user is exposed to. An illustration of this risk assessment and how it has an effect on several pillars is provided below in the form of an image that is very expressive. It makes use of a statistical analysis that makes it possible to visualise the data and the trend it reveals.

Figure 1. Risk analysis based on data

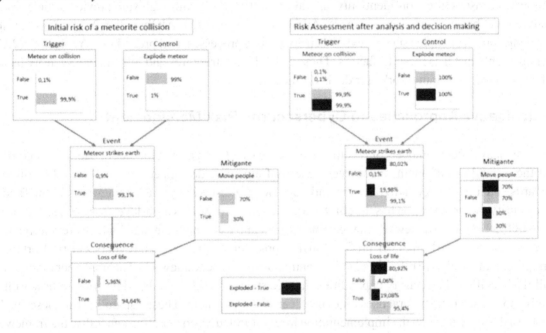

Looking at the values for the probability of "Loss of Life" being false, we found that we jumped from just over 4% (when we do not react) to 81% (when we react). This massive increase in the chance of saving the world clearly explains why it was worth a try.

The main benefits of this approach are:

- Risk measurement is more meaningful in context, in stark contrast to the simple "risk = probability x impact" approach, where none of the concepts has an unambiguous interpretation.
- Uncertainty is quantified, and we can read the current probability values associated with any event at any stage.
- Provides a visual and formal mechanism for recording and testing subjective probabilities. This is especially important for an event with little or no relevant data.

3.2 Risk Management in Cybersecurity and Success Factors

A recent poll conducted by 2021 on cybersecurity trends (Sobers, 2021), Yeoh et al. (2022) found that the majority of business leaders (68%) think that the dangers associated with their company's cybersecurity are growing. However, the installation of security software is necessary in order to successfully integrate cybersecurity within an organisation. The inverse is also true; the project is difficult to complete since it presents a number of obstacles in the areas of organisation, technology, and procedure (Ahmad et al., 2020; Mateus-Coelho & Cruz-Cunha, 2022). Despite the thriving security industry and the myriad of complexities surrounding cybersecurity, there is still a need to establish a comprehensive framework of cybersecurity Critical Success Factors to lead cybersecurity management in organisations. This is the case despite the fact that such a framework would likely be used. The decisions about security are influenced by the 12 aspects listed below: vulnerabilities, compliance and policy, risks, physical security, continuity, infrastructure, confidentiality, and availability (CIA). Although some review articles in the literature on cybersecurity success factors (Atkins & Lawson, 2020; AlGhamdi & Vlahu-Gjorgievska, 2020) concentrate on topics such as cybersecurity policy, processes, and procedures, Yeoh et al. (2022) provides a table that lists these 12 factors. These critical infrastructures and information security factors are based on existing Frameworks for decision-making.

3.3 Qualitative Approaches to Cybersecurity Risk Management

There are many different models of risk management, each of which can either compete with or complement the capabilities of another. The cybersecurity framework developed by the National Institute of Standards and Technology (NIST) is currently one of the most widely used frameworks in the field of cybersecurity. An organisation has the ability to put its own spin on this high-level, easy-to-read information (NIST, 2018). The framework can be broken down into its component parts, which are referred to as the framework core, the framework profile, and the implementation layers. The cybersecurity effort fulfils the requirements of all five roles listed in the centre portion of the framework. The implementation levels detail the specific cybersecurity capabilities that are stated in each level in connection to how well an organization's management practises for cybersecurity display them. These capabilities are described in relation to the level at which the implementation level is located. A corporation can utilise the framework profile to discover ways to strengthen its cybersecurity position by first comparing a "current" profile with a "target" profile. In other words, the "current" profile represents the organisation's current cybersecurity position. Despite the fact that the NIST cybersecurity framework explicitly acknowledges that actions linked to cybersecurity risk management are organization-specific, risk management considerations are only briefly touched upon. One of the advantages of using this framework is that it allows controls to be mapped to ISO 27001, ISA 62443-2-1:2009, ISA 62443-3-3:2013, CIS Controls, and CobIT 5. The process of deciding what kinds of controls should be installed in response to the assessment that has been made is made a great deal easier as a result of this development.

One of the standards that was developed as part of a collaborative effort between the International Organisation for Standardisation (ISO) and the International Electrotechnical Commission (IEC) is designated as ISO/IEC 27005. With the help of the tools and direction it provides, managers may put information security measures into effect and manage the associated risks (ISO/IEC, 2018). It is expected of the organisation that it will define its own strategy to risk management based on the type of information security management system, the status of risk management, and/or industry-specific security challenges. ISO/IEC 27005 does not explicitly apply any particular risk management strategy, despite the fact that it provides an organised sequence of actions to be completed in a certain order. As a consequence of this, businesses are compelled to rely on standards such as the ISO/IEC 31000 risk management standard in order to extend their approach to risk management. This can be accomplished, for example, by taking into consideration factors that are both internal and external to the company.

Cyber Kill Chain® (CKC) seven phase/chain framework is the name of a risk management approach that was developed by Lockheed Martin (Martin, 2009). The model makes predictions about the actions that the cyberattacker will take in order to achieve its objectives and provides recommendations regarding the kind of defenses that the cyberattacker should employ in order to break the chain both early on and later on. The framework places much of its emphasis on the technological component of cybersecurity, which encompasses both attackers and defenders. However, it does not sufficiently cover the human and organisational aspects of cyber risk, such as human error and insider threats. In addition to this, it does not provide any specific suggestions regarding the many investment options available in the field of cybersecurity.

OCTAVE, which stands for Operationally Critical Threat, Asset, and Vulnerability Evaluation, is a security assessment approach that was developed (Alberts & Dorofee, 2002) at the CERT(R) Coordination Centre in Pittsburgh, Pennsylvania, United States of America. An organisation is able to identify and classify its most valuable IT assets with the assistance of OCTAVE. Additionally, the organisation is able to assess the risks that are posed to those assets, investigate the vulnerabilities and impacts of those vulnerabilities, and develop security priorities in order to reduce the risks that are posed to those assets. In accordance with the self-direction principle, which serves as the foundation of OCTAVE, the process of evaluating an organization is carried out by a small team that is comprised of members from different departments inside the organization itself. These individuals get together to form an interdisciplinary group. OCTAVE Allegro, a modified version of the original OCTAVE, was developed (Caralli et al., 2007) with the intention of simplifying the process of installing the framework within an organization. OCTAVE Allegro provides an extensive assessment of the operational risk environment of a company in the context of a collaborative workshop, and it does so without requiring the participant to have abilities in risk assessment that are particularly in-depth.

Comparatively speaking, OCTAVE and the Cybermaturity Platform developed by the CMMI Institute offer equivalent risk management capabilities. The risk-based roadmap, which is a bespoke list of prioritized action items based on the risks that are most critical to the firm, is one of the distinguishing features of the Cybermaturity Platform (CMMI Institute LLC, 2020). In order to develop a risk-based roadmap, the Cybermaturity Platform will first conduct a security gap analysis to evaluate the level of maturity that is currently in place in comparison to the level of maturity that is desired, and then it will prioritize security activities according to the cybersecurity risk profiles of the firm.

Enterprises should apply the 18 critical security controls (CSC) included in the Consensus Audit Guidelines (CAG) released by the Centre for Internet Security (CIS) (CIS, 2019) in order to avoid or reduce the number of cyberattacks.

A few of the goals of the CAG include maximising the use of automation to apply security controls, maximising the use of cyber-offensives to inform cyber-defence, concentrating on high-return areas, ensuring that security investments are targeted to counter the most serious threats, utilizing cyber-offensives to inform cyber-defence, and utilizing a consensus process to gather the best ideas. The implementation layers of the NIST Cybersecurity Framework, which are referred to as Implementation Groups (IGs), are comparable to those of the CAG. IG 1 has the fewest developed resources and the least developed expertise when it comes to cybersecurity, whereas IG 3 has the most developed resources and the most developed knowledge. The IGs are designed to assist businesses in identifying the level of cybersecurity maturity they possess, prioritizing the use of controls, and developing a productive cybersecurity programme.

3.4 Quantitative Approaches to Cybersecurity Risk Management

Quantitative research approaches are usually used in the kinds of studies that concentrate on evaluating the risks posed by cybersecurity. In this particular situation, a framework for controlling network security risk was utilized, and as an example, a Bayesian decision network (BDN) was used (Khosravi-Farmad & Ghaemi-Bafghi, 2020). Increasing a network's level of security requires meticulous execution of a number of critical processes, including risk assessment, risk mitigation, risk validation, and risk monitoring, to name just a few. These procedures are included in the framework that serves as the basis for network security and should each be carried out in their own unique manner. The BDN models the data required to manage security risks, including information on vulnerabilities, risk mitigation measures, and the consequences of their implementation on vulnerabilities. This data may be found in the table below. During the process of risk mitigation, modified Bayesian inference algorithms are utilized in order to carry out a cost-benefit analysis of risk mitigation. Their tests indicate how their methodology significantly improves network security by precisely detecting threats and efficiently minimizing those hazards.

The precise requirements of ISO 27005 are expanded upon by a distinct risk assessment methodology that is referred to as AVARCIBER (Rea-Guaman et al., 2020). The application of the framework requires a series of stages, including beginning the risk assessment, identifying and evaluating assets, detecting cybersecurity threats, defining the damage level for vulnerability-asset tuples (dimension), calculating the risk, and putting countermeasures into place. When measured against ISO 27005, the procedure in its entirety does not stand out as particularly remarkable. However, more in-depth exercises as well as guides that can be of assistance are provided.

Given that the NIST cybersecurity framework lacks a practical financial technique for justifying cybersecurity projects, a framework for a cost-benefit analysis has been produced as a consequence of study into this issue (Gordon et al., 2020). The research led to the establishment of a framework for a cost-benefit analysis. The study demonstrates how organizations can select the most suitable level of NIST implementation level by using cost-benefit analysis, and it illustrates the relationship between levels of NIST implementation level and the appropriate level of investment that an organization can make in cybersecurity activities. Both of these are demonstrated in the study.

The levels of application of the framework provide a condensed description of how "an organization views its cybersecurity risk and the processes in place to manage that risk" (Deloitte, 2018, p. 8). An organization is capable of progressing all the way to each of the following four levels: Level 1 (Partial), Level 2 (Risk Informed), Level 3 (Repeatable), and Level 4 (Adaptive). According to NIST (Deloitte, 2018, p. 8), "the levels describe an increasing degree of rigour and sophistication in cybersecurity risk management practises." These levels range from "Partial" (Level 1) all the way up to "Adaptive" (Level 4) in the scale. In other words, the level of rigour and sophistication of a company's approach to risk management increases as it moves up the levels, from Level 1 all the way up to Level 4.

Tier 1 (Partial) firms do not have a defined and integrated strategy for managing cybersecurity risk, and they are more likely to take a reactive approach to controlling this risk as opposed to a proactive one. When it comes to the management of cybersecurity risks, Tier 1 firms generally have very minimal involvement with other businesses or cybersecurity professional bodies (such an Information Sharing Analysis Centre). Companies that fall into the Tier 2 (risk-informed) category typically have formal risk management processes that are only loosely linked to one another, but these processes are not enforced as official company rules. In addition, Level 2 organizations typically have very limited discussion with other companies or professional bodies regarding the management of their cybersecurity risks.

Organizations who have reached Level 3 (Repeatable) in the Cybersecurity Maturity Model have formalized and integrated their risk management practices, as well as established official lines of contact with other businesses and professional groups working in the subject of cybersecurity. These companies use a mixed approach to the management of the risks posed by cybersecurity; they are both proactive and reactive in their approach. Level 4 (Adaptive) companies have formal, integrated risk management procedures in place in addition to their formal channels of engagement with other companies and industry associations about cybersecurity risk management. In addition to proactive and reactive techniques of managing cybersecurity risk, Level 4 organizations also utilize an adaptive approach to the management of this risk. As a direct consequence of this, these companies continually evaluate the degree to which the cybersecurity threats to which they are exposed have evolved, and they keep their recovery procedures up to date to reflect the modifications. Organizations operating at Level 4 make it a point to think carefully about the effects, both operational and financial, of making any necessary adjustments to their recovery plans.

The four levels of the NIST Cybersecurity Framework each provide businesses with a basic overview of how they should see their cybersecurity risk management process and what has to be done to advance to a higher level. The levels are a useful tool for analyzing the financial costs and benefits associated with the various approaches that businesses take to the management of cybersecurity risks. According to NIST (Deloitte, 2018, p. 15), "The tier selection process takes into account an organization's current risk management practices, business/mission objectives, supply chain cybersecurity requirements, and organizational constraints."

3.5 How to Determine Whether or Not Your Investment in Information Security is Worth It

Calculating the return on investment in information security can be tricky since not all elements associated to information security are easily quantified in terms of their direct financial value. However, there are approaches that may be taken in order to evaluate the value of one's return on investments made in information security. The following is a list of several approaches that can be used to calculate the return on investment in information security:

Determining whether or not there has been a reduction in the number of security incidents that have happened after the new security measures were implemented. This could mean reducing the number of successful assaults, data breaches, system failures, or other bad scenarios. By reducing the frequency of these occurrences, it is possible to save money that would have been spent on things like repairs, data loss, fines, reputational damage, and interruptions to business operations.

Recovery will go more quickly if you first determine how much time it will take to get back up and running after a security incident. The sooner the company is able to recover and get back to normal business, the less of an effect this will have on its finances and operations. The decrease in recovery time can be an indicator that information security is valuable since it helps to prevent financial losses and business interruptions. Information security also helps to lessen the likelihood of a breach occurring in the first place.

To determine the value of the costs that could have been avoided, you must first determine the amount of money that was saved by the implementation of security measures. This can include paying to fix compromised systems, recovering lost data, notifying the public about a data breach, filing a lawsuit, paying regulatory penalties, losing customers, and suffering reputational loss. When compared with investments made in information security, the costs that are avoided provide one way to get a ballpark figure for the financial return that can be expected.

The degree of compliance that has been achieved is one of the metrics that may be used to evaluate an organization's level of conformity with security regulations, statutory requirements, and industry standards. One potential source of financial advantage that might result from enhanced compliance is the avoidance of regulatory infractions, which can result in the imposition of fines, penalties, and financial losses.

Evaluate the procedure for risk reduction both before and after the security measures have been put into place. Conduct an analysis to determine how likely it is that risk occurrences would occur now and how the impact of those occurrences would change if they did. This evaluation has the ability to demonstrate the advantages of implementing information security by lowering the likelihood of suffering a financial loss and increasing the amount of money that could be saved.

Take into consideration the level of satisfaction experienced by the organization's customers as well as the level of public confidence in the organization's ability to protect sensitive information. It is possible that client satisfaction surveys, positive remarks, and an increase in trust are indirect evidence of a favorable return on information security. This is because they may result in monetary gains such as the retention of existing clients, the acquisition of new clients, and an increase in income.

Despite the fact that not all of these aspects can be easily quantified in terms of monetary returns, they can nonetheless provide a comprehensive picture of the benefits and returns of information security. Modifications should be made to metrics as well as measurement methodologies in order to accommodate the specific needs and objectives of the organization.

3.6 In Order to Evaluate the Profitability of our Investments in Information Security and Cybersecurity, What Kinds of Benchmarks and Indicators Should We Develop

When calculating the return on investment in information security and cybersecurity, it is required to monitor and analyze a number of metrics and indicators that may be used to judge the success of measures that have been implemented. This is a requirement for the calculation. The following is a summary of some important signs and measurements to take into consideration:

By keeping track of this data throughout time, you may check the occurrence rate of security incidents over the course of the time period. This can manifest itself in a variety of ways, including data leaks, attacks using malware or hacking software, or efforts to infiltrate a system. If this rate continues to fall over the course of time, it is an indication that there has been an increase in security.

Mean time to detect, abbreviated MTTD, is the amount of time that should be measured to determine how long it takes on average for a security incident to be discovered after it has already taken place. A lower MTTD indicates faster and more accurate detection, which paves the way for a more rapid response.

Determine the average amount of time it takes to respond to and resolve a security issue after it has been discovered (also known as MTTR, or the typical amount of time to reply). A shorter mean time to resolve an incident (MTTR) implies a more effective capability for incident response.

Keep an eye on the percentage of attacks that are thwarted when they are directed at the security infrastructure. This parameter has the potential to be used to evaluate the efficacy of the protection mechanisms that have been put into place.

Find out the extent to which the relevant policies, standards, and legislation concerning information security have been adhered with. This indicator contributes to the process of determining how effectively a company complies with both legal requirements and industry standards and recommendations.

It is important to determine the typical expenses incurred while dealing with a security incident. It is possible that forensic investigation costs, data recovery costs, customer notification costs, lost productivity costs, reputational injury costs, and more charges could be included in this. This cost was reduced, which demonstrates that risks were effectively mitigated as they were being managed.

Determine the level of information security knowledge and training that each person have inside the organization. Using things like surveys, mock phishing attacks, or records of previous involvement in training programmers are all viable options for accomplishing this goal. This rate is growing, which shows that people are becoming more aware of security threats and adopting safer habits as a result of this awareness.

If it is at all possible to do so, you should determine the typical amount of time that passes between malfunctions of safety systems. A higher MTBF for the system is indicative of greater dependability and fewer operational problems because there will be less wear and tear on the components.

It is of the utmost importance to adjust measurements and indicators so that they are in line with the one-of-a-kind goals, known dangers, and operational requirements of the organization. It is also recommended to conduct out routine studies and compare the results over time in order to uncover patterns and areas that need to be improved.

4. CONCEPTUAL MODEL: METHODOLOGY FOR PREDICTIVE CYBER SECURITY RISK ASSESSMENT (PCSRA)

The risk management models that are currently in use are those that are based on previously established standards and frameworks, and they always react in line with the controls that are described by these standards. These models have been in use for quite some time now.

Every time a risk assessment is carried out, it is based on the response to these controls, including whether or not they exist, whether or not they are applied, and the opportunities for improvement.

The topic of predictive risk management models has quickly become one of the most talked-about issues in today's culture. When we talk about cybersecurity, these prediction models, however, continue to be developed using the same way of risk assessment as they were in the past. This is not a new practise. When we talk about this component, we are referring to a component that encompasses the infrastructure of the organisation, networks, the web, and a great lot more; in other words, everything that travels through the well-known realm of Cyberspace.

As a consequence of this, Risk Management needs to adopt a more proactive approach to changing the way that it is approached, and the model that has been presented needs to be developed on this new strategy for reacting to risks.

How is this model distinct from those that have come before it?

At this moment, companies have the opportunity to utilise monitoring systems such as Security Information and Event Management (SIEMs) and Vulnerability Management, amongst other options.

Figure 2. Conceptual model for PCSRA

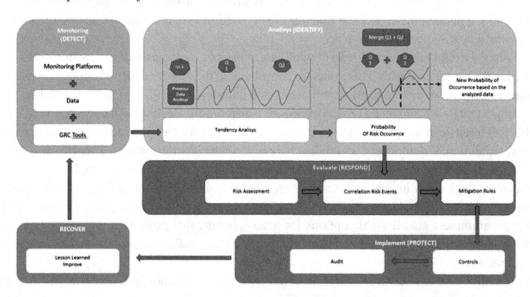

These technologies give them access to data, which, once it has been put through the necessary processing processes, constitutes useful information for conducting a risk assessment based on trends. Since the model has already been presented, it is time to move on to the next step, which is to offer a model that correlates the existing controls and the controls that have been implemented with this data analysis. This will illustrate the propensity for a particular risk to manifest itself once more in the future.

This model makes an effort to have an approach that fulfils other approaches that are already in existence and combines them; doing so will offer value to the process of identifying and managing risks.

The NIST Cybersecurity Framework model was used in this specific instance, and the only reason for doing so was so that it could be explained. This paradigm may be broken down into five distinct phases, which are Detect, Identify, Respond, Protect, and Recover. A potential way of connecting the various phases with the predictive model that was planned to be used is also provided here.

Because it is connected to a number of other reference standards, this framework is utilised as a reference due to the fact that it is connected to those standards.

- Monitoring (DETECTED)
  - The goal of this phase is to make use of the resources that are already available in order to identify potential dangers within the business by utilising monitoring platforms and GRC platforms, which are platforms that are specifically devoted to the controls that are implemented within organisations and their connection to compliance.
  - In this location, we are able to identify any and all potential dangers by either passive or active monitoring.
- Analysis (IDENTIFY)
  - At this point in the process, it is possible to identify which patterns are derived from the monitoring platforms by conducting analysis using the example as a guide. In addition, overlaying the study of trends to anticipate that such a risk will occur again, which will consequently prepare the organisation for a more aggressive answer based on the facts it already

has, leading it to a more consistent answer. At the same time, it gives information on the more actual costs of the actions that need to be taken.

- Evaluate (RESPOND)
  - At this point, the answer is intended to be provided with mitigation measures based on the assessment of the current risk and on the correlation of events originating by the platforms. This is due to the fact that by reconciling these two aspects, we will be able to have more effective and efficient mitigation actions. This will be the goal of implementing controls that are more effective, regardless of the form of such controls.
- Implement (PROTECT)
  - This is the phase in which the controls and measures required to reduce risks and minimise the exposure factor of the organisation to risks of any kind are put into effect. After the controls and procedures have been implemented, they must undergo an audit to confirm that everything adheres to the requirements.
- RECOVER
  - Once all of the potential dangers have been eliminated, the recuperation phase can begin. During this stage, there will be an examination of both the ongoing process of improvement and the lessons that have been gained. That is to say, this stage is an evaluation of the current areas in which improvements are needed, the areas in which it is likely that we will be affected again and the reasons for this, the areas in which we should concentrate our risk management efforts, and the lessons that we will take with us into the future.

In the end, the model that was provided needs to be implemented each and every time a fresh risk assessment is carried out within the business. It should be utilised as a reliable check for carrying out risk assessments about cybersecurity. The sole purpose of this evaluation is not to evaluate risk management based on controls. It should also analyse in a more thorough and cross-cutting manner, looking at things like how deeply ingrained the organization's culture and attitude are in the way it manages risk, how well organised it is, and the level of risk the organisation is willing to take. All of this is designed to help prioritise the appropriate activities and keep track of the steps that need to be taken to implement them. Organisations of any size will have the capability to continuously evaluate the risk management component, and they will also have the ability to take action to resolve the problems that they have identified.

5. DISCUSSION

We chose DSR because it is a problem-solving technique with a clear purpose of expanding human knowledge, generating new artefacts, and solving problems through them (Hevner et al., 2004; Alves et al., 2022). This was done with the intention of helping the resolution of the problems that the research indicated as being problematic (1 and 2).

Within the DSR, we decided to go with the model that was suggested by Peffers (2007), which is a design science technique that has garnered a lot of support from a lot of people. The primary motivation behind this choice is connected to the fact that it is straightforward. Although it is more focused on the theoretical review on the transition from purpose to design than Hevner's (2004) method, it fits better with current research. This is especially true considering that preparedness is not a clearly defined tangible good that can be investigated in the environment of the organisation. At the same time, it offers a process that is both extremely problem-oriented and objectively solution-oriented, guiding us from the identification of the problem (and the relevance of the problem) all the way through the creation and development of a potential solution, as well as its demonstration and communication.

The following is a condensed version of the model's two components, which are known collectively as the Methodology for Predictive Cybersecurity Risk Assessment (PCSRA).

Security-enlightened RoSI - the outcome of the assessment will lead to the identification of risk levels incurred at the calculated state of readiness and the identification of possible actions to be taken as a step towards moving the enterprise to a higher state of readiness. Component 1. Evaluate whether the visualisation of risk-related data simplifies the decision-making process. Component 2. Security-enlightened RoSI - the outcome of the assessment will lead to the identification of risk levels incurred at the calculated state of readiness.

5.1 Future Work

Future study work on the incorporation of this model into the risk management procedures of businesses is something that can be done after the PCSRA has been fully elaborated and validated in its entirety.

This risk management strategy ought to be completely congruent with the governance model and the goals of the company (AlGhamdi & Vlahu-Gjorgievska, 2020).

For this reason, it will be beneficial to conduct additional research on the integration with:

1. Frameworks for the proactive management of the implementation of risk analysis in accordance with any existing standards.
2. Frameworks to continue risk management in an effective manner and to enable the integration of the PCSRA as a model to be used and reference for proactive risk management after the implementation of the PCSRA, answering the questions: is it possible to predict a new risk and thus prevent potential impacts on the organisation? If that is the case, what kind of organisational framework could be employed to steer and oversee the implementation of this risk management programme? (Halima Ibrahim Kure, 2022).
3. The development of frameworks for the risk management strategy and the RBS (Diesch et al., 2020).
4. Using Artificial Intelligence as a value-added resource to proactively identify hazards, adopt risk mitigation and reaction strategies, and finally monitor these processes.

The application of artificial intelligence (AI) in the context of risk management in enterprises has been demonstrating a growing potential for success. AI provides a multitude of tools and methodologies that can help in the discovery, assessment, and mitigation of risks that enterprises are up against.

Data analytics is one of the primary uses of artificial intelligence that can be found in risk management. AI may be used to extract important insights from the huge amounts of information that organisations generate and gather. These insights can be used to find patterns and connections that would be difficult for humans to recognise. Because of this, risk analysis can now be performed in real time and with more precision, which makes it much simpler to make decisions based on correct information.

It has been demonstrated that employing Artificial Intelligence (AI) as a proactive resource in responding to the security risks faced by enterprises is a successful strategy for identifying and preventing cyber threats and other forms of attacks. AI provides more advanced analytics and machine learning capabilities, which enables a faster and more accurate reaction to potential security concerns.

Therefore, AI can be utilised in the process of forecasting potential security issues. AI algorithms can discover trends and patterns that suggest the possibility of certain sorts of attacks or security breaches occurring by drawing on data that is both current and historical in nature. Because of this competence, firms are able to take preventative actions before hazards actually materialise, hence minimising their vulnerability to possible dangers.

Automation of processes is yet another way in which AI may be utilised in risk management. Automating mundane, time-consuming, and low-value-added jobs can be accomplished with the help of AI algorithms, which enables experts to devote their attention to more important, strategic endeavours. Because of this, not only is there an increase in operational efficiency, but there is also a reduction in the possibility of human error.

One thing that can be claimed is that AI has the potential to be employed in the process of automating responses to potential security threats. Once a threat has been identified, AI algorithms have the ability to automatically initiate countermeasures and mitigation steps, such as limiting access, isolating infected systems, or alerting security teams. This both accelerates the time it takes to respond to attacks and lessens their overall impact, which in turn reduces the amount of time spent being exposed to potentially harmful consequences.

AI also has a use in vulnerability assessment, which is another application of the technology. Algorithms powered by AI are able to investigate computer systems and physical infrastructure in the pursuit of finding and naming flaws and openings, thereby locating potential security issues in advance of their being exploited by malicious users. With the help of this proactive analysis, enterprises are able to bolster their defences and put suitable security measures into place, thereby lowering the probability that an attack would be successful.

One other application for artificial intelligence is the identification of fraudulent and suspicious behaviour. This can be accomplished through the usage of the technology. The use of AI algorithms enables the examination of vast volumes of data, which enables the identification of anomalous patterns that may indicate the existence of fraud. This enables speedier detection as well as more effective detection, which in turn helps reduce financial losses and protects the organization's reputation.

The last point to make, but perhaps not the least important, is to underline the importance of taking caution while employing AI to address potential security threats. For artificial intelligence to be effective, it must be kept current and trained with data that is both pertinent and current at all times (data integrity). An additional factor to take into account is the ethical and privacy concerns that are raised by the application of AI data and algorithms in the domain of security, particularly with regard to the handling of personal data.

REFERENCES

ENISA. (n.d.). *Compendium of risk management frameworks.* European Agency for Cybersecurity. https://www.enisa.europa.eu/publications/compendium-of-risk-management-frameworks

Abu, M. S. (2018). Cyber threat intelligence–issue and challenges. *Indonesian Journal of Electrical Engineering and Computer Science, 10*(1), 371–379. doi:10.11591/ijeecs.v10.i1.pp371-379

Ahmad, A., Desouza, K. C., Maynard, S. B., Naseer, H., & Baskerville, R. L. (2020). *How the integration of cyber security management and incident response enables organisational learning.*

Alberts, C., & Dorofee, A. (2002). Introducing OCTAVE Allegro: Improving the Information Security Risk Assessment Process. *Managing Information Security Risks: The OCTAVESM Approach.* Addison Wesley. https://citeseerx.ist.psu.edu/viewdoc/download?doi=10.1.1.461.7807&rep=rep1&type=pdf

AlGhamdi, S., & Vlahu-Gjorgievska, W. K. T. E. (2020). Information security governance challenges and critical success factors. *Computers & Security, 99,* 102030. doi:10.1016/j.cose.2020.102030

Alnatheer, M. (2015). Information Security Culture Critical Success Factors. *Proceedings - 12th International Conference on Information Technology: New Generations, ITNG* (pp. 731-735). IEEE. 10.1109/ITNG.2015.124

Alves, F., Mateus-Coelho, N., & Cruz-Cunha, M. (2022). ChevroCrypto – Security & Cryptography Broker. *2022 10th International Symposium on Digital Forensics and Security (ISDFS),* (pp. 1-5). IEEE. 10.1109/ISDFS55398.2022.9800797

Ashley, C., & Preiksaitis, M. (2022). *Strategic Cybersecurity Risk Management Practices for Information in Small and Medium Enterprises.*

Atkins, S., & Lawson, C. (2020). *An Improvised Patchwork: Success and Failure in Cybersecurity Policy for Critical Infrastructure.*

Bowen, B. M., Devarajan, R., & Stolfo, S. (2011). Measuring the human factor of cyber security. Paper presented at *2011 IEEE International Conference on Technologies for Homeland Security (HST),* (pp. 230–235). IEEE. 10.1109/THS.2011.6107876

Caralli, R. A., Stevens, J. F., Young, L. R., & William, R. (2007). *TECHNICAL REPORT CMU/SEI-2007-TR-012 ESC-TR-2007-012 CERT Program.* CMU. https://resources.sei.cmu.edu/asset_files/TechnicalReport/2007_005_001_14885.pdf

Card, S., Mackinlay, J., & Shneiderman, B. (1999). *Readings in information visualisation: using vision to think.* Morgan Kaufmann.

Cherdantseva, Y., Burnap, P., Blyth, A., Eden, P., Jones, K., Soulsby, H., & Stoddart, K. (2016). A review of cyber security risk assessment methods for SCADA systems. *Computers & Security, 56,* 1–27. doi:10.1016/j.cose.2015.09.009

CIS. (2019). *CIS Controls® V7.1.* CIS. https://www.cisecurity.org/controls/

CMMI Institute LLC. (2020). *Over 1/2 of Cyber Professionals Expect a Cyber Attack within 12 Months.* CMMI Institute. https://cmmiinstitute.com/products/cybermaturity

Conti, M., Dargahi, T., & Dehghantanha, A. (2018). *Cyber threat intelligence: challenges and opportunities. Cyber threat intelligence.* Springer.

Craigen, D., Diakun-Thibault, N., & Purse, R. (2014). Defining Cybersecurity. *Technology Innovation Management Review, 4*(10), 13–21. doi:10.22215/timreview/835

Cruz-Cunha, M. M., & Mateus-Coelho, N. R. (Eds.). (2021). *Handbook of Research on Cyber Crime and Information Privacy.* IGI Global.

Cuchta, T., Blackwood, B., Devine, T., Niichel, R., Daniels, K., Lutjens, C., Maibach, S., & Stephenson, R. (2019). *Human Risk Factors in Cybersecurity*. . doi:10.1145/3349266.3351407

Deloitte. (2018). *Secure IoT by Design*. Deloitte. https://www2.deloitte.com/us/en/pages/operations/articles/iot-platform-security.html

Diesch, R., Pfaff, M., & Krcmar, H. (2020). A comprehensive model of information security factors for decision-makers. *Computers & Security*, *92*, 1–21. doi:10.1016/j.cose.2020.101747

Eigner, W. (2013). Current Work Practice and Users' Perspectives on Visualization and Interactivity in Business Intelligence. In *17th International Conference on Information Visualization*. IEEE. 10.1109/IV.2013.38

Gordon, L.A., Loeb, M.P, & Zhou, L. (2020). Integrating cost–benefit analysis into the NIST Cybersecurity Framework via the Gordon-Loeb Model. *J. Cybersecurity, 6*.

Halima Ibrahim Kure. (2022). An integrated cyber security risk management framework and risk predication for the critical infrastructure protection. *Neural Computing & Applications*.

Hevner, A. R., March, S. T., Park, J., & Ram, S. (2004). Design Science in Information Systems. *Management Information Systems Quarterly*, *28*(1), 75–105. doi:10.2307/25148625

Hussain, A., Mohamed, A., & Razali, S. (2020). *A review on Cybersecurity: Challenges & emerging threats. NISS 2020 Proceedings*. ACM. doi:10.1145/3386723.3387847

ISO27005 Information security risk management

ISO31000 Risk Management.

ISO/IEC. ISO/IEC 27005:2018(en) Information Technology—Security Techniques—Information Security Risk Management. (2018). Available online: https://www.iso.org/obp/ui/#iso:std:iso-iec:27005:ed-3:v1:en

Khosravi-Farmad, M., & Ghaemi-Bafghi, A. (2020). Bayesian Decision Network-Based Security Risk Management Framework. *Journal of Network and Systems Management*, *28*(4), 1794–1819. doi:10.100710922-020-09558-5

Kure, H., & Islam, S. (2019). Cyber Threat Intelligence for Improving Cybersecurity and Risk Management in Critical Infrastructure. *Journal of Universal Computer Science*, *25*(11), 1478–1502.

Lohr, S. (2012). The age of big data. *New York Times, 11*.

Manoj, B., & Baker, A. (2007). Communication challenges in emergency response. *Communications of the ACM*, *50*(3), 51–53. doi:10.1145/1226736.1226765

Martin, L. (2009). *Cyber Kill Chain®*. Lock Heed Martin. https://www.lockheedmartin.com/en-us/capabilities/cyber/cyber-kill-chain.html

Mateus-Coelho, N., & Cruz-Cunha, M. (2022). Serverless Service Architectures and Security Minimals. *2022 10th International Symposium on Digital Forensics and Security (ISDFS)*, (pp. 1-6). IEEE. 10.1109/ISDFS55398.2022.9800779

Moussa Dioubate, B. & Norhayate, W. (2022). *A Review of Cybersecurity Risk Management Framework in Malaysia Higher Education Institutions*.

Munzner, T. (2014). *Visualisation analysis*.

NIST. (2018). Cybersecurity Framework. NIST. https://www.nist.gov/cyberframework

NIST. (n.d.a). *Cybersecurity Framework*. NIST.

NIST. (n.d.b). *800-53 Risk Management Framework*. NIST.

Oltramari, A., & Kott, A. (2018). Towards a reconceptualisation of cyber risk: An empirical and ontological study. *Journal of Information Warfare*, *17*(1).

Peffers, K., Tuunanen, T., Rothenberger, A., & Chatterjee, S. (2007). A design science research methodology for information systems research. *Journal of Management Information Systems*, *24*(3), 45–77. doi:10.2753/MIS0742-1222240302

Ramirez, R., & Choucri, N. (2016). Improving interdisciplinary communication with standardised cyber security terminology: A literature review. *IEEE Access : Practical Innovations, Open Solutions*, *4*, 2216–2243. doi:10.1109/ACCESS.2016.2544381

Ramirez, R. B. (2017). *Making cyber security interdisciplinary: Recommendations for a novel curriculum and terminology harmonisation* [Thesis]. Massachusetts Institute of Technology.

Rea-Guaman, A. M., Mejía, J., San Feliu, T., & Calvo-Manzano, J. A. (2020). *AVARCIBER: A framework for assessing cybersecurity risks*. Clust. Comput.

Fenten, N. (2018). *Risk Assessment and Decision Analysis with Bayesian Networks*. Taylor & Francis.

PEGA. (n.d.). *RMF -Risk Management Framework*. PEGA.

Saraiva, M., & Coelho, N. (2022). CyberSoc Implementation Plan. *2022 10th International Symposium on Digital Forensics and Security (ISDFS)* (pp. 1-6). IEEE. 10.1109/ISDFS55398.2022.9800819

Saraiva, M., & Mateus-Coelho, N. (2022). CyberSoc Framework a Systematic Review of the State-of-Art. *Procedia Computer Science*, *204*, 961–972. doi:10.1016/j.procs.2022.08.117

Sobers, R. (2021). *134 Cybersecurity Statistics and Trends for 2021*. Varonis. https://www.varonis.com/blog/cybersecurity-statistics/

Thomas, M. (2019). *13 IOT security companies you should know*. Bulitin. https://builtin.com/internet-things/iot-security-companies-startups

Von Solms, R., & Van Niekerk, J. (2013). From information security to cyber security. *Computers & Security*, *38*, 97–102. doi:10.1016/j.cose.2013.04.004

Yeoh, W., Huang, H., Lee, W. S., Al Jafari, F., & Mansson, R. (2021). *Simulated phishing attack and embedded training campaign*.

Yeoh, W., Wang, S., Popovic, A., & Chowdhury, N. (2022). A Systematic Synthesis of Critical Success Factors for Cybersecurity. *JCOSE*. doi:10.1016/j.cose.2022.102724

Chapter 4
The Role of Blockchain Technology in Organizational Cyber Security

Dauda Sule

https://orcid.org/0000-0002-8795-4717

Air Force Institute of Technology, Kaduna, Nigeria

Jude Enenche Ameh

https://orcid.org/0009-0001-4523-5204

Sheffield Hallam University, UK

Suleiman Abu Usman

Air Force Institute of Technology, Kaduna, Nigeria

ABSTRACT

Distributed ledger technology (DLT), decentralized finance (DeFi), blockchain – these are terms that have been trending especially in technology circles. Today, blockchain has gained more acceptance, but sceptics continue to raise concerns about the technology's scalability, security, and long-term viability. There are also concerns regarding its being associated with crime and the dark web, which might imply it will have negative consequences if adopted. It has its own peculiar cyber security loopholes, but these can be addressed. That notwithstanding, organizations stand to gain from the blockchain in terms of cyber security; especially its qualities of decentralization and immutability. It has been successfully implemented in some sectors with positive results. This chapter seeks to illustrate how the blockchain can be used to boost and optimize cyber security for organizations.

INTRODUCTION

With comments and arguments of the technology's potential to disrupt multiple industries, including Healthcare, Public Sector, Energy, Manufacturing, and especially Financial Services, where it is predicted to be the beating heart of finance and the ultimate provider of a new industry fabric; blockchain's evolution has been compared to the early rise of the internet. The technology has sparked such interest that

DOI: 10.4018/979-8-3693-1528-6.ch004

financial services and technology organizations around the world invested about $8.7 billion in blockchain as at the first half of 2021 (Statista Research Department, 2022)and it was projected that the market size of blockchain would increasingly grow from 2022 to 2030 at a compound annual growth rate of about 86% (Grand View Research, Inc., 2022). Gartner observed that decentralized blockchain applications were thriving, while there a few successful permissioned blockchains for enterprise, however, there is also a move by countries (like Nigeria, China and the US trying to join in) to create central bank digital currencies (CBDC) based on blockchain technology. It has, therefore, become a top priority for industry leaders to understand how it may transform their business models and value chains to gain a competitive edge and, perhaps more importantly, to stay relevant (Litan, 2021).

However, the technology is currently at the pinnacle of inflated expectations and is poised to plummet into the abyss of disillusionment. Some of the early use cases we saw were deploying blockchain for the sake of deploying blockchain, rather than focusing on the technology's core attributes, which have the potential to generate significant process efficiencies across a wide range of industries and is likely to contribute to entirely new business models. As a result, the blockchain sector is going beyond proof-of-concept to production pilots, with business cases being developed to determine the technology's value. A focus on security and privacy, which must be addressed and tested if this technology is to become the true catalyst for social and industrial change that so many believe it can be, is a necessary component of such studies.

BACKGROUND

Today's increasing reliance on technology and the internet has given rise to new business models and revenue streams for businesses, but it has also created new vulnerabilities and opportunities for cyber criminals to exploit. Due to the use of more sophisticated malware and the growing threat of professional criminal cyber organizations and also nation states using such malicious actors to carry out cyber-attacks against and siphon funds from other nation states; cyber-attacks have grown more targeted and complex (Cybersecurity and Infrastructure Security Agency, 2022)There has also been a surge in use of stolen identity and credentials for malicious activity, reducing reliance on malware, as was observed that 62% of detected malicious cyber activity in the first quarter of 2021 were free of malware (Business Australia, 2022). Cyber criminals now attempt to steal valuable data such as intellectual property (IP), personally identifiable information (PII), health records, and financial data, and are employing highly profitable strategies such as monetizing data access via advanced ransomware techniques or disrupting overall business operations via Distributed Denial of Service (DDoS) attacks.

So, what about blockchain technology? Will technology be an aid or a detriment to cyber security? As a matter of fact, blockchain is seen as an enabler for cybercrime, in that cryptocurrency has been the preferred payment method requested for by criminals for ransomware and even kidnapping based on its perceived anonymity. The CEO of Fireeye observed that increase in ransomware attacks was closely related to the coming of cryptocurrency as a result of anonymity of entry and payment (Singh, 2021). There are also cases of money laundering with cryptocurrency, according to the BBC, money laundering by way of cryptocurrency increased in volume by 30% as at 2021 (BBC News, 2022). Criminals in addition to the usual money laundering tactics (layering, placement integration, money mules and so on) also use mixing services (also known as tumblers) which mix the crypto with others in a pool before sending back, obfuscating source and destination of funds (Stevens, 2022). There is also the technique of chain-hopping whereby funds are siphoned using cheaply acquired or stolen accounts to make tracing difficult (Stevens, 2022).

The chapter will look at how blockchain can be used to mitigate such issues, especially based on its core qualities of immutability, transparency, auditability, data encryption, and operational resilience, blockchains could potentially aid and strengthen cyber security by securing, and preventing fraudulent activities through consensus processes, and detecting data tampering (including no single point of failure). However, the characteristics of blockchain do not provide an impenetrable panacea for all cyber ills; to believe otherwise would be naive at best. Instead, blockchain implementations and roll-outs must include standard system and network cyber security controls, due diligence, practice, and procedures, just like other technologies.

Another issue is that the decentralized nature of blockchain can have adverse effects on the confidentiality of information, as all participants on a blockchain can have access to it (Mani, 2017). Are there ways this can be mitigated, or can there be a trade-off on a cost-benefit-basis? This will also be trashed in the chapter.

The planned chapter will examine the security of blockchain technology as per the following:

- Blockchain's present level of security from a system and data perspective for both public and private blockchains will be reviewed and addressed in this global point of view.
- To analyse the current maturity level of blockchain technology, the CIA (Confidentiality, Integrity and Availability) triad model will be used.
- Secure by design? Blockchain security attacks, hacks, and issues. Does blockchain enable crime, can it be used to fight cybercrime?
- Basic security considerations for securing information and creating/managing new systems and networks, such as authentication, authorization, and auditing (AAA) and non-repudiation, will also be discussed.
- Building secure and resilient cyber risk programs for organizations using blockchain.
- Present and future Industry use case of blockchain in cybersecurity.

The Promises of Blockchain

The primary security features of blockchains are cryptography and hashing. The first iteration of the blockchain was cryptocurrency, bitcoin, which came with the promise of security, anonymity (which ended up encouraging criminal adoption) and decentralization. The selling points of blockchain technology are:

1. Trustless
2. Anonymity
3. Decentralization
4. Fault tolerance
5. Immutability
6. Transparency

Trustless

The blockchain is meant to have enhanced trust by being trustless. This means that the blockchain operates in such a way that a third party is not required to handle and managed records and transactions, as the system is built to inherently give the users independent and freedom to control their data and information. A trustless system is one that does not require trusting in parties that one is dealing with, but rather trust is inbuilt in the system – each transaction gets verified by computers using sophisticated algorithms to confirm transactions and create records. Every transaction has to be confirmed by each node on the network using consensus protocols (Jung, 2019). This ensures confidence in transactions being carried out by an organization, whether financial or otherwise (King, 2018).

Anonymity

Extensive use of hashing and cryptography in blockchain enhance anonymity of transactions carried out, the help minimize exposure to unauthorized and unwanted parties. The blocks in the blockchain are essentially linked with hash functions; each block contains the hash of the previous block (Poston & Bennett, 2018). The hashing creates a situation where it would be difficult for malicious actor make modifications to any block, as a change in a block will result in a change in the hash of previous blocks – to be successful, the actor may have to change the hash of all blocks, which is virtually impossible (Noor et al, 2021). Transactions carried out in the blockchain are cryptographically signed are then organized into blocks at regular intervals, the blocks are also cryptographically signed with a secret before being added to the network (Poston & Bennett, 2018).

The blockchain is said to be pseudonymous – they are not really anonymous. A transaction, for example, could be carried out by an individual without exposing the individual's personal identity, but the profile used would be known and recorded; hence activities can be linked to a specific profile without actually disclosing the actual owner of the profile. Pseudonyms can be used to carry out operations and transactions of the blockchain, which do not collect personally identifiable information, this gives a semblance of anonymity, but in reality activities can be traced to the pseudonym to expose the actual person behind it (Pruden, 2022)

Decentralization

The blockchain operates without a central authority (Poston & Bennett, 2018), making it more democratic in nature. It is also distributed in addition to not having a central control, so nodes are distributed without a central point. The nodes are self-regulatory and enable users to directly access and have more control over their data without a central third party (Noor, Khanum, Anwar, & Ansari, 2021). Decentralization and the distributed nature of the blockchain ensure its trustless nature, and also creates immutability, fault tolerance and transparency.

Fault Tolerance

The blockchain does not have a single point of failure as a resulted of being distributed and decentralized. None of the nodes on the blockchain are mission-critical (Poston & Bennett, 2018), all the nodes are used to store data; hence, unlike a centralized system where one system might be the control or storage centre, the blockchain has everything copied everywhere ensuring continuity in the event a node gets compromised. All the nodes on the blockchain have to be taken out for there to be data or service loss.

Immutability

Data once input on the blockchain, cannot be tampered with, it is append-only (Quaranta, 2020). The cryptographic hashes The nature of the blockchain is such that anything that is entered on the leger cannot be altered, this is guaranteed by the decentralization (no central authority with unilateral veto powers over entries) and distribution (the same data is spread across various nodes that any change on one cannot affect the others). Any attempt to change data on a node would be virtually impossible as the blocks are linked by the cryptographic hashes, hence a change on any node will affect all the nodes (Bigelow, 2021).

Transparency

Contents of the blockchain can be viewed by anyone, and they exist without risk of alteration. Records on the blockchain remain as they are and cannot be tampered with, ensuring that it can be viewed at any point in time. It makes audits easy. The immutable nature ensures records cannot be tampered with or destroyed, records remain as they were entered and can be clearly seen and reviewed. Decentralization eliminates the risk of trail obfuscation arising from a compromise of the central control system.

BLOCKCHAIN TECHNOLOGY FOR CYBER SECURITY IN THE LIGHT OF THE CIA TRIAD

The main objective of cyber security is to ensure confidentiality, integrity and availability (CIA) of data and information. The qualities of blockchain can be used to achieve the cyber security (CIA) objectives.

The use of cryptography in the blockchain which gives anonymity, this can be used to protect restricted data from unauthorized access. However, confidentiality is not the strong point of the blockchain in reality because of the transparency, which can make everything seen and easily traced, the case of it being pseudonymous. The pseudonymity implies that transactions can be seen, but the identity of the user conducting the transaction can be concealed; but the pseudo identity can be used to trace and uncover the user. This is actually a useful security feature, notwithstanding the lack of confidentiality, as this was used to trace criminals and shut down the silk road dark web marketplace (Leonard, 2018). Blockchain has been used to ensure confidentiality of health records by storing various aspects separately and some even being of the blockchain, for example personally identifiable information like name and address stored separate from health records, those who manage and work with the data have access restricted to what concerns their specific job function (Daley, 2022). This approach ensures an attacker cannot compromise the confidentiality of data completely, reducing the risk to health records, and can also be applied to other data other than health data.

Integrity of records is assured in the blockchain by the blocks being linked with hashes, which ensure that any change to any of the blocks would alter the hash of the others, exposing an attempt to compromise integrity. The immutability of the blockchain protects integrity of data recorded on the blockchain, as it is append-only and cannot be easily altered without being exposed. Decentralization prevents a compromise of integrity, by compromising a central command and control centre for example, there would have to be consensus among the various nodes to confirm validity of an entry. Distribution in the blockchain also eliminates having a single point of failure, creating resilience against unauthorized tampering or destruction of records. Where issues can come up is if the records are tampered with, and go unnoticed, before being entered into the blockchain; this could affect integrity, but that is not necessarily the fault of the blockchain. The blockchain is a tool operated by humans, therefore due care has to be taken when entering records unto it, as these errors (intentional or unintentional) would become more or less permanent part of the blockchain. The immutability of the blockchain also ensures non-repudiation with transparency and immutability, as audit trail is created, all activities can be traced by to the profiles that created them.

An organization always wants its systems to be up and running at all times with minimal downtime, the distributed and immutable nature of the blockchain offer resiliency and fault tolerance to achieve this. Probably the part of the CIA-triad blockchain best aids is availability, the immutability, and the decentralization and distribution (which eliminate a single point of failure) guarantee the availability of data and information at all times irrespective of impediments – natural or human (malicious or error/ negligence). Distributed denial of service (DDoS) attacks use distribution as a weapon against corporate or government networks and platforms to bring them down; blockchain serves as a shield against such attacks by also being distributed such that a DDoS attack cannot compromise availability. Other malicious attacks that can affect availability are also mitigated by the blockchain, like viruses, worms and ransomware, and even physical destruction of a data centre. A ransomware attack, especially, would be ineffective against data that is stored on distributed ledger like the blockchain; it would be very difficult to restrict access to all the nodes on which the data is stored at the same time for the attack to have any semblance of success.

Other Security Offers From the Blockchain

There are other security benefits of the blockchain that do not directly impact the CIA triad, although they derive from them. These include:

1. Governance, risk and compliance (GRC)
2. Fraud prevention
3. Incident response and investigations
4. Know Your Customer (KYC) applications

Governance, Risk, and Compliance (GRC)

The blockchain helps a lot when it comes to information governance, managing risks and complying with ethics, laws and regulations. In terms of information governance, the blockchain helps in identity management and contingency management, including disaster recovery and business continuity management, forensic readiness management, data retention management – these are meant to mitigate risks to an acceptable level in the event of negative events and incidents an organization might face. Contingency management is meant to ensure that information and information systems remain available or get quickly restored with minimal in the event of any incident; they also ensure such information is readily available as evidence for investigations or in the event of litigation (in a legally acceptable manner).

Identity management can be enhanced with the blockchain; the incidents of stolen and false identities can be minimized with blockchain – a stolen or forged identity card, for example, can be used to deceive an organization, but having IDs on the blockchain would not allow for that. The IDs can easily be verified, and cannot be easily forged as the blockchain is immutable and transparent. It is also faster and easier to verify and authenticate the identity with blockchain. Blockchain promises Self Sovereign Identity (SSI) whereby identity owners have more control over their identification detail; individual has to give content for data to be accessed, and the need for third party identity managers becomes more unnecessary (Iredale, 2021). This helps the organization gain more trust from their employees who have a good level of comfort that their identities and privacy are safe, and also reduces the risk of employee identity being stolen by a malicious actor to attack or compromise the organization.

The blockchain also helps to ensure compliance with legal and regulatory requirements which also include contingencies like industry related data retention requirements, ensuring electronically stored information is readily available for investigations and audit by regulatory bodies and/or law enforcement agents. Blockchain can be used to protect customer privacy, for example in managing health records as previously mentioned, this not only ensures compliance with privacy laws and regulations (like the European Union's General Data Protection Regulation, and similar in other jurisdictions), but also shows moral and ethical empathy by the organization towards its customers; which also helps improve the organization's reputation and goodwill (a mitigation of reputational risk).

The blockchain also benefits supply chain management, where it is applied in procurement, it helps to establish source of hardware and software used by an organization, enabling them to avoid acquiring these from sources that might be questionable, like organizations that might be suspected of being associated with adversarial nation states. Software and hardware from such sources might have backdoors for spying or spreading malware.

In the light of the Russia-Ukraine conflict that began in 2022, sanctions were meted out against Russia, with sanctions for dealing with some organizations from there. The heavy mix of sources of business, outsourcing and similar, could lead a company to unwittingly engage in a transaction that involves a blacklisted organization; the blockchain can be used to establish the organization that is being dealt with or the source of commodity or service offered.

Fraud Prevention

One of the fundamental issues blockchain was developed to address was double spending in digital currencies. Double spending is a phenomenon whereby an individual can use the digital token for multiple transactions, since the content of the token can be falsified and duplicated (Bennett & Decker, 2019). The issue of double spending was solved by the distributed nature of the blockchain ledger; having a record of every transaction on each of the various distributed nodes on the blockchain which are timestamped and immutable – the records are widespread, so there is not a single point of compromise, and any change to a block would affect the hash which links the blocks (Bansal, 2022). Other than the issue of double spending, the blockchain also ensures easy detection of other types of fraud involving data manipulation or destruction due to the decentralized, distributed and immutable nature. The requirement for a consensus across nodes for transactions to be entered on the blockchain minimize the risk of a malicious individual making a fraudulent entry, the other nodes have to be convinced or also be compromised (which would not be an easy task to achieve given they are dispersed and distributed). An in the event a fraudulent entry manages to pass through, it would be easy to trace it on the blockchain, as covering tracks is also very difficult, the blockchain is transparent. It also prevents any potential miscreant that is aware of its nature from attempting fraudulent actions seeing as it would be a difficult task to achieve and can be easily traced.

The blockchain prevents fraud due to the strong authentication, authorization and auditing (AAA) it offers. The consensus of nodes ensures strong authentication and authorization of transactions, the nodes have to generally agree for a transaction to be authorized, that is to say the nodes authenticate first. The transparent nature ensures easy audit, the data are recorded in decentralized, distributed nodes that cannot be tampered with, this ensures a digital footprint and also helps to ensure non-repudiation.

Incident Response and Investigations

The transparency, auditability, and immutability of the blockchain make it ideal for sourcing electronically stored information (ESI). In the event of any incident that needs to be investigated, be it a cyber-attack or anomaly or litigation, the blockchain helps preserve digital evidence. The hashing of blocks helps to confirm the soundness of digital evidence; and it helps to establish a case against or in favour of a suspect. As was previously mentioned, the blockchain was used to bring down the dark web Silk Road. Another example of blockchain aiding investigations was the case of Mendoza and Diaz in Venezuela, where there was bitcoin theft of about a million dollars from an indigenous cryptocurrency exchange, initial evidence seemed to point out the two as suspects of the crime and were arrested; full investigations by CipherBlade were able to trace the crime to a Russian national due to the transparency of the blockchain (Handagama, 2022). The to two individuals inaptly suspect would probably not have been able to prove their innocence without the blockchain.

The blockchain is also useful to organizations that carry out investigations, law enforcement agencies, regulators, private investigators and so on. The blockchain can be used to record and document evidence collection, preservation, analysis and storage, which help establish chain of custody and show that evidence was collect and handled in a legally acceptable manner, ensuring it is forensically sound. This applies to all forms of evidence – digital and otherwise. Researchers from Alister, Inc. recommended the use of blockchain to augment traditional chain of custody documents in order to minimize evidence tampering leading to false arrests and convictions; the blockchain greatly minimizes the risk of evidence getting damaged, lost or manipulated (by bad police officers for example) by ensuring transparency and immutability (Anderes et al, n.d.). This ensures the evidence presented.

Know Your Customer (KYC) Applications

The blockchain can efficiently aid organizations to properly authenticate their customers and even employees; reducing risk exposure. KYC is the identification and verification of customers by an organization (Sharma, 2022); it essentially ensures the customer is who the customer claims to be, verifying identification, address, employment status and so on, and also to confirm if the customer has issues that can cause damage to the organization (financial, reputational, legal, etc.). KYC is widely used by financial intuitions as a regularity requirement to avoid aiding and abetting criminals, terrorist and the like and also falling victim to these malicious actors, it is one of the first steps in anti-money laundering (AML) and combating terrorist financing (CFT). KYC is, however, not restricted to financial initiations alone, other businesses and organizations (including public, government owned) would also need to verify their customers as well to avoid negative consequences from having criminals as customers, like fraud and reputational damage. Employers can also use KYC techniques to ensure they employ wholesome employees; blockchain can be used to speed up background checks, for example.

Verified identification being stored on the blockchain makes customers' details be available for verification without having access to personally identifiable information that is not need-to-know. Once an organization has KYC'ed (verified and authenticated) a customer, the KYC is also stored on the blockchain; hence when another organization wants to establish relationship with the customer, that data is readily available on the blockchain. The transparency and immutability of the blockchain give confidence to organizations regarding the data they have on customers they are trying to verify.

An illustration of blockchain in KYC is a country having national identification management using blockchain. An individual's details, like biometrics, address and so on, are stored on the blockchain secured with hashing and encryption. The identification management service provider would probably do physical and manual verification of the individual's identity, address and other things; this is then stored in the blockchain. In the event the individual wants to open a bank account, the individual only needs to provide identification details, the bank would verify from the blockchain then authenticate the customer for account opening, the bank would not necessarily need access to the identification details, but the details will be confirmed from the blockchain and also stored there. The individual in question might later want to rent a property; and the landlord' who requires KYC on the individual only needs to refer to the blockchain and get the already verified and authenticated identification by the bank. This makes the process of KYC much cheaper and less cumbersome for the organization making operations more efficient, protecting the organization for establishing a relationship with an unwanted entity that might end up having a negative impact on the organization.

The Security of the Blockchain Itself

The blockchain is being presented as a panacea for organizational cyber security, but how vulnerable or secure is the blockchain itself? To ensure the blockchain is secure, its risks and vulnerabilities need to be known and mitigated against. The following are some major vulnerabilities faced by the blockchain:

1. 51% attacks
2. Denial of Service (DoS) attacks
3. Eclipse attacks
4. Sybil attacks
5. Routing attacks
6. Social engineering attacks

51% Attacks

The consensus algorithm of the blockchain is based on a minimum 51% of the nodes agreeing and confirming the authenticity an entry before it is recorded on the blockchain. The implication is that if a malicious entity is able to control up to 51% of the nodes on a blockchain, such entity can manipulate the entries and records. 51% attacks are peculiar to public blockchains, private blockchains are not susceptible to this as there is more control on who has access to the network. The entity can achieve this by buying, hiring or stealing computational resources to attain at least 1% above half control of a blockchain; and hence initiate a 51% attack (Poston & Bennett, 2018). This attack gives the attackers a monopoly over the blockchain, giving them control over the blockchain. Control of the blockchain enables them to, for example, carry out double spending, carry out frequent reorganizations of the blockchain (rendering the integrity doubtful) or render it impractical by mining empty blocks and making their blocks longer than others' such that they become irrelevant (Noor, Khanum, Anwar, & Ansari, 2021). Entities with mal-intent having monopoly of the blockchain can render it unsecure, unreliable and even crash it completely. Getting the majority (at least 51%) control of the blockchain is much easier when the blockchain is new as there are less miners at that time, giving room for malicious actors to hijack it (Krishna, 2022).

Checkpoints can be used to prevent 51% attacks. Checkpoints specific points in the history of blocks at intervals, of which divergent blockchains would not be accepted without (Poston & Bennett, 2018). This helps minimize the risk of a malicious alteration of the blocks' history. Transactions that are confirmed before and at the checkpoint cannot be reversed (BitFlyer, n.d.).

Denial of Service (DoS) Attacks

Despite the fact that blockchains are solution to DoS attacks, they are also susceptible to the attacks. They protect a network form DoS attack because they are distributed in nature; hence reduce the attack surface by eliminating a single point of failure – all the nodes on the blockchain have to be brought down for the network to become victim to DoS. DoS attacks can take advantage of flaws in the blockchain to service disruption, transaction flooding is an example of a DoS attack against the blockchain.

Transaction flooding attacks are viewed as the main DoS threat to the blockchain, they are perpetrated by creating thousands of spam transactions that cause genuine transactions not to get included in a current block and kept delayed in memory, lading to inefficiency in processing transactions, as the required ones are delayed by the spam (ZebPay, 2022). An example of transaction flooding DoS attack happened in 2021 against the Solana crypto ecosystem which recorded a peak of 400,00 transactions per second leading to queuing of legitimate transactions in the memory, the memory eventually got overloaded and crashed leading to hours of disruption (Shumba, 2021) (ZebPay, 2022). Another transaction flooding attack hit Solana again in early 2022, this time with spam transactions getting u to 6 million transactions per second (Keller, 2022).

DoS attacks can be prevented on the blockchain by ensuring each node has adequate storage, RAM, bandwidth and processing power, this minimizes the effect of a flooding attack. The network administrators can choose to wait for the flooding to end, then continue adding blocks or create emergency blocks to divert and mop up the flood attack, hence clear the congestion (Poston & Bennett, 2018). Spam filters also need to be effectively deployed to filter out spam transactions, especially when there is network congestion; block verification enables choosing which transactions can be added to a block (ZebPay, 2022).

Eclipse Attacks

An eclipse attack is one in which an attacker cuts-off a node or et of nodes form the rest of the blockchain such that control of information transfer to and from them is in the hands of the attacker; essentially the nodes are eclipsed from the rest of the blockchain. The attacker has full control of the information that goes to those nodes, ensuring the eclipsed nodes are in the dark as to the true state of the blockchain. The attacker can also hijack the mining ability of the eclipsed nodes to attack the whole blockchain network (U. & Rajagopalan, 2020). The attacker can use eclipse attacks to carry out DoS attacks, as they can flood the eclipsed nodes with spam transactions to bring them down. They can also carry out double spending transactions against the eclipsed nodes as the nodes are cut-off form the main blockchain preventing them from having records of already carried out transactions; in the same vein, replay attacks can as well be carried out. In the event the attacker is able to eclipse up to 51% of nodes on the blockchain, 51% attacks can also be initiated. The eclipse attack can open doors to other attacks against the blockchain.

Regular vulnerability assessment and penetration testing of nodes on the blockchain helps detect loopholes that can be exploited by attackers to carry out eclipse attacks, which should be immediately plugged. This reduces the attack surface. Another way of preventing eclipse attacks is by increasing connections to the nodes, so as to reduce the probability of an attacker gaining control of nodes users connect to (Poston & Bennett, 2018); this is reduces the attack surface by minimizing the risk of the attacker compromising a node or set of nodes through a single connection point. Whitelisting also helps reduce the incidents of eclipse attacks, a list of trusted nodes is created which must always be connected to at least once (Poston & Bennett, 2018). Being connected to a whitelisted node helps a node to know what is actually correct and on the actual blockchain in the event it is eclipsed; the node will have to confirm every transaction through the whitelisted nodes, which is why it always has to be connected to at least.

Sybil Attacks

A Sybil attack involves a malicious actor creating a large number of nodes and accounts which can be controlled to influence the blockchain. The attackers take advantage of weaknesses in node creation and validation to create multiple fake accounts which can be sued to launch attacks (Fáwọlé & Ciattaglia, 2023b). The malicious actor can use botnets, virtualization and malware to create and control the accounts and nodes (Poston & Bennett, 2018). Sybil attacks can be used to launch eclipse attacks, DoS and 51% attacks.

Similar measures to eclipse attacks, whitelisting can be used against Sybil attacks. Additionally, a single IP address that runs more than one node should not be allowed to validate transactions (Fáwọlé & Ciattaglia, 2023a). A hierarchical system can be used to mitigate against Sybil attacks by assuming all new accounts and nodes on a blockchain are Sybil; hence should have limited power to operate on the blockchain (Fáwọlé & Ciattaglia, 2023b). The new nodes will be under observation for suspicious behaviour, if found trustworthy over time, powers can be increased. In this way, it becomes difficult for the Sybil nodes to carry out actions that can impact the network.

Routing Attacks

Routing attacks target the communication network used by blockchains in order to achieve malicious goals. Routing on the Internet is carried out using Border Gateway Protocol (BGP) in which a node communicates with another by sending a query to over the network for directing the message to the other, the response with the shortest route is taken without any validation (Poston & Bennett, 2018). This can be taken advantage of by an attacker responding to the query by offering the shortest route, which leads the communication to be routed through the attacker. Once, the communication is routed through the attacker, the malicious actor has control over them. Routing attacks can be either used to partition the network or cause delays – both can target the whole network or just the parts routed through the attacker. They can also be sued for eavesdropping on transactions.

Partitioning the blockchain network involves isolating the part of the network routed through the attacker from the rest of the blockchain, which enable the attacker to manipulate the sections as they wish. This can be used to launch eclipse, double spend, DoS and even 51% attacks. The isolated nodes can be subjected to double spend attacks as they do not have access to valid authentication, they can also be subjected DoS as they are essentially cut-off from the network. If a lot of nodes are routed through the attacker, the possibility of creating two versions of the blockchains is high; the real one and the one routed through the attacker (Apostolaki et al, 2017). Routing attacks can also be used to slow down the blockchain by delaying the delivery of blocks to the compromised nodes, resulting in leaving them uninformed (Apostolaki et al, 2017) and waste of resources in mining.

Routing attacks can be avoided by increasing diversity in node connections; nodes should have more than one connection network, for example having more than one VPN for routing traffic (Apostolaki et al, 2017). This reduces the attack surface as the attacker would need to compromise the various connection networks, and even if they do, they become more noticeable. The routing should be done using secure protocols and strong encryption. Network monitoring has to be increased and be more efficient such that abnormal network behaviour patterns can be flagged; for example, the time it takes to respond to a request, like increased round-trip return time (RTT) to a node can indicate hijacked routing.

Social Engineering Attacks

Transactions are carried out on the blockchain and it is operated by humans. The humans are subject to manipulation by malicious actors, the manipulation is so much easier to be done than carrying out attacks that require a lot of resources and technical know-how. One most commonly used form of social engineering is phishing which can be used by malicious actors to steal login credentials or cause malware infestations that can be used to compromise a blockchain. Baiting can also be similarly used; a malicious actor could drop an enticingly labelled malware-infested disk at a strategic location where an unsuspecting victim can pick and insert on a node in the blockchain, compromising the node. Improperly discarded data, whether paper or disks, can be retrieved by malicious actors through dumpster diving, where sensitive data concerning the blockchain are contained in such discarded material, the sky is the limit for the attacker.

Being extra-vigilant and avoiding clicking unsolicited and suspicious links and attachments. Users of the blockchain should be enlightened on social engineering techniques that can be used against them so as to compromise their network and how to avoid falling victim. Disposing data and data sources should be done in a way that is irreversible, done in such that data cannot be restored from them. Awareness of social engineering and the potential devastation they can cause go a long way in ensuring vigilance and is about the best solution to such attacks.

Other Security Concerns

The blockchain has a somewhat notoriety as a result of cryptocurrency (especially Bitcoin) being demanded as payment by malicious actors. For example, ransomware payments being demanded to be paid in cryptocurrency, and also other criminals like kidnappers have demanded ransom payment in cryptocurrency (Uzoho, 2021). This is not really as serious concern as it is based on a misconception that blockchain is something used by criminals, so it is likely to have backdoors or something that can help criminals compromise an organization; the mere fact that criminals adopt a tool does not mean it the tool itself is bad. There are many tools that, in fact probably almost every tool, can be used for both positive and negative purposes – Wireshark, for example, the good guys and the bad guys.

Another issue is the lack of standardization which impacts interoperability. There are no fixed standards for blockchain operations which tends to leaves each blockchain with its own standards, making them independent siloes. Ab initio the blockchains did not communicate with other blockchains, transactions could not be carried out between different blockchains – a hypothetical example is transacting between Bitcoin and Ethereum. Blockchain interoperability is the ability of communicate with one another for transactions like accessing data, sharing data, transferring assets and so on (Breia, 2022). There have been projects that have tried to and are still trying to address the issue of interoperability on the blockchain like Polkadot, Cosmos and Blocknet, among others. Polkadot uses parallel chains (known as parachains) to interact within and with external blockchains, but within its ecosystem, to go out it uses bridges – blockchain bridges are third party intermediaries that convert between blockchains (Merre, 2022). Cosmos uses Inter Blockchain (IBC) communication which works in similar way to Polkdot, it also offers a software development kit (SDK) for coders to develop their own decentralized apps for interoperability (Breia, 2022). There have been security challenges associated with interoperability of the blockchain like what happened to on the Ronin Network in 2022 where their bridge was compromised leading to a loss of $625 million in cryptocurrency; and before that in 2021, Poly Network was also compromised with funds of $600 million stolen across Ethereum, BSC and Polygon blockchain networks - which was later refunded (Merre, 2022). These attacks were able to compromise the bridges and interoperability protocols, probably as a result of lapses in the protocols based on a lack of focus on ensuring these are secure, rather focus being on trying to only satisfy the demand for interoperability.

BLOCKCHAIN ORGANIZATIONAL USE CASES

The Defense Advanced Research Projects Agency (DARPA) of the United States of America, who were the pioneers of the Internet, worked on secure military communications using blockchain technology leveraging on secure transfer of data and encryption to ensure the US Army can have instantaneous anywhere in the wold without fear of eavesdropping or hacking (Daley, 2022). Some instances where organizations have adopted blockchain use, enhancing cyber security, include financial institutions, e-Governance by governments, supply chain management to name a few. The following are some examples of organizations that have adopted blockchain use with improved cyber security:

1. e-Estonia
2. JP Morgan
3. Medicalchain
4. Lockheed Martin

e-Estonia

One organization that has pioneered and successfully implemented blockchain use is the government of Estonia. The Estonian government already had a decentralized solution for data communication between the private and public sectors known as X-Road (Oyetunde, 2023), which made probably aided transition to the blockchain. Estonia uses the Keyless Signature Infrastructure (KSI) blockchain from Guardtime Federal which is stated to have accomplished confidentiality and integrity of sensitive data of citizens, and curbed corrupt practices as well as internal threats (Jackson, 2019). Estonia had been a victim of cyber-attacks, previously, however, the adoption of blockchain technology has helped to produce resilience in the government's digital governance, if only by eliminating a single point of failure.

JP Morgan

JP Morgan uses Quorom (a version of Ethereum focused on enterprises) to process private transactions using smart contracts (Daley, 2022). Large multinationals are constant targets of cyber-attacks from various threat actors ranging from adversarial nation states to common criminals – state sponsored attacks might be meant to cause economic sabotage, common criminals would be interested in stealing funds. The threat actors hunt for loopholes, which are usually single failure points; the blockchain mitigates against single point of failure issues. Cryptography and hashing also help ensure customers transactions have privacy and integrity, which helps promote trust and goodwill for the bank.

Medicalchain

Healthcare records are subject to cyber-attacks by malicious entities out to steal identities of patients and use them incurring cost for the patients or steal patients' data to blackmail patients or any other malicious purpose. Medicalchain is a platform that provides digital health applications and services for patients and healthcare professionals using blockchain technology. Medicalchain runs on two blockchains – Hyperledger Fabric used to control access to health records and an ERC20 token on Ethereum that underlies all applications and services (Southey, 2018). Hyperledger Fabric is closed and permissioned - it is not open to the public only authorised personnel have aces to the blockchain and also has provision for access control on a privileged basis - which ensures increased confidentiality and privacy of patients' data. The ERC20 on Ethereum is accessible by everyone, Ethereum is an open public blockchain that runs smart contract scripts; this is used for transactions and communications in Medicalchain – like consultation interactions between patients and doctors, payments for services and so on. The two blockchains work symbiotically to ensure seamless, efficient and secure communications, transactions and storage.

Lockheed Martin

Defense companies operate with very sensitive data that needs to be protected from eavesdropping and contamination, the blockchain has been identified as way to mitigate against such threats. Lockheed Martin partnered with Guardtime Federal who offer the KSI blockchain (as used by Estonia) to ensure secure communication, high integrity of products and services through mathematically verifiable end-to-end supply chain verification (Lockheed Martin, 2020). This assures customers that software and hardware in Lockheed Martin's products are from genuine sources that are not likely to have loopholes, like backdoors to adversarial nation states or entities.

FUTURE RESEARCH DIRECTIONS

Distributed ledger technology (DLT), blockchain and decentralized finance (DeFi)are continuously developing with more opportunities and loophole being found. Some areas that further research related to this chapter can be carried out as follows:

1. Legal acceptability of electronic evidence from DLT databases across international borders: a look at how electronically stored information on the distributed ledgers (blockchain or otherwise) can be adopted as evidence in court where the blockchain runs in various international jurisdictions. This will help to streamline digital forensics investigations and eDiscovery.
2. Application of blockchain technology in warfare: defense and offense: in warfare, whether electronic or physical, where does blockchain come in, how can it be used to protect a nation and its critical infrastructure, how can it be used to deter or thwart attacks, how can it be weaponised against adversaries?
3. International standardization for blockchain operations: having common internationally accepted baselines for blockchains can help improve their overall efficiency and effectiveness. It can also help boost interoperability.
4. More energy-efficient ways of operating blockchains: mining of blockchain tend to consume a lot of energy, means can be explored to see how they can be made more energy efficient without compromising on efficiency and standards.
5. Integration of artificial intelligence applications into blockchain operations: the rise of artificial intelligence applications is something that can help boost blockchain efficiency. Artificial intelligence algorithms can be inculcated into the blockchain to improve and processing, storage and security.

CONCLUSION

Blockchain technology has come a long way since its first iteration in Bitcoin from Satoshi Nakamoto and the proliferation of digital currencies. These mainly addressed the issue of double spending in electronic currency, but with time more applications of the blockchain other than as means of exchange were developed; like smart contracts, identity management and supply chain management. Blockchain is especially beneficial for an organization in terms of cyber security as it adopts encryption and hashing which ensure confidentiality and integrity of data with the blockchain network. The decentralized and distributed nature of the blockchain give it the qualities of immutably and transparency, and enhance availability of data with less exposure to single points of failure. These also ensure that stored data cannot be easily tampered with and ensure non-repudiation. In the event of incidents that require electronic evidence (digital forensics investigations of litigation), the blockchain provides a readily available, forensically sound data source.

However, the blockchain is not a silver bullet cure to all cyber security problems, it has its own issue and vulnerabilities too. Other than that, it is still managed and operated by human beings; these human beings need to be trained and enlightened on how to properly and optimally administer data on the blockchain to ensure high efficiency and security.

To summarise, blockchain is a highly potent tool for ensuring organizational cyber security by taking advantage of its peculiar qualities, while not losing focus on implementing other regular security measures. A very important measure that should not be ignored is the training and enlightenment of employees as to proper and safe use and deployment.

REFERENCES

Anderes, D., Baumel, E., Grier, C., Veun, R., & Wright, S. (n.d.). *The USe of Blockchain within Evidence Management Systems*. Alister, Inc.

Apostolaki, M., Zohar, A., & Vanbever, L. (2017). *Hijacking Bitcoin: Routing Attacks on Cryptocurrencies*. IEEE. doi:10.1109/SP.2017.29

Bansal, D. (2022). *Double Spending and How It's prevented by Blockchain*. Retrieved March 15, 2023, from Topcoder: https://www.topcoder.com/thrive/articles/double-spending-and-how-its-prevetned-by-blockchain#:~:text=In conclusion%2C the blcokchain stops,quantitatively tied to the earlier ones.

BBC News. (2022, January 26). *Crypto Money Laundering Rises 30%, Report finds*. BBC. https://www.bbc.com/news/technology-60072195#:~:text=Criminals%20laundered%20%248.6bn%20(£,to%20launder%20cryptocurrency%20by%20criminals.

Bennett, K., & Decker, C. (2019). *Certified Blockchain Business Foundations (CBBF), Official Exam Study Guide*. Blcokchain Training Alliance, Inc.

Bigelow, S. J. (2021). *Blockchain: An Immutable Ledeger to Replace the Database*. TechTarget - IT Operations. https://www.techtarget.com/searchitoperations/tip/Blockchain-An-immutable-ledger-to-replace-the-database

BitFlyer. (n.d.). *Checkpoint*. BitFlyer. https://bitflyer.com/en-eu/s/glossary/checkpoint#:~:text=Checkpoints%20are%20when%20block%20hash,to%20the%20checkpoint%20as%20irreversible

Breia, R. (2022). *What Is Blockchain Interoperability*. Sensorium. https://sensoriumxr.com/articles/what-is-blockchain-interoperability

Business Australia. (2022). *Cybercriminals Becoming More Sophisticated: Report*. Business Australia. https://www.businessaustralia.com/resources/news/cybercriminals-becoming-more-sophisticated-report?utm_brand=BA&utm_prodcat=content&utm_p

Cybersecurity and Infrastructure Security Agency. (2022). *2021 Trends Show Increased Globalized Threat of Ransomware*. CISA. https://www.cisa.gov/uscert/ncas/alerts/aa22-040a

Daley, S. (2022). *20 Blockchain in Cybersecurity Examples*. Built In. https://builtin.com/blockchain/blockchain-cybersecurity-uses

Fáwọlé, J., & Ciattaglia, L. (2023a). *Blockchain Secuirty: Common Vulnerabilities and How to Protect Against Them*. Hacken. https://hacken.io/insights/blockchain-security-vulnerabilities/

Fáwọlé, J., & Ciattaglia, L. (2023b). *Sybil Attack in Blockchain: Examples & Prevention*. Hacken. https://hacken.io/insights/sybil-attacks/

Grand View Research, Inc. (2022). *Blockchain Technology Market Size, Share & Trends Analysis Report By Type (Private Cloud, Public Cloud), By Application (Digital Identity, Payments), By Enterprise Size, By Component, By End Use, And Segment Forecasts, 2023 - 2030*. Grand View Research, Inc. https://www.grandviewresearch.com/industry-analysis/blockchain-technology-market

Handagama, S. (2022). *They Were Jailed for Hacking an Exchange. Blockchain Data Cleared Them.* CoinDesk. https://www.coindesk.com/policy/2022/03/01/they-were-jailed-for-hacking-an-exchange-blockchain-data-cleared-them/

Iredale, G. (2021). *Top 7 Benefits Of Blockchain Identity Management.* 101 Blockchains. https://101blockchains.com/blockchain-identity-management-benefits/

Jackson, E. (2019). *What We Can Learn From Estonia's Real-World Use Case of Blockchain.* LinkedIn. https://www.linkedin.com/pulse/what-we-can-learn-from-estonias-real-world-use-case-eric-jackson/

Jung, T. J. (2019). *How Transparency through the Blockchain helps the Cybersecurity Community.* IBM Supply Chain and Blockchain Blog. https://www.ibm.com/blogs/blockchain/2019/04/how-transparency-through-blockchain-helps-the-cybersecurity-community/

Keller, L. (2022). *Solana Loses Consensus after Bots flood Network, SOL takes Hit.* Forkast. https://forkast.news/headlines/solana-loses-consensus-bots-flood-sol/

King, J. (2018). *Trustless Technology: The Core of the Blockchain. Blockchain Beach.* Blockchain Beach. https://www.blockchainbeach.com/trustless-technology-core-blockchain/

Krishna, A. (2022). *Blockchain Security Issues – A Complete Guide.* Astra. https://www.getastra.com/blog/knowledge-base/blockchain-security-issues/

Leonard, M. (2018). *How Blockchain Helped bring down the Silk Road.* GCN. https://gcn.com/emerging-tech/2018/05/how-blockchain-helped-bring-down-the-silk-road/300085/

Litan, A. (2021). *Hype Cycle for Blockchain 2021; More Action than Hype.* Gartner. https://blogs.gartner.com/avivah-litan/2021/07/14/hype-cycle-for-blockchain-2021-more-action-than-hype/

Lockheed Martin. (2020). *Lockheed Martin And Guardtime Federal Join Forces To Thwart Software Cyber Threats.* Lock Heed Martin. https://news.lockheedmartin.com/2020-02-20-Lockheed-Martin-and-Guardtime-Federal-Join-Forces-to-Thwart-Software-Cyber-Threats

Mani, V. (2017). Blockchain Technology from Information Security. *ISACA Journal.* https://www.isaca.org/resources/isaca-journal/issues/2017/volume-4/a-view-of-blockchain-technology-from-the-information-security-radar

Merre, R. (2022). *Blockchain Interoperability: Challenges & Opportunities.* NGRAVE. https://www.ngrave.io/en/blog/blockchain-interoperability-challenges-opportunities

Noor, M. A., Khanum, S., Anwar, T., & Ansari, M. (2021). A Holistic View on Blockchain and Its Issues. In H. Patel & G. S. Thakur (Eds.), *Blockchain Applications in IoT Security* (pp. 23–24). IGI Global. doi:10.4018/978-1-7998-2414-5.ch002

Oyetunde, B. (2023). *7 GovTech trends to watch out for in 2023.* e-Estonia. https://e-estonia.com/7-govtech-trends-to-watch-out-for-in-2023/

Poston, H., & Bennett, K. (2018). *Certified Blockchain Security Professional (CBSP), Official Exam Study Guide.* Blockchain Training Alliance, Inc.

Pruden, A. A. (2022, July 16). *The difference between pseudonymity and anonymity: When zero is more.* Venture Beat. https://venturebeat.com/datadecisionmakers/the-difference-between-pseudonymity-and-anonymity-when-zero-is-more/

Quaranta, R. (2020). *Blockchain Framework and Guidance.* Shuamburg: ISACA.

Sharma, T. K. (2022). *What Is KYC & How KYC On Blockchain Can Help?* Blockchain Council. https://www.blockchain-council.org/blockchain/what-is-kyc-how-kyc-on-blockchain-can-help/

Shumba, C. (2021). *Solana says It is Back Up and Running after a Surge in Transactions caused the Network to Crash the Day Before.* Insider. https://markets.businessinsider.com/news/currencies/solana-crash-network-transaction-volume-sol-crypto-back-running-system-2021-9

Southey, S. (2018). *Medicalchain — The Future of Healthcare.* Retrieved March 28, 2023, from Medium: https://medium.com/medicalchain/medicalchain-the-future-of-healthcare-5b130cbba439

Statista Research Department. (2022). *Blockchain and Cryptocurrency: Global Investments, 2021.* Statista. https://www.statista.com/statistics/1260400/global-investments-in-blockchain-cryptocurrency/

Stevens, R. (2022). *Bitcoin Mixers: How Do They Work and Why Are They Used?* Coindesk. https://www.coindesk.com/learn/bitcoin-mixers-how-do-they-work-and-why-are-they-used/

U., P., & Rajagopalan, N. (2020). Concept of Blockchain Technology and Its Emergence. In H. Patel, & G. S. Thakur (Eds.), *Blockchain Applications in IoT Security* (pp. 1-20). IGI Global. doi:10.4018/978-1-7998-2414-5.ch001

Uzoho, P. (2021). *Nigeria: Terrorists, Kidnappers Demanding Ransom in Cryptocurrency, Moghalu Says.* Arise News. https://www.arise.tv/nigeria-terrorists-kidnappers-demanding-ransom-in-cryptocurrency-moghalu-says/

ZebPay. (2022). *Crypto DDoS Attacks: What, Why and How?* ZebPay. https://zebpay.com/blog/what-is-crypto-ddos-attack-and-how-to-prevent-it#:~:text=Even%20if%20a%20node%20in,creating%20thousands%20of%20spam%20transactions

KEY TERMS AND DEFINITIONS

Blockchain Bridge: Blockchain badges are protocols used to facilitate interoperability between different blockchain networks. Some examples include Polkadot, Cosmos and Blocknet. They enable communication across different blockchains; for example, transaction between Bitcoin and Ethereum.

Blockchain: Blockchain is a distributed ledger technology that is decentralized and immutable. It is immutable because of its decentralized and distributed nature, data is stored across various nodes and a record is confirmed and stored after there is a consensus among the nodes (at least 51%). It is made of blocks linked by hash functions, each block contains the hash of the previous block which creates a situation where it would be difficult to make modifications to any block, as a change in a block will result in a change in the hash of previous block.

Border Gateway Protocol (BGP): BGP is the protocol for routing systems managing how packets get routed in the network; usually by directing the packets from communicating nodes to another the one with the shortest route.

Central Bank Digital Currency (CBDC): CBDC's are digital currencies issued by central banks of countries. They are managed and issued by the central bank just like normal fiat currency.

CIA Triad: CIA in cyber security terms refers to confidentiality, integrity and availability, and these represent the objectives of cyber security as regards data and information. Cyber security is meant to ensure data are confidential (kept away from those not authorized to access); integrity by ensuring data is not tampered with or contaminated; and the data is available to authorized users when they need to access it.

Cryptocurrency: Cryptocurrencies are digital currency that recorded and verification carried on the transactions using decentralized and distributed networks. The first cryptocurrency was Bitcoin. one of the major reasons for developing cryptocurrency was to address the issue of double spending in digital currency.

Decentralized Finance (DeFi): DeFi refers to financial models that operate without a central authority. Cryptocurrencies are examples of DeFi. The decentralization is meant to enhance security and add checks and balances without a single point of failure.

Distributed Ledger Technology (DLT): DLT are technological systems that record transactional data over multiple distributed networked nodes at the same time. This allows for simultaneous recording, validation and updating of transactions. Examples are blockchain and directed acrylic graph (DAG). The technology is applied in DeFi.

Immutability: Immutability is a quality of the blockchain and distributed ledger technologies that arise as a result of their decentralization and distribution, which ensure they do not have a single point of failure and are always up and running and available.

Know Your Customer (KYC): KYC is a way by which service rendering organizations try to ensure their customers are actually who they claim to be by verifying the biodata they provide when being registered on the database of the organization. This can be achieved by verifying means of identification, utility bills and physical address verification.

Pseudonymity: One of the qualities of the blockchain is anonymity, but that is not really the case. A transaction, for example, could be carried out by an individual without exposing the individual's personal identity, but the profile used would be known and recorded; hence activities can be linked to a specific profile without actually disclosing the actual owner of the profile. That is why the blockchain is said to be pseudonymous, that is pseudo-anonymous.

Chapter 5
The Dilemmas of Criminal Liability Regarding Cybercrimes on Wireless Sensor Networks (WSNs)

Joshua Ojo Nehinbe

 https://orcid.org/0000-0002-0098-7437

Edo State University, Uzairue, Nigeria

ABSTRACT

New studies have revealed serious dilemmas that can confront investigators in the arrest and investigations of suspects of complex cybercrimes on wireless sensor networks (WSNs) and whenever they must subsequently institute criminal liability against agents of the crime. Accordingly, some investigators continue to face challenges to criminalize proven suspects and allocate compensations for negligence to lawless complainants. This chapter used mixed methods and different datasets to critically examine and explain the above issues. Datasets that were qualitatively and quantitatively analyzed with Snort IDS suggest that criminal liabilities on WSNs may be settled with concurrent negligence in the ratio of 0.27, comparative negligence in the ratio of 0.32; contributory negligence in the ratio of 0.18 and vicarious negligence in the ratio of 0.23. Similarly, employer may be criminalized for cybercrimes committed by his employee, employee can be criminalized for cybercrimes committed by his employer, and employer with his employee can be criminalized jointly for their negligence to stop cybercrimes on WSNs.

1. INTRODUCTION

Cybercrimes on Wireless Sensor Networks (WSNs) is alarming across the globe. However, significant numbers of them are not reported to the police. The central fact here is that it is hard to discern relevant actors and suspects and further establish all the victims of cybercrimes on Wireless Sensor Networks (WSNs) without technically incurring some tradeoffs. Nonetheless, recent studies have shown that allegations of cybercrimes that involve Wireless Sensor Networks (WSNs) can generate serious orga-

DOI: 10.4018/979-8-3693-1528-6.ch005

nizational conflicts and complex dilemmas in many ways. Complainants may have legal grounds to establish criminal liability and draw their arguments on the existence of "negligence" so that courts can award damages to favour them and simultaneously apportion suitable punishments to proven suspects of cybercrimes that will also commensurate to the degree of the involvement of each suspect in such criminality Kagan, 2022. Cybercrime is the usage of computer system and internet resources in the manner that against the law. Some cybercrimes can cause trifling or severe harm to another entity or a group of entities. The "entity" in this case can be a person, company, nation, etc. The challenge is that while some complainants of cybercrimes on Wireless Sensor Networks (WSNs) that have incurred trifling harm may overlook their unpleasant experience, some victims that have experienced severe harm may seek for compensation from courts of law for the damages they have incurred.

In Figure 1, investigators of cybercrimes can carry out the arrest of the alleged suspects in the morning, afternoon and at night. However, criminal courts would require evidence of forensic facts that can substantiate the actual entities that are criminally liable to the crimes before judges can decide whether or not to allocate compensation for the damages that complainants alleged that they have incurred from the crime.

Figure 1. A model for arresting the suspects of criminal allegations

Criminal liability is a legal term to establish the actor(s) that is/are legally obliged or liable to criminal charge(s) and be held legally responsible for an allegation of crime (Plunkett, 2018; Peno and Bogucki, 2021). The classical basis for criminal liability in cybercrimes is that criminal laws mostly require that law enforcement agents or investigators of cybercrimes must identify, interrogate, prove the suspect(s) or perpetrator of cybercrimes beyond reasonable doubt so that courts can adopt the reports to decide whether to sanction or acquit the suspect(s).

An employee (or employer) can be guilty of cybercrimes due to their negligence on duty. Nevertheless, contemporary studies and some public commentators have shown that negligence as an element of crimes is multifaceted and it is less expressed in the areas of cybercrimes (Eoin, 2014; Peno and Bogucki, 2021). It has been shown that it is often difficult to use negligence to establish criminal liability especially if the allegations are centered around complex cybercrimes and Wireless Sensor Networks (WSNs) (Owen, 2007).

It is a well-establish fact that the sensing aspect of Wireless Sensor Networks (WSNs) and the entire technologies that underlie them often comprise of multiples of subsidiary technologies. Their back-ends consist of interrelated, interoperability and interdependent components of several computing and heterogeneous devices. These heterogeneous devices also possess hardware and computer software components. The hardware aspect of WSNs includes electronic components such as power, wireless link and sensor while the software components include satellite navigator software, communication apps, anti-virus utility and other embedded applications. Furthermore, the power component of the technology supplies energy to wireless sensor devices. The wireless links of the technologies incorporate the radio transceivers that can receive and transmit (convey) radio signals and remote sensors that can collect forensic information from specific locations, The mechanisms underlying the technologies collabora-tively work to handshake with devices that can convert animation and electronically relay them to the sensors. Moreover, the software components of Wireless Sensor Networks (WSNs) are fully integrated with the hardware and they effectively deliver insightful monitoring; recording and communication of suspicious and normal events to the designated surveillance watchers that reside in remotely strategic locations. The information that the surveillance watchers receive can originate from diverse ecological locations such as aerial, maritime and geophysical sources. Mobile devices such as mobile phones, Global Positioning System (GPS) and mobile transmitters, multiple antenna and stationary satellite dishes are some smart devices that are commonly integrated with Wireless Sensor Networks (WSNs). Wireless Sensor Networks (WSNs) with embedded devices have the capability to quickly relay their observations by means of mobile devices.

The dilemma is enormous whenever complex cybercriminals break into the above settings with devastated intrusions (Eoin, 2014). For instance, each of the components of WSNs is manufactured, owned, supported and managed by different employees in different companies. Cybercrimes can involve many service providers despite the awareness they had about the necessity to adhere to best practices regarding data protection, privacy control and security policies. Empirical studies believe that Internet has a notable flaw and it frequently enables cybercrimes to occur and traverse through two or more international boundaries. Nevertheless, some cybercrimes may sometimes be detected and mitigated by some of the above entities of WSNs. But quite often, several of them occur without the notices of their security experts.

The trouble is that some criminal and cyber laws that some nations have purposely designed to punish and deter cybercrimes are restricted to certain jurisdictions (European Parliament, 2019). The above issues have raised two important questions that have not been empirically tested and answered in recent time (Nolan, 2013). Firstly, how should criminal court apportion negligence if the investiga-tions into certain cybercrimes on WSNs substantiate that the complainants and defendants are at fault? Secondly, how can courts apportion negligence whenever it is proved that the companies (entities) that are co-defendants in the allegations of cybercrimes on WSNs did not essentially act recklessly and yet none of them can detect or deter the cybercrimes? Consequently, this chapter combines qualitative and quantitative methods to critically examine and explain the above legal, criminal, electronic and software issues on Wireless Sensor Networks (WSNs). Three categories of TCP dump traces with Kismet were gathered within the intervals of 3 weeks from traffics that migrate across wireless Local Area Networks (LANs) and CCTV footage in University's setting and in a promiscuous mode. The first packets were gathered between 12 am and 8 am to safe storage space. The second packets were gathered between 8am and 12 pm while the third traffic packets were gathered between 4pm and 12 pm. The above three datasets were mixed with defcon 11 dataset and analyzed quantitatively with Snort-IDS. Log analyzer was designed with C++ language to analyze the logs of the intrusion detector. Qualitative analysis of the results was carried out by 16 undergraduate students, 4 software engineers and 2 marketers of software and electronic systems. The contributions of this chapter are as follows. The chapter has empirically substantiated the concept of negligence and how it relates to cybercrimes on Wireless Sensor Networks (WSNs). The chapter empirically discusses three key considerations on lawsuit that is meant to recover damages incurred from negligence of employer, negligence of employee and joint negligence in other to answer the above puzzling questions. The remainders of this chapter are organized as follows. Section 2 provides definitions of related terms while section 3 will discuss the concept of criminal liability in the Wireless Sensor Networks (WSNs). Section 4 discusses the methodology of the survey. Section 5 gives the results and further analyzes them while section 6 concludes the chapter and offers areas for future research.

2. DEFINITION OF TERMS

Cybercrime involves the use of a computer system or mobile device and Internet facility to perform an act that is punishable by law. Examples are illegal disruption of online operations of corporate networks, online fraud, illegal dissemination of hurtful information over Internet, intrusion into supervisory software of private or corporate individuals via Internet and the use of snooping programs to spy or steal corporate (or private) procedures, regulations and associated documentations via Internet resources, etc.

- *Misconduct* represents a situation whereby a person (or an employee) exhibits improper behavior that is unexpected of such a person by law.
- *Negligence* represents a situation whereby a person (or an employee) deliberately fails to ethically take proper action but the action that the person takes ultimately results into damage (Owen, 2007).
- *Complainant* is a plaintiff, litigator or petitioner who seeks for compensation by bringing a criminal allegation against another person, or service provider, company in a police station or court of law.
- *Defendant* is suspect of a crime. A suspect of cybercrime against Wireless Sensor Networks (WSNs) can denote a person (or service provider, agency, institution) that is sued or accused by complaint(s) in a court of law to have caused harm or infringement to the complaint(s).

Third party to Wireless Sensor Networks (WSNs) is a person or organization that provides services to business owners of Wireless Sensor Networks (WSNs).

3. THE CONCEPT OF CRIMINAL LIABILITY IN THE WIRELESS SENSOR NETWORKS (WSNS)

Wireless Sensor Networks (WSNs) are vital technologies for environmental surveillance. In the banking sector for instance, the sensing aspect of the technologies often comprises of multiple and interdependent components of computing and heterogeneous devices. Several hardware (electronic) and software components also work with the technologies and they cooperatively operate with shared services and interdependent service providers. Though, all the service providers may not reside in the same geographic locations but they collaborate and effectively deliver insightful monitoring; recording and communication of suspicious and normal events to assist surveillance watchers in remote (or strategic) locations. Therefore, cybercrimes against any of the above components of WSNs must be thoroughly investigated to expose the entity and elements that are involved in the crime.

Tracking the account of criminal allegations regarding Wireless Sensor Networks (WSNs) is the source of many dilemmas over years. Investigations into allegations of cybercrime against WSNs in the banking sector for instance can indicate the basis, origin, causes, places, people, software and electronic devices that are connected to the crime. Figure 2 provides a schematic diagram of a bank and its customers to illustrate simple applications and entities of Wireless Sensor Networks (WSNs) in banking sector. The outline suggests that certain employees can occupy the position to prevent some cybercrimes from happening to their organizations in the above context. Some roles and responsibilities in corporate settings are designed to directly or indirectly counter the occurrence of cybercrimes. Some business contingency processes must have been built into the roles and responsibilities of certain employees in corporate organizations in order to mitigate cybercrimes and to ultimately lessen the impacts of unpleasant events due to cybercrimes that are bound to happen.

Figure 2. Schematic diagram of bank and customers

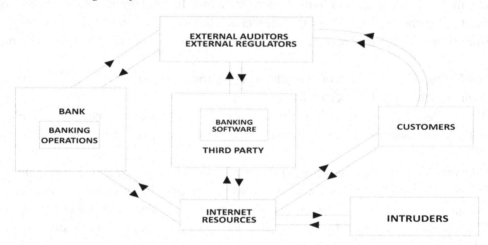

Such cybercrime in the above example must originate from a place (intruder) and it can involve one or many people (banking workers, customers and service providers of the bank, etc), different software (e.g. banking applications, mobile banking apps, virtual conferencing apps, email apps, etc) and numerous electronic systems (e.g. computers, application server, web servers, email server, CCTV, etc). Thus, comprehensive investigations into cases of cybercrime against WSNs should give the initiator of the crime, the accomplice(s) and element(s) of the crime. The investigations should also provide answers to questions such as "who was the architect of the cybercrime?", "where has the cybercrime originated from?", "who fount for the suspects of the cybercrime?", "who might have caused the cybercrime?", "Where are the routine reports on the independent sensor devices that are meant to monitor the environment?", "who should be liable to criminal charges regarding the failure to analyze, monitor or communicate suspicious events that surveillance devices have monitored and recorded at diverse locations from end-to-end of wireless links?", "who can furnish information about the allegation? ", "who should have prevented the cybercrime from happening?".

Thus, most criminal laws and corporate culture would expect employees to act with the prudence and exercise reasonable responsibilities in certain circumstances while discharging their duties on a daily basis. Therefore, the notion of criminal negligence is to apprehend employee that are investigated to have possessed (or demonstrated) the evidence of carelessness, indiscipline, lack of vigilance, willful neglect of their constitutional responsibilities and lack of attention to precautionary measures that should prevent cybercrimes. It is an offence for an employee or employer to be unconcerned in foreseeable or unforeseeable circumstances. Laws expect employers of labour to be legally held accountable for their failure to reasonably and prudently prevent unpleasant situations (events) when and in actual fact they have legal power and positions to do so.

Furthermore, Wireless Sensor Networks (WSNs) encompass many platforms such as hardware system and wireless software. The contractual agreement between vendors and companies that are supporting or marketing wireless sensor devices to the general public, the operating systems and mobile apps that they use to route messages and signals can also vary from one country to another (European Parliament, 2019). Therefore, criminal liability in the above setting should encompass the software and electronic settings and other components of the Wireless Sensor Networks (WSNs) in order to broadly and critical examine the history, sources and genesis of criminal allegations within the technologies.

The outcomes of the investigations on criminal liability on cybercrimes in the areas of the Wireless Sensor Networks (WSNs) can be adopted by litigators and judges on two bases. Firstly, this chapter submits that for the purpose of condemnation or enforcement of punishments, the genesis of cybercrime should be the fundamental basis for detectives and judges to apprehend and apportion blame to proven suspects of cybercrimes in the above environments. Secondly, in the administration of criminal justice, the source(s) of criminal allegations should be the basis that detectives and judges can decide to exonerate and acquit suspects in the above settings.

In addition, some usual and unavoidable cybercrimes on Wireless Sensor Networks (WSNs) and their impacts can raise objectionable comments in courts and in the society. In criminology, investigators of such cybercrimes must thoroughly investigate the grounds, obligations and suitable actions that employees (or employers) must take (or are expected to have taken) in accordance with the laws of contractual and agreement in organizations.

4. METHODOLOGY OF THE SURVEY

Kismet was used to extract three categories of TCP traces in promiscuous mode at the intervals of 3 weeks from traffics that migrated across wireless Local Area Networks (LANs) and CCTV footage of networks to a University. The first packets were gathered between 12 am and 8 am to safe storage space. The second packets were gathered between 8am and 12 pm while the third packets were gathered between 4pm and 12 pm.

The datasets were mixed with defcon 11 dataset and analyzed quantitatively with Snort-IDS. A log analyzer was designed with C++ language to analyze the logs of the intrusion detector. Entropy is demonstrated as a metric that investigators can use to promptly understand the degree of consistency, regularity and distribution of a set of forensic evidence such as the lengths of alerts that originated from Intrusion Detection System (IDS). Mathematically:

$$Entropy = -\sum p(c)\log_2 p(c) \tag{1}$$

In this case, P represents the probability of occurrence of lengths of alerts. Qualitative analysis of the results was carried out by 16 undergraduate students, 4 software engineers and 2 marketers of software and electronic systems. The results that were obtained from the above methods are discussed below.

5. RESULTS AND ANALYSIS

The results demonstrate that the lengths of alerts that can indicate some categories of cybercrimes on Wireless Sensor Networks (WSNs) are not often the same. The degree of homogeneity (or heterogeneity) of such forensic evidence raised a lot of concerns during allocation of criminal liability on cybercrimes against WSNs.

5.1. Quantitative Analysis of Cybercrimes Against Wireless Sensor Networks (WSNs)

Figure 3 to Figure 5 demonstrate that it is possible for Intrusion Detection Systems (IDSs) to use variable lengths of attributes to describe allegations and distributions of cybercrimes against devices or components of WSNs.

For instance, in Figure 3, the entropy grew up to 13.0642 when the length of the messages due to possible allegations of cybercrimes on certain components of WSNs was between 38 and 120.

Figure 3. Entropy analysis of first TCP dump traces

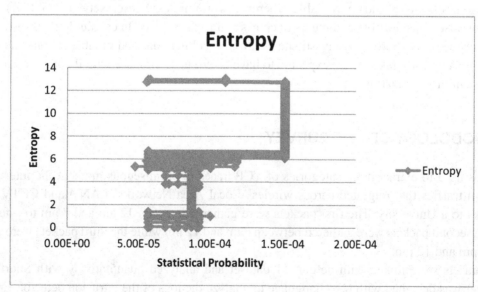

In Figure 4, the entropy grew up to 11.9422 when the length of the messages due to possible allegations of cybercrimes on certain components of WSNs was between 40 and 120.

Figure 4. Entropy analysis of the second TCP dump traces

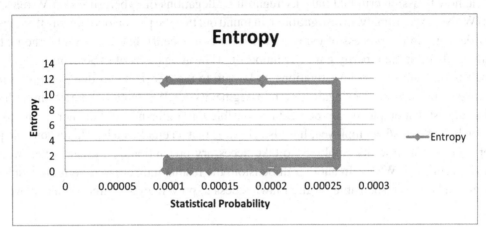

In Figure 5, the entropy grew up to 4.42892 when the length of the messages due to possible allegations of cybercrimes against certain components of WSNs was between 43 and 90. In essence, the lengths of closely related alerts are not the same. The descriptions of such messages are inconsistent and unpredictable. The inconsistency and unpredictability of the cybercrimes may be the rationale behind the inability of employers and their employees to individually and jointly detect and counter the crime. Hence, the challenge of how to detect volatility and unpredictability of the IDS alerts that denote cybercrimes are generating new dilemmas in cyber criminology.

Figure 5. Entropy analysis of the third TCP dump traces

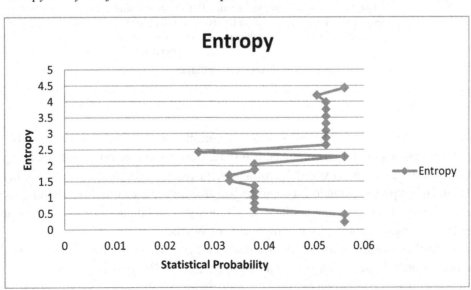

5.2. Qualitative Analysis of Negligence Due to Cybercrimes on Wireless Sensor Networks (WSNs)

Respondents argued that courts and insurance should scrutinize the presence of at least three possibilities to determine how to assign criminal liability regarding allegations of cybercrimes on Wireless Sensor Networks (WSNs). Accordingly, investigations can found out that the person or company that approaches a court for damages in the process of using a device (or component) that works under the platform of WSNs can legally be at fault, partly guilty or innocent of the allegations of cybercrimes.

In Figure 6, the outcomes of investigations on lawsuit to recover damages due to harm or infringements incurred from cybercrimes against certain segment(s) of WSNs can generate three dilemmas. The results suggest that employer can be held responsible for negligence and his/her failure to prevent intrusions on behalf of his/her employee. It is also possible that an employee is held responsible possibly for his/her failure to instruct its employer to take necessary precautionary measures that would have deterred cybercrimes on WSNs. In another dimension, the results indicate that both the employee and its employer can be held responsible for their lawlessness to prevent cybercrimes in the above context.

Figure 6. Outcomes of investigation on lawsuit to recover damages

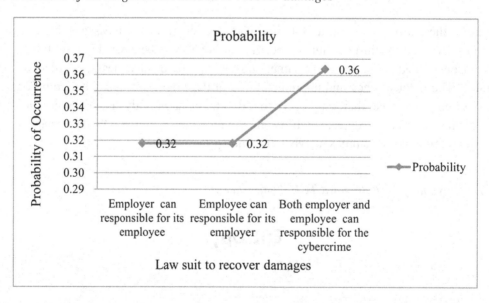

The likelihood that some complex cybercrimes on certain components of WSNs may be attributed to employer being responsible for its employee was 0.32. Conversely, the possibility that employee can be held responsible for its employer was 0.32. Similarly, the results indicate that the possibility that both the employer and its employee being jointly held responsible for certain complex cybercrimes was 0.36. In other words, the results suggest that negligence of employers and their employees may cause certain cybercrimes to occur against some of the components of WSNs.

The results further suggest four potential causes of cybercrimes on Wireless Sensor Networks (WSNs). In other words, Figure 7 suggests that negligence on WSNs may be apportioned on the basis of comparative negligence, concurrent negligence, contributory negligence or vicarious negligence. The

Figure 7. Classification of negligence in WSNs

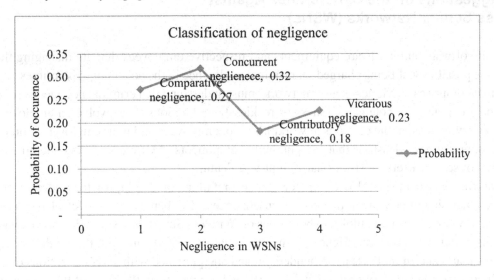

figure summarizes that the likelihood that allegations of complex cybercrimes on entities of WSNs may be attributed to concurrent negligence (0.27), comparative negligence (0.32); contributory negligence (0.18) and vicarious negligence (0.23).

Contributory negligence regarding cybercrimes on Wireless Sensor Networks (WSNs) is awarded against a plaintiff that demonstrated to have failed to exercise reasonable precautionary measure(s) that would have disallowed the cybercrimes from happening to him/her (Kagan, 2021). The participants argued that the failure of plaintiff to act prudently can indicate the contributory factors to the harm or the root cause of the allegations of the complainant. Comparative negligence in the above context conotes the method of aportioning criminal liability (or blame) to multiple parties and whenever it has been proved that the plaintiff and defendant have failed to exercise reasonable precautionary measures that should have prevented the cybercrimes against certain component(s) of WSNS from happening.

Respondents further believe that vicarious liability can occur whenever the negligence due to a company (or person) is proved to have caused the harm(s) to its employee (or another person). Vicarious liability can apply to circumstance whereby investigations have indicted some companies as the entities to be held responsible for the harm(s) of their employees (BOM, 2022). The argument was that the inability of the employees to prevent the cybercrimes on the entity of WSNs can be attributed to the negligence of their employers to properly train them or negligence to hire competent personnel. The result suggest that concurrent negligence is necessary so that the defendants (two or more employees) that have caused the cybercrimes to occur on the entity of WSNs should be penalized (Owen, 2007).

In essence, the above observations indicate that the principles behind award of penalty for negligence in preventing cybercrimes that involve many software and hardware industries vary (Nolan, 2013). Thus, plaintiffs that may intend to approach court of laws for compensations should deeply reflect on their roles. There are instances whereby the plaintiffs can also be found criminally liable and certain percentages of fault can be apportioned to them on certain cybercrimes.

5.3. Suggestions on the Cybercrimes Against Wireless Sensor Networks (WSNs)

Vendors of software and hardware equipments and respective employees that ate managing them can mitigate the possibility of being charged for criminal negligence in the advent of cybercrimes on WSNs. Entities that comprises of wireless sensor networks must understand that criminal negligence in software environment can also connote carelessness or recklessly and actions that involve an employee acting without observing reasonable cautions at workplace. So, employees and their employers should endeavour to abstain from recklessness that can put them, components of wireless sensors and other persons (such users or service users) at risk of harm, injury or death.

The above legal concepts also cover negligence or failure of employees to prudently carry out procedures that should stop or mitigate the consequences of cybercrimes and act of recklessness at workplace. Investigations on complex cybercrimes on Wireless Sensor Networks (WSNs) may generate several misgivings and concerns. Hence, crime investigators should carry out thorough investigations to establish that real criminals are apprehended, judged and punished with suitable sections of criminal codes. Claims must be amicably settled and apportioned to victims on the basis of their severity of the consequences of cybercrimes on them.

Similarly, the degree of innocence or guiltiness of the suspects of cybercrimes on WSNs is assessed at court's trial. Some cybercrimes in the above scenarios may require several trials in the courts of law. Cybercrimes can involve co-defendants to unravel the case. In this case, the investigators must establish that the right defendant is appropriately proved beyond doubt that he/he (or the organization) is legally liable to be joined together with one or additional defendants in the same allegation of cybercrimes on components of WSNs. Therefore, the enforcement and apportioning of the punishments on the proven suspects of the cybercrimes in the above domain should commensurate to the degree of their involvement in the allegations.

6. CONCLUSION

Wireless Sensor Networks (WSNs) are vital technologies for environmental surveillance. Studies have established that the sensing features of the technologies comprise of multiple and interdependent components of computing and heterogeneous devices in diverse locations. However, new studies have revealed that the arrest and investigations of suspects of complex cybercrimes on the above technologies and establish criminal liability and negligence against the perpetrators of the crime, suspects or complainants often generate lots of dilemmas. The study have shown that the arrest of suspects of cybercrimes that involve many service providers, investigations of suspects of cybercrimes and how to establish criminal liability against proven suspects of the crime are constantly adding up to global concerns in recent time. The study made known that individual length of the alerts that originate from IDSs that monitor traffics across wireless nodes and peripheral components of WSNs are not often the same.

Serious dilemmas originate from the fact that the custodians of the sensing aspect of wireless sensor networks are different from the custodians of other components of the technologies. Moreover, the chapter has also shown that each of the various components of WSNs is often manufactured, owned, supported and controlled by different employees in different companies. Cybercrimes against the peripheral components of WSNs become inevitable because each company usually enforces data protection policies to the best of their capability in different manners.

The trouble is that some criminal and cyber laws to punish and deter such illegal act often depend on jurisdiction and the liability of the defendant(s). Similarly, consideration should also be made to possible plaintiff's negligence and the administration of justice on the legal issues, which often vary from one country to another. For these reasons, it is difficult to criminal charge or hold specific companies, and or employees legally responsible for not detecting, stopping or reporting serious cybercrimes within the peripherals of WSNs. Stigmatization and the sensitivity of the problems in the software and hardware industries have made most corporate organizations to rarely involve the law enforcement agents until some victims may decide to approach the court of laws for compensation. New developments that come with novel issues are emerging on the domains of the Wireless Networks on routine basis. As a result, there is no accurate criminal datasets on the above problems across the globe. So, it is difficult to ascertain the various impacts of complex cybercrimes would have had on the past victims and the individual wireless nodes across the globe.

Furthermore, this chapter discovered lawlessness (such as erring complainants and guilty employers) is an emerging issue in WSNs. We observed that investigators of criminal liability involving components of WSNs can explore the likelihood that the allegations can be attributed to the company that is responsible for its employee, employee that is responsible for its employer or combination of both the employer and the employee acting in negligence manners. The study further summarizes that criminal courts and insurance firms may be looking at the criminal cases on cybercrimes in WSNs from the perspectives of concurrent negligence, comparative negligence, contributory negligence or vicarious negligence.

We therefore submit that software companies and their business partners can act with reasonable caution and hope that they are immune of cybercrimes. They should operate without endangering their clients, customers or another person. However, business partners in the above domains can still be victims of some devastated cybercrimes. As a result, future research should evolve models for understanding cybercrimes that can involve many service providers. Finally, the theory of negligence in the domains of Wireless Sensor Networks (WSNs) is calling for urgent empirical substantiation to promote criminal justice system and criminal prosecution of proven suspects of cybercrimes against Wireless Sensor Networks (WSNs) across the globe.

REFERENCES

Block O'Toole and Morphy (BOM). (2022). *Types of Negligence and How They Apply in Different Scenarios*. BOM. https://www.blockotoole.com/negligence/types-of-negligence.

Eoin, Q. (2014). *Torts In Ireland*. Dublin., Gill education.

European Parliament. (2019). Access to legal remedies for victims of corporate human rights abuses in third countries. Policy Department for External Relations. *Directorate General for External Policies of the Union, PE, 603*, 47.

Jay, F. (2010). Law 101. Oxford University Press publisher.

Kagan, J. (2021). *Contributory Negligence*. Investiopedia. https://www.investopedia.com/terms/c / contributory-negligence.asp.

Lawteacher.net. (2022). Principles of Criminal Liability: Intention and Recklessness. *Lawteacher.net.* https://www.lawteacher.net/free-law-essays/criminal-law/principles-of-criminal-liability.php.

Nolan, D. (2013). Varying the standard of care in Negligence. *The Cambridge Law Journal, 72*(3), 651–688. doi:10.1017/S0008197313000731

Owen, D. G. (2007). The Five Elements of Negligence. *Hofstra Law Review, 35*(4), 1–16.

Peno, M. and Bogucki, O. (2021). Principles of Criminal Liability from the Semiotic Point of View. *International Journal for the Semiotics of Law - Revue internationale de Sémiotique juridique, 34*(3). doi:10.1007/s11196-020-09691-z

Plunkett, J. (2018). *The Duty of Care in Negligence* (1st ed.). Oxford and Portland Publisher.

Chapter 6
Hacking:
Evolution, Conceptualization, and the Perpetrators

Carolina Roque
https://orcid.org/0000-0002-7858-6991
Faculty of Law, University of Porto, Portugal

Maria Canudo
https://orcid.org/0009-0008-1733-2366
Faculty of Law, University of Porto, Portugal

Samuel Moreira
https://orcid.org/0000-0002-6873-492X
Faculty of Law, University of Porto, Portugal & Faculty of Law, University Lusíada, Portugal

Inês Sousa Guedes
Faculty of Law, University of Porto, Portugal

ABSTRACT

This chapter aims to present a theoretical foundation on hacking, focusing on the perpetrator's profile, his modus operandi, and typologies. First, a conceptualization and characterization of the phenomenon's key terms is presented. Next, the chapter addresses the historical evolution of the perception of the phenomenon, from the moment of its emergence to the current understanding. The most prominent typologies in the scientific literature will be described, which seek to distinguish the perpetrators of the behaviors according to criteria related to their practice. While focusing on the cybercriminals, the chapter emphasizes the hacker's figure, directing the review on their sociodemographic profile and contextual aspects. Finally, the personality factors prevalent in hackers are characterized, namely according to the big five model and the dark triad model. This chapter, using criminological lens, will increase the knowledge of the hackers and its modus operandi. The implications of this knowledge will be outlined.

DOI: 10.4018/979-8-3693-1528-6.ch006

1. INTRODUCTION

In the last few decades, the use of computers and the Internet has proliferated, profoundly revolutionizing societal dynamics and human behaviors. From these changes, technological resources evolve, creating opportunities for committing criminal behaviors in cyberspace (Maimon & Louderback, 2019). These new activities, as a whole, are commonly called cybercrime, characterized by new contours and by being able to overcome the existing physical barriers, since the perpetrator does not need to perform a proximal action and share the same physical space as its victims (Bossler & Burruss, 2011; Britz, 2013)[1].

One of the fastest-growing crimes is hacking, conceived in the scientific literature as an illegal and unauthorized activity related to the intrusion and manipulation of a computer and/or computer system (Yar, 2006; Sharma, 2007). This conceptualization is included in computer-focused crimes, rather than computer-assisted crimes, since it can only be committed through modern technologies, which did not exist before the emergence of the Internet (Furnell, 2001; Furnell et al., 2015). Moreover, following Wall's (2007) classification criteria, hacking is considered a computer integrity crime, because it is related to altering the integrity of systems. Specifically, it can be described as a cybertrespass conduct, depicting the unauthorized crossing of the boundaries inherent to computer systems (Wall, 2001; Wall & Williams, 2007).

Over the past few years, the frequency of this criminal phenomenon has increased exponentially, and hacking behaviors are responsible for more than half (52%) of existing data breaches (Hiscox, 2022) with approximately 65 thousand computer vulnerabilities discovered in 2022 caused by these behaviors (HackerOne, 2022). As a result of this growth, hacking is becoming problematic and harmful in various sectors of social life. In fact, an analysis of data from the IBM Security and Ponemon Institute (2022) showed that the economic cost derived from these actions was $4.35 million, an increase of 2.6% by 2021.

In the international scientific community, the analysis of hacking and its behaviors has been conducted along several lines of investigation, particularly: (1) the hacker's sociodemographic and psychological characteristics; (2) the subcultural dynamics underlying Hacking Culture; (3) the types of behaviors perpetrated (*e.g.,* creation of malware and computer viruses; identity theft; website defacement); (4) the hacking explicative factors according to the criminological theories (Steinmetz, 2016). However, these advances in theoretical and empirical knowledge on the topic have not accompanied the evolution of hacking and remain underdeveloped. Therefore, this chapter offers a consolidation of hacking and the existing criminological understanding of this issue, addressing the previously mentioned research. First, a conceptualization and characterization of the phenomenon's key terms (*i.e.,* hacking, hack, and hacker) are presented to provide a foundation for the following topics.

The next section presents the historical evolution of the perception of the phenomenon from the moment of its emergence to current comprehension. Regarding the understanding of hacking behaviors, the diverse historical moments are crucial to build an overview and understanding of why it is a phenomenon that generates some lack of consensus. In this sense, the prominent typologies in the scientific literature are described, which seek to share how the perpetrators have been conceptualized and distinguished taking different criteria into consideration (*e.g.,* motivations and act's sophistication). To focus on the cybercriminal, the hacker's figure is emphasized, highlighting the aspects that constitute their sociodemographic profile (*e.g.,* gender, age, ethnicity, academic and professional qualifications) and the dimensions of the context where the individual is inserted (*e.g.,* peer network, family ties).

Finally, the personality factors prevalent in hackers will be characterized, supported by the premises of the Big Five (Costa & McCrae, 1992) and the Dark Triad Models (Paulhus & Williams, 2002).

2. KEY TERMS

Currently, hacking is one of the most studied cybercrime by the scientific community and it is currently at the center of public debates and social concerns (Holt, 2020; Payne, 2020). The present section presents the characterization of the main terms inherent to the phenomenon – 'hacking' and 'hack'. It should be noted that both concepts have been the target of several interpretations and alterations, depending on the author's personal perspectives and the empirical results obtained.

2.1 Hacking

Generally, the term hacking has a malicious connotation, associated with criminal or antisocial behavior. The definition by Taylor (1999), although simplistic, fully captures society's view of the phenomenon, in which it is seen as an *"unauthorized access to and subsequent use of other people's computer systems"* (p. viii). However, special care must be taken when using this term, because its original meaning differs substantially from this premise (Bossler & Burrus, 2011; Holt 2020; Yar, 2006).

Hacking was initially proposed as an ethical concept, linked to the fascination with technological discoveries, computer innovation and sophistication (Levy, 1984; Holt, 2020; Jaquet-Chiffelle & Loi, 2020), in which it would be viewed as *"the act of creative problem solving when faced with complex technical problems"* (Yar, 2016, p.6). This illustrates that the first approach to hacking and its conduct was largely based on fun, resolution, and enthusiasm for the digital and technological environment (Jaquet-Chiffelle & Loi, 2020; Steinmetz, 2016). Although associated with exploring other people's computers and computing systems, the purpose of hacking was curiosity and the desire to learn (Bossler & Burruss, 2011). However, this connotation did not endure, gradually beginning to acquire a malicious label, previously presented.

In light of this, a new concept – *cracking* – was proposed, which would integrate criminal behaviors supported by the individuals' malicious motivations and intentions. More specifically, it was referred to as *"illicitly breaking into someone else's computer through a range of techniques, such as social engineering (tricking someone into giving access) or exploitations of technical faults"* (Jordan, 2017, p.534). The primary goal was to differentiate between both terms, emphasizing that hacking was associated with something positive and beneficial (Yar, 2006). In spite of this distinction, the illicit usage prevailed, continuing to be associated with the term hacking until today (Jaquet-Chiffelle & Loi, 2020; Steinmetz, 2016). This becomes a term that encompasses two key components – vulnerability and exploitation. There are numerous vulnerabilities to be identified in softwares or devices, in which this flaw or error can be used to exploit certain software and/or hardware and, consequently, gain access to the command system and connections (Holt, 2020).

Another perspective emerges, which sees hacking as a subculture, called 'Hacking Culture' (Holt, 2020; Taylor, 1999). This point of view has been widely analyzed, both theoretically and empirically, with numerous authors discovering the existence of certain characteristics associated with this subculture (Bossler & Burruss, 2011; Holt, 2007). The goals and beliefs of this subculture converge in three central elements - technology, knowledge, and secrecy – which are retained regardless of the act's nature (Holt, 2020; Jordan & Taylor, 1998; Steinmetz, 2016; Taylor, 1999; Thomas, 2002).

Technology is one of the focal points of hacking that allows individuals to be deeply connected with each other (Bossler & Burruss, 2011). In this culture, there is a shared passion for technical development and innovation, in which one tries to identify the vulnerabilities of the systems and introduce changes to make them more effective (Taylor, 1999, 2001; Yar, 2006). Concerning the element of knowledge, in this context it refers to wisdom, as it is something constructed and recognized by the members. This enables individuals to understand who possesses the skills necessary to join the subculture (Holt, 2020; Taylor, 1999). Lastly, secrecy is the basis of the phenomenon. On the one hand, despite the desire to share its skills with the world, the subculture operates in a specific environment, reserved only for those who have the mastery of technology. On the other hand, due to the growth of the term's malicious connotation and the extent of law enforcement to encompass hacking behavior, communication is now performed in the online world, not revealing identities as a way to minimize the risk of arrest (Holt, 2020; Taylor, 1999; Yar, 2006).

Additionally, the Hacking Culture is organized in a similar way to gangs, as the bonds between members are formed quickly and informally. In this connection with other hackers, ideas and goals are shared, and action strategies are encouraged (Bossler & Burruss, 2011; Steinmetz et al., 2020). Although there are common characteristics that unite these individuals, the analysis of hacking as a subculture requires further investigation, not only to examine the superficial aspects, but also the historical and structural context in which this phenomenon is located (Steinmetz, 2016).

Despite the various contours that hacking can assume, the dominant perspective is the negative and criminal one, in which it is synonymous with illegal activities associated with the intrusion and manipulation of a computer (Yar, 2006). Moreover, this attempt, whether successful or not, is always unauthorized (Sharma, 2007). Accordingly, Furnell (2001) describes hacking as a *"deliberately gaining unauthorized access to a computer system, usually through the use of communication facilities"* (p.36).

According to several authors, hacking has acquired multiple views over time, and can be seen as a socially constructed term, progressively acquiring the conceptualization that society attributes to it, leading to fear and not allowing society to truly know the intentions behind their actions (Steinmetz, 2016; Taylor, 1999; Thomas, 2002). This societal position leads to a continuous process of labeling the behavior and identity of the individual (Coleman & Golub, 2008), gathering them all under the same conceptualization and neglecting their differences. Considering this, arises the need to conduct an in-depth analysis of the phenomenon and deconstruct the several aspects and terms that hacking involves.

2.2 Hack

Although hack might be considered an act of hacking, this perception is clearly simplistic since this behavior involves multiple details and characteristics that should be further explored (Bossler & Burruss, 2011; Yar, 2006). Originally, the concept was associated with the pranks and jokes that students at the Massachusetts Institute of Technology (MIT) performed, either among themselves or towards the professors and the university (Levy, 1984). Regardless of this earliest and most traditional usage, the term acquired a new life with the members of the Tech Model Railroad Club (TMRC). According to the members of this club, a certain action would be considered a hack if it were a technical and sophisticated procedure that brought enjoyment to its performer (Levy, 1984; Steinmetz, 2016).

In the scientific literature developed in recent decades, hacking has been analyzed according to the technological skills it involves, similar to what has been done with various forms of cybercrime (Bossler & Burruss, 2011). This behavior can range from simple tasks (*e.g.,* trying to guess someone's password) to more complex conducts (*e.g.,* creating and distributing malicious software) (Holt, 2007; Rogers et al., 2006). Nevertheless, the most widely accepted idea is the association of this behavior with the possession of high computer skills (Bossler & Burruss, 2011), which, according to Holt (2020), is aligned with *"more technical methods"* which *"involve the use of programs and tools to facilitate a compromise"* (p.727). Therefore, to successfully perform a hack, individuals must have specialized knowledge of computer systems and be familiar with the attacks to be executed (*e.g.,* phishing; malware; SQL injection; session hijacking) (Bossler & Burruss, 2011; ul Hassan & Ahmad, 2021).

Furthermore, a more characterizing position emerges, highlighting some characteristics inherent to what would be considered a 'good hack' (Peacock, 2013). Here the reference to certain words stands out, namely - simplicity, mastery, and illegality. This means that the act would be simple, but impressive; thoughtful, accomplished using sophisticated techniques; and illicit, violating normative and legal norms (Taylor, 1999; Turkle, 1984).

Yar's (2006) writings illustrate the general picture of this behavior, exemplifying multiple forms that hacking can take, as follows: (a) theft of confidential information or property; (b) theft of computer resources; (c) defacing websites; (d) sabotage, alteration, and/or destruction of systems; (e) denial of access to a service; (f) distribution of malicious software.

These premises allow one to conclude that, similarly to what happened with the concept of hacking, there was a progressive evolution of the sense in which the term is used, from a positive view to an illegal connotation related to *"breaking into a computer particularly in order to steal or damage"* (Peacock, 2013, p.31).

3. HISTORICAL EVOLUTION

When the terms hack, hacking and hacker appeared, they were used with a purely positive connotation (Szpor & Gryszczyńska, 2022). Scientific community has attributed its origin to a student club - the Tech Model Railroad Club (TMRC) – formed at the Massachusetts Institute of Technology (MIT) in 1940 (Levy, 2001), a group composed of enthusiasts of model railroads, showing particular interest in their electronic systems (Steinmetz, 2016). Members of this club would coin the term hacking to refer to the acts they performed as *"goofing around with the models' electrical systems and equipment for fun"* (Holt, 2020, p.728). Eventually, these early hackers were drawn to more complicated technological systems available at the time, namely computers (Steinmetz, 2016). Hacking began to be a term also used by computer programmers and engineers who were also working with these systems at various universities (Holt, 2020).

At that time, the technology used was far different from what is available today. The systems and computers occupied the entire space of a room, described by Levy (1984, p.25) as a *"hulking giant"*, with limited processing power and memory and, moreover, were not connected to each other in any way. Thus, programmers looked for strategies to improve the capacity of these systems and used the term 'hack' to refer to the solutions they found (Levy, 2001). Therefore, as it began to be used by TMRC, the essence of the hack started out as a project or product built for constructive and pleasure purposes. (Levy, 1984). At this time, the main characteristics of a hack were simplicity, as the act had to be simple but impressive; mastery, of sophisticated technical knowledge; and illegality, being an act that violated rules (Taylor, 1999). To constitute a hack, the act had to exhibit *"innovation style, and technical virtuosity"* (Levy, 2010, p.34), and the creators of them would be referred to as hackers.

In its primary sense, in 1960s, hacker was addressed as a 'technological virtuous individual' (Levy, 1984). The prevailing definitions featured a person who enjoyed exploring details in programmable systems and testing their capabilities, as opposed to most users who merely learned the bare minimum necessary to make use of the same systems (Szpor & Gryszczyńska, 2022). In this sense, hacking was used to refer to problems found in the programming of the original computers (Levy, 1984), so that, among hacker circles, hacking was defined as an attempt to make use of any technology in an inventive, unorthodox, and original way (Taylor, 1999).

The first generation of MIT hackers, formed by individuals who were involved in the development of the most primitive programming techniques, were responsible for establishing the ideals of morality within the hacking culture. Their main proposition was that access to computers should be unlimited and spread to the general population. Other premises by which they were ruled were, particularly: (1) the need for freedom of information; (2) distrust of authority; (3) the need to judge other hackers by their hacking activities and not according to certain criteria, such as academic degrees, age, ethnicity, and social status; (4) the possibility of creating art and beauty through a computer; and (5) the utility of computers for a change toward a better life (Levy, 1984).

This set of ideals became known as the 'Hacker Ethic', in which individuals who followed these premises became known as 'True Hackers', since it faithfully represented the spirit and primordial intentions of hacking (Jaquet-Chiffelle & Loi, 2020). One example of True Hackers, pointed out by Landreth and Reingold (1985), was the 'Inner Circle', a hacker's group established in 1982, whose actions embodied this moral code, actively seeking to avoid getting information to other hackers who did not obey to the Hacker Ethic and whose activities may passed for a dishonest use of such information. The group claimed to be *"explorers, not spies"* and further underlined that for them *"damaging computer files was not only clumsy and inelegant – it was wrong"* (Landreth & Reingold, 1985, p.19).

Technology underwent several improvements and, throughout the 1960s, became more prominent in industry, both private and public, and the concept of hacking also followed this evolution, becoming increasingly common (Holt, 2020). Two technological innovations that occurred during this period contributed greatly to this development. First, the computer systems of universities and military services were connected, leading to the creation of the Internet, enabling large-scale information sharing, as advocated by Hacker Etchic. Moreover, computers and their technological systems suffered a decrease in economical and dimensional terms, making it easier for any person to own them (Holt, 2020; Taylor, 1999; Levy, 2001).

With these developments, public and governmental interest in the use of computers and information increased, and debates and statements about citizen's right to privacy are initiated (Levy, 1984; Yar, 2006). A focus on malicious hacks emerged in the *media* and combined with this new social perception, there was an emergence of new laws covering unauthorized access to computer systems and unauthorized detention of information from banking and financial institutions (Hollinger & Lanza-kaduce, 1988; Holt, 2020), seeking to regulate these new interactions.

This is a crucial period in which a more negative connotation associated with hacking emerges, compared to the original, as there is distrust towards the interests of the individuals who perpetrate it, who are now associated with a malicious intent (Holt, 2020; Jaquet-Chiffelle & Loi, 2020; Steinmetz, 2016; Yar, 2006). The increased emphasis on criminal uses of hacking has led to difficulties on the hacker's side in explaining its activities. The tension between their interests those wrongly associated with them by the general public is materialized in 1986 in the periodical magazine Phrack through the publication of the article 'The Conscience of a Hacker', popularly known as 'The Hacker Manifesto'. This was attributed to a hacker operating under the pseudonym 'The Mentor', an original member of the Legion of Doom group, arrested in 1990 (Furnell et al., 1999; Thomas, 2002). This text highlighted the existence of a central interest on behalf of the hackers in acquiring knowledge, even though some of their actions were against the law (Holt, 2020). From the very beginning, it is notable that this article does not use the term hacker in its original meaning, prevalent in the 1960s, but rather takes the more widely prevalent view of nowadays: individuals who gain unauthorized access to computer systems (Furnell et al., 1999). The publication of this work caused a split in the hacker community, creating a divergence from the ethics proposed earlier, granting the use of malicious hacks, however exploratory (Holt, 2020). Here is noted the rise of a new generation of hackers, which Taylor (1999) points out as having less technological skills and less sense of ethics, compared to the original hackers.

With the arrival of the new millennium, transformations have once again hit the technology field, contributing to the development of hacking in its most current version, propagated by hackers with an economic vision. The exponential growth of the Internet allows communicating in real time without any disadvantages caused by geographical barriers, increasing opportunities for online commerce, facilitating the acquisition of assets through technological means, among other innovations. Therefore, economic opportunities are created for hackers who, in their activity, resort to illicit acts. Financial institutions are becoming desirable targets for these individuals, who seek to acquire sensitive information. To this end, terms such as phishing are beginning to appear, due to the greater reliance on email and the web, and various tools are being developed by malware writers to be used by individuals with less technological abilities. Furthermore, hacking has become a useful tool for political and social causes, which, due to the hosting of more sensitive information on web servers, has begun to be targeted by both state and individual actors (Holt, 2020).

4. HACKER'S TYPOLOGIES

With the goal of generating a better understanding, and consequently tackling the problems created by hackers, it is necessary to gain knowledge about the individuals behind the attacks (Furnell, 2001; Skinner & Fream, 1997). Therefore, some authors (*e.g.,* Rogers, 2006, 2010; Moore, 2015; Seebruck, 2015) have attempted to achieve a consensual taxonomy of hackers.

Landreth and Reingold (1985) proposed one of the initial typologies which was based on the individual's level of competence and their motivations, namely mischief, intellectual challenge, thrill, ego boost, and criminal profit. From this derived a classification consisting of five types of hackers: (1) the *novice*, which would be the entry level for hackers, usually young people with the inability to perform sophisticated attacks; (2) the *students*, who would perpetrate hacking for the intellectual challenge, typically without a criminal motivation; (3) the *tourists*, who would perform attacks for the thrill that this practice would bring to them; (4) the *crashers,* who would engage in destructive behavior, seeking to cause damage to the systems with the intention of gaining visibility among their peers and even their victims, frequently signing their attacks with a nickname; and, finally, (5) the *thieves*, who would be professionals, financially motivated, who would carry out strategic attacks against their targets, accessing and illicitly collecting information from the computer system and selling this data to other individuals or companies (Landreth & Reingold, 1985).

Since this first typology was established, several other attempts have been made to categorize hackers. Each is slightly different from the others, but, in general, all are widely based on individual's motivation and skills. Some of the terms used by Landreth and Reingold (1985), such as *novice*, have been used over time and are still in use today by numerous authors, even if they assume different nomenclatures (*e.g.,* Moore, 2015; Rogers, 2006, 2010), while others (*e.g., students*) are no longer used.

Two typologies that emerged shortly after Landreth and Reingold (1985) were from Hollinger (1988) and Chantler (1996, *cited in* Rogers, 1999). The first author distinguished hackers based on the technological skills, thus dividing them into three categories in ascending order of skills: pirates, browsers, and crackers. The second author's work used several characteristics to segment hackers, namely their activities, hacking prowess, knowledge, motivations, and duration of involvement in these activities. All of these dimensions contributed to the allocation of hackers to one of three following categories: the *elite group*, consisting of individuals with a high level of knowledge and primary motivations for success, self-discovery, and intellectual challenge; the *neophytes*, subjects with an intermediate level of knowledge, mostly followers of the elite group; and the *losers and lamers*, characterized by a low level of knowledge and motivated primarily by profit, revenge, theft, and espionage (Chantler, 1996, *cited in* Rogers, 1999).

Based on these and other studies, Rogers (1999) published his first classification attempt, which was later updated in 2006, and again in 2010. In the first one, the author distinguishes between seven categories: *newbie/tool kit* and *cyber-punks* (with these two having an identical characterization to Landreth and Reingold's, 1995, novice and crasher categories, respectively); *internals*; *coders*; *old guard hackers*; *professional criminals*; and *cyberterrorists*. These categories are formed around the hacker's technological abilities, from the lowest level, consisting of the newbie/tool kit, to the highest, which highlights the last three categories presented (Rogers, 1999).

As for the *newbie/tool kit*, this is a category composed of individuals with very limited technological skills who conduct their attacks by using "tool kits", which are pieces of software, already built by other hackers. On the other hand, *cyber-punks* are already individuals who demonstrate a higher level of programming skills, able to create software on their own in order to attack a certain system, about which they have some insight. *Internals* are individuals with high technical skills, usually employees or ex-employees in a company, possibly in technology-related jobs, who have the opportunity to put in place attacks against certain systems to which their position grants them access. As for the *old guard*, although they do not have any criminal intent, they do have a disrespect for personal property and a desire for intellectual challenge, referring to the ideology of the first generation of hackers, from which their activities derive. Rogers (1999) also classifies *professional criminals* and *cyber-terrorists*, these being the trained professional criminals with access to the best equipment, often engaging in activities such as corporate espionage. Despite not being included in the typology put forward in 1999, the author also presents as a possible category the *political activists*, a type that will eventually be included in his later publication, in 2006.

In this regard, the taxonomy he published in 2006, based on his original work, will consist of nine categories. In addition to technological skills, which can oscillate on a gradual scale, depending on whether the hacker has more or less technical abilities, it now also includes the aspect of motivation, with four motivational aspects to look at: (a) curiosity, characterized by the desire for knowledge, thrill seeking, and intellectual gain; (b) notoriety, directed toward media visibility and fame or status; (c) revenge, which can be directed against a company/institution, an individual, or a nation; (d) financial, essentially aiming for monetary benefit and greed (Rogers, 2006). To portray these two central aspects, the author conceives a two-dimensional circumplex model. These models are used to represent different concepts and the relationships between them and are displayed in a circle divided into four quadrants, in this case each representing a motivation (Seebruck, 2015).

Five of the categories were reused from his previous work and retained its characterization, these being *novice* (which replaces the previous category newbie/tool kit), *old guard* hackers, both assigned the curiosity motivation; *cyberpunks*, who hold the notoriety motivation; *internals*, motivated by revenge, acting against their institution; and *professional criminals*, who are financially motivated. To these, the author adds four other categories: *petty thieves*, which have an identical characterization to the thief category of Landreth and Reingold (1985), being a financially driven category, that is, they are opportunists with technological skills, who take advantage of the lack of internal organization of a certain organization, managing to dominate some aspects of computer systems; *virus writers*, coders who use automated tools, seeking prestige and power and having the ability to use advanced malware, also often being employees or ex-employees with technological knowledge of the system to cause a threat to its security; *information warriors* are funded to participate in cyber-attacks that are often politically motivated; the latter are very similar to *political activists*, individuals or groups whose behavior is claimed to be morally justified, namely by political issues. Despite this, their true motivation is undetermined (Rogers, 2006).

In this new categorization, the author highlights the *information warriors*, *professional criminals*, *political activists*, and *old guard hackers* as having the highest level of technical expertise, and the *novice* group as presenting the lowest. As for the motivations, in summary: the *internals* and the *virus writers* would be motivated by revenge; the behavior of the *information warriors*, *petty thieves* and *professional criminals* would have a financial purpose; the notoriety would be the main motivation of the *cyber punks* and *political activists*; and, finally, the *novice* and *old guard hackers* would be motivated by curiosity (Rogers, 2006).

Lastly, in 2010 the author updated his typology one last time, composed of seven categories, excluding the *internals* and *old guard* groups, and re-titling his categories as *script kiddies* (which replaces the *novice* category), *cyber-punks*, *professionals*, *virus writers*, *cyber-terrorists*, a category recovered from 1999's work, and *hacktivists*.

The typologies presented by Rogers (2006, 2010) have largely influenced future classifications, including Seebruck's (2015) who, like Rogers (2006), also uses a circumplex model, in what he calls the 'Weighted Arc Circumplex Model' (Seebruck, 2015). To create his typology, the author focused on the recent increase in cyberattacks motivated by social and ideological causes, and from this, several authors also begin to pay more focus to this issue (*e.g.,* Thackray et al., 2016).

Seebruck (2015), due to the vast multiplicity of hacker's typologies that have emerged over the years, proposed to achieve a *"unified and updated view"* (p. 37) on this topic, noting, conversely, the need for constant reform in existing typologies to be able to embrace new developments in the phenomenon. In this sense, he intended to incorporate ideology as a motivation, because at the time he presents his proposal, a growing importance of this motivation in cyber-attacks had been observed. Thus, even though Rogers (2010) included *political activists* in his categorization as a subgroup of hackers, Seebruck (2015) sought to extend this idea and provide ideology with its own category as a motivating factor for hacking.

In this way, the author redefined and updated the motivations of hackers to include: (a) recreation, that is, hacking practiced for pleasure such as intellectual curiosity, excitement, or malice; (b) prestige, encompassing non-material gains such as notoriety, primary motivation for non-malicious coders; (c) revenge, which can be both personal and motivated by social problems; (d) profit, consisting of material gain, which is the main motivation for criminals; and (e) ideology, whether political or social (Seebruck, 2015).

In addition to highlighting the category of ideologically motivated hackers, the *hacktivists*, he also created a new category, the *crowdsourcers*, whose movements consist of collective efforts to solve a problem, sometimes with dubious goals and methods. Combining the two aspects, Seebruck (2015) built a classification consisting in eight types of hackers, in ascending order of act sophistication, the following categories: (1) *novices* – individuals who use basic and simple techniques pre-existent on the internet, and are driven by mere curiosity; (2) *crowsourcers* – those who do not possess sophisticated skills, but merely move collective efforts to execute revenge; (3) *punks* – individuals who are motivated by the excitement of the deviant act and by revenge, and may have low to high skills; (4) *hacktivists* – those who possess intermediate technological skills and act according to political ideology; (5) *insiders* – individuals who act for revenge and profit, possessing medium skills; (6) *criminals* – individuals who act for financial gain from crime, aided by medium-high skills; (7) coders – those who are non-malicious hackers who seek prestige in their act and they are able to achieve this by their high technological abilities; (8) *cyber warriors* – individuals who carry out sophisticated attacks based on ideology and financial profit.

Finally, due to its importance, Moore's (2015) typology should be mentioned. In fact, this is currently the most widespread typology in the scientific community, which addresses the contours of legality and ethics in hacking. Moore (2015) distinguishes between six types of hackers, according to how they perform their attacks on computer systems. In addition to the categories of *script kiddies*, *hacktivists* and *cyberterrorists*, whose characterization he reuses from the works of Landreth and Reingold (1985), Rogers (2006; 2010) and Seebruck (2015), the author also presents three distinct typologies: *black hat hackers*, *white hat hackers* and *grey hat hackers*, which have gained popularity among hacker communities, academic institutions and the media.

According to the author, *black hat hackers* are *"the epitome of all that the public fears in a computer criminal"* (Moore, 2015, p.66). These are individuals who write programs to damage computer systems and networks, thus breaching computer security, either out of malice or for personal gain. These individuals are thus situated in the illegality of the law, and their only purpose is to destroy and damage the systems, taking advantage of their vulnerabilities to obtain financial benefit from the affected companies. To do so, these individuals have an advanced technological knowledge (Moore, 2015). The activity developed by this type of hackers increases the need to improve security strategies and develop antivirus products. It also causes businesses to form around the need for protection of technological systems, as individuals are paid to develop networks and operating systems with better protection, something of the white hat hacker's competence.

Contrary to the former, their main goal is to provide programs that protect systems from being illegally and maliciously penetrated (Moore, 2015). These individuals are often hired by companies in an attempt to prevent attacks by malicious hackers, or even for the purpose of countering them (Abeoussi, 2019). They sometimes behave like the other types of hackers, seeking an entry into the system (*i.e.,* Pen Testing), however, upon success, they cease their activity and alert the owner to vulnerabilities that have been discovered (Moore, 2015). Individuals who constitute this category can therefore be viewed as ethical hackers, as their activities have legal and moral boundaries (Abeoussi, 2019).

Finally, *grey hat hackers* are considered *"a combination of white hat and black hat"* (Moore, 2015, p. 67). According to the author, these are opportunistic hackers, who seek out targets and once they gain access to their system, will notify the owners, proposing a reparation through a pecuniary amount. Other authors (*e.g.,* Kirsch, 2014; Jaquet-Chiffelle & Loi, 2020) disagree with this intent to profit as a distinction from *white hat*, but rather derive it from unethical purposes, as they are prepared to break the law through their technological exploits, with the justification of achieving better security, notwithstanding the lack of prior consent or authorization. The lack of ethics is related to the the fact that they often expose flaws publicly, not only offering solutions to companies on how to rectify such flaws, but also demonstrating to other hackers the possibility and ways to exploit them (Kirsch, 2014).

The above-mentioned lines of work have been suporting the development of more recent hacker typologies. Moeckel's (2019) classification is a clear example, in which he establishes the following types of hackers: (1) *toolkit users*; (2) *system challengers*; (3) *supporters*; (4) *insiders*; (5) *ideologists*; (6) *officials*; (7) *professionals I* (groups and gangs); (8) *professionals II* (small groups and individuals).

Although the categorization of hackers succeeds in clarifying and deconstructing the actions of these individuals, it is important to reinforce that human beings are complex and not one-dimensional. Consequently, they can belong to more than one typology, driven by diverse intentions (Moeckel, 2019; Rogers, 2010).

5. MOTIVATIONS

Several investigations have been conducted on the topic of motivations or intentions, complementing the previously mentioned studies. In addition to classifying the hacker's motivations, this body of research allows to understand what leads individuals to initiate and maintaining the hacking practice. The studies produced in this area have been diverse, adopting both quantitative (*e.g.*, Madarie, 2017; Rogers, 2006) and qualitative (*e.g.*, Taylor, 1999; Xu et al., 2013) approaches.

In a groundbreaking study, Madarie (2017) aimed to quantify the motivations of hackers by analyzing the relationships between the frequency of various hacking behaviors and the motivations for committing them. A survey was administered to a sample of 127 male hackers and potential hackers, and the results revealed that 51% claimed to be motivated primarily by enjoyment, a result that is in line with the HackerOne (2020) report, which shows a prevalence of 49%. Madarie (2017) also found that sensation-seeking (51%) was a relevant motivation. This motivation has also been mentioned by several authors (*e.g.*, Rogers, 2006; Gaia et al., 2021), and Taylor (1999) calls it 'feeling of power', related to the sensation obtained, having one of his interviewees mentioned that with the practice of hacking *"you got a thrill out of knowing how much power you had"* (Taylor, 1999, p. 58). Profit is another motivation identified in the literature. Regarding its importance, it is observed a wide variation between studies. For instance, from 18% (Madarie, 2017) to 53% (HackerOne, 2020). Some research also indicates that 'being challenged' is a prominent motivation for hackers, being prevalent in 68% of the HackerOne (2020) sample and in 30% of the Bachmann (2010) sample. HackerOne (2020) report next lists the 'learn new techniques' motivation, with a prevalence of 51%, an intention also advanced by Turgeman-Goldschmidt (2005). Rogers (2006) adds ego, a motivation also supported by Turgeman-Goldschmidt (2005), which refers to 'feeling smarter than others'.

HackerOne (2020), further enumerates 'advancing one's career' (44%), 'protecting and defending' (29%), 'doing good in the world' (27%), and 'helping others' (25%) as relevant motivations. Taylor (1999) also points out feelings of addiction, political acts (corroborated by authors such as Seebruck, 2015), recognition by peers, annoyance with the education system, and curiosity. Concerning the latter, the author states it is present in the 'hacker mentality' and *"seen as a positive attribute that drives forward technological development"* (Taylor, 1999, p. 53).

Additional motivations that develop in a dynamic process were identified by Xu and colleagues (2013). Drawing on six case-studies of young Chinese hackers, the researchers sought to understand the trajectories of hackers and how they evolve. The findings revealed that the intentions that lead to the practice of hacking tend to be of an innocent nature, presenting as examples the ones already mentioned by Taylor (1999). Moreover, the results showed that the technological talent that these youngsters had, combined with other factors (such as opportunity, deficiencies in system security, association with other hackers), will lead to a progression of behaviors over time. That is, the initially innocent motivations end up undergoing a subsequent change, leading to the practice of behaviors with the purpose of exploitation. The authors illustrate this progression through a scheme that portrays an initial affection for computers, which leads to curious exploitation which, in turn, eventually in illicit excursion and, finally, criminal exploitation. This escalation, which takes place over time, also leads to a progressive potential harm to society. Thus, when studying motivations, it is important to keep in mind that they may not be permanent (Xu et al., 2013).

6. HACKER'S FIGURE

Since its advent, the term hacker(s) has undergone mutations in its identity as a result of the historical and technological changes experienced in society (Furnell, 2001). In the 60's of the 20th century, its connotation was associated with a positive and uplifting representation – someone with technological and creative skills that provided solutions to computational problems (Levy, 1984, 2001; Yar, 2006). This view is described by Levy (1984) as the first generation of hackers, becoming known as the pioneers of programming techniques and computer mastery. Alongside, the discourse of these hackers included liberal ideas, as seen by certain words which used to describe their actions, namely: free speech; the individual; freedom; privacy; meritocracy (Coleman & Golub, 2008).

Due to the computational evolution, a second generation emerged, bringing the desire for total immersion in technological knowledge, especially in hardware and software operations. The goal of these hackers was to gather computer knowledge and return it to large companies, spreading tools to help cybersecurity strategies (Taylor, 1999). Later on, with the improvement of graphical functionalities of the devices, a third generation appeared, known as programmers. These dedicated themselves exclusively to computer games and its architecture, becoming vanguardists in the area (Levy, 1984).

However, a fourth generation of hackers arose, revolutionizing the meaning of the hacker(s) concept. With this generation, the hacker(s) become linked to a negative view – that of cybercriminal (Levy, 1984). This is the current dominant image, whereby the hacker is seen as someone who illegally accesses someone else's computer (Taylor, 1999; Holt, 2020). This image is illustrated by Richet (2013), mentioning that the media uses the term to refer to *"an intruder breaking into computer systems to steal or destroy data"* (p. 54).

While the contribution of the generational distinction is noteworthy, the analysis of these individuals should not be reduced to this kind of actions. The hacker behavior is based on several goals, justifications, and intentions that exist simultaneously (Moeckel, 2019; Rogers, 2010). Thus, it should be noted, as previously mentioned, that not all hacking behaviors should be viewed as criminal. In other words, not all individuals who engage in these acts have malicious intentions (Rogers et al., 2006). In that sense, according to Richet (2013), for greater conceptual clarity it would be crucial to apply the concept 'hacker(s)' in its original meaning and the concept 'cracker(s)' to refer to individuals who use their skills to create and use malware, as well as to infiltrate security systems illegally with the intent to cause damage to them. Moore (2015) also highlights this issue, distinguishing the cracker as the individual who *"violates software copyright protections and gains inappropriate access to password-protected files and services"* (p. 19).

That said, a more comprehensive and appropriate conceptualization would be that presented by Fox and Holt (2021), who describe hackers as individuals who have a deep interest in technology, using their knowledge to access computer systems, either with or without the permission of the system owner. Other authors also adopt this position, stating that it is inappropriate to represent hackers according to a dichotomy of benign or malignant individuals (Coleman & Golub, 2008). The term encompasses different groups, intentions, and purposes. Thus, these individuals should not be reduced to *"visionaries or sinister devils"* (Bossler & Burruss, 2011, p. 65).

6.1 Sociodemographic Profile

In order to deepen the understanding of the individual who practices hacking behaviors, empirical research has been exploring the hacker's profile, although always compromised and hampered by the anonymity associated with these individuals and low participation in studies (Marcum et al., 2014; Taylor, 1999). Nevertheless, the scientific literature has pointed out some characteristics that are frequently associated with these individuals, determining a common profile.

Regarding gender, a greater tendency for males to be involved in hacking behaviors is observed (Holt et al., 2020). For instance, Fox and Holt (2021) conducted an international quantitative study, relying on data from 66,820 youngsters from the ISRD-2[2], and found that of the 5081 individuals considered hackers, 75% (n = 3780) were boys. This finding is consistent with the results obtained in several other studies and sources (*e.g.,* Bachmann, 2008; HackerOne, 2020, 2021; Holt et al., 2010; Marcum et al., 2014; Nodeland & Morris, 2020; Skinner & Fream, 1997; Steinmetz, 2016; Taylor, 1999). Authors such as Hutchings and Chua (2016), Steinmetz (2016) and Taylor (1999) propose that a possible justification for this result is the socialization of the male gender towards technology and its devices since early adolescence.

As for age it is found that hackers tend to be more heterogeneous and dispersed. Studies revealed hacking practice from both young individuals, in their pre-teens, and older individuals, in their 60's (Schell & Holt, 2010; Steinmetz, 2016). For example, the study of Payne and colleagues (2018) showed that the average age was 36 years for male hackers and 52 years for female hackers. However, most studies found that the average age tends to be between 20 and 30 years old (Bachmann, 2010; Fox & Holt, 2021; HackerOne, 2020, 2021; Steinmetz, 2016). Despite this, it should be noted that the average ages obtained in the studies varies depending on the type of sample that is being used, since research around hacking has concentrated on: a) young people in high school; b) university students; c) employed individuals.

Regarding socioeconomic status, this is a sociodemographic characteristic that has not received much attention in empirical research on cybercrime compared to traditional crimes (Park et al., 2019). With regard to hacking, studies on socioeconomic status are limited, which may be due to the difficulty in operationalizing and measuring this variable (Holt et al., 2020). However, the qualitative research of Steinmetz (2016) stands out in this scope. The researcher analyzed the perceived social class of hackers, finding that most individuals positioned themselves in the middle class and some even in a higher class. According to the author, in general, people tend to position themselves in such classes, meaning that this proves to be a non-exclusive finding, and there may be hacker in other classes. The study by Holt and researchers (2020), in turn, measured socioeconomic status through the ownership of a vehicle by the participant's families. Through this indicator, it was concluded that young people from families with a higher status were more likely to report hacking behavior. Based on this, the authors suggested that those subjects inserted in higher social classes and economic statuses have greater and privileged access to technologies, increasing opportunities to perform cybercriminal behaviors, such as hacking (Holt et al., 2020; Steinmetz, 2016).

Concerning racial-ethnic characteristics, studies have presented disparate results. Several empirical studies show that individuals with involvement in hacking behaviors are generally Caucasian (Bachmann, 2008; Nodeland & Morris, 2020; Steinmetz, 2016) However, other investigations found divergent results. Marcum and colleagues (2014), in their study with a sample of 1617 youths, found that Caucasian subjects were less prone to hacking compared to non-Caucasian subjects. Another study that obtained divergent findings was that of Woo (2003) with a sample of 729 self-reported hackers, in which was observed that 60.4% of the individuals were Asian, and only 18.8% were Caucasian. The aforementioned results demonstrate that, unlike gender, there is no generalized data regarding the relationship between hacking behaviors and different ethnicities (Edwards et al., 2022).

Other aspects that have been analyzed in scientific research are the education and employment status of individuals. With respect to the educational qualifications, most hackers have completed their studies, especially higher-level degrees (*e.g.,* bachelor's, master's, and doctorate degrees) (Bachmann, 2010; HackerOne, 2020, 2021; Steinmetz, 2016). Steinmetz's (2016) study illustrates this, in which was found that all 14 respondents had at least a higher education degree. Woo (2003), in turn, observed that 26.6% of his study sample held a college degree. In general, studies have revealed that individuals tend to position hacking as a part-time or a hobby, with few individuals being fully employed in this way (Bachmann, 2008; Taylor, 1999). However, a large portion of the participants in hacking conferences tend to perform these behaviors professionally within technology jobs (Steinmetz, 2016), inherent to financial services and computer software organizations, educational institutions, and health and medical technology services (HackerOne, 2021).

6.2 Contextual Aspects

After the analysis of the individual's personal and intrinsic sphere, a more comprehensive domain follows – the context surrounding hackers. The results obtained in various studies allow to break with the idea of introversion and isolation originally associated with hacking (Holt et al., 2020; Steinmetz, 2016), since it is showed that these individuals build diverse peer networks, whether online (*e.g.,* internet forums and groups) and/or offline (*e.g.,* school context and international hacking conferences[3]) friendships (Fitch, 2004; Leukfeldt et al., 2017; Skinner & Fream, 1997).

The social facet of hackers has also been evidenced in the *"presence of marital and familial ties"* (Steinmetz, 2016, p. 45). These individuals commonly engage in long-term loving relationships (*e.g.,* dating, marriage, divorce), with multiple individuals constituting families and assuming parental responsibilities (Steinmetz, 2016; Taylor, 1999). Furthermore, these individuals exhibit a close relationship with their parents, having a positive and intimate perception of it (Steinmetz, 2016). This relational and contextual information substantiates the evidence that *"hackers have a number of social relationships that influence their willingness to engage in different forms of behavior over time"* (Holt et al., 2017, p. 91). In the last two decades, the scientific community found the influence that the peer network and family members hold on the practice of hacking, allowing the recovery of Aker's Social Learning Theory's (1998)[4] ideas.

Similar to what happens with traditional crime, the practice of these acts is driven by the presence and influence of deviant peers, considering that several studies conclude that having a network of friends involved in these behaviors, or other cyberdeviant acts, increases the likelihood of hacking (*e.g.,* Holt et al., 2010; Kim et al., 2022; Morris & Blackburn, 2009; Rogers, 2001; Young & Zhang, 2005). Skinner and Fream's (1997) study drove these findings, serving as the basis for the empirical development of this relationship. The authors collected data from 581 college students in order to examine the predictive role of the components of Aker's (1998) Social Learning Theory in explaining hacking behaviors. The main finding was the moderate support they hold, with special emphasis on differential association. This translates to hackers, versus non-hackers, as having proximal and intimate relationships with individuals associated with hacking and other cyberdeviant acts.

Additionally, empirical studies found that these associations create the possibility for the transmission of a set of definitions and justifications favorable to crime, creating a fertile ground for the imitation of these behaviors (Holt et al., 2010; Leukfeldt et al., 2017; Morris & Blackburn, 2009; Rogers, 2001; Skinner & Fream, 1997). In that sense, Bossler and Burruss (2011) explain that to commit these behaviors *"most individuals needed to associate with computer hackers, learn hacker values, and be socially reinforced in this domain"* (p.57).

One of the aspects that enhances this interest and involvement in hacking is the profession of the mother and/or father figure. Based on the conduction of interviews, Steinmetz (2016) found that 12 of the 14 participants had at least one of these parental figures employed in the technology sector. Several individuals reported that their parents encouraged them to certain behaviors by applying positive reinforcement when using a computer or the internet. Their narratives also suggested that they were exposed to technology at an early age, and this is consistent with other studies (e.g., Holt et al., 2020; Taylor, 1999). Holt (2007), through qualitative data from 13 interviews, found that all hackers reported having developed an early interest in technology and computers during adolescence, or even earlier. Several interviewees mentioned that the existence of this curiosity early in their lives allowed them to engage in multiple online behaviors, such as hacking.

Considering these empirical results, it can be deduced that *"just like most other groups"* hackers are *"social creatures who may seek affection, intimacy, camaraderie, and even familial bonding"* (Steinmetz, 2016, p.45).

6.3 Personality Traits

While rapid advances in cybercrime research are evident, there are still particular aspects that need further analysis, namely cyberdependent crimes and the explanatory role of psychological factors in them. From an applied perspective, such research would allow for more informed cyberdefense practices (Jones et al., 2021). According to Loch and Conger (1996), *"individual characteristics all appear to be important in determining ethical computing decisions"* (p. 82). Despite the growth of the hacking phenomenon and the association of personality theories with crime, little empirical research has been conducted to investigate the psychological composition of cybercriminals and cyberdeviant individuals (Rogers, 1999) and as such, the literature on their personality characteristics, particularly as it relates to hacking, is still scarce.

6.3.1 Five-Factor Model of Personality

Regarding the Five Factor Model, also known as the Big Five, it was originated from Costa and McCrae's work (1992), and postulates that personality is segmented into five traits: neuroticism; extroversion; openness to experience; agreeableness; and conscientiousness. Briefly: (1) *neuroticism* reflects individual differences in negative emotion, including vulnerability to stress, anxiety, depression, and other adverse feelings (Costa & McCrae, 1992); (2) *extroversion* is associated with positive emotionality and an energetic approach to the social world, including traits such as activity, sociability, and assertiveness (Clark & Watson, 1999); (3) *openness to experience* manifests itself in *"the breadth, depth, and permeability of consciousness, and in the recurrent need to enlarge and examine experience"* (McCrae & Costa, 1991, p. 826) and is observed in traits such as artistic sensitivity, intellectual curiosity, and unconventional attitudes, among others (McCrae, 1996); (4) *agreeableness* is defined by traits such as altruism, trust, conformity, and concern for others (Costa & McCrae, 1992); finally, (5) *conscientiousness* is materialized in the ability to concentrate, to stay focused on tasks, and to be goal oriented (Costa & McCrae, 1992).

The literature has been trying to establish which traits are most associated with delinquent and criminal behavior. Regarding hacking, some authors have tried to identify which traits are present in hackers that distinguish them from individuals who do not engage in this type of conducts (*e.g.,* Jabłońska & Zajdel, 2020; Rogers et al., 2006, 2006a; Seigfried-Spellar & Treadway, 2014; Whiters, 2019). Although existent, empirical research is still scarce and some inconsistencies are found, which will be presented next.

The media has described hackers and cyber deviant individuals as introverts, who derived from their antisocial natures tend to spend more time on the internet and engage in unethical internet use (Karim et al., 2009). Rogers and colleagues (2006) conduct an exploratory study by administering a pen-and-paper self-report survey to a sample of 381 undergraduate students in the liberal arts department at a university in Canada. The authors' main purpose was to examine whether cyber deviant individuals differ from non-cyber deviant individuals in terms of the traits of openness to experience, extroversion, and neuroticism. Although they do not specifically analyze hackers, but rather individuals in the broader term, "cyber deviant", many behaviors they analyzed correspond to the behaviors that Yar (2006) points out as typical of hackers. Thus, they question participants about: (a) guessing passwords; (b) using someone else's password without authorization; (c) accessing someone else's files without authorization; (d) changing someone else's files without authorization; (e) using or writing viruses; (f) getting someone else's credit information without authorization; and (g) using a device to get free calls. The results did not prove insightful, as they revealed no significant relationship between the practices of these behaviors and any of the mentioned traits.

Rogers and colleagues (2006a) carried out a study with 77 college students from the Information Technology department of a Western American university in which they replicated Rogers et al. (2006) investigation, described above. This research led to different conclusions, especially regarding the extroversion trait that showed a negative relationship with the analyzed behaviors, allowing the authors to conclude that individuals who practice those behaviors tend to be more introverted, compared to those who do not. This result is in line with the ideas that were once held about the hacker, since *"hackers have often been perceived to be introverted, friendless individuals (...) who have sought solace in the company of machines, or who cannot socially interact without the anonymity offered by cyberspace"* (Peacock, 2013, p. 35).

Additionally, hackers have also been found to possess a greater hostility and propensity to exhibit selfish qualities (Schell & Holt, 2010), reflecting lower levels of agreeableness. Seigfried-Spellar and Treadway (2014) conducted a quantitative study using self-report online surveys administered to a convenience sample of 398 college students in the southern United States of America who were at least 19 years old. The purpose of the study was to determine whether there are individual differences between subjects who commit different forms of cyber deviancy, namely hacking, virus writing, cyberbullying, and identity theft. They also analyzed the existence of personality differences between cyberdeviant and non-cyberdeviant individuals, namely between hackers (n = 170) and non-hackers. Only the agreeableness trait was found to be (negatively) related to the commission of hacking, suggesting that hackers are more antagonistic compared to non-hackers. Despite being a separately measured behavior, virus writing is something that some authors place on the hacking spectrum, and this study also revealed it was significantly related to agreeableness and conscientiousness. This result elucidates that those individuals who write viruses have lower levels of agreeableness, meaning that they are more antagonistic, but revealed higher levels of conscientiousness, *i.e.,* are able to exhibit greater discipline, compared to individuals who do not commit this cyber-deviant act.

Seigfried-Spellar et al. (2017) conducted a quantitative study with a sample of 235 individuals with the main purpose of exploring the relationships between cybercriminal behavior and psychopathy, the five-factor model of personality, and other types of antisocial behavior. To do this, the authors tested the correlations between the Big Five traits and several behaviors that fall on the hacking spectrum, namely: (a) unauthorized access; (b) writing viruses; (c) monitoring network traffic; and (d) defacing websites. The study revealed several relationships between behaviors falling within the hacking domain and some personality traits, namely: unauthorized access was shown to be related to lower levels of agreeableness; writing viruses was associated with higher levels of neuroticism; monitoring network traffic was associated with lower agreeableness; and finally, defacing websites was shown to be associated with higher levels of neuroticism and lower levels of openness to experience and agreeableness.

6.3.2 Dark Triad

Another of the most widespread personality models in scientific research, whose application to hacking is still in its early days, is the Dark Triad proposed by Paulhus and Williams (2002). The Dark Triad consists of personality traits that are intercorrelated and are described predominantly, as the name implies, as negative traits. These traits are associated with a tendency to engage in unethical and criminal behavior (Jones & Paulhus, 2014; Paulhus & Williams, 2002). While these traits are often being studied with reference to interpersonal harm, they have not been extensively studied in the cybersecurity context (Jones et al., 2021). The Dark Triad is a set of personality traits - machiavellianism, narcissism, and psychopathy – that fall within the negative spectrum of personality disorders (Paulhus & Williams, 2002).

As for *machiavellianism*, individuals with high levels of this trait see other people, more or less, as objects to be manipulated to achieve their goals. Machiavellians are therefore cold, manipulative, and rational individuals in their behavior. They are goal-oriented, characterized by being strategic and manipulative to a certain extent, which allows them to achieve their goals (Jones & Paulhus, 2014), having been described as possessing *"moral flexibility"* (Jonason et al., 2015, p. 103). *Narcissism*, on the other hand, describes someone who needs admiration and lacks empathy for others. Additional attributes are a sense of grandeur and self-centeredness (American Psychiatric Association, 2013), possessing an inflated belief in their own competence and ability (Jones & Paulhus, 2014; Paulhus & Williams, 2002) and a sense of entitlement, through which they take advantage of others (American Psychiatric Association, 2013). Finally, there is *psychopathy*. Psychopathic tendencies lead to disregard for long-term consequences. Individuals with high levels of psychopathy also show high levels of impulsivity and sensation seeking that are associated with criminal attitudes. Furthermore, they manifest low ability to show empathy, remorse, and anxiety (Paulhus & Williams, 2002).

This theory has just recently been applied to cybercrime and it was observed, for example, that a psychopathic tendency predicts behaviors such as cyber aggression and trolling (Lopes & Yu, 2017;

Pabian et al., 2015). Also, some studies have applied this model to behaviors that fall under hacking, such as phishing (*e.g.,* Curtis et al., 2018; Jones et al., 2021), being found that those traits can act as facilitators of strategies often employed by hackers, such as social engineering. Thus, the Dark Triad model, albeit sparsely, has been tested to explain hacking and evidence has been found regarding its relevance (Gaia et al., 2021).

Whiters (2019) conducted a quantitative investigation, aiming, on the one hand, to explore the existence of significant relationships between Dark Triad personality traits and specific cybercriminal behaviors on social media (namely, unethical hacking, conceptualized in the study as 'accessing a computer system or network without authorization'), and, on the other hand, to understand which traits are related to each type of defined behavior. The study sampled offensive and cyber-deviant security engineers from hacker conferences (Black Hat, DefCon, and BSides, conferences in Las Vegas) and from websites that discuss and/or promote cyber-deviant behavior (*e.g.,* hacking). An additional sample was collected from the general population of social media users. In total, 235 individuals completed an online self-report survey that included items related to cyberdeviance, personality traits, and demographic characteristics. As for the results, only one Dark Triad personality trait – machiavellianism – proved to be negatively related to unethical hacking, meaning that individuals who engage in unethical hacking behaviors present themselves as less strategic and manipulative.

This link between machiavellianism and hacking was also verified in the findings of the study by Jabłońska and Zajdel (2020), but in the opposite direction. The authors administered an online survey to 384 individuals from Poland and the goal was to examine the relationship between each Dark Triad trait and online behavior, among them 'wanting to hack a website'. The study found that all the Dark Triad traits were related to this behavior, most notably machiavellianism and psychopathy. Thus, this study suggested that the behavior of 'wanting to hack a website' tends to be associated with individuals who are colder, manipulative, and strategic, which contradicts the results found previously by Whiters (2019), as well as with individuals who are impulsive and less empathetic.

7. CONCLUSION

Hacking and its behaviors have changed dramatically in the last few decades and are constantly evolving from the moment they first appeared. The information presented in this chapter shows that the scientific community and other entities have made a remarkable effort to learn about hacking and produce scientific knowledge on the subject. However, this knowledge is still at an early stage and further research is needed to better understand what aspects characterize hacking and the predictors that can explain its commission. As previously discussed, the difficulty in conceptualizing and describing the phenomenon remains, since the way hacking is viewed may involve an ethical and beneficial personification or a malicious and criminal one. Although in recent years there has been an increase in the complexity and diversification of behaviors, at the same time there has been an extension of these acts to individuals with low levels of computer knowledge (*e.g.,* script kiddies), in contrast to the highly skilled performers associated with the emergence of hacking (*e.g.,* old guard).

Based on existing empirical studies, it is possible to trace a hacker's sociodemographic profile, being mostly young males with high academic qualifications (*e.g.,* master's degree). When it comes to personality traits, the results obtained have not been conclusive. However, the Big Five Model of Costa and McCrae (1992) highlights the relationship between low levels of extroversion and agreeableness and hacking (*e.g.,* Rogers et al., 2006a; Seigfried-Spellar et al., 2017). Concerning Paulhus and William's (2002) Dark Triad, the machiavellianism trait is emphasized, which although research does not yield similar results (*e.g.,* Jabłońska & Zajdel, 2020; Whiters, 2019), is understood to hold an influence on the performance of hacking behaviors. Moreover, if on the one side, some studies have associated hacking with introverted and solitary individuals, on the other side, studies that analyze the relational and contextual aspect have obtained divergent results, in that hackers constitute family, have a vast network of friendships (offline and online) and learn from other hackers the definitions and techniques inherent to the commission of the behaviors (*e.g.,* Leukfeldt et al., 2017; Skinner & Fream, 1997; Steinmetz, 2016).

Regarding typologies, various classifications of hackers have been proposed over the years, having support in criteria such as: (a) illegality and ethics in behaviors (e.g., Moore, 2015); (b) level of computer expertise (e.g., Landreth & Reingold, 1985); and (c) motivations (*e.g.,* Seebruck, 2015). Concerning the last criteria, intentions have been the subject of in-depth analysis, since it is information that allows for an understanding of why hackers engage in these acts and their durability in the lives of these individuals. Specifically, research has identified fun, challenge, and learning as the main reasons for hackers to engage in those behaviors (e.g., Bachmann, 2010; HackerOne, 2021; Madarie, 2017; Turgeman-Goldschmidt, 2005).

REFERENCES

Abeoussi, J. M. D. (2019). *Black Hat and White Hat Hacking - The thin line of ethics*. EC-Council University.

American Psychiatric Association. (2013). *Diagnostic and statistical manual of mental disorders* (5th ed.).

Bachmann, M. (2008). *What makes them Click? Applying the Rational Choice Perspective to the Hacking Underground*. University of Central Florida.

Bachmann, M. (2010). The risk propensity and rationality of computer hackers. *International Journal of Cyber Criminology*, *4*(1), 643–656.

Baitha, A. K., & Vinod, S. (2018). Session hijacking and prevention technique. *Int. J. Eng. Technol*, *7*(2.6), 193-198.

Bossler, A. M., & Burruss, G. W. (2011). The general theory of crime and computer hacking: low self-control hackers. In T. J. Holt & B. H. Schell (Eds.), *Corporate Hacking and Technology-Driven Crime: Social Dynamics and Implications* (pp. 38–67). IGI Glob. doi:10.4018/978-1-61692-805-6.ch003

Britz, M. T. (2013). Introduction and overview of computer forensics and cybercrime. In Computer Forensics and Cyber Crime: An Introduction (pp. 1 -20), South Carolina, Pearson (3).

Clark, L. A., & Watson, D. (1999). Temperament: A new paradigm for trait psychology. In L. A. Pervin & O. P. John (Eds.), *Handbook of personality: Theory and research* (pp. 399–423). Guilford Press.

Coleman, E. G., & Golub, A. (2008). Hacker practice: Moral genres and the cultural articulation of liberalism. *Anthropological Theory*, *8*(3), 255–277. doi:10.1177/1463499608093814

Costa, P. T. Jr, & McCrae, R. R. (1992). The five-factor model of personality and its relevance to personality disorders. *Journal of Personality Disorders*, 6(4), 343–359. doi:10.1521/pedi.1992.6.4.343

Curtis, S. R., Rajivan, P., Jones, D. N., & Gonzalez, C. (2018). Phishing attempts among the dark triad: Patterns of attack and vulnerability. *Computers in Human Behavior*, 87, 174–182. doi:10.1016/j.chb.2018.05.037

Fitch, C. (2004). *Crime and Punishment: The Psychology of Hacking in the New Millennium*. SANS Institute.

Fox, B., & Holt, T. J. (2021). Use of a Multitheoretic Model to Understand and Classify Juvenile Computer *Hacking* Behavior. *Criminal Justice and Behavior*, 48(7), 943–963. doi:10.1177/0093854820969754

Furnell, S., Emm, D., & Papadaki, M. (2015). The challenge of measuring cyber- dependent crimes. *Computer Fraud & Security*, 2015(10), 5–12. doi:10.1016/S1361-3723(15)30093-2

Furnell, S. M. (2001). Categorising cybercrime and cybercriminals: The problem and potential approaches. *Journal of Information Warfare*, 1(2), 35–44.

Furnell, S. M., Dowland, P. S., & Sanders, P. W. (1999). Dissecting the "Hacker Manifesto". *Information Management & Computer Security*, 7(2), 69–75. doi:10.1108/09685229910265493

Gaia, J., Sanders, G. L., Sanders, S. P., Upadhyaya, S., Wang, X., & Yoo, C. W. (2021). Dark Traits and Hacking Potential. *Journal of Organizational Psychology*, 21(3), 23–46.

HackerOne. (2020). *The 2020 Hacker Report*. Available at: https://www.hackerone.com/resources/reporting/the-2020-hacker-report

HackerOne. (2021). *The 2021 Hacker Report*. Available at: https://www.hackerone.com/resources/reporting/the-2021-hacker-report

HackerOne. (2022). *The 2022 Hacker Report*. Available at: https://www.hackerone.com/resources/reporting/the-2022-hacker-report

Hardaker, C. (2013). "Uh....not to be nitpicky,but…the past tense of drag is dragged, not drug.": An overview of trolling strategies. *Journal of Language Aggression and Conflict*, 1(1), 58–86. doi:10.1075/jlac.1.1.04har

Hiscox. (2022). *Cyber Readiness Report 2022*. Hiscox. https://www.hiscoxgroup.com/sites/group/files/documents/2022-05/22054%20-%20Hiscox%20Cyber%20Readiness%20Report%202022-EN_0.pdf

Hollinger, R. (1988). Computer hackers follow a Guttman-Like Progression. *Phrack Inc.*, 2(22).

Hollinger, R. C. (1991). Hackers: Computer Heroes or Electronic Highwaymen? *Computers & Society*, 21(1), 6–17. doi:10.1145/122246.122248

Hollinger, R. C. (1992). Crime by Computer: Correlates of Software Piracy and Unauthorized Account Access. *Security Journal*, 4(1), 2–12.

Hollinger, R. C., & Lanza-Kaduce, L. O. N. N. (1988). The process of criminalization: The case of computer crime laws. *Criminology*, 26(1), 101–126. doi:10.1111/j.1745-9125.1988.tb00834.x

Holt, T. J. (2007). Subcultural Evolution? Examining the Influence of On and Offline Experiences on Deviant Subcultures. *Deviant Behavior, 28*(2), 171–198. doi:10.1080/01639620601131065

Holt, T. J. (2020). Computer Hacking and the Hacker Subculture. In T. J. Holt & A. M. Bossler (Eds.), *The Palgrave Handbook of International Cybercrime and Cyberdeviance* (pp. 725–742). Palgrave Macmillan. doi:10.1007/978-3-319-78440-3_31

Holt, T. J., Bossler, A. M., & Seigfried-Spellar, K. C. (2017). *Cybercrime and digital forensics: An introduction*. Routledge. doi:10.4324/9781315296975

Holt, T. J., Burruss, G. W., & Bossler, A. M. (2010). Social learning and cyber- deviance: Examining the importance of a full social learning model in the virtual world. *Journal of Crime and Justice, 33*(2), 31–61. doi:10.1080/0735648X.2010.9721287

Holt, T. J., Navarro, J. N., & Clevenger, S. (2020). Exploring the moderating role of gender in juvenile hacking behaviors. *Crime and Delinquency, 66*(11), 1533–1555. doi:10.1177/0011128719875697

IBM Security and Ponemon *Institute* (2022). *Cost of a Data Breach Report 2022*. IBM. https://www.ibm.com/downloads/cas/3R8N1DZJ

Jabłońska, M. R., & Zajdel, R. (2020). The Dark triad Traits and Problematic Internet Use: Their Structure and Relations. *Polish Sociological Review, 4*, 477–496.

Jaquet-Chiffelle, D. O., & Loi, M. (2020). Ethical and unethical hacking. In M. Christen, B. Gordjin, & M. Loi (Eds.), *The Ethics of Cybersecurity* (pp. 179–204). Springer Nature. doi:10.1007/978-3-030-29053-5_9

Jonason, P. K., Strosser, G. L., Kroll, C. H., Duineveld, J. J., & Baruffi, S. A. (2015). Valuing myself over others: The *Dark triad* traits and moral and social values. *Personality and Individual Differences, 81*, 102–106. doi:10.1016/j.paid.2014.10.045

Jones, D. N., Padilla, E., Curtis, S. R., & Kiekintveld, C. (2021). Network discovery and scanning strategies and the Dark Triad. *Computers in Human Behavior, 122*, 1–10. doi:10.1016/j.chb.2021.106799

Jones, D. N., & Paulhus, D. L. (2014). Introducing the Short Dark triad (SD3): A brief measure of dark personality traits. *Assessment, 21*(1), 28–41. doi:10.1177/1073191113514105 PMID:24322012

Jordan, T. (2017). A genealogy of hacking. *Convergence (London), 23*(5), 528–544. doi:10.1177/1354856516640710

Jordan, T., & Taylor, P. (1998). A sociology of hackers. *The Sociological Review, 46*(4), 757–780. doi:10.1111/1467-954X.00139

Karim, N. S. A., Zamzuri, N. H. A., & Nor, Y. M. (2009). Exploring the relationship between Internet ethics in university students and the big five model of personality. *Computers & Education, 53*(1), 86–93. doi:10.1016/j.compedu.2009.01.001

Kinkade, P. T., Bachmann, M., & Bachmann, B. S. (2013). Hacker Woodstock: Observations on an off-line Cyber Culture at the Chaos Communication Camp 2011. In T. J. Holt (Ed.), *Crime On-line: Correlates, Causes, and Context* (2nd ed., pp. 19–60). Carolina Academic Press.

Kirsch, C. (2014). The Grey Hat Hacker: Reconciling cyberspace reality and the law. *Northern Kentucky Law Review, 41*(3), 383–403.

Landreth, B., & Rheingold, H. (1985). *Out of the inner circle: a hacker's guide to computer security.* Microsoft Press.

Leukfeldt, R., Kleemans, E. R., & Stol, W. (2017). Origin, growth, and criminal capabilities of cyber-criminal networks. An international empirical analysis. *Crime, Law, and Social Change, 67*(1), 39–53. doi:10.100710611-016-9663-1

Levy, S. (1984). *Hackers: Heroes of the computer revolution* (Vol. 14). Anchor Press/Doubleday.

Levy, S. (2001). *Hackers: Heroes of the computer revolution.* Penguin.

Levy, S. (2010). *Hackers: Heroes of the computer revolution.* O'Reilly.

Loch, K. D., & Conger, S. (1996). Evaluating Ethical Decision Making and Computer Use. *Communications of the ACM, 39*(7), 74–83. doi:10.1145/233977.233999

Lopes, B., & Yu, H. (2017). Who do you troll and Why: An investigation into the relationship between the *Dark triad* Personalities and online trolling behaviours towards popular and less popular Facebook profiles. *Computers in Human Behavior, 77*, 69–76. doi:10.1016/j.chb.2017.08.036

Madarie, R. (2017). Hackers' Motivations: Testing Schwartz'S Theory Of Motivational Types Of Values In A Sample Of Hackers. *International Journal of Cyber Criminology, 11*(1), 78–97.

Marcum, C. D., Higgins, G. E., Ricketts, M. L., & Wolfe, S. E. (2014). Hacking in high school: Cyber-crime perpetration by juveniles. *Deviant Behavior, 35*(7), 581–591. doi:10.1080/01639625.2013.867721

McCrae, R. R. (1996). Social consequences of experiential openness. *Psychological Bulletin, 120*(3), 323–337. doi:10.1037/0033-2909.120.3.323 PMID:8900080

McCrae, R. R., & Costa, P. X. Jr. (1991). Conceptions and correlates of Openness to Experience. In R. Hogan, J. A. Johnson, & S. R. Briggs (Eds.), *Handbook of personality psychology.* Academic Press.

Moeckel, C. (2019). Examining and constructing attacker categorisations: an experimental typology for digital banking. In *Proceedings of the 14th International Conference on Availability, Reliability and Security* (pp. 1-6). 10.1145/3339252.3340341

Moore, R. (2015). *Cybercrime: Investigating High-Technology Computer Crime.* Routledge.

Morris, R. G., & Blackburn, A. G. (2009). Cracking the code: An empirical exploration of social learning theory and computer crime. *Journal of Crime and Justice, 32*(1), 1–34. doi:10.1080/073564 8X.2009.9721260

Nissenbaum, H. (2004). Hackers and the contested ontology of cyberspace. *New Media & Society, 6*(2), 195–217. doi:10.1177/1461444804041445

Nodeland, B., & Morris, R. (2020). A test of social learning theory and self-control on cyber offending. *Deviant Behavior, 41*(1), 41–56. doi:10.1080/01639625.2018.1519135

Pabian, S., De Backer, C. J. S., & Vandebosch, H. (2015). *Dark triad* personality traits and adolescent cyber-aggression. *Personality and Individual Differences, 75*, 41–46. doi:10.1016/j.paid.2014.11.015

Paulhus, D. L., & Williams, K. M. (2002). The *Dark triad* of personality: Narcissism, Machiavellianism, and psychopathy. *Journal of Research in Personality, 36*(6), 556–563. doi:10.1016/S0092-6566(02)00505-6

Payne, B. K. (2020). Defining Cybercrime. In T. J. Holt & A. M. Bossler (Eds.), *The Palgrave Handbook of International Cybercrime and Cyberdeviance* (pp. 1–25). Palgrave Macmillan. doi:10.1007/978-3-319-78440-3_1

Payne, B. K., Hawkins, B., & Xin, C. (2019). Using labeling theory as a guide to examine the patterns, characteristics, and sanctions given to cybercrimes. *American Journal of Criminal Justice, 44*(2), 230–247. doi:10.100712103-018-9457-3

Peacock, D. (2013). *From underground hacking to ethical hacking*. University of Northumbria at Newcastle.

Richet, J. L. (2013). From Young *Hacker*s to Crackers. *International Journal of Technology and Human Interaction, 9*(3), 53–62. doi:10.4018/jthi.2013070104

Rogers, M. (1999). *Psychology of hackers: Steps toward a new taxonomy*. InfoWar. http://www.infowar.com

Rogers, M., Smoak, N. D., & Liu, J. (2006). Self-reported deviant computer behavior: A big-5, moral choice, and manipulative exploitive behavior analysis. *Deviant Behavior, 27*(3), 245–268. doi:10.1080/01639620600605333

Rogers, M. K. (2001). *A social learning theory and moral disengagement analysis of criminal computer behavior: An exploratory study* [Doctoral dissertation].

Rogers, M. K. (2006). A two-dimensional circumplex approach to the development of a hacker taxonomy. *Digital Investigation, 3*(2), 97–102. doi:10.1016/j.diin.2006.03.001

Rogers, M. K. (2010). The psyche of cybercriminals: A psycho-social perspective. In S. Ghosh & E. Turrini (Eds.), *Cybercrimes: A multidisciplinary analysis* (pp. 217–235). Springer Berlin Heidelberg.

Rogers, M. K., Seigfried, K., & Tidke, K. (2006a). Self-Reported Computer Criminal Behavior: A Psychological Analysis. *Digital Investigation, 3*, 116–120. doi:10.1016/j.diin.2006.06.002

Schell, B. H., & Holt, T. J. (2010). A profile of the demographics, psychological predispositions, and social/behavioral patterns of computer hacker insiders and outsiders. In T. J. Holt & B. H. Schell (Eds.), *Corporate hacking and technology-driven crime: Social dynamics and implications* (pp. 144–168). IGI Global.

Seebruck, R. (2015). A typology of hackers: Classifying cyber malfeasance using a weighted arc circumplex model. *Digital Investigation, 14*, 36–45. doi:10.1016/j.diin.2015.07.002

Seigfried-Spellar, K. C., & Treadway, K. N. (2014). Differentiating *Hackers*, Identity Thieves, Cyberbullies, and Virus Writers by College Major and Individual Differences. *Deviant Behavior, 35*(10), 782–803. doi:10.1080/01639625.2014.884333

Seigfried-Spellar, K. C., Villacís-Vukadinović, N., & Lynam, D. R. (2017). Computer criminal behavior is related to psychopathy and other antisocial behavior. *Journal of Criminal Justice*, *51*, 67–73. doi:10.1016/j.jcrimjus.2017.06.003

SharmaR. (2007). Peeping into a Hacker's Mind: Can Criminological Theories Explain Hacking? SSRN, 1-20. doi:10.2139/ssrn.1000446

Skinner, W. F., & Fream, A. M. (1997). A social learning theory analysis of computer crime among college students. *Journal of Research in Crime and Delinquency*, *34*(4), 495–518. doi:10.1177/0022427897034004005

Steinmetz, K. F. (2016). Hacked: A radical approach to hacker culture and crime. New York University Press.

Steinmetz, K. F., Holt, T. J., & Holt, K. M. (2020). Decoding the binary: Reconsidering the hacker subculture through a gendered lens. *Deviant Behavior*, *41*(8), 936–948. doi:10.1080/01639625.2019.1596460

Szpor, G., & Gryszczyńska, A. (2022). Hacking in the (cyber)space. *GIS Odyssey Journal*, *2*(1), 141–152.

Taylor, P. A. (1999). *Hackers: Crime and the digital sublime*. Routledge.

Taylor, P. A. (2001). Hacktivism: in search of lost ethics? In D. S. Wall (Ed.), *Crime and the Internet* (pp. 59–74). Routledge.

Thackray, H., McAlaney, J., Dogan, H. Z., Taylor, J., & Richardson, C. N. (2016). *Social Psychology: An under-used tool in Cybersecurity. Proceedings of the 30th International BCS Human Computer Interaction Conference*. IEEE. 10.14236/ewic/HCI2016.64

Thomas, D. (2002). *Hacker culture*. U of Minnesota Press.

Turgeman-Goldschmidt, O. (2005). Hackers' Accounts: Hacking as a Social Entertainment. *Social Science Computer Review*, *23*(1), 8–23. doi:10.1177/0894439304271529

Turkle, S. (1984). The Second Self: Computers and the Human Spirit. Granada.

ul Hassan, S. Z., & Ahmad, S. Z. (2021). The Importance of Ethical Hacking Tools and Techniques in Software Development Life Cycle. *International Journal*, *10*(3).

Wall, D. S. (2001). *Cybercrime and the Internet*. Routledge. doi:10.4324/9780203164501_chapter_1

Wall, D. S. (2007). Policing cybercrimes: Situating the public police in networks of security within cyberspace. *Police Practice and Research*, *8*(2), 183–205. doi:10.1080/15614260701377729

Wall, D. S., & Williams, M. (2007). Policing diversity in the digital age: Maintaining order in virtual communities. *Criminology & Criminal Justice*, *7*(4), 391–415. doi:10.1177/1748895807082064

Wang, Z., Zhu, H., Liu, P., & Sun, L. (2021). Social engineering in cybersecurity: A domain ontology and knowledge graph application examples. *Cybersecurity*, *4*(1), 31. doi:10.118642400-021-00094-6

Whiters, K. L. (2019). *A Psychosocial Behavioral Attribution Model: Examining the Relationship Between the "Dark Triad" and Cyber-Criminal Behaviors Impacting Social Networking Sites* [Unpublished doctoral dissertation, College of Engineering and Computing, Nova Southeastern University].

Xu, Z., Hu, Q., & Zhang, C. (2013). Why computer talents become computer hackers. *Communications of the ACM, 56*(4), 64–74. doi:10.1145/2436256.2436272

Yar, M. (2006). *Cybercrime and society*. Sage Publications. doi:10.4135/9781446212196

Yar, M. (2016). Online crime. In Oxford Research Encyclopedia of Criminology and Criminal Justice. (pp. 1-27). doi:10.1093/acrefore/9780190264079.013.112

Young, R., & Zhang, L. (2005). Factors affecting illegal hacking behavior. *AMCIS*, 3258-3264.

ADDITIONAL READING

Akers, R. L. (2010). *Social learning and social structure: A general theory of crime and deviance*. Transaction Publishers.

Akers, R. L., & Jennings, W. G. (2016). Social Learning Theory. In A. R. Piquero (Ed.), *The handbook of criminological theory* (pp. 230–240). John Wiley & Sons.

KEY TERMS AND DEFINITIONS

Malware: Is a variety of computer codes, like viruses, trojan horses, and logic bombs, which are designed to interfere or disrupt the computer's normal operation (Yar, 2006).

Phishing: Form of cyberattack that, usually through messages or emails, seeks to trick people into giving up sensitive information or installing harmful software (Curtis et al., 2018).

Session Hijacking: It consists of the exploitation of a computer session, also called a session key. Allowing to gain unauthorized access to information or services on a computer system (Baitha & Vinod, 2018).

Social Engineering: Type of attack in which human vulnerabilities are exploited, through interaction, to breach cybersecurity (Wang et al., 2021).

SQL Injection: Type of online security flaw that allows interference with an online database query (ul Hassan & Ahmad, 2021).

Trolling: It consists in the deliberate use of aggression, mislead and/or manipulation in a way to create a context able to trigger a conflict (Hardaker, 2013).

ENDNOTES

[1] For more information about the configurations associated with cybercrime see: Yar (2006).

[2] Second International Self-Report of Delinquency Study

[3] In the USA, the DefCon conference stands out, addressing aspects related to hacking and computer security (Holt, 2007). In Germany the Chaos Communication Congress (CCC) is held, dedicated to sharing information about technology and creating a space for hackers to meet (Kinkade et al., 2013).

[4] For more information on the influence of social learning components on hacking practice see: Akers, 2010; Akers & Jennings, 2016; Hollinger, 1992; Morris & Blackburn, 2009; Skinner & Fream, 1997.

Chapter 7
Methodologies Based on Hardware Performance Counters for Supporting Cybersecurity

Pablo Philipe Pessoa
Federal University of Pernambuco, Brazil

Aline do Monte
Federal University of Pernambuco, Brazil

Camila Dantas
Federal University of Pernambuco, Brazil

Paulo Maciel
Federal University of Pernambuco, Brazil

ABSTRACT

Cybersecurity is a critical area of information technology, where prevention, detection, and mitigation of cyberattacks are crucial to ensure system and data integrity. This chapter presents several methods and strategies that adopt hardware performance counters (HPCs) as the paramount protection utility, with the aid of analysis and advanced techniques from several areas of statistics and computing, to support cybersecurity. Furthermore, the chapter discusses the need for broader approaches, including preventive and protective measures, regular penetration testing, user awareness, implementation of robust security policies, and advanced threat detection techniques. While traditional security tools such as implementing IDSs, IPSs, firewalls, antivirus, and other solutions are critical, they must be complemented with more comprehensive approaches to deal with the increasing sophistication of cyberattacks, and HPCs provide this support with efficiency.

DOI: 10.4018/979-8-3693-1528-6.ch007

INTRODUCTION

In recent years, cyberattacks have become increasingly complex and frequent, posing a significant threat to the security and privacy of individuals and organizations. Traditional Intrusion Detection Systems (IDS) that rely on signature-based detection are inadequate against zero-day attacks and new and previously unknown threats that can bypass traditional security measures. Therefore, researchers are exploring alternative methodologies to supplement traditional IDSs and improve their effectiveness. Hardware Performance Counters (HPCs) have emerged as promising engineers for enhancing Cybersecurity. HPCs are low-level hardware components that track various system performance metrics (Chigada & Madzinga, 2021; Lee, 2021; Bunker, 2020).

HPCs can detect zero-day attacks because they do not rely on predefined signatures. Additionally, HPCs can provide real-time information on system performance, enabling faster and more accurate detection of cyberattacks. Another advantage of using HPCs for cybersecurity is their ability to provide detailed insights into system behavior. This information can help security teams understand how an attack was executed and identify potential weaknesses in the system's security. HPCs can also detect attacks designed to evade traditional security measures, such as those that use low-bandwidth traffic or multiple stages of infection (Wang et al., 2020; Abdel-Basset, 2022).

HPCs generate large amounts of data that must be processed and analyzed in real time, which can be computationally intensive. By analyzing the data collected by HPCs, security teams can develop new strategies and tools to prevent similar attacks from occurring in the future. Additionally, HPCs perform low-level access to the system, which can create security risks if not properly implemented. Therefore, it is essential to plan and configure HPCs properly to maximize their effectiveness and minimize the risks (Alam et al., 2020; Kadiyala et al., 2020; Kuruvila et al., 2022).

There are different methodologies for using HPCs for Cybersecurity, and good planning is essential to determine the best configuration to be implemented in the infrastructure. This chapter will explore the eight deployment methods of HPCs, discuss their emerging potential to detect different types of cyberattacks and address the challenges and limitations associated with their use in each methodology. We will demonstrate the application with practical examples in developed works to provide a broader view of the potential of HPCs in combating cyberattacks (Nascimento et al., 2021).

Overall, HPCs have evidence of great potential to enhance Cybersecurity and detect previously unknown threats. However, it is crucial to plan and configure HPCs properly to maximize their effectiveness and minimize the risks associated with their use. By exploring the different deployment methods of HPCs and addressing their associated challenges and limitations, this chapter aims to provide a comprehensive understanding of the potential of HPCs in combating cyberattacks (Mushtaq et al., 2020; Li & Gaudiot, 2021).

HARDWARE PERFORMANCE COUNTERS

Hardware performance counters (HPCs) are low-level hardware components that track various system performance metrics, providing detailed information about system performance (AMD, 2019; ARM, 2019; Intel, 2020; MICROSOFT, 2022; The Linux kernel documentation, 2022). For example, HPCs can collect data about various system activities, such as CPU usage, memory usage, and network traffic. This data can then be analyzed to detect anomalous behavior that could indicate the presence of a cyberattack (Botacin & Grégio, 2022; Omotosho et al., 2022).

HPCs are built into the hardware of a computer system and are used to monitor its performance. They work by counting the number of hardware events that occur while the system is running. These events can include CPU cycles, memory accesses, and cache hits. HPCs provide a way to collect low-level data on system performance that can be used to identify bottlenecks and optimize system performance. Also known as PCL, LPE, or perf events, HPCs are an event-driven observation tool capable of capturing advanced performance functions in the system. Among the events the utility can monitor are *Hardware Events*, CPU-only performance monitoring counters, and *Software Events*, which are based on kernel counters such as CPU migrations and crashes (Bazm et al., 2018; IBM, 2021; BSD Manuals, 2022).

These characteristics are part of a specific and dedicated unit of the CPU structure called the Performance Monitoring Unit, also called the Performance Monitoring Counter. A PMU is a hardware built into a processor to measure performance parameters, such as instruction cycles, cache hits, cache misses, and branch misses, among many others. In addition, PMUs and HPCs can collect and analyze data to detect incorrect system behavior, such as crashes, errors, and anomalous behavior (Gregg, 2019a, 2019b, 2021). In this way, it is possible to identify adverse situations in the system, in the execution of applications and processes, exactly when the patterns created later in the diagnosis differ from those classified as typical (Mushtaq et al., 2018; Krishnamurthy et al., 2019; Banerjee et al., 2021).

Data Collection and Monitoring

Accurately and reliably, collecting and monitoring data from HPCs requires careful data engineering. This data is usually contained in real time and can generate large amounts of information that must be processed and analyzed. Data filtering and aggregation are standard data engineering techniques used to reduce the amount of data generated and facilitate analysis. However, it is essential to note that although today's microprocessors have many performance counters, it is only possible to collect a limited number. These counters perform a cumulative count of related events (Basu et al., 2019; Nascimento et al., 2021).

In addition, data visualization is a valuable technique to make information more accessible to users and assist in decision-making. HPCs were initially designed to perform hardware and performance debugging, helping developers better understand the behavior of applications running on the system and, in this way, adjust their performance. The utility uses these performance counters to count specific events on the processor. Each approach must be modeled individually, collecting hardware events and other variables at runtime and automatically counting monitored events. They are accumulated and measured over time between predetermined intervals (Das et al., 2019).

Collecting samples triggered by CPU hardware events is also a form of CPU behavioral profiling, which can be used to shed light on cache misses and memory lock cycles. However, it is essential to note that the number and types of HPCs events depend mainly on the processor in use, which makes it interesting to use common subsets of options to develop methodologies that can be applied to most CPUs. Likewise, data engineering is critical to accurately and reliably collecting and monitoring data from HPCs. Data filtering and aggregation techniques, data visualization, and sampling triggered by CPU hardware events are techniques used to facilitate analysis and improve system performance (Garcia-Serrano, 2015; Woo et al., 2018; Li & Gaudiot, 2018).

To use HPCs in Linux environments, it is necessary to have the Linux kernel compiled with support for HPCs, which can be done during the kernel configuration process. Although HPCs have been available in the Linux kernel since version 2.6.31, support for different types of HPCs can vary depending on the kernel version and Linux distribution in use. Therefore, checking the distribution and kernel documentation to determine which HPCs are supported and which kernel modules need to be loaded to enable support is essential. In addition, some tools may have limited or no permission for HPCs (Linux kernel documentation, 2022).

In Windows operating systems, to use them, it is necessary to check if the processor and the operating system support HPCs. Next, the HPCs must be enabled via the "Typeperf" command line tool. Finally, it is essential to carefully choose which performance counters to monitor to ensure the data collected is relevant to monitoring objectives. Then, the collected data can be analyzed using performance analysis tools such as Windows Performance Analyzer or PerfView. It is important to note that the proper use of HPCs is essential for identifying performance problems and anomalous behavior in the system, which can lead to significant improvements in system performance. In addition, it is necessary to have technical knowledge in configuring and using HPCs to ensure proper collection and analysis of performance data (Microsoft, 2022).

The appropriation of native system utilities for collecting and processing data is a recommendation to ensure the accuracy and reliability of the information provided. Preferring these tools causes a low interference in the collection, which avoids introducing noise in the collected data; the construction and implementation of scripts helped this process. Furthermore, this approach is fundamental in performance- and availability-critical environments where running third-party or resource-intensive tools can affect the system's ability to perform other tasks. Therefore, using these tools consistently and systematically during the data collection and processing process is recommended to obtain more accurate and complete information about the system without affecting its operation or causing additional problems.

Types of HPCs

System performance monitoring is essential to ensure maximum efficiency and optimization in high-performance environments or as protective countermeasures. Several types of HPCs can be used to measure and analyze the performance of a system and track projection anomalies (Wang et al., 2020; Bourdon et al., 2020; Li & Gaudiot, 2018).

HPCs can be classified into different categories, each with a specific purpose. Among the main types of HPCs, we can highlight the following:

Hardware Events: These performance monitoring counters are in the CPU's hardware and store information regarding process elements such as the number of cycles, cache misses, and execute instructions. These events are accounted for by the hardware and provide accurate and detailed information about the CPU performance.

Software Events: These are events related to occurrences at the kernel level of the operating system and are counted from the affairs of CPU migrations, minor failures, and serious failures. They help measure operating system and memory performance, allowing the identification of bottlenecks and performance issues that affect system performance.

Tracepoints: These are predefined kernel-level static instrumentation software events encoded into various logical locations in the kernel, such as TCP/UDP exchange, scheduler, and system call instances. They help measure operating system activity in real time, allowing the identification of performance issues and bottlenecks.

Dynamic Tracepoints: These are dynamically instrumented tracing software events for user-level programs and applications through the *kprobe* for *kernel* software and *uprobe* for user-level software interfaces. They help measure the performance of specific applications, allowing the identification of performance issues and code optimization.

Each type of HPCs has its specific purpose and use, and their proper use is critical to diagnosing and optimizing system performance. Choosing the right HPCs should be based on the needs and objectives of the system to be monitored. With the correct selection of HPCs, it is possible to identify performance problems and anomalous behavior in the system, which includes cyber threat situations (Cho et al., 2020; Woo et al., 2018). The table show some counters and their descriptions (Table 1).

Information about hardware performance counters is specific to each processor architecture and manufacturer, so their references will vary by the platform in question (The Linux kernel documentation, 2022). For Intel (2020) processors, official documentation can be found in the Intel® 64 and IA-32 Architectures Software Developer's Manual Volume 3: System Programming Guide, available from the Intel website. For AMD (2019) processors, official documentation can be found in the AMD64 Architecture Programmer's Manual Volume 3: General-Purpose and System Instructions, available from the AMD website. ARM (2019) processors, official documentation can be found in the ARM Architecture Reference Manual, available on the ARM website. Each manufacturer may have documentation but also make information available on their websites, forums, and developer communities. It is essential to check the official documentation for the specific processor architecture for accurate information on available performance counters (NVIDIA, 2021, IBM, 2021; Oracle, 2022; Apple, 2022; BSD Manuals, 2022).

CYBERSECURITY CHALLENGES

Cybersecurity has become a growing concern for individuals, businesses, and governments worldwide. It protects computer systems and networks from malicious attacks, theft, and logical data damage. Cyber threats can be intentional or accidental and can occur through various methods, including phishing scams, ransomware, viruses, and denial-of-service attacks (Foreman, 2018; Alam et al., 2020; Mantha & Soto, 2019).

One of the significant challenges in cybersecurity is the increasing sophistication of cyber-attacks. Cybercriminals are continually developing new methods to evade detection and exploit vulnerabilities, making it challenging for security professionals to keep up with the constantly evolving threat landscape. For instance, ransomware attacks have increased, and cybercriminals encrypt files and demand payment in exchange for a decryption key, causing significant financial losses for individuals and organizations (Fischer, 2017; Hasan et al., 2023).

Another challenge is the human factor. Employees who lack cybersecurity training or do not follow best practices can inadvertently expose their organization to cyber threats. Social engineering attacks, such as phishing, are becoming more prevalent, targeting susceptible individuals through email, text messages, or social media (Basu et al., 2019). Indeed, one of the challenges in cybersecurity is balancing security measures with user convenience. Security measures such as two-factor authentication or complex password requirements can frustrate users and even lead them to circumvent them altogether. This is a delicate balance for security professionals, who must provide adequate protection without sacrificing user experience.

Table 1. Description of performance counters

Name	Event Description	Event Type
cpu-cycles OR cycles	Count CPU cycles	Hardware event
instructions	Count instructions	Hardware event
cache-references	Count cache accesses	Hardware event
cache-misses	Count cache misses	Hardware event
branch-instructions OR branches	Count branch instructions	Hardware event
branch-misses	Count mispredicted branches	Hardware event
bus-cycles	Count bus cycles	Hardware event
ref-cycles	Count reference cycles	Hardware event
cpu-clock	Clock ticks of CPU core	Software event
task-clock	Clock ticks of process	Software event
page-faults OR faults	Count page faults	Software event
minor-faults	Count minor page faults	Software event
major-faults	Count major page faults	Software event
context-switches OR cs	Count context switches	Software event
cpu-migrations OR migrations	Count CPU migrations	Software event
alignment-faults	Count alignment faults	Software event
emulation-faults	Count emulation faults	Software event
bpf-output	Count BPF output	Software event
cgroup-switches	Count cgroup switches	Software event
dummy	Dummy event	Software event
L1-dcache-loads	Count L1 data cache loads	Hardware cache event
L1-dcache-load-misses	Count L1 data cache load misses	Hardware cache event
L1-dcache-stores	Count L1 data cache stores	Hardware cache event
L1-dcache-store-misses	Count L1 data cache store misses	Hardware cache event
L1-dcache-prefetches	Count L1 data cache prefetches	Hardware cache event
L1-dcache-prefetch-misses	Count L1 data cache prefetch misses	Hardware cache event
L1-icache-loads	Count L1 instruction cache loads	Hardware cache event
L1-icache-load-misses	Count L1 instruction cache load misses	Hardware cache event
L1-icache-prefetches	Count L1 instruction cache prefetches	Hardware cache event
L1-icache-prefetch-misses	Count L1 instruction cache prefetch misses	Hardware cache event
LLC-loads	Count last level cache loads	Hardware cache event
LLC-load-misses	Count last level cache load misses	Hardware cache event
LLC-stores	Count last level cache stores	Hardware cache event
LLC-store-misses	Count the last level cache store misses	Hardware cache event
sched:sched_stat_runtime	CPU time of a task	Tracepoint event
sched:sched_pi_setprio	Change in scheduling priority	Tracepoint event
syscalls:sys_enter_socket	Socket system call entry	Tracepoint event
syscalls:sys_exit_socket	Socket system call exit	Tracepoint event

Another challenge is the issue of data privacy. With the increasing amount of data generated and stored by individuals and organizations, the risk of data breaches and leaks also increases. This can lead to significant financial losses, reputational damage, and legal liabilities. Implementing robust data encryption and access control measures is crucial in safeguarding sensitive information and maintaining trust with customers and clients.

Moreover, as technology advances and more devices connect to the internet, the attack surface for cyber threats also expands. The Internet of Things (IoT) devices, which include everything from home appliances to medical devices, are vulnerable to cyber-attacks, posing a severe threat to individuals' privacy and safety. Therefore, effective cybersecurity measures require a multifaceted approach involving individuals, organizations, and governments.

To address the cybersecurity challenges, continuing education and training, regular software updates and patching, and proactive monitoring and detection of cyber threats are necessary (He et al., 2021; Zhou et al., 2018; Sobb et al., 2020). By adopting such measures, individuals and organizations can enhance their security posture and reduce the risks associated with cyber threats. Cybersecurity challenges are pervasive, and addressing them requires a collaborative effort from all stakeholders.

Furthermore, the rapid pace of technological advancements also challenges cybersecurity professionals. As new technologies emerge, so do new vulnerabilities and attack vectors. For example, the rise of artificial intelligence and machine learning brings new opportunities for cybercriminals to exploit vulnerabilities and launch sophisticated attacks. Keeping up with these emerging threats requires continuous learning and the development of new cybersecurity strategies and technologies.

Addepalli (2020) highlights the importance of identifying the most suitable defense strategy for a given environment to implement security measures and define their levels effectively. Among the designs available, they mention Origin and Extremity Defense, Intermediate Network Defense, and Host-Based Defense.

- **Origin and Extremity Defense (OED):** This approach can be implemented on the user's computer, whether in a hardware or software device, limiting and optimizing the sending and receiving of network packets to ensure greater control over the connection. However, it is crucial to note that a malicious actor who manages to disable or bypass the security device can easily circumvent this approach before launching, for example, a DoS/DDoS attack. To enhance the effectiveness of OED, multiple layers of security measures should be implemented, regularly tested, and updated. Incident response plans should be implemented to respond quickly and mitigate the impact of potential attacks.

- **Intermediate Network Defense (IND):** IND includes the use of intermediary mechanisms within the infrastructure and environment, such as Intrusion Detection Systems (IDS) and Intrusion Prevention Systems (IPS), to offer various means of protecting the infrastructure and service. They are widely used in Software-defined networking (SDN) technologies. While effective, adding assets to the network increases the structural complexity of the infrastructure. It can create or increase single points of failure, making these devices targets of attacks resulting in service unavailability. To mitigate such risks, network architects and engineers should follow a defense-in-depth approach by implementing multiple layers of security, including but not limited to IND.

- **Host-Based Defense (HBD):** This defense method does not involve adding assets to the traffic path. Instead, the host is responsible for its defense, which can prevent, detect, and mitigate threats. Additionally, the host can perform protective countermeasures by itself, using parameters and hardware characteristics such as CPU, RAM, and network bandwidth consumption to increase the accuracy of triggers. Usually, they are implemented using some intelligence mechanism so that, through the observed data, it is possible to execute protection actions. While HBD is effective, it increases the complexity and resource costs of the system. Furthermore, a compromised host can become a source of threats and attacks in the network.

These countermeasure strategies can increase the accuracy and speed of detecting attacks, providing better mitigation solutions. However, it is crucial to note that the asset's anomalous behavior can cause system failures, and malware in the environment can be identified in various ways. HPCs have already shown significant results in capturing the system's behavior, making them an excellent resource for diagnosing these threats. It is essential to continuously monitor the system and implement necessary security measures to prevent or mitigate the impact of potential attacks. Regular vulnerability assessments and penetration testing can identify weaknesses in the design and help strengthen the security posture.

There are two main categories of defense mechanisms in cybersecurity: proactive mechanisms and reactive mechanisms.

- **Proactive mechanisms:** Focus on prediction and detection techniques that add features to ensure service availability. These mechanisms can include traditional network administration practices, such as load balancing, service replication, and firewall rules. Proactive means aim to prevent cyberattacks from occurring or mitigate their impact.
- **Reactive mechanisms:** Reactive mechanisms are executed after detecting malicious activities. These mechanisms seek to control the flow of requests, block malicious traffic, and locate the responsible malicious agents. Reactive mechanisms are often used to support decision-making by administrators as they analyze the best approach to dealing with threats. Reactive mechanisms include intrusion detection systems (IDS) and intrusion prevention systems (IPS), which detect and respond to threats by analyzing network traffic and applying appropriate rules to block malicious traffic.

An emerging category of defense mechanisms is adaptive mechanisms. Adaptive mechanisms are designed to automatically adjust their behavior based on the changing conditions of the system or the environment. These mechanisms use machine learning algorithms to learn from experiences and adapt to new threats. Adaptive mechanisms can be proactive or reactive, depending on their design and implementation. For example, adaptive firewalls can learn from past traffic patterns and adjust their rules to prevent future attacks. In contrast, adaptive IDS/IPS can dynamically adapt their regulations based on the changing threat landscape.

Overall, the use of multiple defense mechanisms, including proactive, reactive, and adaptive mechanisms, can enhance the security stance of a system or network. However, the effectiveness of these mechanisms depends on their proper configuration and tuning, as well as regular updates and maintenance to keep up with the evolving threat landscape.

Utilizing HPCs in Cybersecurity

Hardware Performance Counters (HPCs) are promising means for engineers to enhance cybersecurity. By monitoring various low-level system metrics, HPCs can provide valuable insights into system behavior and help identify potential cyber threats (Kuruvila et al., 2020). HPCs are capable of detecting zero-day attacks that bypass traditional security measures, and they are also capable of detecting attacks that are designed to evade standard security measures. Additionally, HPCs can provide real-time information on system performance, enabling faster and more accurate detection of cyberattacks (Alam et al., 2020).

One of the advantages of using HPCs for cybersecurity is their ability to perform low-level access to the system, allowing for monitoring various performance metrics such as cache utilization, memory bandwidth, and instruction execution (Li & Gaudiot, 2021). By analyzing this data, HPCs can identify anomalies and potential threats that traditional signature-based IDSs may not detect. Moreover, HPCs can be used with conventional IDSs to improve their effectiveness against known and unknown threats.

HPCs can help detect various types of cyberattacks, such as Distributed Denial of Service attacks (DDoS), malicious code injection attacks (SQL injection), side-channel attacks, and phishing attacks. By using HPCs to monitor system activity, it is possible to identify suspicious and abnormal behavior that could indicate the presence of an ongoing attack. For example, HPCs can detect increased network traffic or system resource utilization, indicating a possible DDoS attack. Likewise, HPCs can detect attempts to inject malicious code into a database by monitoring processor behavior during the execution of SQL queries. With the use of HPCs, it is possible to detect these attacks more quickly and accurately, allowing a more efficient and tolerant response to the damage caused by the actions of intruders.

However, some challenges and limitations are associated with using HPCs for cybersecurity. One of the main challenges is the high computational cost of processing and analyzing large amounts of data generated by HPCs in real time. This can be addressed by implementing efficient algorithms and data compression techniques (Nascimento et al., 2021). Another challenge is ensuring the security of the HPCs themselves, as they have low-level access to the system and can potentially be exploited by attackers. Therefore, it is crucial to implement appropriate security measures and protocols to protect HPCs from unauthorized access and manipulation (Pan et al., 2022; Elnaggar et al., 2021; Tan & Karri, 2020).

Despite these challenges, the potential benefits of using HPCs for cybersecurity make them a promising area of research. In addition to these uses, HPCs can be used for performance optimization and tuning. By monitoring system behavior and identifying bottlenecks and inefficiencies, HPCs can help optimize system performance and improve resource utilization. HPCs can help identify potential threats and vulnerabilities, maximize system performance, and enhance the effectiveness of cybersecurity measures. As technology advances, HPCs will likely play an increasingly important role in cybersecurity and system analysis (Maciel, 2023 Vol. 2; Borba et al., 2022).

METHODOLOGIES

Hardware Performance Counters (HPCs) are addressed in many ways in information security. In a literature review, eight significant approaches use performance counters and their events to detect, classify, and mitigate attacks and malware (Foreman, 2018; Das et al., 2019; Basu et al., 2019; Nascimento et al., 2021; Kuruvila et al., 2022; Maciel, 2023 Vol. 1).

Several methodologies are proposed in the literature for using hardware performance counters (HPCs) in the context of information security. These methodologies leverage the valuable performance data collected by HPCs to identify patterns of behavior associated with malicious activity and prevent attacks before they cause significant damage.

Some standard methods include anomaly detection, signature-based detection, and behavior-based detection. Overall, these methodologies demonstrate the potential of HPCs in improving information security, allowing the detection and mitigation of cyberattacks in real time. Each approach has its strengths and weaknesses, and the choice of methodology depends on specific security requirements and the nature of the threats faced. However, the common goal of all these methodologies is to provide effective and efficient protection against cyber threats and ensure the security and integrity of critical information assets. This section will present and discuss the methods, presenting their main characteristics.

Subscription-Based

The subscription-based approach is another significant methodology that uses HPCs for cybersecurity. This approach relies on subscribing to a list of known threats and creating profiles with signatures of reference situations and behavior characteristics corresponding to these attacks. By comparing the current situational profile of the system with the registered conditions of the attack signatures, this approach can identify abnormal behavior caused by known threats. This methodology is commonly used in credit card fraud detection, system failure detection, surveillance, and data validation. However, it requires high computational power to process large volumes of data and may not be effective against new and emerging threats.

Another way to use this methodology is to correlate data from multiple sources, such as network traffic, system logs, and user behavior, and analyze it in real-time to detect previously unknown threats. By detecting and mitigating threats in real time, this approach reduces the workload on security analysts and provides early warning of an attack. This methodology is particularly effective in detecting complex and sophisticated attacks that involve multiple stages and techniques.

This is a traditional technique used by antivirus and antimalware to detect and block known threats. They compare system traffic patterns against a list of known viruses and other malware signatures. If there is a match, the device blocks or alerts the user to malware on the system. However, this technique may be less effective against unknown threats and new types of malware. Therefore, other methods, such as anomaly detection and event correlation, are used in conjunction with signature detection to improve the effectiveness of malware detection.

Heuristics-Based

The heuristic-based approach is widely used in cybersecurity threat detection. It is an effective methodology that provides direct detection when events exceed predefined thresholds, individually or in combination. This method is advantageous in detecting attacks such as jump-oriented, which exploits the execution of instructions that jump from one memory address to another, redirecting the program's execution flow to malicious codes, like stack-oriented return attacks (ROP - Return Oriented Programming). It is important to note that these solutions may result in more false positives, especially when running a wide range of potentially valid processes. However, these solutions are easy to implement and can be a pre-filter for more advanced and resource-intensive detection approaches.

Another advantage of the heuristics-based approach is its ability to be implemented in real-time, allowing rapid response to potential threats. Plus, it's a solution that doesn't require a significant investment in specialized hardware or specific cybersecurity expertise, making it affordable for businesses of all sizes. However, it is essential to emphasize that the heuristic-based approach should not be the only line of defense against cyberattacks. It should be used with other security techniques, such as firewalls, antivirus, and data access policies, to ensure complete system protection.

Hybrid Methodologies

Hybrid approaches have become standard practice in cybersecurity, where different techniques are combined to improve effectiveness in detecting and preventing threats. This technique usually involves using traditional protection techniques, such as IDS, IPS, and Firewalls, in conjunction with artificial intelligence and machine learning techniques, taking advantage of the ability of these techniques to adapt to different scenarios. In addition, hybrid approaches can support other frontline techniques, providing an additional line of countermeasure protection on top of existing ones.

In the context of threat protection, especially in the case of DoS/DDoS attack detection, hybrid approaches combine different detection and prevention techniques to maximize effectiveness in combating threats, considering the limitations of each method individually. The hybrid system, therefore, offers a significant advantage in terms of protection and security compared to using a single technique.

Statistics-Based

The detection of anomalies in systems is a critical area of information security, and one of the most used methodologies using HPCs is statistics. For its application, the procedures are divided into three primary stages: data collection, treatment of these data with statistical and mathematical methods, and, finally, decision-making and classification of the data collected about the observed situations. There are two types of statistical methods: detection based on a fixed threshold value of specific parameters and detection based on behavioral profiles, which focus on previously captured behavioral characteristics and compare them with current ones, interpreting the most significant deviations as anomalies in the system. A typical example of this methodology is using Time Series to detect malware.

This approach is commonly used in conjunction with creating run profiles while the system is in regular operation. Deviations from the collected profiles are constantly measured and compared with the current system behavior to detect anomalous behavior. For this, probabilistic models are built, and mathematical and statistical methods are used based on probability theories. Anomaly detection is essential to protect systems against cyberattacks and maintain information security.

One of the main advantages of statistical methods for detecting anomalies using HPCs is their ability to handle large volumes of data. With the growing amount of information generated in different systems, statistical techniques have become essential to identify anomalies that may go unnoticed by traditional security methods. In addition, these methods can be easily implemented in various designs and platforms, making them an affordable and effective option for protecting sensitive information.

Knowledge-Based

Knowledge-based or rule-based methods detect system anomalies based on prior knowledge of the system's HPC resource utilization pattern. For this, previously established standards are used to classify the system's current state as suspicious activity or everyday use. Expert administrators identify these situations, using their expertise to understand and tag system behavior. These methods can be classified into two basic types: anomaly detection by established rules and rule-based intrusion identification.

The first type records the audit history of generating new automated regulations and identifying new patterns. In the second type, data from already identified anomalies are used to identify and classify signatures of known anomalies.

Another way of using this methodology is to use it in conjunction with signature-based methods. This approach analyzes system behavior over time and identifies deviations from the expected behavior pattern. These deviations can indicate malicious or anomalous activity on the system.

Soft Computation-Based

Methods based on Soft Computing are known to have low computational costs or require minimal knowledge. Several techniques for this methodology include feature selection/reduction techniques and unsupervised classification techniques, such as Artificial Neural Networks (ANNs) and SVM (Support Vector Machines) methods. ANNs are mainly used to develop new non-linear systems that accept many input and output variables and their relationships. These networks can learn from input data, allowing the system to recognize patterns and make decisions. SVM methods are used to classify data based on independent and target relationships of variables, allowing the detection of patterns in complex data. Both techniques are widely used in anomaly detection applications in computational systems using HPCs.

Another technique used in Soft Computation-based methods for anomaly detection is fuzzy logic. This approach allows for the creation of rule-based systems that handle uncertain or ambiguous data to HPCs, often encountered in the real world. Fuzzy logic is a mathematical tool that uses linguistic variables and membership functions to deal with imprecise or uncertain data. By using fuzzy sets, the system can represent a range of values rather than a binary classification, which makes it more suitable for real-world applications where data may be incomplete or uncertain. Fuzzy logic has been applied in various anomaly detection applications, such as intrusion detection in computer networks, fault detection in industrial systems, and fraud detection in financial transactions, using data obtained through performance counters.

Data-Mining-Based

Methods based on data mining are typically used in more complex environments and systems, which require more processing and the use of more significant resources. Typically, lower anomaly detection rates are achieved compared to signature-based methods, which detect patterns in large amounts of data and use these patterns to detect future anomalies in similar data. This countermeasure method primarily detects new threats or uncommon events in denser datasets. A challenge for techniques that use this approach is dealing with large amounts of data, requiring much computational power.

In addition to detecting new or uncommon events, data mining-based methods also have the advantage of handling heterogeneous data sources, using data from HPCs and several other system variables. These methods can combine data from different sources and formats, such as structured and unstructured data, to detect anomalies more comprehensively. However, this requires a more advanced approach, such as deep learning algorithms, to handle the complexities of the data. Another challenge in data mining-based anomaly detection is the need for domain knowledge to identify relevant features and reduce the number of variables to be analyzed. The detection rate may be compromised without proper feature selection, and the algorithm may become too computationally intensive.

Machine-Learning-Based:

Machine learning has become a powerful tool for detecting various cyberattacks, including malware, phishing, and other malicious activities. Furthermore, there are two configurations of use, supervised and unsupervised learning. Supervised learning is an approach in which data from HPCs are obtained and trained against previously classified valid and malicious situations. In this way, the classification engine can detect malicious behavior. On the other hand, unsupervised learning involves online learning during runtime based on accumulated information, such as information from HPCs. In addition, context sensitivity is essential for machine learning in cybersecurity, as it requires knowledge of the operating environment and application to validate the proper operation of the compiled application. By providing a more advanced detection scheme that carries off false positives and negatives, machine learning can be an effective second layer to a signature or heuristic first layer, minimizing the performance impact while improving the accuracy of threat detection. Methods based on machine learning are made possible with the use of advanced and specific statistical techniques for data analysis and classification. This method employs a comprehensive combination of Artificial Intelligence techniques and mathematical models, such as Artificial Neural Networks (ANNs), K-Nearest Neighbors (KNN), and Random Forests (RF).

Despite the many benefits of machine learning in cybersecurity, some challenges still need to be addressed. One of the biggest challenges is the issue of data quality and quantity. Machine learning algorithms require large amounts of high-quality data to be trained effectively. However, collecting and labeling data for cybersecurity can take time and effort, particularly for newer, more sophisticated threats. In addition, machine learning algorithms are vulnerable to adversarial attacks, where malicious actors intentionally manipulate data to mislead or confuse the algorithm. Hostile attacks can lead to false positives or negatives and weaken the effectiveness of the machine learning system. Therefore, new approaches and techniques are being developed to address these challenges and improve the accuracy and reliability of machine learning in cybersecurity.

It is important to emphasize that using Machine Learning methods is a promising technique for detecting and preventing cyber-attacks, such as DDoS attacks. With the evolution of technology, ML will continue to be an area of great interest and development. However, this evolution will need supervision by information security specialists so that the achieved growth makes sense for application in the real world.

Examples for Implementations

Over the more than a decade since the availability of HPCs, several applications have been proposed for their use. The first works investigated code changes (Malone et al., 2011). However, soon there were proposals for profiles for configuring environments (Weaver, 2013), monitoring application performance (Gravelle et al., 2022), and energy modeling (Zamani & Afsahi, 2012). Research efforts have focused on proving the effectiveness of HPC data for efficiently capturing these impacts (Zhang et al., 2007) with source code changes (Tinetti & Méndez, 2014) or through non-invasive methodologies that do not require this change (do Nascimento, 2021), often combined with pure statistical approaches to search for patterns and apply tests (Chen & Baer, 1995; Gravelle et al., 2022; Yu et al., 2019).

Consolidated the effectiveness of HPCs data for efficient performance monitoring, then the relationship between security threats and their reflections on this performance captured by HPCs revealed several possibilities for applications in information security. Numerous advances were driven by the increasing difficulties with performance faced by existing threat detection software, each time in search of collection strategies with low computational cost and less time in detections. Krishnamurthy (2019) proposed an effective method for real-time software monitoring in embedded systems, using time series analysis and supervised learning classifiers. Other alternatives also sought to eliminate the need for additional hardware. Wang et al. (2015) presented a tool for host-based anomaly detection, proposing to eliminate additional hardware by using integrated hardware resources to characterize system behavior in embedded systems. The device uses exclusively HPCs at runtime (Nascimento et al., 2021).

The encounter of this emerging area of research with the advancement of machine learning took place at a fertile moment for the growth of threats resulting from the difficulties faced by traditional detection software, which already indicated a decline in performance when dealing with large amounts of information. In real-time, in addition to the inefficiency in detecting zero-day attacks, in exponential growth (Xin et al., 2018; Choi et al., 2018). For this reason, much of the literature on HPCs available so far is dedicated to the combination of data collection techniques and their application to the training of machine learning models, breaking down into the general categories of attacks and their specificities, demonstrating results for the expansion of detection tools based on this proposal (Krishnamurthy et al., 2019). Some types of attacks most investigated by variations of this methodology are intrusion (Kuruvila et al., 2022; Das et al., 2021), side channel (Sayadi et al., 2020; Wang et al., 2020; Alam et al., 2017), firmware (Wang et al., 2015), hijacking (Yu et al., 2019), ransomware (Ganfure et al., 2022), adversarial attacks (Derasari et al., 2020), DDoS (Atasever et al.,2020) and malware (Gao et al., 2021; Zhou et al., 2021).

The accelerated advance of machine learning research has enabled the incorporation of several products into the information security market, paving the way for the current state of the art. There are two primary methodologies for model optimization to face significant challenges in threat detection. The first is oriented towards explanatory results and uses feature selection and extraction techniques and metaheuristic methods that reduce dimensionality and eliminate overfittings, redundancies, and multicollinearities. This approach contributes to understanding decision-making processes and the behavior of features involved in the detection. The second approach uses automatic selection methods, prioritizing detection accuracy and reducing the time required to the detriment of understanding the decision-making processes, which are considered a black box.

Facing the significant challenges in research with machine learning for threat detection currently finds two primary methodologies for model optimization. Both track recent trends in machine learning research. The first is oriented towards explaining the results and is explored in work such as (Kuruvila et al., 2022). For this, the application of techniques such as selection and selection of features (Chen et al., 2006) or metaheuristic methods that lead to the reduction of dimensionality (Anzueto-Ríos et al., 2022), the elimination of overfittings, redundancies, and multicollinearities (Chan et al., 2022) are used to select as main features for training the models, also confident for the understanding of the decision-making processes and the behavior of the components involved in the detection. Numerous tools have gained results by comparing models before and after applying feature reduction or guarantee techniques (Gao et al., 2021; Khasawneh et al., 2015). In one of them, He et al. (2021) propose a model for zero-day malware detection. The proposal combines models with different approaches and covers an RFE stage for selecting the main features. Sayadi et al. (2018) also submitted a joint machine learning-based model for zero-day malware detection. In addition, the proposal seeks to eliminate the need for multiplexing to collect data from several HPCs. The result presents an Ensemble model that uses data from only 2 HPCs.

The second approach uses automatic selection methods, prioritizing detection accuracy and reducing the time required to the detriment of understanding the decision-making processes, which are considered a black box. For this line, in the current state of the art, we find unsupervised learning models, such as those based on artificial neural networks (Gulmezoglu et al., 2019; Xue et al., 2019), potentially exploring neuron optimization techniques (Van Geit et al., 2008). Other proposals suggest approaches with joint entropy (Rahmani et al., 2009), fuzzy logic (Chowdhury et al., 2022), evolutionary computation (Sahoo et al., 2020), genetic algorithms (Ling et al., 2022), the use of digital twins (Ling et al., 2022), or even pointing out future paths for quantum logic.

CONCLUSION AND RECOMMENDATIONS

Cybersecurity is a shared responsibility between all parties, including users, IT managers, and security experts. Organizations must proactively approach Cybersecurity by implementing preemptive protection measures such as encryption, two-factor authentication, and software patch management. Additionally, organizations need to conduct regular penetration testing to assess the effectiveness of their security solutions and detect potential vulnerabilities.

Traditional security tools, such as IDSs, IPSs, Firewalls, Antivirus, and other protection solutions, are essential to prevent, detect and mitigate cyber-attacks. However, more comprehensive approaches are needed with the increasing sophistication of attacks and the constant threats to Cybersecurity. An effective strategy should also include user education and awareness, implementing robust security policies, and using advanced threat detection techniques such as statistical analysis, behavioral analysis, and artificial intelligence. This is the only way to guarantee the security and integrity of systems and data, protecting the organization against the severe and often irreparable consequences of a successful cyber-attack.

It is concluded that combining HPCs and ML techniques can be a highly effective approach to preventing and detecting cyber-attacks, including DOS/DDoS attacks. The use of hardware performance counters and data engineering techniques can make data more accessible and easier to analyze, while ML-based approaches can better adapt to unfamiliar situations. However, Cybersecurity is an ever-evolving field, and staying current on the latest security techniques and technologies is essential. Furthermore, implementing cybersecurity solutions must be holistic, involving security policies, risk management, and user education.

REFERENCES

Abdel-Basset, M., Gamal, A., Sallam, K. M., Elgendi, I., Munasinghe, K., & Jamalipour, A. (2022). An Optimization Model for Appraising Intrusion-Detection Systems for Network Security Communications: Applications, Challenges, and Solutions. *Sensors (Basel)*, 22(11), 4123. doi:10.339022114123 PMID:35684744

Addepalli, S. K., Karri, R., & Jyothi, V. (2020). U.S. Patent No. 10,735,438. Washington, DC: U.S. Patent and Trademark Office.

Alam, M., Bhattacharya, S., Mukhopadhyay, D., & Bhattacharya, S. (2017). *Performance counters to rescue: A machine learning based safeguard against micro-architectural side-channel-attacks*. Cryptology ePrint Archive.

Alam, M., Sinha, S., Bhattacharya, S., Dutta, S., Mukhopadhyay, D., & Chattopadhyay, A. (2020). *Rapper: Ransomware prevention via performance counters.* arXiv preprint arXiv:2004.01712.

AMD. (2019). *AMD64 Architecture Programmer's Manual, Volume 3: General-Purpose and System Instructions.* AMD. https://www.amd.com/system/files/TechDocs/24594.pdf

Anzueto-Ríos, A., Gómez-Castañeda, F., Flores-Nava, L. M., & Moreno-Cadenas, J. A. (2022, November). Metaheuristic Method for Dimensionality Reduction Tasks. In *2022 19th International Conference on Electrical Engineering, Computing Science and Automatic Control (CCE)* (pp. 1-5). IEEE. 10.1109/CCE56709.2022.9975991

Apple. (2022). *Performance Counters.* Apple. https://developer.apple.com/documentation/performance

ARM. (2019). *Armv8-A Architecture Reference Manual.* ARM. https://developer.arm.com/documentation/ddi0487/latest/

Atasever, S., Özçelik, İ., & Sağiroğlu, Ş. (2020, October). An Overview of Machine Learning Based Approaches in DDoS Detection. In *2020 28th Signal Processing and Communications Applications Conference (SIU)* (pp. 1-4). IEEE. 10.1109/SIU49456.2020.9302121

Banerjee, S. S., Jha, S., Kalbarczyk, Z., & Iyer, R. K. (2021, April). BayesPerf: minimizing performance monitoring errors using Bayesian statistics. In *Proceedings of the 26th ACM International Conference on Architectural Support for Programming Languages and Operating Systems* (pp. 832-844). ACM. 10.1145/3445814.3446739

Başkaya, D., & Samet, R. (2020, September). Ddos attacks detection by using machine learning methods on online systems. In *2020 5th International Conference on Computer Science and Engineering (UBMK)* (pp. 52-57). IEEE. 10.1109/UBMK50275.2020.9219476

Basu, K., Krishnamurthy, P., Khorrami, F., & Karri, R. (2019). A theoretical study of hardware performance counters-based malware detection. *IEEE Transactions on Information Forensics and Security, 15,* 512–525. doi:10.1109/TIFS.2019.2924549

Bawazeer, O., Helmy, T., & Al-hadhrami, S. (2021, July). Malware detection using machine learning algorithms based on hardware performance counters: Analysis and simulation. []. IOP Publishing.]. *Journal of Physics: Conference Series, 1962*(1), 012010. doi:10.1088/1742-6596/1962/1/012010

Bazm, M. M., Sautereau, T., Lacoste, M., Sudholt, M., & Menaud, J. M. (2018, April). Cache-based side-channel attacks detection through intel cache monitoring technology and hardware performance counters. In *2018 Third International Conference on Fog and Mobile Edge Computing (FMEC)* (pp. 7-12). IEEE. 10.1109/FMEC.2018.8364038

Borba, E., Tavares, E., & Maciel, P. (2022). A modeling approach for estimating performance and energy consumption of storage systems. *Journal of Computer and System Sciences, 128,* 86–106. doi:10.1016/j.jcss.2022.04.001

Botacin, M., & Grégio, A. (2022, December). Why We Need a Theory of Maliciousness: Hardware Performance Counters in Security. In *Information Security: 25th International Conference, ISC 2022, Bali, Indonesia,* (pp. 381-389). Cham: Springer International Publishing.

Bourdon, M., Alata, E., Kaâniche, M., Migliore, V., Nicomette, V., & Laarouchi, Y. (2020, January). Anomaly detection using hardware performance counters on a large-scale deployment. In *10th European Congress Embedded Real Time Systems (ERTS 2020)*. IEEE.

Bunker, G. (2020). Targeted cyber-attacks: How to mitigate the increasing risk. *Network Security*, *2020*(1), 17–19. doi:10.1016/S1353-4858(20)30010-6

Chan, J. Y. L., Leow, S. M. H., Bea, K. T., Cheng, W. K., Phoong, S. W., Hong, Z. W., & Chen, Y. L. (2022). Mitigating the multicollinearity problem and its machine learning approach: A review. *Mathematics*, *10*(8), 1283. doi:10.3390/math10081283

Chen, T. F., & Baer, J. L. (1995). Effective hardware-based data prefetching for high-performance processors. *IEEE Transactions on Computers*, *44*(5), 609–623. doi:10.1109/12.381947

Chen, Y., Li, Y., Cheng, X. Q., & Guo, L. (2006). Survey and taxonomy of feature selection algorithms in intrusion detection system. In Information Security and Cryptology: Second SKLOIS Conference, Inscrypt 2006, Beijing, China.

Chigada, J., & Madzinga, R. (2021). Cyberattacks and threats during COVID-19: A systematic literature review. *South African Journal of Information Management*, *23*(1), 1–11. doi:10.4102ajim.v23i1.1277

Cho, J., Kim, T., Kim, S., Im, M., Kim, T., & Shin, Y. (2020). Real-time detection for cache side channel attack using performance counter monitor. *Applied Sciences (Basel, Switzerland)*, *10*(3), 984. doi:10.3390/app10030984

Choi, J., Park, G., & Nam, D. (2018, September). Efficient classification of application characteristics by using hardware performance counters with data mining. In *2018 IEEE 3rd International Workshops on Foundations and Applications of Self* Systems (FAS* W)* (pp. 24-29). IEEE.

Chowdhury, A. B., Mahapatra, A., Soni, D., & Karri, R. (2022). Fuzzing+ Hardware Performance Counters-Based Detection of Algorithm Subversion Attacks on Post-Quantum Signature Schemes. *IEEE Transactions on Computer-Aided Design of Integrated Circuits and Systems*.

Das, S., Saha, S., Priyoti, A. T., Roy, E. K., Sheldon, F. T., Haque, A., & Shiva, S. (2021). Network intrusion detection and comparative analysis using ensemble machine learning and feature selection. *IEEE Transactions on Network and Service Management*.

Das, S., Werner, J., Antonakakis, M., Polychronakis, M., & Monrose, F. (2019, May). SoK: The challenges, pitfalls, and perils of using hardware performance counters for security. In *2019 IEEE Symposium on Security and Privacy (SP)* (pp. 20-38). IEEE. 10.1109/SP.2019.00021

Derasari, P., Koppineedi, S., & Venkataramani, G. (2020, August). Can Hardware Performance Counters Detect Adversarial Inputs? In *2020 IEEE 63rd International Midwest Symposium on Circuits and Systems (MWSCAS)* (pp. 945-948). IEEE.

Do Nascimento, P. P., Colares, I. F., Maciel, R., Da Silva, H. C., & Maciel, P. (2021). Prediction, detection, and mitigation of DDOS attacks using hpcs: Design for a safer adaptive infrastructure. Handbook of Research on Cyber Crime and Information Privacy, 523-538.

Elnaggar, R., Servadei, L., Mathur, S., Wille, R., Ecker, W., & Chakrabarty, K. (2021). Accurate and Robust Malware Detection: Running XGBoost on Runtime Data From Performance Counters. *IEEE Transactions on Computer-Aided Design of Integrated Circuits and Systems*, *41*(7), 2066–2079. doi:10.1109/TCAD.2021.3102007

Fadhlillah, A., Karna, N., & Irawan, A. (2021, January). IDS performance analysis using anomaly-based detection method for DOS attack. In *2020 IEEE International Conference on Internet of Things and Intelligence System (IoTaIS)* (pp. 18-22). IEEE. 10.1109/IoTaIS50849.2021.9359719

Fischer, E. (2017, January). *Cybersecurity Issues and Challenges.* LIBRARY OF CONGRESS WASHINGTON DC.

Foreman, J. C. (2018). *A survey of cyber security countermeasures using hardware performance counters*. arXiv preprint arXiv:1807.10868.

Furfaro, A., Pace, P., & Parise, A. (2020). Facing DDoS bandwidth flooding attacks. *Simulation Modelling Practice and Theory*, *98*, 101984. doi:10.1016/j.simpat.2019.101984

Ganfure, G. O., Wu, C. F., Chang, Y. H., & Shih, W. K. (2022). Deepware: Imaging performance counters with deep learning to detect ransomware. *IEEE Transactions on Computers*, *72*(3), 600–613.

Gao, Y., Makrani, H. M., Aliasgari, M., Rezaei, A., Lin, J., Homayoun, H., & Sayadi, H. (2021, June). Adaptive-hmd: Accurate and cost-efficient machine learning-driven malware detection using microarchitectural events. In *2021 IEEE 27th International Symposium on On-Line Testing and Robust System Design (IOLTS)* (pp. 1-7). IEEE.

Garcia-Serrano, A. (2015). *Anomaly detection for malware identification using hardware performance counters*. arXiv preprint arXiv:1508.07482.

Gogoi, P., Bhattacharyya, D. K., Borah, B., & Kalita, J. K. (2011). A survey of outlier detection methods in network anomaly identification. *The Computer Journal*, *54*(4), 570–588. doi:10.1093/comjnl/bxr026

Gravelle, B. J., Nystrom, W. D., & Norris, B. (2022, November). Performance Analysis with Unified Hardware Counter Metrics. In *2022 IEEE/ACM International Workshop on Performance Modeling, Benchmarking and Simulation of High-Performance Computer Systems (PMBS)* (pp. 60-70). IEEE. 10.1109/PMBS56514.2022.00011

Gregg, B. (2019). *BPF Performance Tools*. Addison-Wesley Professional.

Gregg, B. (2019, October). Linux systems performance. In USENIX Association.

Gregg, B. (2021). *Computing Performance: On the Horizon*. USENIX Association, červen.

Gulmezoglu, B., Moghimi, A., Eisenbarth, T., & Sunar, B. (2019). *Fortuneteller: Predicting microarchitectural attacks via unsupervised deep learning*. arXiv preprint arXiv:1907.03651.

Hasan, M. K., Habib, A. A., Shukur, Z., Ibrahim, F., Islam, S., & Razzaque, M. A. (2023). Review of cyber-physical and cyber-security system in smart grid: Standards, protocols, constraints, and recommendations. *Journal of Network and Computer Applications*, *209*, 103540. doi:10.1016/j.jnca.2022.103540

He, Z., Miari, T., Makrani, H. M., Aliasgari, M., Homayoun, H., & Sayadi, H. (2021, April). When machine learning meets hardware cybersecurity: Delving into accurate zero-day malware detection. In *2021 22nd International Symposium on Quality Electronic Design (ISQED)* (pp. 85-90). IEEE.

He, Z., Miari, T., Makrani, H. M., Aliasgari, M., Homayoun, H., & Sayadi, H. (2021, April). When machine learning meets hardware cybersecurity: Delving into accurate zero-day malware detection. In *2021 22nd International Symposium on Quality Electronic Design (ISQED)* (pp. 85-90). IEEE.

IBM. (2021). *PowerPC Microprocessor Family: The Programming Environments for 64-bit Microprocessors*. IBM. https://www.ibm.com/docs/en/aix/7.2?topic=processors-powerpc-microprocessor-family

Intel. (2020). *Intel 64 and IA-32 Architectures Software Developer's Manual: Volume 3A - System Programming Guide, Part 1*. Intel. https://software.intel.com/content/www/us/en/develop/articles/intel-sdm.html

Kadiyala, S. P., Jadhav, P., Lam, S. K., & Srikanthan, T. (2020). Hardware performance counter-based fine-grained malware detection. [TECS]. *ACM Transactions on Embedded Computing Systems*, 19(5), 1–17. doi:10.1145/3403943

Khasawneh, K. N., Ozsoy, M., Donovick, C., Abu-Ghazaleh, N., & Ponomarev, D. (2015, December). Ensemble learning for low-level hardware-supported malware detection. *In Research in Attacks, Intrusions, and Defenses: 18th International Symposium, RAID 2015*, (pp. 3-25). Cham: Springer International Publishing. 10.1007/978-3-319-26362-5_1

Krishnamurthy, P., Karri, R., & Khorrami, F. (2019). Anomaly detection in real-time multi-threaded processes using hardware performance counters. *IEEE Transactions on Information Forensics and Security*, 15, 666–680. doi:10.1109/TIFS.2019.2923577

Kuruvila, A. P., Arunachalam, A., & Basu, K. (2020, December). Benefits and Challenges of Utilizing Hardware Performance Counters for COPPA Violation Detection. In *2020 IEEE Physical Assurance and Inspection of Electronics (PAINE)* (pp. 1-6). IEEE.

Kuruvila, A. P., Meng, X., Kundu, S., Pandey, G., & Basu, K. (2022). Explainable machine learning for intrusion detection via hardware performance counters. *IEEE Transactions on Computer-Aided Design of Integrated Circuits and Systems*, 41(11), 4952–4964. doi:10.1109/TCAD.2022.3149745

Lee, G., Shim, S., Cho, B., Kim, T., & Kim, K. (2021). Fileless cyberattacks: Analysis and classification. *ETRI Journal*, 43(2), 332–343. doi:10.4218/etrij.2020-0086

Li, C., & Gaudiot, J. L. (2018, September). Online detection of spectre attacks using microarchitectural traces from performance counters. In *2018 30th International Symposium on Computer Architecture and High-Performance Computing (SBAC-PAD)* (pp. 25-28). IEEE. 10.1109/CAHPC.2018.8645918

Li, C., & Gaudiot, J. L. (2021). Detecting spectre attacks using hardware performance counters. *IEEE Transactions on Computers*, 71(6), 1320–1331. doi:10.1109/TC.2021.3082471

Ling, Y., Yang, C., Li, X., Xie, M., & Ming, S. (2022, September). WEB Attack Source Tracing Technology Based on Genetic Algorithm. In *2022 7th International Conference on Cyber Security and Information Engineering (ICCSIE)* (pp. 123-126). IEEE. 10.1109/ICCSIE56462.2022.00032

Linux kernel documentation. (2022). perf events. https://www.kernel.org/doc/html/latest/perf/index.html

Maciel, P. R. M. (2023). Performance, reliability, and availability evaluation of computational systems, Volume 1: Performance and Background. CRC Press.

Maciel, P. R. M. (2023). Performance, reliability, and availability evaluation of computational systems, Volume 2: Reliability, availability modeling, measuring, and data analysis. CRC Press.

Malone, C., Zahran, M., & Karri, R. (2011, October). Are hardware performance counters a cost effective way for integrity checking of programs? In *Proceedings of the sixth ACM workshop on Scalable trusted computing* (pp. 71-76). ACM. 10.1145/2046582.2046596

Mantha, B. R., & de Soto, B. G. (2019). Cyber security challenges and vulnerability assessment in the construction industry. In *Creative Construction Conference 2019* (pp. 29-37). Budapest University of Technology and Economics. 10.3311/CCC2019-005

Microsoft. (2022). *Performance Counters*. Microsoft. https://docs.microsoft.com/en-us/windows/win32/perfctrs/performance-counters

Mirchev, M. J., & Mirtchev, S. T. (2020). System for DDoS attack mitigation by discovering the attack vectors through statistical traffic analysis. *International Journal of Information and Computer Security*, *13*(3-4), 309–321. doi:10.1504/IJICS.2020.109479

Mushtaq, M., Akram, A., Bhatti, M. K., Chaudhry, M., Lapotre, V., & Gogniat, G. (2018, June). Nightwatch: A cache-based side-channel intrusion detector using hardware performance counters. In *Proceedings of the 7th International Workshop on Hardware and Architectural Support for Security and Privacy* (pp. 1-8). ACM. 10.1145/3214292.3214293

Mushtaq, M., Benoit, P., & Farooq, U. (2020, October). Challenges of using performance counters in security against side-channel leakage. In *5th International Conference on Cyber-Technologies and Cyber-Systems (CYBER 2020)*. ACM.

NVIDIA. (2021). *NVIDIA Tegra Linux Driver Package Development Guide*. NVIDIA. https://developer.nvidia.com/embedded/dlc/tegra-linux-driver-package-development-guide

Omotosho, A., Welearegai, G. B., & Hammer, C. (2022, April). Detecting return-oriented programming on firmware-only embedded devices using hardware performance counters. In *Proceedings of the 37th ACM/SIGAPP Symposium on Applied Computing* (pp. 510-519). IEEE. 10.1145/3477314.3507108

Oracle. (2022). *Performance Analysis Guide*. Oracle Solaris 11.4 https://docs.oracle.com/en/operating-systems/solaris/solaris-11-4/perf-anal-guide/

Pan, Z., Sheldon, J., & Mishra, P. (2022). Hardware-assisted malware detection and localization using explainable machine learning. *IEEE Transactions on Computers*, *71*(12), 3308–3321. doi:10.1109/TC.2022.3150573

Rahmani, H., Sahli, N., & Kammoun, F. (2009, August). Joint entropy analysis model for DDoS attack detection. In *2009 Fifth International Conference on Information Assurance and Security* (Vol. 2, pp. 267-271). IEEE. 10.1109/IAS.2009.298

Sahoo, K. S., Tripathy, B. K., Naik, K., Ramasubbareddy, S., Balusamy, B., Khari, M., & Burgos, D. (2020). An evolutionary SVM model for DDOS attack detection in software defined networks. *IEEE Access: Practical Innovations, Open Solutions, 8*, 132502–132513. doi:10.1109/ACCESS.2020.3009733

Sayadi, H., Patel, N., Sasan, A., Rafatirad, S., & Homayoun, H. (2018, June). Ensemble learning for effective run-time hardware-based malware detection: A comprehensive analysis and classification. In *Proceedings of the 55th Annual Design Automation Conference* (pp. 1-6). IEEE. 10.1145/3195970.3196047

Sayadi, H., Wang, H., Miari, T., Makrani, H. M., Aliasgari, M., Rafatirad, S., & Homayoun, H. (2020, August). Recent advancements in microarchitectural security: Review of machine learning countermeasures. In *2020 IEEE 63rd International Midwest Symposium on Circuits and Systems (MWSCAS)* (pp. 949-952). IEEE.

Sobb, T., Turnbull, B., & Moustafa, N. (2020). Supply chain 4.0: A survey of cyber security challenges, solutions and future directions. *Electronics (Basel), 9*(11), 1864. doi:10.3390/electronics9111864

Tan, B., & Karri, R. (2020, August). Challenges and new directions for ai and hardware security. In *2020 IEEE 63rd International Midwest Symposium on Circuits and Systems (MWSCAS)* (pp. 277-280). IEEE. 10.1109/MWSCAS48704.2020.9184612

Tinetti, F. G., & Méndez, M. (2014, March). An automated approach to hardware performance monitoring counters. In *2014 International Conference on Computational Science and Computational Intelligence* (Vol. 1, pp. 71-76). IEEE. 10.1109/CSCI.2014.19

Van Geit, W., De Schutter, E., & Achard, P. (2008). Automated neuron model optimization techniques: A review. *Biological Cybernetics, 99*(4-5), 241–251. doi:10.100700422-008-0257-6 PMID:19011918

Wang, H., Sayadi, H., Rafatirad, S., Sasan, A., & Homayoun, H. (2020, July). Scarf: Detecting side-channel attacks in real-time using low-level hardware features. In *2020 IEEE 26th International Symposium on On-Line Testing and Robust System Design (IOLTS)* (pp. 1-6). IEEE.

Wang, M., Zheng, K., Yang, Y., & Wang, X. (2020). An explainable machine learning framework for intrusion detection systems. *IEEE Access: Practical Innovations, Open Solutions, 8*, 73127–73141. doi:10.1109/ACCESS.2020.2988359

Wang, X., Konstantinou, C., Maniatakos, M., & Karri, R. (2015, November). Confirm: Detecting firmware modifications in embedded systems using hardware performance counters. In *2015 IEEE/ACM International Conference on Computer-Aided Design (ICCAD)* (pp. 544-551). IEEE. 10.1109/ICCAD.2015.7372617

Weaver, V. M. (2013, April). Linux perf_event features and overhead. In The 2nd international workshop on performance analysis of workload optimized systems. *FastPath, 13*(5).

Woo, L. L., Zwolinski, M., & Halak, B. (2018, March). Early detection of system-level anomalous behaviour using hardware performance counters. In *2018 Design, Automation & Test in Europe Conference & Exhibition (DATE)*, (pp. 485-490). IEEE.

Xin, Y., Kong, L., Liu, Z., Chen, Y., Li, Y., Zhu, H., Gao, M., Hou, H., & Wang, C. (2018). Machine learning and deep learning methods for cybersecurity. *IEEE Access : Practical Innovations, Open Solutions*, *6*, 35365–35381. doi:10.1109/ACCESS.2018.2836950

Xue, Y., Tang, T., & Liu, A. X. (2019). Large-scale feedforward neural network optimization by a self-adaptive strategy and parameter-based particle swarm optimization. *IEEE Access : Practical Innovations, Open Solutions*, *7*, 52473–52483. doi:10.1109/ACCESS.2019.2911530

Yu, M., Halak, B., & Zwolinski, M. (2019, July). Using hardware performance counters to detect control hijacking attacks. In *2019 IEEE 4th International Verification and Security Workshop (IVSW)* (pp. 1-6). IEEE. 10.1109/IVSW.2019.8854399

Zamani, R., & Afsahi, A. (2012, June). A study of hardware performance monitoring counter selection in power modeling of computing systems. In *2012 International Green Computing Conference (IGCC)* (pp. 1-10). IEEE. 10.1109/IGCC.2012.6322289

Zhang, X., Dwarkadas, S., Folkmanis, G., & Shen, K. (2007, May). Processor hardware counter statistics as a first-class system resource. In HotOS.

Zhou, B., Gupta, A., Jahanshahi, R., Egele, M., & Joshi, A. (2018, May). Hardware performance counters can detect malware: Myth or fact? In *Proceedings of the 2018 on Asia conference on computer and communications security* (pp. 457-468). IEEE. 10.1145/3196494.3196515

Zhou, B., Gupta, A., Jahanshahi, R., Egele, M., & Joshi, A. (2021). A cautionary tale about detecting malware using hardware performance counters and machine learning. *IEEE Design & Test*, *38*(3), 39–50. doi:10.1109/MDAT.2021.3063338

Chapter 8
How Can Cyberhate Victimization and Perpetration Be Understood?
Towards a Psychological Approach

Maria Vale

Psychology Research Centre (CIPsi), School of Psychology, University of Minho, Braga, Portugal

Marlene Matos

Psychology Research Centre (CIPsi), School of Psychology, University of Minho, Braga, Portugal

ABSTRACT

The freedom of expression enabled through information and communication technologies (ICT) has been misused to create, (re)produce, and distribute cyberhate. Otherwise known as online hate speech, it refers to all forms of ICT-mediated expression that incites, justifies, or propagates hatred or violence against specific individuals or groups based on their gender, race, ethnicity, religion, sexual orientation, or other collective characteristics. This chapter aims to contribute to a comprehensive analysis of cyberhate among adolescents and adults. It is structured into three main sections. The first operationalizes the key conceptual characteristics, disentangles the similarities and differences between cyberhate and other forms of violence, and presents the known prevalence of victimization and perpetration. The second identifies the main sociodemographic correlates and discriminates the risk and protective factors with theoretical frameworks. The chapter concludes with recommendations for prevention and intervention strategies that demand a multi-stakeholder approach.

INTRODUCTION

Modern societies live in the digital age, with access to and use of information and communication technologies (ICT) ubiquitously integrated into their quotidian experiences. Early in 2023, there were 5.44 billion mobile phone or smartphone users worldwide, 5.16 billion Internet users, and 4.76 billion social media users, which is equivalent to 68%, 64.4%, and 59.4% of the world's total population, respectively (Kemp, 2023).

DOI: 10.4018/979-8-3693-1528-6.ch008

The adolescent generation has often stood out in these statistics (Gen Z, born 1997–2009; Dimock, 2019). In the United States of America, the most recent survey of the Pew Research Center on the Internet and Technology documented that nearly all adolescents had access to smartphones (95%), desktop or laptop computers (90%), and gaming consoles (80%). YouTube (95%), TikTok (67%), Instagram (62%), and Snapchat (59%) dominated their social media landscape, with 97% of them accessing the Internet daily and 46% almost constantly (Vogels et al., 2022; $N = 1316$, 13-17 years old). The cross-cultural report conducted by the EU Kids Online Network identified similar digital patterns among 25,101 adolescents aged 9 to 16 years old from nineteen European countries (Smahel et al., 2020). Specifically, in Portugal, most households with adolescents up to 15 years of age had Internet access at home (99.2%), and 97% surfed via mobile broadband (Instituto Nacional de Estatística [Statistical National Institute], 2022; $N = 6594$ households, with at least one person aged 16 to 74 years old). Fully 87% of adolescents logged on via smartphones, 41% via desktop or laptop computers, and 25% via tablets (Ponte & Batista, 2019; $N = 1974$, 9-16 years old). Their top online activities included consulting or sharing content on TikTok (43.1%), exchanging messages on WhatsApp (38.8%), consulting or sharing content on Instagram (37.1%), watching series (37%), playing online games (36.4%), and watching videos on YouTube (32.7%), accounting for two or more hours on a typical weekday (Gaspar et al., 2022; $N = 5809$, 11-15 years old).

Adults' generations have also embraced these digital tools and habits (Millennials, born 1981–1996; Gen Xers, born 1965–1980; Baby Boomers, born 1946–1964; Silent Generation, born 1945 and earlier; Dimock, 2019; Vogels, 2019). In the United States of America, a Pew Research Center survey on the Internet and Technology revealed that smartphone ownership (85%) and home broadband subscriptions (77%) were increasingly common (Perrin, 2021; $N = 1502$, 18-65 years old or older). More than eight-in-ten adults were online at least daily (85%), and about three-in-ten were online almost constantly (31%; Perrin & Atske, 2021; $N = 1502$, 18-65 years old or older). A majority used YouTube (81%) and Facebook (69%), with Instagram, Snapchat, and TikTok being more popular among those under 30 years old (Auxier & Anderson, 2021; $N = 1502$, 18-65 years old or older). The annual statistics on ICT access and use by individuals and households throughout the member states of the European Union revealed consistent trends (Eurostat, 2022). Specifically, in Portugal, 88.2% of households had an Internet connection at home, and 84.6% had a broadband connection. The most common Internet activities among adults were exchanging instant messages (91.8%, e.g., WhatsApp, Messenger), sending or receiving emails (87.9%), searching for information about goods or services (86.1%), reading online news (81.8%), making calls (81.5%, e.g., video calls), participating in social network sites (79%), listening to music (69.5%), and banking services (68.0%; Instituto Nacional de Estatística [Statistical National Institute], 2022; $N = 6594$ households, with at least one person aged 16 to 74 years old).

This level of network immersion allows people to easily exchange their opinions, ideas, and information, but it has also led to information disorder and its associated perils. Overall, the conceptual framework of information disorder considers three elements: a) the agent, which is the person, group, or organization that creates, (re)produces, and distributes the message, as well as their motivations, intention to mislead and/or harm, and audience; b) the message, which is information, and its formats, characteristics, and duration; and c) the interpreter, which is the reader, and how they interpret the message (Wardle & Derakhshan, 2017; Wardle, 2018). Three stages can also lead to information disorder: a) creation, when the message is produced; b) (re)production, when the message is turned into a media product; and c) distribution, when the media product is made available to the public (Wardle & Derakhshan, 2017; Wardle, 2018). Based on the falseness and harm dimensions, information disorder can be distinguished into three types: a) misinformation, which is information that is false but not intended to cause harm (e.g., false connection[1], misleading content[2]); b) disinformation, which is information that is false and intended to cause harm (e.g., false context[3], imposter content[4], manipulated content[5], and fabricated content[6]); and c) malinformation, which is truthful information that is intended to cause harm (e.g., some forms of leaks, harassment, and cyberhate; see the full theoretical model in Wardle & Derakhshan, 2017; Wardle, 2018).

This conceptual chapter aims to contribute to a comprehensive and integrated analysis of cyberhate among adolescents and adults. It is structured into three main sections. The first operationalizes the key conceptual characteristics, disentangles the theoretical similarities and differences between cyberhate and other forms of violence, and presents the known prevalence of victimization and perpetration among adolescents and adults. The second identifies the main sociodemographic correlates and discriminates the risk and protective factors with theoretical frameworks and the unique effects of ICT. The chapter concludes with recommendations for prevention and intervention strategies that demand a multi-stakeholder approach.

CYBERHATE: (IN)DEFINITION AND PREVALENCE OF VICTIMIZATION AND PERPETRATION

Cyberhate (otherwise known as "online hate", "online hate speech", or "online extremism"; Bauman et al., 2021; Bernatzky et al., 2022; Costello & Hawdon, 2018) lies in a complex nexus of misused, unmediated, and unregulated freedom of speech (Bauman et al., 2021; Castaño-Pulgarín et al., 2021; Chetty & Alathur, 2018). The debate about its universal conceptualization is still ongoing (Bauman et al., 2021; Windisch et al., 2022). Meanwhile, cyberhate has been defined as all forms of ICT-mediated expression that incite, justify, or propagate hatred or violence against individuals or groups based on their gender, race, ethnicity, religion, sexual orientation, or other collective characteristics (Anti-Defamation League, 2016; Bauman et al., 2021; Bernatzky et al., 2022; Blaya & Audrin, 2019; Bliuc et al., 2018; Castaño-Pulgarín et al., 2021; Chetty & Alathur, 2018; Council of Europe, 2016; Costello et al., 2019; Wachs et al., 2021a; Wachs et al., 2021b). Considering the complexity of this phenomenon, each of its conceptual components will be examined in further depth in the following paragraphs.

Firstly, the authors of cyberhate may be individuals or members of organized hate movements. The Internet has facilitated an easier and more affordable process for any ordinary individual to create, (re) produce, and disseminate hateful content, as well as engage in communication with hate groups without the need for a formal affiliation (Blaya & Audrin, 2019; Blaya et al., 2020; Bernatzky et al., 2022; Costello & Hawdon, 2018; Southern Poverty Law Center, 2020, 2021). At the same time, organized hate groups swiftly recognized the Internet as a valuable tool for their activities. It provided them with the means to operate anonymously, disseminate and popularize their hateful and radicalized ideologies, indoctrinate and recruit new sympathizers, reinforce transnational identities, acquire funding, and coordinate acts of hate-based violence (Bauman et al., Wachs, 2021; Blaya & Audrin, 2019; Costello & Hawdon, 2018; Hawdon et al., 2014). Although some of them have been banned and have resurfaced on encrypted platforms (Southern Poverty Law Center, 2020, 2021), the most recent report from the Southern Poverty Law Center listed 733 active hate groups in the United States of America, including General Hate ($n = 65$), White Nationalist ($n = 98$), Anti-LGBTQ ($n = 65$), Antisemitism ($n = 61$), Neo-Nazi ($n = 54$), Anti-Muslim ($n = 50$), Neo-Völkisch (n = 32), Ku Klux Kan ($n = 18$), Anti-Immigrant

($n = 18$), Racist Skinhead ($n = 17$), Neo-Confederate ($n = 16$), and Christian Identity ($n = 9$; Southern Poverty Law Center, 2021).

Secondly, the intended targets of cyberhate reflect historical, social, and cultural movements, along with their status within different societies. Cyberhate is most commonly manifested as the expression of prejudices, stereotypes, and/or extrapolations based on the characteristics of minority, oppressed, and marginalized individuals or groups (Bauman et al., 2021). These characteristics can be alleged or identified, assigned or selected, and include, but are not limited to: gender (e.g., sexism, misogyny, transphobia), race or ethnic background (e.g., racism, regionalism, nativism, xenophobia), religion (e.g., anti-Christianity, anti-Islamism, anti-Muslim, anti-Hinduism), sexual orientation (e.g., homophobia), immigrant status, and political affiliation (Bauman et al., 2021; Bedrosova et al., 2022; Blaya & Audrin, 2019; Blaya et al., 2020; Bliuc et al., 2018; Castaño-Pulgarín et al., 2021; Chetty & Alathur, 2018; Fortuna & Nunes, 2018; Hawdon et al., 2014).

Thirdly, cyberhate can manifest itself in both subtle expressions (e.g., humor, irony, sarcasm, and generalizations), and overt incitements to hatred (e.g., hostile, resentful, or angry tone); various forms of hate can be observed, including text, memes, stickers, images, videos, and/or graphic representations, all of which can appear in both the main content and comment sections of online platforms; it can be encountered on video sharing sites (e.g., YouTube), social networking sites (e.g., Instagram, Facebook, Twitter, Tumblr), personal blogs, public forums, newspaper message boards, interactive online games, and even on the deep or dark web (e.g., 4chan, 8chan, EndChan; Bauman et al., 2021; Blaya & Audrin, 2019; Costello & Hawdon, 2018; Fortuna & Nunes, 2018; Hawdon et al., 2014; Reichelmann et al., 2021; Rieger et al., 2021). The selection of these online channels appears to vary. For instance, Bliuc and colleagues (2018) conducted a comprehensive systematic review spanning ten years of research on cyber-racism. They revealed that individual cyber-racism is communicated through diverse channels, including forums, chat rooms, social networking sites, blogs, and YouTube videos. In contrast, group-based cyber-racism appears to be predominantly confined to websites associated with specific groups. Furthermore, political fringe communities such as Reddit, 4chan, and 8chan have repeatedly been linked to right-wing extremist terrorists (Rieger et al., 2021).

Subsequently, although cyberhate may consist of a single act without explicitly highlighting its repetitive nature, Windisch and colleagues (2022) argued that comprehending it necessitates the recognition of a continuum of processes encompassing both victimization and perpetration, thereby establishing connections across varying degrees of severity. Building upon an adapted version of Allport's scale of prejudice (1954), the manifestation of cyberhate may begin with anti-locution (or cyberhate, which involves expressing prejudice against friends or strangers) and subsequently progress through avoidance (the act of avoiding individuals or members of certain social groups), discrimination (the act of distinguishing and excluding them based on prejudice), physical attacks (the act of physically assaulting them), and finally culminate in eradication (the act of eradicating them; Windisch et al., 2022). With that in mind, there are some examples of how online extremist narratives spilled over into hate-fueled real-life acts of violence, such as the mass shootings that took place at the Walmart store in El Paso (Texas, United States of America), at the synagogue in Poway (California, United States of America), and at the mosques in Christchurch (New Zealand, Australia; Castaño-Pulgarín et al., 2021; Rieger et al., 2021; Windisch et al., 2022). Additional related insights are put forth by Chetty and Alathur (2018). As per their propositions, cyberhate can unfold in distinct stages following trigger incidents: a) influence stage (immediately after the incident, there will be a heavy flow on social networking sites); b) intervention stage (after a few days, it will decrease); c) response stage (after a few more days, it will subside to nil); and d) rebirth stage (after a considerable time, there is a possibility of it resurfacing; Chetty & Alathur, 2018).

Still, the harmfulness experienced by individuals as victims of or witnesses to cyberhate depends on the specific persons and circumstances involved (Chetty & Alathur, 2018). For example, in a study involving 2,592 individuals aged 18-25 years old from the United States of America, the United Kingdom, Finland, Poland, France, and Spain, it was observed that 70.7% of respondents had been exposed to hateful or degrading writings or speech online that attacked individuals or groups of people in the preceding three months (Reichelmann et al., 2021). Subsequently, after such exposition, a significant majority of respondents reported experiencing emotions of anger (65%), sadness (64.8%), and shame (51.0%), with a substantial proportion also indicating feelings of guilt (22.6%) and pride (17%; Reichelmann et al., 2021). Through an exploration of the impact of LGBTQ+ cyberhate on 175 individuals aged 13-25 years old, predominantly from the United Kingdom, one study documented adverse effects on their well-being and social interactions. These effects included experiences of sadness and depression, shame and self-blame, feelings of inferiority and invalid identities, fear and a sense of lack of safety, as well as instances of isolation and withdrawal from online and offline spaces (Keighley, 2022). However, cyberhate carries the potential to cause serious repercussions not only for individuals but also for communities. In addition to subjecting the targets of cyberhate to humiliation, degradation, stigmatization, and dehumanization, these acts also present a threat to human rights, fundamental freedoms, democratic outcomes, and social cohesion (Bauman et al., 2021; Bliuc et al., 2018; Blaya & Audrin, 2019; Blaya et al., 2020; Chetty & Alathur, 2018).

Examining the similarities and differences between cyberhate and other forms of violence can offer valuable insights into the intricacies of this phenomenon. Among these concepts are cyber-aggression, cyber-harassment, cyber dating abuse, and cyberbullying. Additionally, there are broader constructs such as extremism, hate crimes, terrorism, and cyber-terrorism that also warrant consideration.

Cyber-aggression (also known as cyberviolence) is an umbrella term that encompasses a wide range of ICT-mediated interpersonal aggressive behaviors, including subsets such as cyberhate, cyber-harassment, cyber dating abuse, and cyberbullying (Bedrosova et al., 2022; Vale et al., 2018).

Cyber-harassment has been conceptualized as any kind of repeated, intentional, and unwanted ICT-mediated interpersonal aggression that entails dominance, coercion, and emotional harm. This includes behaviours labeled as cyber sexual harassment (e.g., pressuring someone to send erotic or pornographic messages or to share nude images, as well as engaging in phone sex), cyber obsessional relational intrusion[7] (e.g., sending exaggerated messages of affection), cyberstalking(e.g., initially meeting online and then improperly approaching, intimidating, or pursuing the victim physically), and cyberbullying (e.g., sending insulting, humiliating, or threatening messages; Pereira & Matos, 2015; Pereira & Matos, 2016; Pereira et al., 2016; Vale et al., 2022).

Cyber dating abuse refers to a pattern of repeated, intentional, and unwanted abusive behaviours that a current and/or former partner exerts over the other through ICT: threats (e.g., intimidating to emotionally and/or physically harm the current and/or former partner, their families, or their friends); humiliation (e.g., starting a social networking page for posting negative information about the current and/or former partner); monitoring or control (e.g., making the current and/or former partner disclose digital conversation(s) they've had with another person(s); and sexual coercion (e.g., sharing a nude photo or video of the current and/or former partner without their permission; Brown & Hegarty, 2021; Brown et al., 2021; Vale et al., 2020; Vale et al., 2021).

Researchers have also highlighted the urgent need to distinguish between cyberbullying and cyberhate. Despite both using similar online channels, sharing the intention to inflict harm upon specific individuals or groups, and occasionally overlapping in their manifestations, they are not identical in all theoretical components (Blaya et al., 2020; Bedrosova et al., 2022). Cyberbullying is characterized as recurring behavior that takes place over an extended period with a focus on targeting individuals rather than communities (i.e., individual focus; typically involves peers within the same school environment or extracurricular activities). It involves an asymmetric power imbalance between the victim and the perpetrator (e.g., which may stem from physical strength, psychological confidence, or technological expertise). The motivation behind cyberbullying can be diverse, including internal and external factors (e.g., seeking entertainment, dealing with boredom, feelings of jealousy, seeking revenge, desiring acceptance; Aboujaoude et al., 2015; Blaya et al., 2020; Hinduja & Patchin, 2011; Smith et al., 2008; Smith, 2012; Vale et al., 2020; Varjas et al., 2010). On the other hand, cyberhate does not have to be repetitive and long-lasting, tends to target communities rather than individuals (collective focus; (un) known individuals, selected based on identified or assumed group characteristics), is driven by the perpetrator's prejudices and stereotypical ideas, and aims to stigmatize and dehumanize the identity and the community to which the victim belongs (Bedrosova et al., 2022; Blaya et al., 2020). An examination of the structural relationship between these two types of violence revealed that cyberbullying and cyberhate share some common factors, such as higher age, time spent online, exposure to harmful online content, and emotional symptoms. However, they are also different from each other and, to some degree, related by different correlates. Specifically, individual-based discrimination (e.g., height, weight, appearance, behaviour, opinions, or beliefs) was associated with cyberbullying but did not predict cyberhate involvement, while group-based/community-based discrimination (e.g., family background, skin colour, religion) predicted cyberhate and, to a lesser extent, cyberbullying (Bedrosova et al., 2022; N = 3,855, aged 11–17 years old, from the Czech Republic, Poland, and Slovakia).

Briefly, extremism refers to racial, religious, political, social, and/or other ideologies that deviate from accepted societal norms and are often linked to hate organizations and extremist movements (Chetty & Alathur, 2018; Fortuna & Nunes, 2018). Hate crimes are crimes against a person, group, or property with an added element of bias. These offenses may include threats, arson, vandalism, assault, and homicide (Chetty & Alathur, 2018). According to the Federal Bureau of Investigation's Uniform Crime Reporting Program's annual report, there were 8,763 bias-motivated offenses and 7,314 reported hate crimes in the United States of America (FBI, 2021). Under the Portuguese legal framework, cyberhate is criminally punishable[8], but it is only considered a hate crime when it takes this form of conduct, being a criminal offense with an aggravating circumstance (Lei n.º 94/2017, de 23 de agosto [Law no. 94/2017, of 23 August]). Still, terrorism can be characterized as the intimidation or coercion of the civilian population through life-threatening acts or the commitment of real-life acts of violence that have the potential to cause mass destruction, homicide, abduction, or other serious crimes (Chetty & Alathur, 2018). When those acts of terrorism are facilitated through ICT, they become known as cyber-terrorism. Similar to extremist movements, cyberhate and the process of radicalization can be prevalent elements in (cyber) terrorist activities (Chetty & Alathur, 2018).

Regardless of the operational definition of cyberhate, different roles can be played, such as those of bystanders (i.e., those who see or hear cyberhate), victims (i.e., those who are and/or feel targeted by cyberhate), and/or perpetrators (i.e., those who create, (re)produce, and disseminate cyberhate; Bedrosova et al., 2022; Hawdon et al., 2014; Machakova et al., 2020; Reichelmann et al., 2021; Wachs & Wright, 2018; Wachs et al., 2019). Exposure to cyberhate seems inevitable, with existing research suggesting that being a bystander is the most prevalent form of experiencing cyberhate (Bedrosova et al., 2022; Blaya & Audrin, 2019; Hawdon et al., 2015; Machakova et al., 2020; Wachs & Wright, 2018; Wachs et al., 2019). While not all instances of exposure to cyberhate result in becoming a victim or perpetrator, the evidence suggests that these rates are also alarming. The following are some research-survey studies from different American, Asian, and European countries that illustrate these issues.

Studies with samples of adolescents found that of 9,459 adolescents aged 11-17 years old from the Czech Republic, Finland, Flanders, France, Italy, Lithuania, Norway, Poland, Romania, and Slovakia, the percentage who had received hateful and degrading messages or comments online against them or their community in the last 12 months varied from 3% (Italy) to 13% (Poland). In all countries, less than 2% of adolescents reported experiencing victimization on a daily or weekly basis (Machakova et al., 2020); and, of 6,829 adolescents aged 12-18 years old from the United States of America, South Korea, Thailand, India, Cyprus, Greece, Germany, and Spain, 14.2% reported posting hateful or degrading writing or speech online, which inappropriately attacked individuals or certain groups based on their sex, race, sexual orientation, and religious affiliation, at least once within the last 12 months. Prevalence rates of cyberhate perpetrators varied from 4.2% among South Korean adolescents to 32.2% among Thai adolescents (Wachs et al., 2019).

Studies with samples of adults found that of 10,093 adults aged 18-65 years old or older from the United States of America, 20% reported being harassed online due to their political views, 14% due to their gender, 12% due to their race or ethnicity background, 8% due to their religion, and 7% due to their sexual orientation (Vogels, 2021); and of, 4,878 adults aged 18-26 years old from the United States of America, the United Kingdom, Finland, Poland, France, and Spain, the percentage who reported experiencing at least one attack online based on their characteristics (e.g., gender, ethnicity, religion, political views) in the preceding three months varied from 43.33% (Finland) to 72.95% (United States of America), and the percentage of adults who reported producing hateful or degrading writings or speech online that attacked specific individuals or groups varied from 8.78% (Poland) to 19.29% (United States of America; Celuch et al., 2022).

Portugal is still in an embryonic stage regarding the conduct of this kind of studies focused on cyberhate victimization and perpetration. However, the latest annual reports have documented alarming figures. Out of 27,887 crimes and other reported situations, 210 were related to discrimination and incitement to hate and violence. Moreover, 190 out of 810 reports of illegal content available on the Internet were related to cyberhate (Associação Portuguesa de Apoio à Vítima [Portuguese Association for Victim Support], 2022a, 2022b). Additionally, 60 of the 418 reported situations of alleged discrimination occurred on social networking websites or the Internet. Most of these incidents did not target specific individuals but rather communities or social groups, such as Brazilian nationality, Roma ethnicity, and Black skin color (Comissão para a Igualdade contra a Discriminação Racial [Portuguese Comission for Equality Against Racial Discrimination], 2021).

The variability in the estimation of prevalence rates of cyberhate is often attributed to conceptual and methodological differences among various studies. These differences can include the definition of cyberhate (using a broad definition or focusing on specific behaviours targeting some minorities, oppressed, and marginalized individuals or groups), measures of cyberhate (employing specific items developed for this purpose or adapting items from other scales), time frames of experiences (e.g., the last three months, the last year, lifetime), response options (e.g., categorical, continuous), perspectives considered (victimization and/or perpetration), as well as the characteristics of the samples (e.g., gender identity, age, race, and ethnic background; Bauman et al., 2021). Additionally, cultural and legal differences can also contribute to this variability in the prevalence of cyberhate. For example, in the United States of America, the First Amendment ensures the protection of freedom of speech, which can influence tolerance for certain forms of expression. On the other hand, member states of the European Union have been taking specific measures to regulate and combat cyberhate (e.g., the EU Hate Speech Code of Conduct; Project Hate No More: training and awareness raising to combat crime and hate speech; and, the Lisbon Declaration: Digital Democracy with a Purpose, an initiative recently developed by the Portuguese Presidency of the Council of the European Union).

CYBERHATE: SOCIODEMOGRAPHIC CORRELATES AND THEORETICAL FRAMEWORKS

The literature on the sociodemographic characterization of those involved in cyberhate shows unclear or inconsistent findings. Some studies suggest that gender may not be a significant predictor of involvement in cyberhate (e.g., Görzig et al., 2023; Wachs et al., 2020; Wachs et al., 2021). On the other hand, other studies indicated that females were more often victims, while males tended to be perpetrators of cyberhate (e.g., Blaya & Audrin, 2019; Costello & Hawdon, 2018; Wachs & Wright, 2018; Wachs et al., 2019). These findings align with the insights of Celuch and colleagues (2022), where females were less likely to report accepting cyberhate in half of their samples in Finland, Poland, and the United States of America. These results also resonate with the dominant male-oriented and patriarchal social structure, where males have a greater tendency to engage in other cyber criminal behaviors (Pereira et al., 2016; Vale et al., 2018). Regarding age, some studies have found that increasing age is associated with higher odds of being a victim or perpetrator of cyberhate (e.g., Wachs et al., 2019). Particularly in the context of adolescents, this may be attributed to older adolescents exhibiting specific developmental needs, curiosities, and desires, which can lead to more frequent engagement in cyber-practices and risks, where there is also a decrease in parental mediation (Pereira et al., 2016; Vale et al., 2018; Vale et al., 2022).

Additionally, beyond sociodemographic correlates, scholars in the fields of psychology and criminology have emphasized the need for comprehensive theoretical frameworks to identify the individual, relational, and contextual factors influencing the likelihood of cyberhate victimization and perpetration.

According to Bauman and colleagues (2021), Erikson's Theory of Stages of Psychosocial Development (1963) is essential in explaining why children and adolescents are at a heightened risk of cyberhate involvement. This theory proposes that the development of a person's personality may be broken down into eight sequential stages that begin in childhood and continue into late adulthood. In each of these stages, there is a psychosocial crisis that must be resolved by the successful completion of a developmental task. These tasks have an impact on how individuals relate to their inner and outer worlds. During the fourth psychosocial stage (industry vs. inferiority, 5-12 years old), children develop skills in (extra) curricular activities, and their classmates' recognition of their accomplishments is critical to their self-esteem and self-concept (Bauman et al., 2021; Erikson, 1963). However, those who do not acquire this sense of competence develop a sense of inferiority. When this occurs, children may doubt their abilities, feel like they don't fit in with their peers, and be vulnerable to hate content and hate-groups recruiting strategies. Through this interaction, they begin to attribute their feelings of inferiority to certain social groups and diminish them, and when they are appreciated for engaging in cyberhate, they get a sense of competence that they have never felt before (Bauman et al., 2021).

In the fifth psychosocial stage (identity vs. role confusion, 12-18 years old), adolescents are developing their sense of self in diverse domains (e.g., gender, ethnicity, religion, and sexuality; Bauman et al., 2021; Erikson, 1963). If access to and use of ICT can help them meet this developmental task by allowing them to identify and differentiate, develop critical thinking, self-explore intellectual, entertainment, and sexual interests, and refine socio-emotional skills (Gaspar et al., 2022; Ponte & Batista, 2019; Smahel et al., 2020; Vale et al., 2018; Vogels et al., 2022), they might also interfere with these processes. Adolescents who are struggling to establish their different identities and feel isolated can be vulnerable to individuals or organized hate movements. These groups offer them acceptance when it may be lacking elsewhere (Bauman et al., 2021) and disseminate content that can be aesthetically appealing and tailored to their cultural trends. Proof of that can be found in the percentage of cyberhate exposure in online multiplayer games. According to the latest report from the Anti-Defamation League in the United States of America, 26% of adolescents reported exposure to white supremacist ideologies on social media networks, and 16% encountered these ideologies in online multiplayer games (e.g., Dota 2, PUBG: Battlegrounds, Valorant, World of Warcraft, Grand Theft Auto, Overwatch, or Call of Duty; Anti-Defamation League, 2022).

Other insights are derived from major victimology and criminology paradigms. For example, Cohen and Felson's Lifestyle-Routine Activities Theory (1979) considers structural opportunities as a causal mechanism for crimes. Victimization occurs because of the intersection, in time and space, between the exposure or proximity to motivated perpetrators, attractive targets, and the absence of capable guardianship (Cohen & Felson, 1979; Eck & Clarke, 2003; Hindelang et al., 1978; Miethe & Meier, 1990; Reyns et al., 2011). Although some questions remain unexplored about their usefulness in ICT-mediated interpersonal aggressive behaviors (e.g., Yar, 2005), this theory has been gaining empirical support in understanding factors that lead individuals to fall victim to cyberhate (e.g., Wachs et al., 2021a; Wachs et al., 2021b).

Individuals who act on their pre-existing criminal tendencies are considered motivated perpetrators. While exposure alludes to how accessible an individual is to a perpetrator, proximity alludes to the likelihood of coming into contact with a perpetrator (Cohen & Felson, 1979; Hindelang et al., 1978; Miethe & Meier, 1990). Studies that tested this theory with samples of adolescents found that excessive Internet use and witnessing cyberhate seemed to increase the visibility of and the likelihood of contact with motivated perpetrators, thereby increasing the likelihood of cyberhate victimization (Wachs et al., 2021a; Wachs et al., 2021b).

Once an individual is exposed or in proximity, the target's attractiveness represents how the individual's characteristics and individual lifestyle choices and activities make them appear like a potentially rewarding opportunity to motivated perpetrators (Cohen & Felson, 1979; Hindelang et al., 1978; Miethe & Meier, 1990). Similarly, specific cyber risky routines, such as disclosing personal information, contacting unknown people online, and experiencing data misuse, seem to increase the target's suitability, thereby increasing the likelihood of cyberhate victimization (Wachs et al., 2021a; Wachs et al., 2021b).

Considering such exposure and attractiveness, this theory focuses on how capable guardianship can prevent the occurrence of victimization (Cohen & Felson, 1979; Hindelang et al., 1978; Miethe & Meier, 1990). Findings support the hypothesis that adolescents' experience of problematic sharenting facets (e.g., "I received negative or hurtful comments from someone because of something my parent or caregiver published online") was positively related to the risk of being a victim of cyberhate (Wachs et al., 2021b). Furthermore, while the adolescents' perception of being subjected to the restrictive strategies of parental mediation on the Internet also increased such vulnerability (i.e., implementing rules without dialogue, restricting the use of the Internet or access to specific websites; e.g., "My parents check my Facebook, WhatsApp, or other profiles on other networks"), the instructive strategies of parental mediation demonstrated the opposite effect (i.e., parental guidance, collaboration, and support; e.g., "My parents show me how to use the Internet and warn me about its risks"; Wachs et al., 2021a). Other studies have also supported the usefulness of these instructive strategies, revealing a positive association between them and the use of problem-focused coping strategies in response to cyberhate. Therefore, these adolescents' capability to cope included strategies such as distal advice (e.g., "go to the police"), close support (e.g., "spending time with my friends to take my mind off it"), assertiveness (e.g., "tell the person to stop it"), and technical coping (e.g., "block that person so that he or she cannot contact me anymore"; Wachs et al., 2020; Wright et al., 2021). The adolescents' perception of family support was found to strengthen the positive relationship between instructive strategies of parental mediation and problem-focused coping strategies towards cyberhate (Wright et al., 2021). Other studies explored the role of friends in relation to cyberhate. For example, Bedrosova and colleagues (2022) found a certain tendency for perceived friend support to be negatively associated with cyberhate in two countries (Czech Republic and Poland). Furthermore, a supportive peer environment emerged as a protective factor against cyberhate victimization due to perceived discrimination and lower life satisfaction (Görzig et al., 2023).

Lifestyle-Routine Activities Theory is often used to explain victimization. However, the acknowledged overlap of roles between victims and perpetrators (Jennings, Piquero, & Reingle, 2012; Lauritsen, Sampson, & Laub, 1991; Posick, 2013) has led researchers to think that exposure to online hate materials and participation in group attacks would have a positive relationship (Hawdon et al., 2019). The theory's applicability received no support. High social networking site usage did not demonstrate a significant relationship, time spent online per day exhibited a negative relationship, and living alone also failed to show a significant association with joining an online attack on a targeted group when witnessing such an attack occurring (Hawdon et al., 2019).

Gottfredson and Hirschi's General Theory of Crime (1990) offers an insightful explanation for cyberhate perpetration. The theory revolves around the concept of "self-control", which refers to an individual's ability to regulate their own emotions, thoughts, and behaviours. This trait or characteristic is believed to be established in early childhood through parental or caregiver supervision and the transmission of social values and norms. Individuals who experience a lack of parental mediation and inadequate socialization are more likely to possess lower levels of self-control. Consequently, they may exhibit certain characteristics, including impulsivity, insensitivity, risk-taking, and nonverbal behaviours. These characteristics can predispose them towards delinquency, criminal acts, and other problem behaviours, whenever opportunities materialize in the direction of such deviation, especially when they perceive immediate or near-term gratification for engaging in them (Gottfredson & Hirschi, 1990). Findings suggest that low levels of self-control played an important role in the decision to joining an online attack on a targeted group when witnessing such an attack occurring (Hawdon et al., 2019), as well as in the decision to engage in cyberhate production (Bernatzky et al., 2022). However, the explanatory effect of low self-control on cyberhate production lost significance after controlling for the core variables of the Social Structure-Social Learning Theory (Bernatzky et al., 2022).

Akers' Social Structure-Social Learning Theory (2009), an extension of Social Learning Theory, focuses on how macro-level structural factors can influence social learning processes at the micro-level, leading to deviant and criminal behaviours. Akers (2009) identified four interrelated elements of social structure through which social learning processes might occur: a) differential location, which involves the individuals' sociodemographic characteristics and the influence of social stratification patterns on social learning processes (e.g., gender, age, race, ethnicity, economic status); b) differential social location, which considers group relationships, social ties, and institutional affiliations that may influence individuals' inclinations towards or away from engaging in cyberhate (e.g., family, peers, work groups); c) differential association, which focuses on exposure, interaction, and proximity to individuals who legitimize norm-violating activities and/or commit deviant or criminal behaviours; and d) differential reinforcement, which alludes to (non)social rewards received for engaging in the deviant or criminal behaviours.

The study conducted by Bernatzky and colleagues (2022) examined the elements of the social structure that might account for individuals producing online material that others might interpret as hateful or degrading. The authors observed that factors such as being white, male, less educated, and economically disengaged did not significantly predict cyberhate production (although right-wing individuals and extremist movements have been playing a very active role online; differential location; Bernatzky et al., 2022; Costelo et al., 2019; Hawdon et al., 2014; Southern Poverty Law Center, 2020, 2021). Moreover, they noted that proximity to friends or religious groups did not show a significant relationship. However, being close to one's family was found to be associated with a reduced likelihood, while being close to online communities was associated with an increased likelihood of producing cyberhate (differential social location). Furthermore, they found that joining an online attack on a targeted group when witnessing such an attack occurring and agreeing with deviant definitions of behavior were both correlated with producing cyberhate (differential association). Nonetheless, expressing agreement with cyberhate witnessed was positively associated with producing such content, while copying one's friends did not demonstrate a significant relationship (differential reinforcement; Bernatzky et al., 2022).

Other studies have provided substantial support for the aforementioned aspects of the theory: differential social location, association, and reinforcement. These studies have shown that spending more time on websites that are populated by hate, belonging to an online community and a deviant youth group, holding favorable attitudes toward violence and racism, witnessing cyberhate, and having less trust in institutions are associated with a greater likelihood of engaging in cyberhate perpetration (Blaya & Audrin, 2019; Celuch et al., 2022; Costello & Hawdon, 2018; Hawdon et al., 2019; Wachs & Wright, 2018; Wachs et al., 2019). These findings align with the Internet hate-crime typology developed by Jacks and Hadler (2015). The authors argue that Internet users may initially start as browsers (i.e., accidentally or intentionally watching online hate, without interacting with other users or the online community); however, due to repeated exposure and acceptance within the group, their prejudices and bigotries may strengthen, leading them to take on roles as commentators (i.e., watching online hate content, (re)posting hateful or other comments, and interacting with the online community), activists (i.e., uploading overtly hateful material and, perhaps, interacting with hate organizations offline), and even leaders (i.e., advocating for one's own extreme views, building websites, purchasing extremist material, planning and organizing hate-related activities both online and offline, and potentially engaging in illegal activities).

Agnew's General Strain Theory (1992) can be promising in explaining the overlapping roles of victims and perpetrators (i.e., double involvement). According to this theory, experiences of strain (e.g., failure to reach valued goals, loss of positive stimuli, and exposure to negative stimuli) can lead to negative emotions (e.g., sadness, anger, and frustration). In the absence of effective coping skills, these emotions may lead individuals to engage in deviant, criminal, or other problem behaviors (Agnew, 1992). Strain has been shown to have a relationship with cyberhate. For example, research has shown that individuals who were exposed to cyberhate and experienced victimization were more likely to join in on hateful behavior online or to be perpetrators of cyberhate (Blaya & Audrin, 2019; Costelo & Hawdon, 2018; Hawdon et al., 2019; Wachs & Wright, 2018).

Sociological theoretical frameworks, such as Tajfel and Turner's Social Identity Theory (1979), offer valuable insights. According to this theory, an individual's social identity is formed through group membership. In this process, individuals perceive those who are similar to them as part of their in-groups ('us'), while those perceived as different become out-groups ('them'). Cyberhate amplifies groups identities, leading to favorable judgments of in-groups and derogation of out-groups (Costello et al., 2019). Empirical evidence supports these propositions, as studies have shown that females and individuals who identify as political moderates or liberals were substantially more likely than males and political conservatives to rate cyberhate as more disturbing (Costello et al., 2019). Notably, right-wing groups tend to target females, non-conservatives, racial and ethnic minorities, Jews, Muslims, immigrants, and other marginalized groups (Costelo et al., 2019; Hawdon et al., 2014; Southern Poverty Law Center, 2020, 2021). These findings suggest that individuals who are already vulnerable or at risk appear to be particularly affected by cyberhate (Costello et al., 2019).

To deepen our understanding of cyberhate, it is essential to consider the unique mechanisms of ICT that can exacerbate polarization and limit users' exposure to alternative information, viewpoints, and positions. These mechanisms include algorithms that customize and direct individuals' Internet experiences based on data collected about their profiles, interests, and behaviors, creating a "filter bubble effect" (Pariser, 2011). In addition, exposure to environments that validate and strengthen certain ideologies and behaviours can lead to an "echo chamber effect" (Cinelli, 2021). Consequently, initial exposure to cyberhate can create hate-filter bubbles and contribute to echo chambers. Moreover, the presence of (real or perceived) anonymity, asynchronous communication, de-individuation, a lack of social cues, and an apparent lack of repercussions and impunity can further encourage such behavior, known as the "online disinhibition effect" or "toxic online disinhibition effect" (Suller, 2004; Wachs & Wright, 2018). Studies have confirmed a link between the belief that one is less inhibited while engaging in certain cyber-practices and the posting of hateful or degrading speech online that targets individuals or groups based on their gender, race, sexual orientation, or religious affiliation, with the toxic effect of online disinhibition moderating the relationship between being bystanders and becoming perpetrators of cyberhate (Wachs & Wright, 2018).

CYBERHATE: RECOMMENDATIONS FOR PREVENTION AND INTERVENTION

Cyberhate is a pressing societal problem that requires attention due to its alarming prevalence rates (victims, perpetrators, and bystanders), multicausal origins (individual, relational, and contextual variables), and potential detrimental consequences. With that in mind, addressing cyberhate demands comprehensive prevention and intervention efforts that involve a concerted, long-term commitment from society. Adolescents, as a group with distinct developmental characteristics and needs, are especially vulnerable to a variety of risks. To protect them, it is crucial to foster a warm, available, and responsive home environment that facilitates trusting relationships. Parents play a vital role in educating their adolescents about mutual respect, socio-cultural diversity, and boundaries of expression, making them aware of the responsibilities that come with exercising their human rights and fundamental freedoms. In addition, parents should adopt instructive mediation strategies on the Internet (e.g., stimulating open dialogue, staying around, and teaching adolescents about netiquette and safety rules). Educational institutions also have significant responsibilities. This includes prioritizing the creation of an inclusive socio-cultural climate and the implementation of anti-cyberhate policies. Equally important is the restructuring of the pedagogical curriculum to promote single-sessions about critical thinking abilities (e.g., educating students on distinguishing between accuracy, misinformation, disinformation, and malinformation), emotional regulation and conflict management (e.g., enabling students to handle sadness, anger, and frustration in constructive ways), empathy (e.g., encouraging students to adopt the perspective of victims and become proactive upstanders), and comprehensive digital literacy and citizenship education (e.g., teaching students about the nature, dynamics, myths, and consequences of cyberhate). Additionally, they should leverage their support services to provide appropriate support to victims, perpetrators, and bystanders of cyberhate incidents. Collaborative efforts and specialized training are crucial for professionals from various fields, including teachers, health professionals, psychologists, criminologists, police officers, prosecutors, and judges, to enhance their sensitivity and practices. To reduce the risk of secondary victimization, key recommendations include learning about the specificities of cyberhate, using simple and inclusive language, being attentive to victims' needs, considering multiple social identity characteristics (e.g., intersectionality[9]), and adopting non-critical and respectful approaches. Researchers must urgently produce an integrative mapping of cyberhate, encompassing its prevalence, characterization, and impact through a combination of quantitative and qualitative studies. This holistic and mixed-methodological approach is essential for promoting best practices in the field, including risk assessment and the development of prevention and intervention measures for adolescents and adults (primary prevention), vulnerable groups (secondary prevention), and victims and/or perpetrators (tertiary intervention). Linguistics and computer engineers should continue to develop efforts to identify, classify, and quantify cyberhate using different techniques (e.g., lexicons, semantic analysis, syntactic, and n-grams). Technological industries and web developers must redesign platforms with long-term solutions to anticipate, classify, report, and mitigate cyberhate in a timely and effective manner. Social organizations should persist in addressing cyberhate in their initiatives, while media campaigns sensitize the general public with appropriate information and language, including victim's rights, legal proceedings, and available services. Lawmakers should seek to update and enforce laws discouraging these behaviours, holding individuals criminally responsible, and promoting the social reintegration of perpetrators to prevent revictimization experiences. Global institutional efforts are of paramount importance (e.g., United States of America: Federal Bureau of Investigation's Uniform Crime Reporting, Southern Poverty Law Center, Anti-Defamation League; Member states of the European Union: European Union Agency for Fundamental Rights, European Office for Democratic Institutions and Human Rights, European Commission against Racism and Intolerance; Portugal: Associação Portuguesa de Apoio à Vítima [Portuguese Association for Victim Support], Comissão para a Cidadania e Igualdade de Género [Portuguese Commission for Citizenship and Gender Equality], ILGA Portugal - Observatório da Discriminação contra Pessoas LGBTI+ [ILGA Portugal - Observatory for Discrimination against LGBTI+ People] and Comissão para a Igualdade contra a Discriminação Racial [Portuguese Comission for Equality Against Racial Discrimination]). In conclusion, to efficiently combat this urgent societal issue, all communities must consider cyberhate a fundamental priority and place it at the forefront of their scholarly, practical, scientific, media, political, and public agendas.

FUNDING

This study was conducted at the Psychology Research Centre (PSI/01662), School of Psychology, University of Minho, supported by the Foundation for Science and Technology (FCT) through the Portuguese State Budget (UIDB/PSI/01662/2020) and a PhD fellowship awarded to Maria Vale (Ref. 2021.07545. BD) co-funded by the FCT under the POCH/FSE Program.

REFERENCES

Aboujaoude, E., Savage, M. W., Starcevic, V., & Salame, W. O. (2015). Cyberbullying: Review of an Old Problem Gone Viral. *The Journal of Adolescent Health*, *57*(1), 10–18. doi:10.1016/j.jadohealth.2015.04.011 PMID:26095405

Agnew, R. (1992). Foundation for a General Strain Theory of Crime and Delinquency. *Criminology*, *30*(1), 47–88. doi:10.1111/j.1745-9125.1992.tb01093.x

Akers, R. (2009). *Social learning and social structure: A general theory of crime and deviance*. Routledge. doi:10.4324/9781315129587

Allport, G. W. (1954). *The Nature of Prejudice*. Addison-Wesley.

Anti-Defamation League. (2016). *Responding to Cyberhate: Progress and trends*. https://www.adl.org/sites/default/files/documents/assets/pdf/combating-hate/2016-ADL-Responding-to-Cyberhate-Progress-and-Trends-Report.pdf

Anti-Defamation League. (2022). *Hate Is No Game Hate and Harassment in Online Games 2022*. ADL Center for Technology & Society. https://www.adl.org/sites/default/files/documents/2022-12/Hate-and-Harassment-in-Online-Games-120622-v2.pdf

Associação Portuguesa de Apoio à Vítima [Portuguese Association for Victim Support]. (2022a). *Estatísticas APAV. Relatório Anual 2022* [APAV Statistics. Annual Report 2022]. https://apav.pt/apav_v3/images/pdf/Estatisticas-APAV_Relatorio-anual-2022.pdf

Associação Portuguesa de Apoio à Vítima [Portuguese Association for Victim Support]. (2022b). *Estatísticas 2022. Linha Internet Segura* [Statistics 2022. Safe Internet Line.]. https://internetsegura.pt/sites/default/files/2023-02/lis_2022_final-1.pdf

Auxier, B., & Anderson, M. (2021). *Social Media Use in 2021*. Pew Research Center On Internet & Technology. https://www.pewresearch.org/internet/2021/04/07/social-media-use-in-2021/

Bauman, S., Perry, V. M., & Wachs, S. (2021). The rising threat of cyberhate for young people around the globe. In M. F. Wright & L. B. Schiamberg (Eds.), *Child and Adolescent Online Risk Exposure: An Ecological Perspective* (pp. 149–175). Academic Press. doi:10.1016/B978-0-12-817499-9.00008-9

Bedrosova, M., Machackova, H., Šerek, J., Smahel, D., & Blaya, C. (2022). The relation between the cyberhate and cyberbullying experiences of adolescents in the Czech Republic, Poland, and Slovakia. *Computers in Human Behavior*, *126*, 107013. doi:10.1016/j.chb.2021.107013

Bernatzky, C., Costello, M., & Hawdon, J. (2022). Who produces online hate? An examination of the effects of self-control, social structure, & social learning. *American Journal of Criminal Justice, 47*(3), 421–440. doi:10.100712103-020-09597-3

Blaya, C., & Audrin, C. (2019). Toward an understanding of the characteristics of secondary school cyberhate perpetrators. *Frontiers in Education, 4*(46), 46. Advance online publication. doi:10.3389/feduc.2019.00046

Blaya, C., Audrin, C., & Skrzypiec, G. (2020). School bullying, perpetration, and cyberhate: Overlapping issues. *Contemporary School Psychology, 26*(3), 341–349. doi:10.100740688-020-00318-5

Bliuc, A. M., Faulkner, N., Jakubowicz, A., & McGarty, C. (2018). Online networks of racial hate: A systematic review of 10 years of research on cyber-racism. *Computers in Human Behavior, 87*, 75–86. doi:10.1016/j.chb.2018.05.026

Brown, C., & Hegarty, K. (2021). Development and validation of the TAR Scale: A measure of technology-facilitated abuse in relationships. *Computers in Human Behavior Reports, 3*, 100059. doi:10.1016/j.chbr.2021.100059

Brown, C., Sanci, L., & Hegarty, K. (2021). Technology-facilitated abuse in relationships: Victimisation patterns and impact in young people. *Computers in Human Behavior, 124*, 106897. doi:10.1016/j.chb.2021.106897

Castaño-Pulgarín, S. A., Suárez-Betancur, N., Vega, L. M. T., & López, H. M. H. (2021). Internet, social media and online hate speech. Systematic review. *Aggression and Violent Behavior, 58*, 101608. doi:10.1016/j.avb.2021.101608

Celuch, M., Oksanen, A., Räsänen, P., Costello, M., Blaya, C., Zych, I., Llorent, V. J., Reichelmann, A., & Hawdon, J. (2022). Factors associated with online hate acceptance: A cross-national six-country study among young adults. *International Journal of Environmental Research and Public Health, 19*(1), 534. doi:10.3390/ijerph19010534 PMID:35010794

Chetty, N., & Alathur, S. (2018). Hate speech review in the context of online social networks. *Aggression and Violent Behavior, 40*, 108–118. doi:10.1016/j.avb.2018.05.003

Cinelli, M., De Francisci Morales, G., Galeazzi, A., Quattrociocchi, W., & Starnini, M. (2021). The echo chamber effect on social media. *Proceedings of the National Academy of Sciences of the United States of America, 118*(9), 2023301118. doi:10.1073/pnas.2023301118 PMID:33622786

Cohen, L. E., & Felson, M. (1979). Social change and crime rate trends: A routine activity approach. *American Sociological Review, 44*(4), 588–608. doi:10.2307/2094589

Comissão para a Igualdade contra a Discriminação Racial [Portuguese Comission for Equality Against Racial Discrimination]. (2021). *Relatório Anual 2021: Igualdade e Não Discriminação em Razão da Origem Racial e Étnica, Cor, Nacionalidade, Ascendência e Território de Origem* [Annual Report 2021: Equality and Non-Discrimination on the grounds of Racial and Ethnic Origin, Color, Nationality, Ascendancy and Territory of Origin]. https://www.cicdr.pt/documents/57891/574449/20220809+-+Relat%C3%B3rio+Anual+CICDR+2021_.pdf/a7777160-f69a-48dd-8156-80d6bfcc93d0

Costello, M., & Hawdon, J. (2018). Who Are the Online Extremists Among Us? Sociodemographic Characteristics, Social Networking, and Online Experiences of Those Who Produce Online Hate Materials. *Violence and Gender*, *5*(1), 55–60. doi:10.1089/vio.2017.0048

Costello, M., Hawdon, J., Bernatzky, C., & Mendes, K. (2019). Social Group Identity and Perceptions of Online Hate. *Sociological Inquiry*, *89*(3), 1–26. doi:10.1111oin.12274

Council of Europe. (2016). *The European Commission against Racism and Intolerance (ECRI): Recommendation No. 15 on Combating Hate Speech*. https://rm.coe.int/ecri-general-policy-recommendation-no-15-on-combating-hate-speech/16808b5b01

Dimock, M. (2019, January 17). *Defining generations: Where Millennials end and Generation Z begins*. Pew Research Center. https://www.pewresearch.org/fact-tank/2019/01/17/where-millennials-end-and-generation-z-begins/

Eck, J. E., & Clarke, R. V. (2003). Classifying common police problems: A routine activity theory approach. In M. J. Smith & D. B. Cornish (Eds.), Crime prevention studies: Vol. 16. Theory and practice in situational crime prevention (pp. 7-39). Monsey, NY: Criminal Justice Press.

Erikson, E. H. (1963). *Childhood and society* (2nd ed.). Norton.

Eurostat. (2022). *Digital economy and society statistics - Households and individuals*. https://ec.europa.eu/eurostat/statistics-explained/index.php?title=Digital_economy_and_society_statistics_-_households_and_individuals

Federal Bureau of Investigation's Uniform Crime Reporting. (2022, December 12). *FBI Releases 2021 Hate Crime Statistics*. FBI National Press Office. https://www.fbi.gov/news/press-releases/fbi-releases-2021-hate-crime-statistics

Fortuna, P., & Nunes, S. (2018). A Survey on Automatic Detection of Hate Speech in Text. *ACM Computing Surveys*, *51*(4), 1–30. doi:10.1145/3232676

Gaspar, T., Matos, G. M., Guedes, B. F., Cerqueira, A., Branquinho, C., Simões, C., Tomé, G., Reis, M., Ramiro, L., Marques, A., Camacho, I., Loureiro, N., Gaspar, S., Carvalho, M., Raimundo, M., Ramos, M., Moraes, B., Noronha, C., Sousa, B. S., . . . Costa, R. (2022). *A saúde dos adolescentes portugueses em contexto de pandemia*: Dados nacionais do estudo HBSC 2022 [The health of Portuguese adolescents in a pandemic context: HBSC 2022 national report]. https://aventurasocial.com/wp-content/uploads/2022/12/HBSC_Relato%CC%81rioNacional_2022.pdf

Görzig, A., Blaya, C., Bedrosova, M., Audrin, C., & Machackova, H. (2023). The amplification of cyberhate victimisation by discrimination and low life satisfaction: Can supportive environments mitigate the risks? *The Journal of Early Adolescence*, *43*(1), 5–36. doi:10.1177/02724316221078826

Gottfredson, M., & Hirschi, T. (1990). *A General Theory of Crime*. Stanford University Press., doi:10.1515/9781503621794

Hawdon, J., Oksanen, A., & Räsänen, P. (2014). Victims of online hate groups: American youth's exposure to online hate speech. In J. Hawdon, J. Ryan, & M. Lucht (Eds.), *The causes and consequences of group violence: From bullies to terrorists* (pp. 165–182). Lexington Books.

Hindelang, M. J., Gottfredson, M. R., & Garofalo, J. (1978). *Victims of personal crime: An empirical foundation for a theory of personal victimization.* Ballinger.

Hinduja, S., & Patchin, J. W. (2011). *Electronic dating violence: A brief guide for educators and parents.* US Cyberbullying Research Center. https://cyberbullying.org/electronic_dating_violence_fact_sheet.pdf

Instituto Nacional de Estatística [Statistical National Institute]. (2022). *Sociedade da Informação e do Conhecimento. Inquérito à Utilização de Tecnologias da Informação e da Comunicação pelas Famílias 2022* [Information Society and Knowledge. Survey on the Use of Information and Communication Technologies by Families in 2022]. https://www.ine.pt/xportal/xmain?xpid=INE&xpgid=ine_destaques&DESTAQUESdest_boui=541053235&DESTAQUESmodo=2

Jacks, W., & Adler, J. R. (2015). A proposed typology of online hate crime. *Open Access Journal of Forensic Psychology, 7,* 64–89.

Jennings, W. G., Piquero, A. R., & Reingle, J. M. (2012). On the overlap between victimization and offending: A review of the literature. *Aggression and Violent Behavior, 17*(1), 16–26. doi:10.1016/j.avb.2011.09.003

Keighley, R. (2022). Hate Hurts: Exploring the Impact of Online Hate on LGBTQ+ Young People. *Women & Criminal Justice, 32*(1), 29–48. doi:10.1080/08974454.2021.1988034

Kemp, S. (2023). *Digital 2023: Global Overview Report.* DataReportal. https://www.slideshare.net/DataReportal/digital-2023-global-overview-report-summary-version-january-2023-v02

Lauritsen, J. L., Sampson, R. J., & Laub, J. H. (1991). The link between offending and victimization among adolescents. *Criminology, 29*(2), 265–292. doi:10.1111/j.1745-9125.1991.tb01067.x

Lei n.º 94/2017, de 23 de agosto [Law no. 94/2017, of 23 August]. *Diário da República – I Série,* N.º 162. Quarta alteração ao Código Penal, aprovado pelo Decreto-Lei n.º 48/95, de 15 de março [Fourth amendment to the Penal Code, approved by Decree-Law no. 48/95 of March 15]. https://dre.pt/dre/legislacao-consolidada/decreto-lei/1995-34437675-108044756?_ts=1680220800034

Machackova H. Blaya C. Bedrosova M. Smahel D. Staksrud E. (2020). *Children's experiences with cyberhate.* EU Kids Online: The London School of Economics and Political Science. https://doi.org/ doi:10.21953/lse.zenkg9xw6pua

Miethe, T. D., & Meier, R. F. (1990). Opportunity, choice, and criminal victimization: A test of a theoretical model. *Journal of Research in Crime and Delinquency, 27*(3), 243–266. doi:10.1177/0022427890027003003

Pariser, E. (2011). *The Filter Bubble: What the Internet Is Hiding From You.* Penguin Press.

Pereira, F., & Matos, M. (2015). Ciberstalking entre adolescentes: Uma nova forma de assédio e perseguição? [Cyberstalking among adolescents: A new form of harassment and stalking?]. *Psicologia, Saúde & Doenças, 16*(1), 57–69. doi:10.15309/15psd160207

Pereira, F., & Matos, M. (2016). Cyberstalking victimization: What predicts fear among Portuguese adolescents? *European Journal on Criminal Policy and Research, 22*(2), 253–270. doi:10.100710610-015-9285-7

Pereira, F., Spitzberg, B., & Matos, M. (2016). Cyber-harassment victimization in Portugal: Prevalence, fear and help-seeking among adolescents. *Computers in Human Behavior, 62*, 136–146. doi:10.1016/j. chb.2016.03.039

Perrin, A. (2021). *Mobile Technology and Home Broadband 2021*. Pew Research Center. https://www. pewresearch.org/internet/2021/06/03/mobile-technology-and-home-broadband-2021/

Perrin, A., & Atske, S. (2021, March 26). *About three-in-ten U.S. adults say they are 'almost constantly' online*. Pew Research Center. https://www.pewresearch.org/fact-tank/2021/03/26/about-three-in-ten-u-s-adults-say-they-are-almost-constantly-online/

Ponte, C., & Batista, S. (2019). *EU Kids Online Portugal. Usos, competências, riscos e mediações da internet reportados por crianças e jovens (9-17 anos)* [EU Kids Online Portugal. Internet uses, skills, risks, and mediations reported by children and youth (9-17-years-old)]. EU Kids Online. Lisboa: Faculdade de Ciências Sociais e Humanas da Universidade Nova de Lisboa. http://pnl2027.gov.pt/np4/%7B$client ServletPath%7D/?newsId=676&fileName=relatoriofinaleukidsonline.pdf

Posick, C. (2013). The Overlap Between Offending and Victimization Among Adolescents: Results From the Second International Self-Report Delinquency Study. *Journal of Contemporary Criminal Justice, 29*(1), 106–124. doi:10.1177/1043986212471250

Reichelmann, A., Hawdon, J., Costello, M., Ryan, J., Blaya, C., Llorent, V., Oksanen, A., Räsänen, P., & Zych, I. (2020). Hate knows no boundaries: Online hate in six nations. *Deviant Behavior, 42*(9), 1100–1111. doi:10.1080/01639625.2020.1722337

Reiger, D., Kümpel, A., Wich, M., Kiening, T., & Groh, G. (2021). Assessing the extent and types of hate speech in fringe communities: A case study of alt-right communities on 8chan, 4chan, and Reddit. *Social Media + Society, 7*(4), 1–14. doi:10.1177/20563051211052906

Reyns, B. W., Henson, B., & Fisher, B. S. (2011). Being pursued online: Applying cyber lifestyle routine activities theory to cyberstalking victimization. *Criminal Justice and Behavior, 38*(11), 1149–1169. doi:10.1177/0093854811421448

SmahelD.MachackovaH.MascheroniG.DedkovaL.StaksrudE.ÓlafssonK.HasebrinkU. (2020). *EU Kids Online 2020: Survey results from 19 countries*. EU Kids Online: The London School of Economics and Political Science. doi:10.21953/lse.47fdeqj01ofo

Smith, P. K. (2012). Cyberbullying and cyber aggression. In. S. R. Jimerson, A. B. Nickerson, M. J. Mayer, M. J. Furlong (Eds.), Handbook of school violence and school safety: International research and practice (pp. 93-103). New York: Routledge.

Smith, P. K., Mahdavi, J., Carvalho, M., Fisher, S., Russell, S., & Tippett, N. (2008). Cyberbullying: Its nature and impact in secondary school pupils. *Journal of Child Psychology and Psychiatry, and Allied Disciplines, 49*(4), 376–385. doi:10.1111/j.1469-7610.2007.01846.x PMID:18363945

Southern Poverty Law Center. (2020). *The Year in Hate & Extremism 2020*. https://www.splcenter.org/sites/default/files/yih_2020-21_final.pdf

Southern Poverty Law Center. (2021). *The Year in Hate & Extremism 2021*. https://www.splcenter.org/sites/default/files/splc-2021-year-in-hate-extremism-report.pdf?utm_source=web

Spitzberg, B. H., & Cupach, W. R. (2014). *The dark side of relationships pursuit. From attraction to obsession and stalking* (2nd ed.). Routledge. doi:10.4324/9780203805916

Spitzberg, B. H., & Hoobler, G. (2002). Cyberstalking and the technologies of interpersonal terrorism. *New Media & Society*, *4*(1), 71–92. doi:10.1177/14614440222226271

Suler, J. (2004). The online disinhibition effect. *Cyberpsychology & Behavior*, *7*(3), 321–326. doi:10.1089/1094931041291295 PMID:15257832

Tajfel, H., & Turner, J. C. (1979). An integrative theory of intergroup conflict. In W. G. Austin & S. Worchel (Eds.), *The social psychology of intergroup relations* (pp. 33–47). Brooks-Cole.

Vale, A., Matos, M., & Pereira, F. (2021). Ciberabuso nas relações de intimidade dos adolescentes: Um diálogo entre a Psicologia e a Criminologia [Cyber dating abuse among adolescents: A dialogue between Psychology and Criminology]. In I. S. Guedes & M. A. Gomes (Eds.), *Cibercriminalidade: Novos Desafios, Ofensas e Soluções* (pp. 119–129). Pactor-Edições de Ciências Sociais, Forenses e da Educação.

Vale, A., Pereira, F., Gonçalves, M., & Matos, M. (2018). Cyber-aggression in adolescence and internet parenting styles: A study with victims, perpetrators and victims-perpetrators. *Children and Youth Services Review*, *93*, 88–99. doi:10.1016/j.childyouth.2018.06.021

Vale, A., Pereira, F., & Matos, M. (2020). Adolescents digital dating abuse and cyberbullying. In S. Caridade & A. Dinis (Eds.), *Adolescent Dating Violence: Outcomes, Challenges, and Digital Tools* (pp. 89–112). Nova Science Publishers.

Vale, M., Pereira, F., Spitzberg, B. H., & Matos, M. (2022). Cyber-harassment victimization of Portuguese adolescents: A lifestyle-routine activities approach. *Behavioral Sciences & the Law*, *40*(5), 604–618. doi:10.1002/bsl.2596 PMID:36102898

Varjas, K., Talley, J., Meyers, J., Parris, L., & Cutts, H. (2010). High school students' perceptions of motivations for cyberbullying: An exploratory study. *The Western Journal of Emergency Medicine*, *11*(3), 269–273. PMID:20882148

Vogels, A. E. (2019, September 9). *Millennials stand out for their technology use, but older generations also embrace digital life*. Pew Research Center. https://www.pewresearch.org/fact-tank/2019/09/09/us-generations-technology-use/

Vogels, A. E., Gelles-Watnick, R., & Massarat, N. (2022). *Teens, Social Media, and Technology 2022*. Pew Research Center. https://www.pewresearch.org/internet/2022/08/10/teens-social-media-and-technology-2022/

Vogels, E. (2021). *The State of Online Harassment*. Pew Research Center. https://www.pewresearch.org/internet/2021/01/13/the-state-of-online-harassment/

Wachs, S., Costello, M., Wright, M. F., Flora, K., Daskalou, V., Maziridou, E., Kwon, Y., Na, E. Y., Sittichai, R., Biswal, R., Singh, R., Almendros, C., Gámez-Guadix, M., Görzig, A., & Hong, J. S. (2021a). "DNT LET'EM H8 U!": Applying the routine activity framework to understand cyberhate victimization among adolescents across eight countries. *Computers & Education, 160,* 104026. doi:10.1016/j.compedu.2020.104026

Wachs, S., Mazzone, A., Milosevic, T., Wright, M. F., O'Higgins Norman, J., & Blaya, C. (2021b). Online correlates of cyberhate involvement among young people from ten european countries: An application of the routine activity and problem behaviour theory. *Computers in Human Behavior, 123*(3), 106872. doi:10.1016/j.chb.2021.106872

Wachs, S., & Wright, M. F. (2018). Associations between bystanders and perpetrators of online hate: The moderating role of toxic online disinhibition. *International Journal of Environmental Research and Public Health, 15*(9), 2030. doi:10.3390/ijerph15092030 PMID:30227666

Wachs, S., Wright, M. F., Sittichai, R., Singh, R., Biswal, R., Kim, E. M., Yang, S., Gámez-Guadix, M., Almendros, C., Flora, K., Daskalou, V., & Maziridou, E. (2019). Associations between witnessing and perpetrating online hate in eight countries: The buffering effects of problem-focused coping. *International Journal of Environmental Research and Public Health, 16*(20), 3992. doi:10.3390/ijerph16203992 PMID:31635408

Wardle, C. (2018). The Need for Smarter Definitions and Practical, Timely Empirical Research on Information Disorder. *Digital Journalism (Abingdon, England), 6*(8), 951–963. doi:10.1080/2167081 1.2018.1502047

Wardle, C., & Derakhshan, H. (2017). *Information disorder: Toward an interdisciplinary framework for research and policy making.* Council of Europe. https://rm.coe.int/information-disorder-toward-an-interdisciplinary-framework-for-researc/168076277c

Windisch, S., Wiedlitzka, S., Olaghere, A., & Jenaway, E. (2022). Online interventions for reducing hate speech and cyberhate: A systematic review. *Campbell Systematic Reviews, 18*(2), e1243. doi:10.1002/cl2.1243 PMID:36913206

Wright, M. F., Wachs, S., & Gámez-Guadix, M. (2021). Jóvenes ante el ciberodio: El rol de la mediación parental y el apoyo familiar [Youths' coping with cyberhate: Roles of parental mediation and family support]. *Comunicar, 67,* 21–33. doi:10.3916/C67-2021-02

Yar, M. (2005). The Novelty of 'Cybercrime': An Assessment in Light of Routine Activity Theory. *European Journal of Criminology, 2*(4), 407–427. doi:10.1177/147737080556056

ENDNOTES

[1]   Headlines, images, and captions that do not correspond to the article's content. Clickbait headlines can be the most common examples (Wardle & Derakhshan, 2017; Wardle, 2018).

[2]   Information that is used to paint a false picture of a person or an issue. This can happen when a story is retold, a quote or statistic is cut up, or an image is cropped to support a broader point of view and get rid of essential arguments (Wardle & Derakhshan, 2017; Wardle, 2018).

3   True information that is distributed with false contextual information (Wardle & Derakhshan, 2017; Wardle, 2018).

4   Impersonation of true sources, such as well-known figures, journalists, or logos (Wardle & Derakhshan, 2017; Wardle, 2018).

5   True information that is manipulated to cause deception (Wardle & Derakhshan, 2017; Wardle, 2018).

6   False information intended to deceive and cause harm (Wardle & Derakhshan, 2017; Wardle, 2018).

7   Both cyber obsessional relational intrusion and cyberstalking reflect a continuum process of unwanted harassment. However, while the former entails achieving a heightened level of intimacy, typically in a romantic context, the latter involves persist harassment leading to feelings of threat or fear (Spitzberg & Cupach, 2014; Spitzberg & Hoobler, 2002).

8   Lei n.º 94/2017, de 23 de agosto [Law no. 94/2017, of 23 August]: "Discrimination and incitement to hatred and violence. 1 - Whoever: a) Founds or constitutes an organization or develops organized propaganda activities that incite discrimination, hate, or violence against a person or group of persons because of their race, color, ethnic, or national origin, ancestry, religion, sex, sexual orientation, gender identity, or physical or mental disability, or encourages it; or b) Participates in or provides assistance to the organization or activities referred to in the previous paragraph, including their financing, is punishable by one to eight years in prison. 2 - Whoever, publicly, by any means intended for dissemination, namely through apologia, denials, or gross trivialization of crimes of genocide, war, or against peace and humanity: a) Provoke acts of violence against a person or group of persons because of their race, color, ethnic or national origin, ancestry, religion, sex, sexual orientation, gender identity, or physical or mental disability; b) Defaming or insulting a person or group of people because of their race, color, ethnic or national origin, ancestry, religion, sex, sexual orientation, gender identity, or physical or mental disability; c) Threatening a person or a group of persons because of race, color, ethnic or national origin, ancestry, religion, sex, sexual orientation, gender identity, or physical or mental disability; or d) Inciting violence or hatred against any person or group of persons because of their race, color, ethnic or national origin, ancestry, religion, sex, sexual orientation, gender identity, or physical or mental disability, is punishable by imprisonment from 6 months to 5 years".

9   The convergence of social categorizations (e.g., gender, race, ethnicity, sexual orientation, or other characteristics) results in interconnected and interdependent experiences of oppression, discrimination, or disadvantage.

Chapter 9
A Black Hole Attack Protection Approach in IoT-Based Applications Using RLNC

Abidhusain Syed
VTU Belagavi Karnataka, India

Baswaraj Gadgay
VTU Kalburgi, India

ABSTRACT

Smart environments have recently transformed the standard of human existence by increasing comfort and efficiency. IoT, or the internet of things, has become an instrument for developing intelligent environments. But because of security vulnerabilities in IoT-based systems, applications for smart environments are in danger. Harmful items have a significant effect on cyber defence mechanisms. In order to stop security attacks against IoT that exploit some of these security vulnerabilities, IoT-specific intrusion detection systems (IDSs) are crucial. Due to the limited computing and storage capacities of IoT devices and the specific protocols used, it's conceivable that conventional IDSs are not an option for IoT environments.

1. INTRODUCTION

The most recent trends and updates notify us of the fast-growing IoT population that is connecting to the internet all around the world. The risk associated with cybersurveillance has increased, and malicious programmes now have access to personal data. Inappropriate system key usage and a dearth of system modernisation are to blame. The database was mostly cracked as a result of authoritarian surveillance measures that were put in place. According to a network surveillance expert, the IoT is especially susceptible to cyber invasion. It'sa result of inadequate surveillance regulations and practises. Numerous types of malware have been developed by hackers to compromise IoT devices. To get consumers to reveal personal information, hackers send deceptive emails that appear to be from reliable companies (Monther, A.A.& Tawalbeh,2020). The implementation of

DOI: 10.4018/979-8-3693-1528-6.ch009

IoT encompasses numerous sectors such as resourceful homes, smart supply chains, customizable environments, and intelligent monitoring (A. V. Dastjerdi and R. Buyya, 2016; J. Li.et.a,2019), so network surveillance is obvious. There are a number of cybersurveillance risks for enterprises when real items are included in wireless networks. Denial of Service (DoS), Man-in-the-Middle (MITM), and other tactics can be used against crucial IoT infrastructures to bring down the entire system and compromise it. IDS plays a crucial role as a key element in the IoT surveillance architecture for information systems and traditional networks to overcome these difficulties. Therefore, it is essential to develop a high-performance IoT invasion detection system element in order to increase the surveillance of the IoT (Z. Jinsheng 2018).

The four main groups of surveillance-related issues for IoT systems are authentication and physical threats, secrecy risks, data integrity issues, and privacy concerns (Liu et al., 2017). Figure 1 depicts the relationships among these categories. The following succinct discussion addresses the surveillance issues that arise in the various IoT levels.

1. Authentication and physical threats are fundamental issues faced by IoT system.
2. These are the risks associated with confidentiality between IoT devices and the gateways in the network layer (Trappe W, Howard R & Moore RS, 2015).

Figure 1. Surveillance challenges in various IoT layers

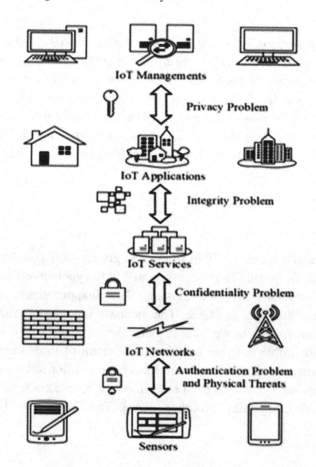

3. Data consistency across apps and services When spoofing attacks or noise influence an IoT device, data integrity issues arise.

4. The fourth category of challenges has to do with privacy. In IoT networks, information privacy is a crucial component of surveillance (Hassan AM, Awad AI, 2018).

2. BACKGROUND

The intricacy of modern convocation (such online gaming, video conferencing etc) that demand consistent QoS assurances has increased the need for precise and timely network monitoring tools. This makes monitoring network performance easier for network engineers and Internet service providers (ISPs). There are many crucial network elements to comprehend and account for, including loss rate, delay distribution, bandwidth availability, and origin-destination traffic. Only a few of these traits, such origin-destination traffic, may, however, be directly retrieved from network hardware viz switches and routers. The direct evaluation of some characteristics by network devices, however, includes the link-level loss rate, delay distribution, and available bandwidth. It is often impractical to do so in a large network spanning many independent systems due to security and other factors. Data packet buffering during the route discovery process might also cause packet losses as a result of buffer overflow. With single link routing, this problem becomes severe as the network becomes more dynamic. As the rate of connection failures rises, so does the frequency of route discoveries. Additionally, as each route discovery results in significant packet overhead, its frequency affects the network's QoS performance.

A network is expected to be robust in nature, as it can withstand failures in hostile environments. The response of the network to the removal of nodes or links is the focus of robustness. Given a network and a link failure pattern, it is straightforward to consider the network obtained by eliminating the failing links, which is analogous to examining static solutions. The network is not aware of the precise failure pattern in a static condition. In order for the functions to be independent of the present failure pattern, each node is expected to broadcast a function of the observed random processes on its outgoing edges. Consequently, failed connections should display the link constant as zero. Network coding is a robust technique that can overcome any difficult situation in communication networks to improve throughput, reliability, and latency by combining multiple data packets into a single transmission entity. This method enables more efficient utilisation of network resources and offers increased flexibility in handling diverse traffic patterns. Network reliability is a critical aspect of modern communication systems. Among various techniques to improve reliability, Random Linear Network Coding (RLNC) has emerged as a promising solution. In this article, we will discuss the concept of link failure in the context of RLNC, its impact on network performance, and methods to mitigate and detect such failures. We will also explore the advantages of RLNC and its applications in various domains. The next section includes some of the most recent research related to our subject.

2.1 Otherworks

An explanation in-depth of a smart home system that employed deep learning to spot surveillance flaws (E. Gelenbe & Y. Yin, 2017) covers the subject of DRNNs. The study in (O. Brun et al., 2018) focused mostly on Denial of Service and Denial of Sleep assaults on a simple IoT site. Here we first exhibit dense random neural networks. Yu et al. developed an XOR network coding surveillance solution that can immediately identify pollution attacks using message authentication codes (MACs) and probabilistic key pre-distribution techniques (Monther, A.A. & Tawalbeh, 2020). Data surveillance is essential when service providers and customers use the cloud, according to Shafagh et al.'s observation in (Shafagh et al., 2017), since the cloud is used to store data collected by an IoT application. An algorithm for sharing data has been created and tested by the authors of this work. In contrast to the traditional network invasion detection algorithm, the genetic algorithm is used to identify network invasions. This algorithm's training sampling time is shorter, and the effects of invasion identification and detection are excellent (G. Ke & Y. H. Hong, 2014). Raman and other academics proposed an invasion detection system based on the Online Sequential Extreme Learning Machine (OS-ELM). It makes use of a number of feature selection techniques based on filtration, association, and consistency, as well as alpha analysis and other time-efficient methods, to eliminate extraneous features. This method has been successfully used in experiments to find network breaches (R. Singh, H. Kumar, & R. K. Singla, 2015). By recovering the original message from packets that comprise the attacked "look-like-valid" packets, authors in (Bandyopadhyay D, Sen J, 2011) propose a method for identifying attacked packets among the packets that are received at a target location. Workers at construction site are at serious risk like injuries life threating accidents. This is preventable using Internet of Things (IoT)-based sensors. Supervisors or site managers should keep an eye on employees and warn them when they are in danger in order to protect them. Data will be directed from a site worker to a supervisor; however, due to wireless communication, this routing method exposes data to assaults like a black hole attack and others. The issue of black hole attack that occurs during wireless transmission between nodes and the base station (BS) of IoT-based civil construction is discussed in (Estrada, D. Tawalbeh, L.Vinaja, R, 2020).

2.2 IoT Basics

2.2.1 System Architectures

According to (Bandyopadhyay D, Sen J, 2011, Han C et al.,2013, Khan R, Khan S, Zaheer R, 2012) the three domains that make up the overall architecture of the IoT are the application domain, the network domain, and the physical domain. As a result, the IoT may be adjusted to meet the requirements of different smart environments.

The application field also covers use and administration. The network domain is responsible for data transfer. The physical domain is in charge of gathering information. The tiers of the overall IoT architecture are shown in Figure 2. The various levels' operations are covered in the next section.

The application domain, network domain, and physical domain are the three domains that make up the overall design of the IoT, according to (Bugeja, J. Jacobsson, A. Davidsson, P., 2016, Culbert, D, 2019, Gemalto, 2020). Because of this, the IoT may be modified to suit the needs of various smart settings. The application domain also includes management and utilisation.

The network domain is responsible for data transfer. The physical domain is in charge of gathering information. The tiers of the overall IoT architecture are shown in Figure 2. The various levels' operations are covered in the next section.

Our strategy is likewise valid when using error-processing methods, assuming transmission errors. To put it another way, while packets with defects rectified by error correction methods are counted as regular arrivals at the destination, packets with specific faults will be ignored by error detection methods there, resulting in no arrivals. A node in a network system distributes packets that have been arbitrarily

Figure 2. IoT architecture

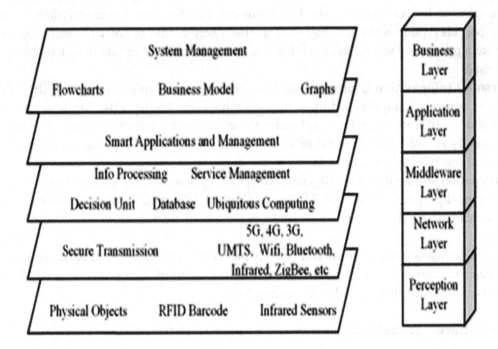

network coded by combining the packets it just received with a random linear combination. A packet in this context is a component of a message that has been separated into segments of a predetermined length for transmission, whereas a message in this context is any quantity of data generated by a source. An illustration of data obtained in this way can be found in Figure 1.

2.2.2 Functioning

Devices and items with built-in sensors are connected to an Internet of Things platform that collects and analyses the data from a large number of devices. One of the most simple instances is the use of sensors in stores. Customers' time spent in various store areas, the items they frequently use, and the route they take can all be ascertained. This data can be used to identify trends, offer suggestions, and foresee issues before they arise.

2.2.3 Surveillance Threats

IoT provides companies with numerous options, but some aspects may pose surveillance risks. For instance, when there are numerous open code sources accessible, such as Magento React, hackers are fully aware of the complexities of the code. Several extra dangers include:

1. **Using Pre-Programmed Passwords:** Most companies send devices with pre-programmed passwords and do not even advise changing them. For instance, this occurs frequently with house routers, surveillance cameras, and light control systems.. One of the greatest threats to IoT surveillance is the fact that default passwords are frequently used and are susceptible to being cracked.

2. **Unsafe Communication:** IoT surveillance flaws are caused by regularly unsecure messages sent by connected devices over networks. Using protocols like Transport Layer surveillance (TLS) and transport encryption is the best way to guarantee a secure link. In order to separate devices and ensure a private and secure link as authorll as the confidentiality of sent data, multiple networks are used.

3. **Personal Information Leaks:** IoT devices with unpatched internet protocol (IP) addresses can be severely compromised by skilled data hackers. The specific location and residential address of a user can be found using these addresses. Internet surveillance specialists frequently advise using a virtual private network (VPN) to encrypt the IoT connection and conceal our internet protocol address.

4. **Automation and artificial intelligence:** AI technologies are already widely used. The downside of automation is that it leaves all AI networks and the infrastructure they authorre in control of vulnerable to a single programming mistake or flaauthord algorithm.

Artificial intelligence and automation are merely pieces of code. Therefore, if hackers obtain access, they can take over the automation and do whatever they want. Therefore, it is essential to make sure the instruments are shielded from such threats and attacks.

2.2.4 Illustrative Cyberattacks

Hackers have the ability to launch attacks and infiltrate thousands or millions of unsecured connected devices, causing infrastructure to be destroyed, networks to go down, or allowing them to access private data. Below we have discussed few of the cyberattacks that best illustrate IoT vulnerabilities:

- **The Mirai Botnet**

The worst DDoS assault on Dyn, a provider of Internet performance management services, occurred in October 2016 and was carried out with the help of an IoT botnet. (a network of computers, each of which runs a bot). As a consequence, many authorbsites, including authorll-known ones like CNN, Netflix, and Twitter, authorre unavailable.

Using authorll-known default usernames and passwords, computers infected with the Mirai malware constantly search the authorb for IoT devices that are vulnerable before infecting them. Two instances of these gadgets authorre digital cameras and DVR players.

- **The Verkada Hack**

In March 2021, hackers obtained access to Verkada, a cloud-based video surveillance system. The attackers gained access to private information kept by Verkada software users as well as live feeds from more than 150,000 cameras placed in factories, hospitals, schools, jails, and other locations using genuine admin account credentials they found online. Later it was discovered that over 100 workers had "super admin" access, giving them access to thousands of client cameras and illuminating the dangers of having overly privileged users.

- **Cold in Finland**

In the Finnish city of Lappeenranta in November 2016, cybercriminals cut off the heating in two buildings. A second DDoS attack was conducted after that, forcing the heating controllers to restart the system numerous times and stopping the heating from ever turning on. Given that Finland has extremely low temperatures at that time of year, this attack was severe.

- **The Jeep Hack**

A team of experts examined the Jeep SUV's surveillance in July 2015. They used the Sprint cellular network to take control of the vehicle by taking advantage of a flaw in a firmware upgrade. The pace of the car could then be controlled, and it could even be forced off the road.

- **Stuxnet**

Probably the most authorll-known IoT assault is Stuxnet. A uranium enrichment facility in Natanz, Iran, was its intended target. The Windows-based Siemens Step7 software was hacked during the attack, allowing the worm access to the industrial programme logic controllers. This gave the worm's creators access to crucial industrial data and control over various machinery at the industrial locations.The first signs of a computer system issue at the nuclear poauthorr plant appeared in 2010. IAEA inspectors observed an oddly high percentage of uranium enrichment centrifuges breaking when they visited the Natanz complex. Later, in 2010, several malicious files authorre discovered on Iranian computer systems. These files are infected with Stuxnet virus

2.2.5 Futures

Currently, objects and systems have network connectivity and the computing ability to interact with similarly connected devices and machines (Bugeja, J. Jacobsson, A. Davidsson, P., 2016). Our lives will be more productive and cost-effective if the network's capabilities are expanded to include all potential physical places. However, using the Internet puts you in contact with possible online threats. Cybercriminals start to target goods with internet connectivity. As the IoT market expands, more potential risks that could affect our privacy, productivity, and gadget safety become available. Data leaks have reportedly become much more frequent since 2015, with 60% of them occurring only in the USA (Culbert, D,2019). Another study performed in France, the United States, Australia, Canada, and Japan found that 63% Research being done now has looked at a number of novel ways to improve privacy protection and reduce cyberattacks. The following is a list of some of the solutions discovered through the study; using encryption methods: Enforcing modern, robust encryption methods can improve safety. the encryption protocol put into use in both device and cloud contexts (He, H,2016).As a result, hackers are unable to abuse the unreadable protected data formats. Ongoing investigation into new threats; frequent evaluation of surveillance risks. Different teams for surveillance research have been created by organisations and device manufacturers.

Increase the frequency of updates: Device makers should create minor patches rather than significant updates. A approach like this can make patch installation less difficult. Additionally, regular updates will assist users in avoiding online threats from various sources (Al Shuhaimi, F. Jose & M. Singh, A.V, 2016).

Implement robust device monitoring techniques: The majority of recent study suggested doing this in order to quickly track and manage any suspicious activity. To identify threats, many IT organisations launched specialised tools for device monitoring. These tools are very helpful for risk evaluation, which helps organisations create complex control mechanisms.

To increase surveillance awareness, create user instructions manual. Most data breaches and Internet of Things attacks are the result of a lack of user awareness. IoT surveillance policies and guidelines are usually not addressed when users purchase these devices. Users can steer clear of these problems if device manufacturers explicitly specify the possible IoT threats. Additionally, organisations can create efficient training programmes to raise surveillance awareness. Such tools assist users in creating secure passwords and reminding them to change them frequently. Additionally, users are urged to routinely update surveillance patches. Users authorre also instructed to stay away from scam emails and other sources that could jeopardise IoT surveillance (Estrada, D. Tawalbeh, L. Vinaja, R, 2020).

Everyone is interested in the IoT's future prospects and where it will go. Over 30 billion IoT devices will exist by 2025. The IoT project was previously known to people, but they ignored it because they believed it would be challenging to execute. The level of IoT development is rising to new heights every day, so it is now becoming clear to people that this was not impossible after the growth of technology. For example, in 2020 and beyond, intelligent thermostats and smart lighting are just a couple of instances of how IoT is being used to reduce bills while also preserving energy, which helps to improve the environment (Estrada, D. Tawalbeh, L.Vinaja, R, 2020).

A large number of communities will become smart. The use of IoT will open up entirely new possibilities for city growth. By implementing IoT on a large scale, better traffic management, congestion-free roads, decreased pollution in cities, and high-standard surveillance will all be achieved.

3. COUNTER MEASURES FOR IOT VULNERABILITIES

If our company employs a large number of IoT devices, we must assess the monitoring of our information systems and the data processed by these devices. We must think about effective surveillance steps that can shield our company from cyberattacks and ransomware attacks that might be brought on by IoT surveillance flaws.

One of the best ways to address IoT risk concerns is to speak with and abide by the recommendations of a cyber surveillance specialist. If you're just beginning to raise the level of cyber surveillance maturity inside your company, a flexible and cost-effective solution like Cyber Management Alliance's Virtual Cyber Assistant service is appropriate. Using the following methods author can defend against IoT vulnerabilities and dangerous software:

1. Using a Cyber Health Check to evaluate the overall cyber health of our company.
2. Assisting you in developing new Cybersurveillance Incident Response Plans or reviewing and updating our current ones.
3. Use Cyber assault Tabletop Exercises to evaluate whether these preparations will work against a DDoS assault, phishing attack, or other attack brought on by an IoT surveillance flaw.

4. Get you going on our journey towards ransomware prevention and surveillance.

5. Helps to obtain company's Cyber Essentials certification. Our IoT devices will then be at least secured against the most frequent internet-based assaults, giving you some peace of mind (Alex Husar, 2022).

4. SYSTEM MODEL

4.1 Basic

An IoT system model is shown in Figure 3.The various application services integrated to form the IoT model, sends information in the form of packets viz u1,u2,...un, which are encoded using GF(2^q) where q is integer with values 2,4,8,16.The filed size refers to the no of elements used for encoding eg q=2 then author do have {0,1}, for encoding. The collection of original and coded packets can be combined and recombined by the source and intermediate nodes in the network. The group formed by the initial M packets is known as a generation. The generation size is the sum of the initial packets combined and recombined.

Figure 3. IoT system model

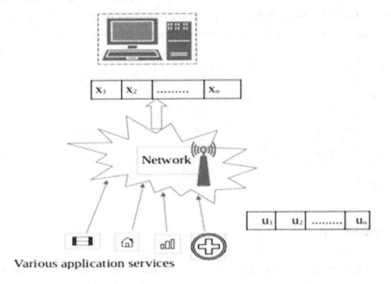

Various application services

With a single transmitter and numerous recievers, author examine the multicast scenario. A packet's link delay is the length of time it takes for a packet to pass through multiple links on a channel before being received. The n-symbol sequence U = (u1, u2,... uK) from GF(2^q), where q is a prime integer such that, it can be used to represent a source packet. Equation (1) is used to describe the coded packet, as shown in Figure 4:

$$xj = \sum_{i=0}^{n} gijui \tag{1}$$

Figure 4. Generation of coded packets

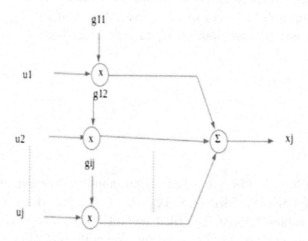

where g_{ij} - packet coefficient.

4.2 Message Recovery at Destination

The receiver attempt to reproduce the coding coefficients from the received message using linear equations as shown in equation (2). As each linear equation comprises of 'b' original packets. These packets forms a subset of n packets produced by the source are linearly independent:

$$\begin{bmatrix} g_{11} & g_{12}\cdots g_{1b} \\ g_{21} & g_{22}\cdots g_{2b} \\ \cdots\cdots\cdots \\ g_{n1} & g_{n2}\cdots g_{nb} \end{bmatrix} \begin{bmatrix} u_1 \\ u_2 \\ . \\ . \\ . \\ u_n \end{bmatrix} = \begin{bmatrix} x_1 \\ x_2 \\ x_j \end{bmatrix} \tag{2}$$

4.3 An Attack Situation

Consider an attack situation in the model outlined in the previous section. Assume a source produces packets while performing a mod 4 operation with GF = {0, 1, 2,3}. The source divides a message into two packets, P1 and P2, and then computes a linear equation for each of them with duplicates, r ji. Then, as shown in equation, it generates and sends the combinations x_1, x_2, x_3 and x_4 as shown in equation(3):

$$\begin{bmatrix} g_{11}u_1 + g_{12}u_2 = x_1 \\ g_{21}u_1 + g_{22}u_{22} = x_2 \\ g_{31}u_1 + g_{32}u_2 = x_3 \\ g_{41}u_1 + g_{42}u_2 = x_4 \end{bmatrix} \tag{3}$$

Assume that packet u_4 is attacked and becomes xe as shown in equation (4):

$$r_1^e u_1^w + r_2^e u_2^w = x_e \qquad (4)$$

No node could identify this attacked packet, xe, until they reached the destination and carried out the recovery procedure since it seems to be a "look-like-valid" with a valid digital signature and a valid encrypted value. author presume that the network is error-free and that all packets sent from the source can reach the destination without any problems. Eventually, x_1, x_2, x_3, and x_e are all received by the destination:

$$\begin{bmatrix} g_{11}u_1 + g_{12}u_2 = x_1 \\ g_{21}u_1 + g_{22}u_{22} = x_2 \\ g_{31}u_1 + g_{32}u_2 = x_3 \\ g_{41}u_1 + g_{42}u_2 = x_e \end{bmatrix} \qquad (5)$$

the receiver 6 possible outcomes are likely, corresponding to equation(5) above, therefore author have:

$$\begin{bmatrix} g_{11}u_1 + g_{12}u_2 = x_1 \\ g_{21}u_1 + g_{22}u_{22} = x_2 \end{bmatrix} \begin{bmatrix} \grave{g}_{11}u_1 + g_{12}u_2 = x_1 \\ g_{31}u_1 + g_{32}u_{22} = x_3 \end{bmatrix} \begin{bmatrix} g_{21}u_1 + g_{22}u_2 = x_2 \\ g_{31}u_1 + g_{22}u_{32} = x_3 \end{bmatrix}$$

these equations imply that (p_1, p_2):

$$\begin{bmatrix} g_{11}u_1 + g_{12}u_2 = x_1 \\ g_1^e u_1^w + g_2^e u_2^w = x_e \end{bmatrix} \text{implies } (u'_1, u'_2)$$

$$\begin{bmatrix} g_{21}u_1 + g_{22}u_2 = x_1 \\ g_1^e u_1^w + g_2^e u_2^w = x_e \end{bmatrix} \text{implies } (u''_1, u''_2)$$

$$\begin{bmatrix} g_{31}u_1 + g_{32}u_2 = x_3 \\ g_1^e u_1^w + g_2^e u_2^w = x_e \end{bmatrix} \text{implies } (u'''_1, u'''_2)$$

As can be seen all reconstruction outcome are not similar, indicating possible errors. As a priori x_4 is corrupted, the reconstruction process may not show the results expected. In the next section author will see the outcome of the implementation of few of the these ideas. Here author have considered link failure due to pollution attack as a case study.

5. RESULTS AND DISCUSSION

In this section we discuss few of our finding based on the concept adopted from (Bandyopadhyay D, Sen J, 2011). Few of the system parameters worth discussing here are: i)No of packets corrupted as traffic grows ii) Packet loss.

5.1 No. of Packets Corrupted

Field size do have an impact on no of packet corrupted. As can be evidently seen in fig with the advent in field size packet corruption can be prevented. When field size=16, the packet corruption is minimal.

Figure 5a. Packets corrupted due to link failure attack

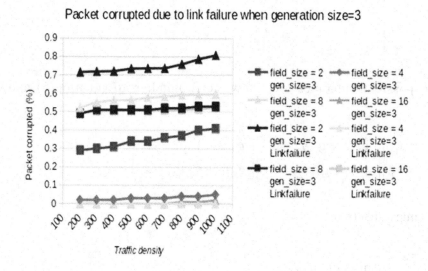

Figure 5b. Packets corrupted due to link failure attack

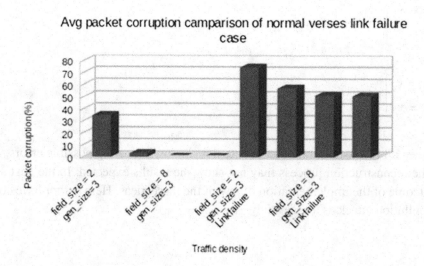

Figure 6. Packet loss due to link failure attack

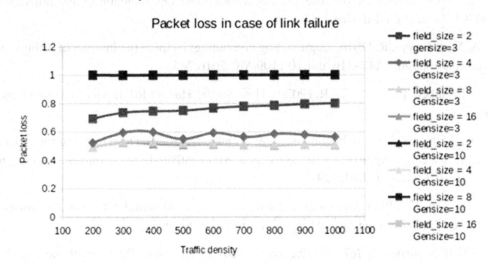

5.2 Packet Loss

A link failure condition due to pollution attack results in packet loss. As can be seen in packet loss is very high when there is pollution attack resulting in link failure, under different field size and generation size.

REFERENCES

Al Shuhaimi, F., Jose, M., & Singh, A. V. (2016). Software-defined network as a solution to overcome surveillance challenges in IoT. *Proceedings of the Reliability, Infocom Technologies and Optimization (Trends and Future Directions) (ICRITO), Noida, India, 7–9 September 2016*, 491–496.

Alex Hussar. (2022). www.cm-alliance.com/cybersurveillance-blog/iot-surveillance-5-cyber-attacks-caused-by-iot-surveillance-vulnerabilities

Bandyopadhyay, D., & Sen, J. (2011). Internet of things: Applications and challenges in technology and standardization. *Wireless Personal Communications*, 58(1), 49–69. doi:10.100711277-011-0288-5

Brun, O., Yin, Y., Gelenbe, E., Kadioglu, Y. M., Augusto-Gonzalez, J., & Ramos, M. (2018). Deep learning with dense random neural networks for detecting attacks against IoT-connected home environments. *Proceedings of the 2018 ISCIS surveillance Workshop, Imperial College London. Recent Cybersurveillance Research in Europe. Lecture Notes CCIS, 821*. 10.1007/978-3-319-95189-8_8

Bugeja, J., Jacobsson, A., & Davidsson, P. (2016). On privacy and surveillance challenges in smart connected homes. *Proceedings of the European Intelligence and surveillance Informatics Conference (EISIC)*, 172–175.

Cibersurveillance, C. I., & Dataset, I. D. S. (2018). *CSE-CIC-IDS2018 on AWS*. https://www.unbca/cicdatas ets/ids-2018 html

Culbert, D. (2020). *Personal Data Breaches and Securing IoT Devices*. Available online: https://betanews.com/2019/08/13/securing-iot-devices/

Dastjerdi, A. V., & Buyya, R. (2016, August). Fog computing: Helping the Internet of Things realize its potential. *Computer, 49*(8), 112–116. doi:10.1109/MC.2016.245

Estrada, D., Tawalbeh, L., & Vinaja, R. (2020). How Secure Having IoT Devices in Our Home. *J. Inf. Secur., 11*.

Ferrag, M. A., Maglaras, L., Moschoyiannis, S., & Janicke, H. (2020). Deep learning for cyber surveillance invasion detection: Approaches, datasets, and comparative study. *J. Inform. Secur. Appl., 50*, 102419. doi:10.1016/j.jisa2019.102419

Gelenbe, E., & Yin, Y. (2017). Deep learning with dense random neural networks. In *Proceedings of the International Conference on Man–Machine Interactions.* Springer.

Gemalto. (2020). *Securing the IoT-Building Trust in IoT Devices and Data.* Available online: https://www.gemalto.com/:https://www.gemalto.com/iot/iot-surveillance

Han, C., Jornet, J. M., Fadel, E., & Akyildiz, I. F. (2013). A cross-layer communication module for the internet of things. *Computer Networks, 57*(3), 622–633. doi:10.1016/j.comnet.2012.10.003

Hassan, A. M., & Awad, A. I. (2018). Urban transition in the era of the internet of things: Social implications and privacy challenges. *IEEE Access : Practical Innovations, Open Solutions, 6*, 36428–36440. doi:10.1109/ACCESS.2018.2838339

He, H., Maple, C., Watson, T., Tiwari, A., Mehnen, J., Jin, Y., & Gabrys, B. (2016). The surveillance challenges in the IoT enabled cyber-physical systems and opportunities for evolutionary computing & other computational intelligence. *Proceedings of the Evolutionary Computation (CEC), 1015–1021.*

Jinsheng, Z. (2018). Design of software architecture stability testing system in IoT framework. *Mod. Electron. Technique, 41*(20), 118–121.

Ke, G., & Hong, Y. H. (2014, August). The research of network invasion detection technology based on genetic algorithm and bp neural network. *Applied Mechanics and Materials, 599–601*, 726–730. doi:10.4028/www.scientific.net/AMM.599-601.726

Khan, R., Khan, S., & Zaheer, R. (2012) Future internet: The internet of things architecture, possible applications and key challenges. In *2012 10th International Conference on Frontiers of Information Technology.* IEEE.

Koroniotis, N., Moustafa, N., Sitnikova, E., & Turnbull, B. (2019). Towards the development of realistic botnet dataset in the Internet of Things for network forensic analytics: Bot-IoT dataset. *Future Generation Computer Systems, 100*, 779–796. doi:10.1016/j.future.2019.05.041

Li, J., Zhang, L., Feng, X., Jia, K., & Kong, F. (2019). Feature extraction and area identification of wireless channel in mobile communication. *J. Internet Technol., 20*(2), 545–553.

Liu, X., Zhao, M., Li, S., Zhang, F., & Trappe, W. (2017). *A surveillance framework for the internet of things in the future internet architecture.* Academic Press.

Monther, A. A., & Tawalbeh, L. (2020). surveillance techniques for intelligent spam sensing and anomaly detection in online social platforms. *Iranian Journal of Electrical and Computer Engineering, 10*, 2088–8708.

Shafagh, H., Hithnawi, A., Burkhalter, L., Fischli, P., & Duquennoy, S. (2017). Secure Sharing of Partially Homomorphic Encrypted IoT Data. *Proceedings of the 15th ACM Conference on Embedded Network Sensor Systems ACM SenSys'17.*

Singh, R., Kumar, H., & Singla, R. K. (2015). An invasion detection system using network traffic profiling and online sequential extreme learning machine. *Expert Systems with Applications, 42*(22), 8609–8624. doi:10.1016/j.eswa.2015.07.015

Srinivas, T. A. & Manivannan, S. S. (2020). Preventing Collaborative Black Hole Attack in IoT Construction Using a CBHA–AODV Routing Protocol. *International Journal of Grid and High Performance Computing, 12*(2), 25-46. http://doi.org/ . 2020040102 doi:10.4018/IJGHPC

Sun, Y., Song, H., Jara, A. J., & Bie, R. (2016). *Internet of Things and Big Data Analytics for Smart and Connected Communities.* Available online: https://ieeexplore.ieee.org/stamp/stamp.jsp?tp=&arnumber=7406686

Trappe, W., Howard, R., & Moore, R. S. (2015). Low-energy surveillance: Limits and opportunities in the internet of things. *IEEE Security and Privacy, 13*(1), 14–21. doi:10.1109/MSP.2015.7

Chapter 10
Exploratory Research of Cyber Security Dimensions:
Selected Use Cases Analysis

Abhishek Vaish
Indian Institute of Information Technology, Prayagraj, India

Vatsala Upadhyay
Indian Institute of Information Technology, Prayagraj, India

Samo Bobek
Faculty of Economics and Business, University of Maribor, Slovenia

Simona Sternad Zabukovsek
(iD) https://orcid.org/0000-0002-7651-7706
Faculty of Economics and Business, University of Maribor, Slovenia

ABSTRACT

Cybersecurity research is gaining a lot of importance in recent times. Bibliometric analysis of cyber security research showed major areas and their overlapping. Due to overlapping research areas with allied areas like system engineering, networking, computer science, information technology, management science, etc., the impact of cyber security research is often hard to gauge. This chapter aims to present the research dimension of cyber security as a number of use cases and an attempt to connect the researcher to understand research areas of cyber security and its complexities through use cases to make them visualize the problem better. In this chapter, the following use cases are presented and analyzed: the role of social media in cyber security issues, how traditional network-based attacks influence the IoT environment, the dynamics of malware and its impact on AI-based detection systems, and security in embedded systems.

DOI: 10.4018/979-8-3693-1528-6.ch010

INTRODUCTION

The exponential growth in the number of incidents in cyberspace has become a concern for every individual. Organizations are investigating enormous resources to tackle the menace of cyber-attack; however, they are still not foolproof. The economics of cyber security is a very interesting domain for researchers to study the causal relationship of heterogonous factors. One of the dominating factors that the attackers exploit cyberspace is financial gain. The variety of cybercrimes can be seen as a product line with different values to be realized if seen from the context of consumerism. It is also interesting to observe that the nature of cyber incidents is changing and evolving from simple logic based to malicious code to tricking human minds. The sophistication of attacks is increasing over time and becoming more and more complicated (Li & Liu, 2021).

Cyber security has become the top priority for the organization, governments and other stakeholders. The rough estimates show that the market reached 173.5 billion in 2022 (Markets and Markets, 2023). Protecting information in cyberspace is highly challenging. The data leakage alone was USD 4.35 million in 2022 (IBM Security, 2022). Ransomware attacks have become a revenue generation industry for many involved in such businesses, with a whopping $ 14 billion in the 2022 global market size (Searchlogistics, 2023). Some industries vulnerable to ransomware attacks are the health sector, financial institutions, ICT companies, etc.

Similarly, if we look at the attacks landscape in the critical infrastructure sector, the highly sophisticated malware targets ways to penetrate the system without getting detected. Another threat that is quite a concern is the insider threat, and therefore critical infrastructure companies are using techniques like design in privacy to handle it. Another attack vector surfacing in the threat landscape is using social engineering techniques to exploit information systems. Attackers are using tricks and techniques to compromise the human decision-making process and compromising information systems. Social engineering-based attacks have become quite popular, and countries with significant populations are the most affected.

Cyber security as a field of research is trending. Researchers are trying to explore directly, indirectly and associative areas of research in the domain of cyber security as the potential domain of research which is scientific and has a future potential. Cybersecurity research is categorized as fundamental research, mainly cryptography. However, this research domain is relatively essential but limited in its way, and researchers are looking more into the applied side of cyber security. Applied cyber security requires much of experimental and validation aspects. Researchers must also find a robust framework for validating the outcome in real-time. There is also a lot of interdisciplinary research. This category of cyber security research is linked with overlapping areas, e.g., computer vision is used in cyber security space, and natural language processing (NLP) is applied in securing cyberspace. Similarly, digital signal processing is used in biometric systems. The fundamental point of differentiation is that the application of the research is in the domain of cyber security, but the scientific model is being adopted from other fields of research.

The complexities involved in cyber security research are a careful consideration for the researchers planning to enter the domain. The researchers should prepare for many essential things before opting for this domain. The complexity is inherently different in sub-categories of cyber security research. The fundamental cyber security researches require proving theories, building up theorems and particular comparison of results against the available research in the field. The study should aim to prove the theory through scientific methods, e.g., any cryptographic techniques should have a theorem as the foundation and then be tested through reverse engineering to test the robustness. The factor critical in advancing research in the applied side of cyber security is the selection of the datasets. Researchers should be careful in choosing the dataset. The factors important in selecting the dataset are versatility, duration and system design. The versatility means that the dataset should have the presence of multiple attack vectors in the respective domain. The duration means the dataset should be considered a time series with an extended period. This increases the size of the dataset and is usually helpful in training the artificial intelligence (AI) model for better accuracy. The third factor is system design. Researchers should be careful to know the topology and configuration of the simulations generated by the dataset. A high system density ensures a realistic scenario, which is vital for real-time detection.

The interdisciplinary research in cyber security suffers from scientific complexities and non-scientific issues, e.g., a very often asked question is to justify the problem as a "cybersecurity" domain. Usually, it is linked with the field's scoping problem and across-discipline issues. The researchers should be ready to answer this question and should be prepared accordingly. Though the field itself is pretty disciplinary, using causal relationship analysis, the researcher can successfully address such questions.

This chapter aims to create a body of knowledge for potential researchers in this direction that will assist them in developing critical thinking. The chapter is organized in the following section. The Introduction part will give insight into the periphery of the research aspects of cyber security. Bibliometrics analysis will serve as state-of-the-art in different aspects of cyber security. The use cases will serve as a specific example for research to get a deeper understanding, aiming to consider those use cases as the potential research direction. Finally, the Conclusion will serve as a short summary and expert recommendation for the researchers.

Bibliometric Analysis

Discussions about bibliometrics began in the 1950s (Wallin, 2005). They refer to applying various quantitative techniques to bibliometric data (e.g., publication units and citations) (Pritchard, 1969; Broadus, 1987). Bibliometric analysis is a rigorous and prevalent technique for analyzing and researching large sizes of scientific literature (Donthu et al., 2021). It has been very popular in Natural Sciences, Biomedical Research and Engineering for a long time (Hicks and Wang, 2011, Mongeon and Paul-Hus, 2015), but recently it has also become very popular in social sciences(Donthu et al., 21020, 2021; Khan et al., 2021). Bibliometric analyses are popular due to: (1) the availability of scientific databases such as Scopus and Web of Science (WoS), (2) free bibliometric software such as VOS viewer, Gephi, Leximancer, etc., and (3) because of the possibility of using in various research fields and the interdisciplinary fields. Bibliometric analyses enable the processing of large amounts of scientific data and generate a significant research impact (Donthu et al., 2021). Bibliometric analysis helps interpret and represent well-established fields' aggregate scientific knowledge and evolutionary distinctions by strictly making sense of enormous quantities of unstructured data. Consequently, fine-performed bibliometric analyses can shape a solid basis for evolving the field in innovative and meaningful ways. It allows researchers to get an overview of the research area in one place, identify gaps in the research area, get new research ideas and place their intended contributions in this research area.

It is important to use bibliometric analysis and other commonly used alternative methods such as meta-analysis and systematic literature review. Aguinis et al. (2011) pointed out that meta-analysis concerns the strength and direction of effects or relationships and the variance between studies in the distribution of effect size estimates and the factors that explain that variance. Meta-analysis also considers large volumes of literature and delivers an accurate summary of a given area. However, the literature considered is less diverse, and the collection of existing publications and publication bias can affect the validity of the results obtained through meta-analysis (Junni, Sarala, Taras & Tarba, 2013). Systematic literature reviews are usually performed manually (Lim, Yap, & Makkar, 2021). They can be theoretical, methodological, or field studies that involve searching, organizing, and evaluating existing literature using systematic procedures (Palmatier, Houston, & Hulland, 2018). They require a narrow scope of study and typically include fewer review articles (Snyder, 2019). They involve qualitative techniques and are more suitable for limited or niche research areas. Donthu et al. (2021) pointed out in their comparison that it makes sense to use bibliometric analysis when the scope of the review is enormous, and the dataset is too big for manual evaluation. Meta-analysis is used when the focus of the study is to summarize the results and not to engage with content that can be broad or specific. And systematic literature review is used when the scope of the study is detailed, and the dataset is small and manageable enough that content can be reviewed manually.

There are two major categories of bibliometric analysis techniques scientific mapping and performance analysis. Scientific mapping focuses on the relationships between research components (e.g. relationship among publications, among cited publications, among topics etc.), while performance analysis considers the impacts of the research components (e.g. total publication, number of contributing authors, co-authored publication, total citations, average citations etc.).In our study, we will also use performance analysis techniques related to publications, such as total publications and the number of active years of publications. We also will use one of the techniques of scientific mapping named co-word analysis. Co-word analysis refers to the analysis of co-words. Words in that analysis are often derived from author keywords. Still, without relevant keywords, essential words can also be extracted from article titles, abstracts and/or full texts (Donthu et al., 2020). Co-word analysis supposes that words that often show together are thematically related. Chang, Huang, and Lin (2015) and Donthu et al. (2021) pointed out that co-word analysis is suitable for enriching the understanding of thematic clusters derived from co-citation analysis and predicting future research in this area.

In addition to the basic bibliometric techniques mentioned above, more advanced methods such as clustering, network analysis and visualization can also be used in the bibliometric analysis (Donthu et al., 2021). The primary goal of clustering is to create thematic or social clusters (depending on the type of analysis being performed). Editing network clusters and observing their evolution can help understand how a research field manifests and evolves. Network analysis illuminates the relative importance of research constituents (e.g., authors, associations, countries) that may not necessarily be reflected in publications or citations. In contrast, visualization is often associated with network visualization software, where most tools are free and open source. The most important visualization tools are VOS viewer, Bibliometrix, Pajek, Bibexcel, Sci2, Gephi, SciMat, UCINET etc.

In our bibliometric analysis, we used the free and open-source tool VOS viewer (van Eck and Waltman, 2023). It was used for the keyword co-occurrence technique (i.e., co-word) for clustering and network visualization. We performed a bibliometric analysis on data from the Scopus database on 15 March 2023. We used the Scopus database because, based on comparative analysis, Mongeon and Paul-Hus (2016) concluded that Scopus also includes the majority of journals that are indexed in WoS and that Scopus has a larger number of exclusive journals than WoS in all fields.

Using the keyword "cybersecurity,[1]" we got 21,392 document results. If we limit ourselves to the subject area of computer science, social sciences and business, management and accounting, we get 12,792. In 2023 alone, 492 documents were already published, which shows the great interest of researchers in this field. Nevertheless, we will exclude 2023 from further analysis as we cannot cover the entire year.

We also limited ourselves to articles, book chapters and books. We got 4,233 document results: 3769 articles (89.0%), 425 book chapters (10%) and 39 books (1%). Document results are distributed according to the subject area: 3,556 documents for computer science (69%), 1,181 for social sciences (23%) and 1,338 for business, management and accounting (8%). Individual documents can be divided into several subject areas. As shown in Figure 1, the first publication dates back to 1999, when there was one paper. Since 2009, the number of documents in this field has increased. In 2020 there were 487 documents. The following year the number of documents almost doubled to 827. Also, in 2022, compared to the previous year, the number of documents doubled (1,640 documents). The first publication, titled "Cyberspace Security Management", by authors Chou, Yen, Lin, and Cheng, was published in the Journal Industrial Management and Data Systems in 1999. The article refers to the problem of internet security. The authors point out that the open environment of the internet contributes significantly to its success but also creates inherent security problems (Chou et al. 1999). The article explores the security framework implemented in the cyberspace setting and current stages and future movements involving this issue.

Figure 1. The time series of published items in the Scopus database, 15 March 2023, with the keyword "cybersecurity"
Source: Authors' research, based on Scopus data

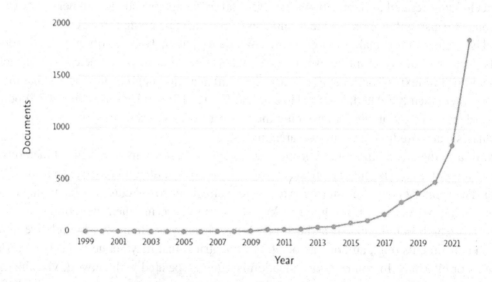

The largest number of documents were written in the United States (1,246), followed by the United Kingdom (402), China (388), India (363), Australia (259), Saudi Arabia (258), Spain (168), Canada (159), Italy (150), South Korea (135) etc., which can be seen in Figure 2.

The most cited article with 1,118 citations is from 2017, titled "DDoS in IoT: Mirai and other botnets" by authors Kolias, Kambourakis, Stavrou, and Voas. The article addresses the Mirai botnet and its variants and imitators as a warning to the industry better to protect internet of things (IoT) devices or risk exposing internet infrastructure to increasingly disruptive distributed denial of service attacks (DDoS) (Kolias et al., 2017). The following is an article with 821 citations entitled "Cyber-physical system security for the electric power grid" by authors Sridhar, Hahn, and Govindarasu from 2012. The article concerns the development of a trusted smart grid that needs a more profound recognition of the

Figure 2. Published items by countries in the Scopus database, 15 March 2023, with the keyword "cy-bersecurity"
Source: Authors' research, based on Scopus data

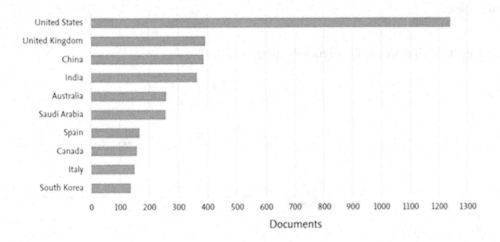

potential impacts of successful cyber-attacks. Assessing an attack's possible impact requires evaluating a network's dependence on its cyber infrastructure and its competence to withstand potential failures.

Further assessment of the cyber-physical relations within the smart grid with a specific investigation of potential attack vectors is needed to verify the appropriateness of cybersecurity efforts. This article highlights the importance of cyberinfrastructure security in conjunction with powering application security to prevent, mitigate and tolerate cyber-attacks (Sridhar et al., 2012).In third place is an article titled "Can Blockchain Power the Internet of Things?" by author Kshetri from 2017, with 537 citations. The paper evaluates blockchain's role in enhancing IoT security. The paper covers the fundamental underlying mechanisms involved in the security link between blockchain and the IoT. From a security perspective, the paper highlights how blockchain-based solutions could be superior to the current IoT ecosystem, which relies primarily on centralized cloud servers. With practical applications and real-world examples, the article explains that decentralized the nature of the blockchain will result in a low susceptibility to manipulation and falsification by malicious participants. Particular attention is paid to how blockchain-based identity and access management systems can address some of the critical challenges related to IoT security (Kshetri, 2017). The last paper, with more than 500 citations, is the paper entitled "Machine Learning and Deep Learning Methods for Cybersecurity" by authors Xin, Kong, Liu, Hou, and Wang from 2018. With the maturity of the internet, cyber-attacks are shifting rapidly, and the state of cyber security is not favorable. This paper describes essential literature research on deep learning (DL) and machine learning (ML) methods for network analysis for intervention detection. It gives a brief lesson explanation for each DL/ML method. Because data is so crucial in DL/ML methods, the authors explain some commonly used network datasets used in DL/ML, highlight the challenges of applying DL/ML to cybersecurity and make suggestions for future research (Xin et al., 2018).

Document results in a total of 21,392, including 21,742 keywords. 122 keywords appear 35 times or more, and 46 are repeated at least 100 times. The most frequently occurring keyword is cybersecurity with 5,722 (26.32%) repetitions, followed by network security with 1,138 (5.23%) repetitions, internet of things (IoT) with 933 (4.29%) repetitions, intrusion detection with 762 (3.50%) repetitions, computer crime or cyber-crime with 719 (3.31%) repetitions, machine learning (ML) with 584 (2.69%) repetitions, cyber- attacks with 505 (2.32%) repetitions etc. Keywords with 100 or more repetitions are shown in Figure 3. The treemap analysis was prepared in Microsoft Excel based on data obtained from the Scopus database.

Figure 3. Treemap of keywords for keyword "cybersecurity"

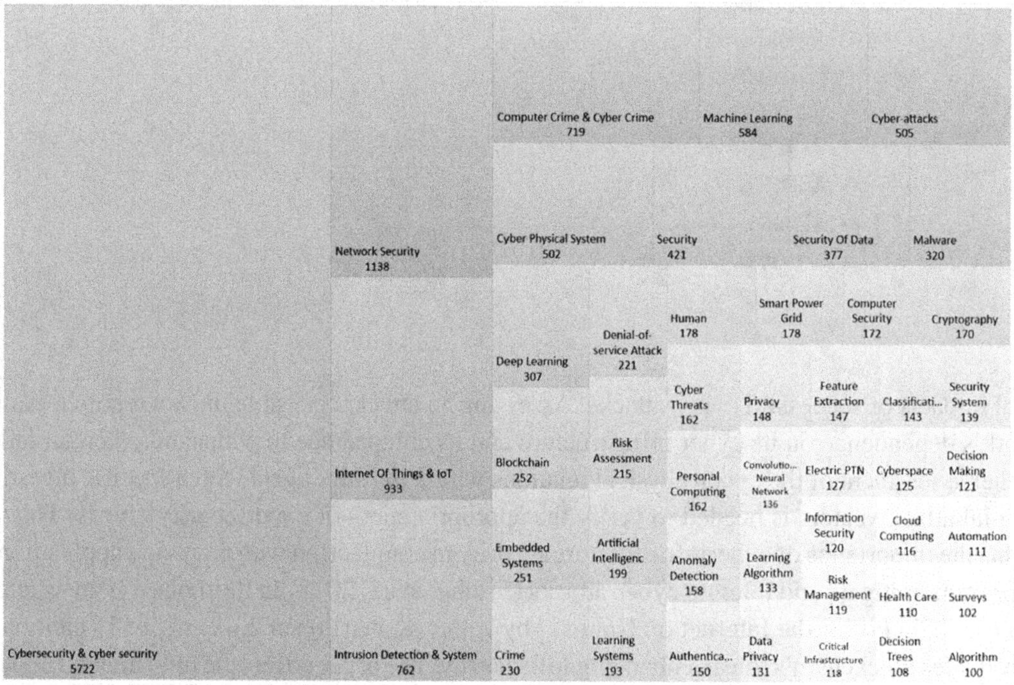

Mapping is the primary method in bibliometric analysis. It aims to produce various bibliometric maps that provide an impression of the organization of scientific publications in a particular research field. One of the most popular ways of using bibliometric mapping is the identification of detailed research areas in a selected scientific field, intending to increase the understanding of the scope of the field and its linked subfields as well as their interconnections (van Eck, 2011). Visualization of Similarity (VOS) is a mapping process used to design bibliometric maps in various analyses. To create bibliometric maps, we used the VOSviewer program, which, in addition to good visualization, can also import data from multiple sources (Moral-Munoz, Herrera-Viedma, Espejo, & Cobo, 2020). Steps for creating bibliographic maps based on data from, e.g., the Scopus database are: (1) recognition of noun phrases, (2) selection of the most relevant noun phrases, (3) mapping and grouping of concepts, (4) visualization of the mapping and (5) clustering results (van Eck, 2011; Moral-Munoz et al., 2020; van Eck & Walterman, 2014). Due to the limitations of the VOSviewer program, that only 2000 bibliographic units can be imported at a time (van Eck, 2023), we divided the documents into three groups according to the period. The first group includes documents from 1999 to 2017 (428 records), the second group contains data from 2018 to 2021 (1,988 records), and the third group includes data for 2022 (1,640 records).

The first period (1999-2017) includes 428 records where 1,098 keywords appear. There are 38 such keywords where the keyword is repeated at least five times. If we limit ourselves to a minimum cluster size of 5, we get four clusters (Figure 4) associated with the keyword cybersecurity:

Figure 4. Bibliometric mapping of clusters for the first period based on the Scopus database, 15 March 2023, keywords "cybersecurity"
Source: Authors' research, based on Scopus data

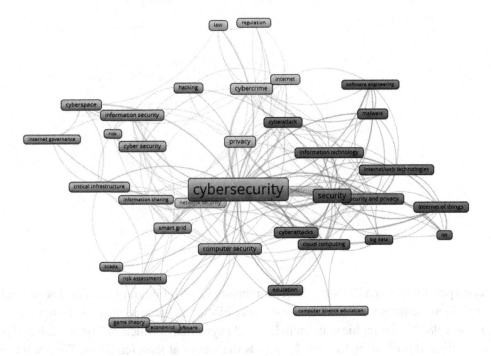

- Cluster 1 (red color) includes big data, cloud computing, cyberattacks, education, IT, internet of things (IoT), internet/web technology, intrusion detection, malware, security and privacy and engineering.
- Cluster 2 (green color) includes critical infrastructure, cyber security, cyberspace, hacking, information security, information sharing, internet governance, network security, risk and smart grid.
- Cluster 3 (blue color) includes computer science education, computer security, cybersecurity, economics, game theory, risk assessment, SCADA and software.
- Cluster 4 (yellow color) includes cybercrime, the internet, law, privacy and regulation.

Figure 5 shows the research over the years. Initially, researchers have focused on computer security, network security, IT and computer education, security and privacy, internet, and regulation. Between 2013 and 2014, research focused on information sharing, smart grid, economy, critical infrastructure, cloud computing, privacy, cyber-attacks, cyber security, internet governance, hacking, cybercrime and cyber-attacks. From 2014 to 2017, researchers focused on information security, malware, software engineering, internet/web technologies, the internet of things (IoT) and big data.

Figure 5. Bibliometric mapping with the time component for the first period based on the Scopus data-base, 15 March 2023, keywords "cybersecurity"
Source: Authors' research, based on Scopus data

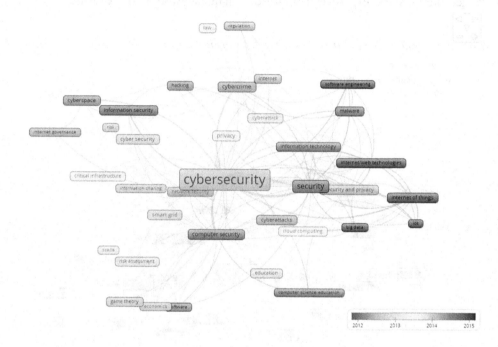

The second period, between 2018 and 2021, comprises 1,988 bibliographic units. The second studied period spanned four years but included 4.6 times more bibliographic units than the first, which spanned 19 years. These 1,988 bibliographic units include 5,333 keywords, of which 241 appear at least five times. Therefore, we limited processing to those keywords that occur at least ten times. We got 93 keywords arranged in 6 clusters (Figure 6).

From Figure 6, we can see which keywords are in the same clusters:

- Cluster 1 (red color) includes the following keywords: 5g, AI, cyberattack, cyber-physical systems, data breach, data security, ethics, hacking, healthcare, internet of things (IoT), privacy, risk assessment, risk management, safety, security, smart cities, threats and vulnerabilities.
- Cluster 2 (green color) includes the following keywords: authentication, big data, blockchain, cloud computing, cryptography, cyber risk, cybersecurity, cyber threats, cyber-physical system, digitalization, game theory, IoT, IIoT, industry 4.0, smart city and vulnerability.
- Cluster 3 (blue color)) includes attack detection, awareness, data mining, education, framework, IDS, industrial control system, information security, network, resilience, SCADA, smart grid, standards, technology, training and trust.
- Cluster 4 (yellow color)) includes bitcoin, cybercrime, cyberspace, data privacy, data protection, digital economy, digital transformation, governance, human rights, IIoT, internet, national security and risk.

Figure 6. Bibliometric mapping of clusters for the second period based on the Scopus database, 15 March 2023, keywords "cybersecurity"
Source: Authors' research, based on Scopus data

- Cluster 5 (violet color)) includes AI, botnet, covid-19, critical infrastructure, cyberattack, cyber threat, digital forensics, incident response, information sharing, malware, phishing, ransomware, social engineering and threat intelligence.
- Cluster 6 (light blue color) includes anomaly detection, classification, cyberattacks, deep learning (DL), feature selection, intrusion detection, machine learning (ML), malware detection, natural language processing (NLP), network security and neural networks.

From Figure 7, we can see that in 2018 and the first part of 2019, the most keywords and research were around data security, industrial control systems, data mining, AI, ethics, security, privacy, bitcoin, safety and safety risk. Then in the second part of 2019 to 2020, most research were focused on cyber-security in connection with risk, education, trust, cyber-physical systems, threats, big data, SCADA, cyberattack, internet, national security, data protection, internet, cyberspace, data breach, Internet of Things (IoT) and IoT, malware, information sharing, human rights, cybercrime, information security, governance, smart cities, cyber risk, vulnerability and cloud computing (Aqeel et al., 2022) . And in the period between 2020 and 2021, studies were oriented to cybersecurity with the following keywords: digital transformation, ransomware, threat intelligence botnet, social engineering, network security,

Figure 7. Bibliometric mapping with the time component for the second period based on the Scopus database, 15 March 2023, keywords "cybersecurity"
Source: Authors' research, based on Scopus data

cyberattack, industry 4.0, blockchain, awareness, IDS, incident response, network, digital forensics, digital economy, machine learning and malware detection. During the year 2021, the following keywords appear in connection with cybersecurity: digitalization, data privacy, cyberattacks, machine learning, malware detection, digitalization, cyberattacks, healthcare, neural networks, cyber-physical system, 5G, authentication, smart city, cyber threats, classification, feature selection, infusion detection system, deep learning, intrusion detection and natural language processing (NLP).

The year 2022 contains 1,640 bibliographic units, almost double 2021, when there were 836. 4,556 keywords appear in 1,640 bibliographic units, with 195 appearing at least five times. We limited the processing to those keywords that occur at least ten times. We obtained 66 keywords, classified into four groups (Figure 8):

- Cluster 1 (red color) includes the following keywords: attacks, authentication, big data, blockchain, cloud computing, cryptography, cyberattacks, encryption, healthcare, IDS, industry 4.0, IoT, intrusion detection and intrusion detection systems, machine learning, privacy, risk assessment, security, smart city, smart grid and vulnerability.
- Cluster 2 (green color) includes the following keywords: adversarial machine learning, anomaly detection, classification, convolutional neural network, cyber threat intelligence, deep learning, ensemble learning, feature selection, IoT, intrusion detection system, malware analysis, malware detection, ransomware and transfer learning.

Figure 8. Bibliometric mapping of clusters for the third period based on the Scopus database, 15 March 2023, keywords "cybersecurity"
Source: Authors' research, based on Scopus data

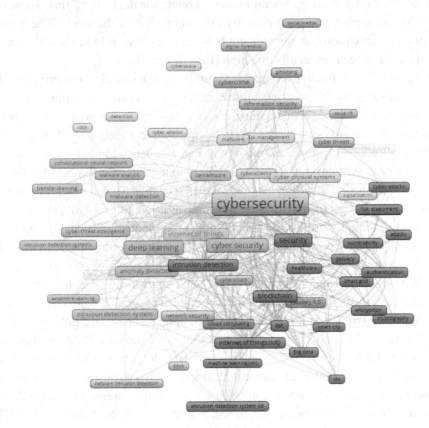

- Cluster 3 (blue color) includes the following keywords: artificial intelligence (AI), computer security, covid-19, cyber threats, cyberattacks, cybercrime, DDoS, digital forensics, information security, machine learning, network intrusion detection, network security, phishing, social media.
- Cluster 4 (yellow color) includes the following keywords: attack detection, critical infrastructure, cyber-attacks, cyber-physical systems, cyberspace, detection, digitalization, industrial control system, malware and risk management.

Based on the bibliometric analysis, we can conclude that cybersecurity has become increasingly important over the years. Conducted bibliometric analysis shows that research is growing fast, reflected in the increased number of articles and book chapters. On the other hand, we can see that research is becoming broader dimensions. The bibliometric analysis shows that many new research areas are emerging and that interdisciplinarity is gaining importance. In the rest of the chapter, four areas are explained and discussed.

Use Case 1: The Role of Social Media in Cyber Security Issues

The popularity of social media among researchers is gaining a lot of importance in the digital era. Social media has become a gold mine for researchers to mine different data types. Social media has emerged as a participatory platform wherein users share their views, post content, use it to establish connections, etc. Social media is used for more than just social contact and communication. It's also used for entertainment and information gathering. Social media accounts for the bulk of time spent on the internet. Social media users are rapidly and geometrically expanding all over the world. The use of social media as a medium of communication and engagement between people worldwide is widespread. Conversely, negative social media usage is at an all-time high (Eriksson et al., 2022).

It has given people more freedom to express themselves, particularly in politics. Furthermore, businesses have adopted social media to varied degrees in their operations, assuming it substantially impacts corporate development. Because social media users have so much freedom of speech, spreading abuse or hate speech toward individuals, groups, or society has become relatively easy. The term "hate speech" is "public communication that expresses hatred or advocates violence toward a person or group based on something such as race, religion, sex, or sexual orientation," states the Cambridge Dictionary (2023). On the internet, it is defined as insulting language directed against a particular group of individuals who share a similar attribute. Social media has been identified as a valuable tool for planning and carrying out hate-related actions. Examples are Delhi Riots in India (Wikipedia, 2020) and Capitol Hill Riots in the US (Reuters, 2022). YouTube removed approximately 500 million comments that violated its stated hate speech policy in September 2019, a two-fold increase from the previous quarter. Given the prevalence of young children using YouTube to share films, this isn't comforting (Bruch, 2019).

The bibliometric analysis shows that social media and hate speech are also becoming essential areas within cybersecurity (Alkomah & Ma, 2022). In the Scopus database, we got 1,736 documents where the keywords "social media" and "attack" appear by the end of the year 2022. We limited subject areas to computer science (1,146 documents), social sciences (639documents), engineering (512documents), decision sciences (219documents), mathematics (212documents), and business, management and accounting (86documents). The same document can be in several subject areas. We added the keyword "hate speech" in our search. We got 65 documents, of which three were in 2016 and one in 2017. The number of documents per year increased yearly until 2022 when 23 documents were published (see Figure 9). Of those 65 documents, 49 documents are from the computer science subject area, 21 documents are from the social sciences subject area, 17 documents are from engineering subject area, followed by decision sciences (13), mathematics (7), and business, management and accounting (1). 159 keywords appear in 65 documents. The keyword social media appears most often (35 times), followed by the keywords social networking (online) (33), hate speech (26), speech recognition (20), machine learning (13), deep learning (12), search detection (12), social media platforms (8), natural language processing (NLP)systems (7), offensive languages (7), text processing (6), classification (of information) (5), decision trees (5), deep neural networks (5), learning algorithms (5), long-short term memory (5), machine learning (5), text classification (5). Other keywords appear less than five times.

We need a smart system to recognize offensive or manipulated social media news. Because many responses can be sent and retrieved on multiple social media sites daily, manually screening out this data is impossible. For example, WhatsApp handles 4 billion daily messages (Shetty, 2012). The researcher is motivated to create an AI-based system because of the requirement for an automated system.

The problem we face in detecting manipulative content is that it is a very complex operation since there is so much content on social media or in the news that it is difficult to interpret whether it is manipulative after analyzing all of the words and sentences.

Let's say that when you put black men in a phrase, you get racism and manipulative content, but when you separate the words black and men, you don't receive manipulative content. As a result, determining

Figure 9. The number of publications over the years in the Scopus database, 27 March 2023, with key-words "social media", "attack", and "hate speech"

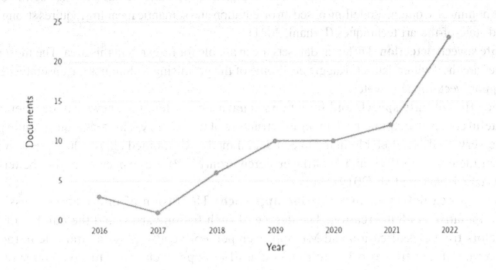

the solution is a complex job. In 2007, Estonia was at a standstill. Fifty-eight websites were offline at once, an outrageous act linked with the disputed relocation of the soviet-era Brownz Soldier monument (McGuinness, 2017).

Natural language processing (NLP) is a branch of computer science that applies machine learning (ML) techniques to natural human languages (Lutkevich, 2023). Sentiment analysis, sarcasm identification, machine translation, speech recognition, automated dialogue systems, topic categorization, false tweet detection, and other NLP applications attempt to analyze printed verbal human languages automatically. NLP approaches have recently been used to investigate the thoughts and social media users' reactions to the COVID-19 outbreak. We can use ML and NLP to classify news stories into many sections and implement the same logic. Even with these, distinguishing between hate speeches and false news can be tricky since these pieces may contain a range of facts that might spread hatred and ignorance among the public, leading to a chaotic scenario in society.

There has been a lot of advancement in online social life, well-being and security during the last decade. This study is beneficial for identifying and avoiding various sorts of offensive language in online journals, blogs, and social media platforms (Uchendu et al., 2021).

Social media and its associated cyber security issues/challenges could lead the researchers to find a research gap as a potential scientific problem. The literature review of this research is quite diverse. To reach the epicentre of the research gap, it is necessary to look into various subdomains. The significant concentration of the review is to understand the impact of manipulative news in destabilizing the social order, the use of hate speech to spread hatred, use of ML, AI, NLP and software tools that have been used to mitigate either fake news or hate speech in the web environment (Rastogi et al., 2022). The correlation between manipulative content and the virality of information metrics to measure the impact (Geldiyev et al., 2020). Multimodal systems for detecting it and exploring the past work in fusion datasets. Some of the subdomains in this direction of research are as follows:

1. **Framework to measure manipulative content:** The contents and their orientation are a complex problem because the output of the information system and its interaction with the cognitive system are nonlinear. Content modelling based on orientation and semantic meaning requires strong models and state-of-the-art techniques (Lohani, 2021).
2. **Hate speech detection:** Different datasets are available for research in this area. The most popular ones are the Twitter dataset, Kaggle etc. Some of the promising techniques are ensemble learning, support vector machine etc.
3. **Detection of hate speech and fake news separately:** Often, fake news can be oriented with hateful content to exploit the democratic structure of the country. This technique is quite popular and very easily exploitable in the age of social media. Combined approaches like Long short-term memory (LSTM), and Multilayer Perceptron(MLP) are expected to give better results (Pereira-Kohatsu et al., 2019).
4. **Hate speech detection using fusion approach:** The fusion of information in essence for manipulative content creation. The degree of such fusion varies, and the number of feature vectors from classification and ML approach perceptive also plays a vital role in the detection rate of any framework. Multiclass classifiers approach proof to give better results in such scenarios. These classifiers include logistic regression (LM), random forest (RF) and support vector machine (SVM). They used deep learning to extract features, which they combined with other syntactic and n-gram features before using a simple baseline classifier (SVM, LR, RF) for training and prediction.
5. **Virality:** The semantics structure of the content and the use of bots in social media are the drivers for content propagation (Aldwairi et al., 2018). The phenomena can be explained by a quantitative technique like power law to see if exponential growth is observed. The power law is an important function to measure nonlinear relationships and is expressed by the equation given: $y = a \times x \times k$, where x and y have a nonlinear relationship and k and a are constants, respectively (Calderón, 2019; Roman & Bertolotti, 2022).

Finally, an example that could be useful for the research to scope their research problem is indicated in Table 1. The researcher can use it as a small concept which prepares the research objective. Table 1 facilitates the research to the scope of the research problem. Usually, in applied research, the challenge is to differentiate between the functionality and the novelty; therefore, researchers can follow to scope of their research problem.

Table 1. Concept for scoping research in hate speech detection

Objective	Functionality	Novelty
To classify a text based on the orientation of the content.	✓	
Fusion of the dataset to increase the accuracy and efficiency of the model.		✓
Classify based on multiple algorithms, compare their performances in detail, and dig deep into why a certain algorithm performs better than the others.	✓	
Implement one of the latest algorithms and techniques for the problem.	✓	
Build the algorithm.		✓

Use Case 2: How Traditional Network-Based Attacks Influence the IoT Environment

Distributed Denial-of-Service (DDoS) attack is one type of overwhelming attack originating from multiple sources, which is targeted different segments of information systems. For example, network components, applications, servers and other intermediary devices forming part of the information system are subject to denial-of-service (DoS) attacks. DDoS attacks can be seen as a many-to-one network problem and are considered one of the top attack vectors against organizations. Researchers are looking at various dimensions of research potentially suitable for scientific requirements, e.g., detection of DDoS attacks using ML approaches, backtracking of multiple proxy addresses, etc. DoS and DDoS are getting a lot of attention in ubiquitous computing, especially in IoT environments, because these systems suffer from the drawback of resource constraints of all kinds, making them a suitable environment to launch DDoS attacks.

In the Scopus database, we checked the number of bibliometric documents for the keywords "Internet of things (IoT)" and "attack". We got 14,721 document results. We supplemented the keyword "attack" with "cyberattack" and add the keyword "security", and we got 1,636 document results, where we limited ourselves to the subject areas of computer science, computer science (1,475 documents), social sciences (116 documents), engineering (915 documents), decision sciences (286 documents), mathematics (261 documents), and business, management and accounting (46 documents). The same document can be in several subject areas. From these numbers, we can conclude that many documents are interdisciplinary (including several subject areas). The first publications appeared in 2014 (6 documents), then increased yearly until 2022, when 474 bibliographic units were published (Figure 10). 142 keywords were used at least 20 times, of which the keyword "network security" appeared the most (1,230 times), followed by the following keywords Internet of things (IoT) (1,208), cyber-attacks (642), cybersecurity (471), computer crime (453), crime (349), intrusion detection (314), machine learning (256) and security (242).

Figure 10. The number of publications over the years in the Scopus database, 27 March 2023, with keywords "internet of things (IoT)", "cyberattack", and "security"

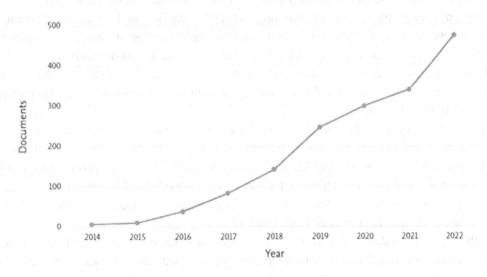

When researching DDoS detection for IoT devices, several critical issues should be considered, including:

1. **Scalability:** From a few devices to very large-scale deployment, IoT devices are used to create ad hoc interconnected networks and generate a lot of data from every individual device. Such voluminous data requires essential consideration, and research should plan for an excellent preprocessing technique for further necessary action.

2. **Diversity of IoT devices:** IoT devices are highly heterogeneous regarding their hardware, software, and communication protocols (Lee et al., 2021). Any DDoS detection mechanism should be able to handle the diversity of IoT devices and their communication patterns.

3. **Overhead cost:** It's pretty evident that IoT is resource constraints ad hoc network of interconnected devices. The researcher should be careful in designing lightweight detection frameworks to be practical. They suffer from the drawback of power, memory, and battery life, so resource-intensive solutions will not be suitable. Another DDoS detection mechanism should be designed to minimize resource consumption.

4. **Design consideration:** There are mainly two schools of thought in detection frameworks, i.e., real-time or near real-time detection frameworks. They are both linked with designing the system. Sophisticated IoT devices are controller enabled in a limited sense and, therefore, can be used for real-time detection under certain situations. However, it has also been seen that resource-intensive detection frameworks opt to use a decentralized-based environment and push the many processing into servers fetched in a specific time delay. So, depending on the requirements, the framework's design is essential for the researchers.

5. **Privacy and security:** IoT devices use much data for different application needs. Therefore, the security and privacy of the data are the paramount concern. The IoT devices are compatible with TCP/IP protocol, and when connected to the public network, it can lead to many security concerns for the data, e.g., botnets.

The research direction in DDoS detection in IoT environments falls under ML techniques, such as deep learning, for improving the accuracy and speed of DDoS detection. ML has shown promising results in other security domains and can potentially enhance DDoS detection in IoT networks.

ML approaches are pretty suitable for handling IoT device traffic and their use for detecting DDoS attacks. The number of features is relatively high, and the sophistication of attacks often uses the evasive method to avoid getting detected. Therefore, the traditional rule-based methods are not remarkably optimized. ML models can learn from the traffic patterns of IoT devices and automatically identify anomalies that indicate DDoS attacks. These models can also adapt to changes in traffic patterns over time and improve their accuracy.

Therefore, future research in this domain should focus on developing ML techniques that are scalable, adaptable, and can handle the diverse traffic patterns of IoT devices. Researchers should also address the privacy and ethical concerns of using ML on IoT data. Overall, ML has the potential to significantly improve the accuracy and speed of DDoS detection in IoT networks and is a promising direction for future research in this domain. The various ML and deep learning techniques used in the detection of DDoS attack in IoT environment is placed in Figure 11.

One of the types of models in the deep learning domain is known as the transformer model (He, 2020). The transformer model is a type of deep learning architecture with excellent performance in

Figure 11. Classification of ML approaches in DDoS detection in IOT systems

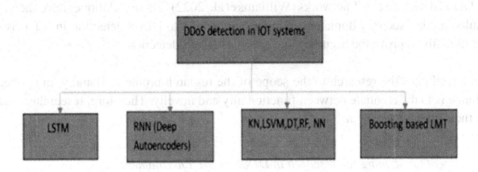

natural language processing (NLP) tasks, such as language translation and text generation. However, recent research has also demonstrated the potential of transformer models for non-NLP tasks, including network traffic analysis, intrusion detection, and DDoS detection, as the network traffic has text strings.

The transformer model is particularly well-suited for DDoS detection in IoT devices for several reasons:

- **Attention mechanism:** The attention mechanism focuses on the query vector of the input sequence and ensures optimized patterns. In a DDoS attack, the complexity generates the relationship in IoT communication and draws patterns to find correlations in different device network traffic.
- **Sequence modelling:** DDoS attacks are many-to-one flooding problems the sequence modelling can effectively measure the flow dynamics. The transformer model can effectively learn the traffic patterns associated with DDoS attacks.
- **Agile:** The transformer model can be adapted to different types of network traffic data, making it highly flexible and adaptable to the diverse traffic patterns of IoT devices.

However, it's important to note that the use of transformer models for DDoS detection in IoT devices is still an active area of research. While initial results are promising, researchers must continue to explore and refine these models to optimize their performance and address the unique challenges of IoT networks.

The topic of DDoS detection for IoT devices is essential for researchers for several reasons:

1. **Increasing prevalence of IoT devices:** The number of IoT devices is rapidly growing, and these devices are becoming more prevalent in our daily lives (Rajmohan et al., 2022). With more IoT devices being deployed, the risk of DDoS attacks targeting these devices also increases, making it essential for researchers to study and develop effective DDoS detection techniques for IoT networks.
2. **The growing threat of DDoS attacks:** DDoS attacks are a significant threat to organizations and individuals alike. These attacks can cause financial and reputational damage, disrupt services, and compromise data. As IoT devices become more interconnected, they become more vulnerable to DDoS attacks, which can result in severe consequences.
3. **Unique challenges of IoT networks:** IoT networks present unique challenges for DDoS detection, such as the heterogeneity of IoT devices, the diversity of traffic patterns, and the limited resources of these devices. Researchers must develop innovative and practical approaches to overcome these challenges and develop robust DDoS detection systems for IoT networks.

4. **Advancement in technologies:** There have been advancements in ML techniques that can be used for DDoS detection in IoT networks (Williams et al., 2022). These techniques have shown promising results in other security domains, and their application to DDoS detection in IoT networks could significantly improve the accuracy and speed of DDoS detection.

Table 2 facilitates the research to the scope of the research problem. Usually, in applied research, the challenge is to differentiate between functionality and novelty. Therefore, researchers can follow to scope of their research problem.

Table 2. Concept for scoping the research in DDoS in IoT Environment

Objective	Functionality	Novelty
Creation of new rules to detect the presence of traces of DDoS attacks on the known dataset.	✓	
Classify based on multiple algorithms, compare their performances in detail, and dig deep into why a certain algorithm performs better than the others.		✓
Developing a real-time test bed with multiple IoT devices and validating the algorithm for some known attacks.		✓
Build the algorithm.		✓

Use Case 3: The Dynamics of Malware and Its Impact on AI-Based Detection Systems

Malware is "any code added, changed, or removed from a software system to intentionally cause harm or subvert the system's intended function" (Zhou et al., 2005). (Spinellis, 2003) has proved that detecting bounded-length viruses is a Non-deterministic Polynomial-time (NP) complete problem. So, we may use heuristic knowledge to identify malware with higher accuracy. The feature extraction detects non-signature-based malware. The code that shows such features is categorized as a malware threat in these recent technologies that predict this: machine learning (ML) and deep learning.

In the Scopus database, we search for the keyword "malware". We got 18,723 document results up to, including, the year 2022. If we include the keyword "detection system", we get 1,510 document results. The first document appeared in 2007; since then, the documents have been increasing yearly. In 2022, there were 234 publications (Figure 12). We limited ourselves to the subject areas of computer science (1,384), social sciences (116), engineering (643), decision sciences (181), mathematics (303), and business, management, and accounting (29). The same document can be in several subject areas. From these numbers, we can conclude that many documents are interdisciplinary (including several subject areas). There are 128 keywords that appear more than 20 times. The keyword malware appears the most (1,158 times), followed by intrusion detection (583), computer crime (525), malware detection (513), network security (492), intrusion detection systems (411), machine learning (364), learning systems (274), Android (operation system) (217) and detection system (208).

Cybercriminals are now using different modes of attacks. It is convenient, and efficacy and stealth mode are the main challenges for the security team. In this way, cybercriminals execute the malicious code using legitimate tools in stealth mode. In this way, exploiting legitimate tools leaves few footprints for detecting the malware. Metamorphic malware is a type of malware that changes its code to avoid

Figure 12. The number of publications in the Scopus database over the years, 27 March 2023, with the keyword "malware"

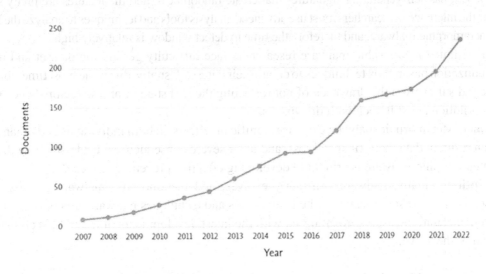

detection by antivirus software. Research in this domain involves understanding how metamorphic malware operates, developing techniques to detect and analyze it, and exploring ways to prevent its spread.

Research often uses one of the following techniques for analysis:

1. **Static malware analysis:** Information is extracted from code to determine whether the software contains malicious code using reverse engineering, which involves analyzing the code structure and understanding how it works.
2. **Dynamic malware analysis:** Malicious codes are run in a virtual environment to observe their behavior and to design actions against the observed behavior.
3. **Hybrid malware analysis:** Firstly, the software is observed by code analysis by checking the malware signature, and then it is run in a virtual environment to keep its actual behavior.

Some of the critical issues involved in the research domain of metamorphic malware are:

1. **Hard to detect:** Metamorphic malware is very sophisticated as it can signify the file using a self-generating engine module to randomize it, making it hard to detect. This is an open problem before researchers and various researchers in the domain of its detection are conducted. Some of the techniques presently being used for detection are:
    a. **Signature-based:** A sequence of bits is embedded in the code and then verified from which family the malicious code belongs. The antivirus program dissembles the code of the infected file and searches for the pattern that belongs to the malicious family.
    b. **Heuristic-based:** Detects or differentiates between the system's normal and abnormal behavior. It consists of two steps. (1) Behavior of the system in the absence of attack is observed, and valuable information is recorded. (2) Malware of a particular family is detected.
    c. **Specification-based:** It is derived from a heuristic-based detection technique. Instead of AI and ML methods, it is based on an analysis of behavior described in the system specification.

2. **Randomness:** The concept of building a model in ML requires an adequate amount of data. Metamorphic because it has self-generating signatures that create randomness, and the features are pretty sparse to draw the inference. Researchers must use advanced analysis tools and techniques to analyze the behavior of metamorphic malware, and therefore the time to detect window is relatively high.

3. **Simulation:** Metamorphic malware researchers face difficulty getting the dataset and must use virtualization or sandbox techniques to create their dataset. Usually, this is the most time-consuming task and suffer from the drawback of not reflecting the real state of attack vectors hence the real-time solution are still open with drawbacks.

4. **Impact:** Metamorphic malware can have significant effects on both individuals and organizations. It can result in data theft, financial loss, and other severe consequences. Understanding the impact of metamorphic malware is critical to developing effective preventative measures.

5. **Evolution:** Finally, malware constantly evolves, and metamorphic malware is no exception. Researchers must stay current on the latest trends and techniques malware creators use to develop effective countermeasures. Keeping up with the latest developments in the field is crucial to stay ahead of the curve.

Metamorphic malware detection is an ever-evolving field of research due to the constantly changing nature of malware. Here are some potential new directions for research in metamorphic malware detection:

1. **Machine learning and artificial intelligence:** One potential new direction for research in metamorphic malware detection is ML and AI. By training models to recognize patterns in malware code and behavior, researchers could develop more accurate and effective methods for detecting metamorphic malware (Zhang et al., 2022).

2. **Behavioral analysis:** Another approach to metamorphic malware detection is to analyze the behavior of the malware rather than its code. By studying how malware interacts with a system and identifying unusual or suspicious behavior, researchers could develop more effective methods for detecting and preventing the spread of metamorphic malware.

3. **Hardware-based solutions:** A potential new direction for research in metamorphic malware detection is the development of hardware-based solutions. By incorporating malware detection and prevention mechanisms into hardware components such as processors or network cards, it could be possible to detect and prevent metamorphic malware before it even reaches the operating system.

4. **Blockchain-based solutions:** Another potential direction for research is using blockchain technology for malware detection. By creating a distributed ledger of known malware signatures and behaviors, detecting and preventing the spread of metamorphic malware across a network could be possible.

5. **Collaborative approaches:** Finally, a potential new direction for research is the development of collaborative approaches to metamorphic malware detection. By bringing together experts from multiple disciplines, including computer science, cybersecurity, and psychology, researchers could develop more comprehensive and effective methods for detecting and preventing the spread of metamorphic malware.

Table 3, indicated below, facilitates the research to use it to scope the research problem. Usually, in applied research, the challenge is to differentiate between functionality and novelty. Therefore, researchers can follow to scope of their research problem.

Table 3. Concept for scoping the research in malware analysis

Objective	Functionality	Novelty
Development of a test bed for dataset generation and simulation of malignant codes		✓
Testing the algorithm's accuracy in the existing dataset, e.g., portable executable (PE) file write headers or other malware codes dataset.	✓	
Implementation of the algorithm in real-time scenarios.		✓
Use of collaborative approaches for detection and prevention in optimized time delay		✓

Use Case 4: Security in Embedded Systems

With the growing dependence on embedded systems in health care applications, business management, industry and home automation, etc., a need arises to protect the entities associated with them, mainly data, things, and processes. Embedded systems security protects the system's hardware and software from attacks (Rajendran et al., 2019; Papp et al., 2015).

We searched for the keywords "embedded system" and "cyber security" in the Scopus database. We got 1,090 documents (articles, conference papers, books and book chapters are included). The first published document was a conference paper published in the year 2003. Figure 13 shows that the number of publications grew until 2019 when 169 documents were published.

Figure 13. The number of publications in the Scopus database over the years, 27 March 2023, with the keywords "embedded system" and "cybersecurity"

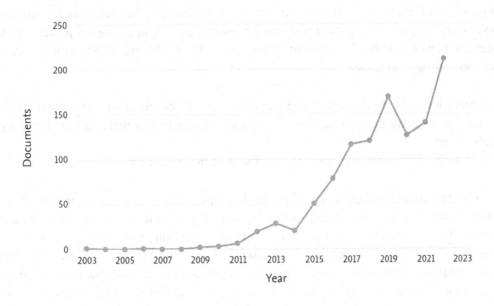

In years 2020 was, 126 documents published. In 2021 140 and in the year 2022, 211 documents were published. Most documents are from the computer science subject area (853), followed by engineering (665), mathematics (245), decision science (101), social sciences (72), and business, management and accounting (16). A hundred keywords are used 20 times or more. The most used keyword is embedded system (1,059), followed by cyber security (848), cyber-physical system (CPS) (541), network security (459), computer crime (239), electric power transmission network (183), cyberattack (154), IoT (153), crime (145), smart power grids (138), security of data (136), risk assessment (108) etc.

Security in embedded systems addresses the following (Aloseel et al., 2020):

1. Tamper resistance
2. Content security
3. Secure storage of data
4. Secure network access
5. User authentication and identification

This section aims to bring the issues regarding securing embedded devices to reality. These attacks occur on the devices through some use cases, along with discussions on the solutions and improvement of the existing methods.

Embedded systems software is programmable and is designed to perform specific tasks. For example, to fulfil a particular purpose like a pacemaker to control the heart beats; ATM (Automated Teller Machine) to perform money transactions, automatic washing machines, digital cameras, etc. In these systems, the property of fulfilling the required functionality brings some loopholes. The manufacturers of these systems focus on the design aspect, as given below:

- **Compact designing:** Since a specific functionality has to be addressed, manufacturers of the systems opt for small device sizes.
- **Portability:** So that it is easy to carry around and is available to the user as and when needed.
- **Low computing power:** Manufacturers look for cost-cutting by employing low power consumption.
- **Short memory capacity:** For efficient system usage, the RAM and ROM of the devices usually have short storage capacities.

These properties make the devices vulnerable to attacks, which can occur directly on the device or by compromising the software of the device. The system's design is such that attackers can compromise the device's security.

Some of the attacks that directly affect the hardware of the system are:

1. **Side channel attacks (Apriorit, 2023):** In this type of attack, the attacker extracts information by comprehending the cryptographic keys (a template attack). An attacker can access the device's data by intercepting the electromagnetic radiation from the hardware, such as the monitor or hard drive. Attackers look for a security exploit in the device and try to extract the secret key from the system's chip. The current flowing from the system's supply, the electromagnetic emissions coming out from the system, etc., contribute to this type of attack (also known as an "electromagnetic attack").

2. **Timing attacks:** Another way the data can be compromised is by analyzing the time the machine takes to respond to different inputs and execute the cryptographic algorithm. The device mostly affected by this attack is the cryptosystems. To attack using this technique, a hacker needs to have

a deep knowledge of the system's architecture and gain physical access. Nowadays, the most commonly used device in every sector, smartcards, are more prone to this type of attack.

3. **Fault injection attack:** An attacker temporarily tampers with the processor's electrical inputs, disrupting the program counter, modifying the device's firmware, etc. Usually, this type of attack requires hardware modification of the target device. It is typically done to alter the intended behavior of the system. The term "glitch" is used to define this type of attack. Voltage glitching means changing the initial voltage parameters-decreasing or increasing the voltage. Clock glitching means altering the synchronizing timing between the operations being performed. Optical glitching means exposing the chip to the infrared laser. All glitches are the different ways the fault injection attack takes place. By violating the safe ranges of these operating parameters, a fault occurs within the processor, resulting in skipped instructions or corrupt memory transactions, incorrect data fetch, and failed execution.

4. **Hardware trojans:** It is pre-installed inside the device without the user's information. It is malicious and is triggered at unpredictable times. It has two components: trigger and payload to determine the trojan's purpose.

The attacks described above occur in the physical presence of the device with the attacker. One way the attacks can be reduced is to look out for electromagnetic radiation coming out from the device and employ robust cryptographic algorithm methods for the encryption and decryption of data.

Some of the methods which can assist the researchers in addressing the security issue in embedded systems are listed below:

1. **Hardware Security Modules (HSMs):** As the name implies, HSMs are physical computing devices that manage the security of the secret keys shared between the embedded devices to provide strong authentication. These have tampered-resistant hardware devices that can help secure the generation of secret keys, digital signatures, and certificates. It is an external device which can be attached to the system. These days, HSMs are widely used in Public Key Infrastructure (PKI) environments and financial sectors.

2. **Physical Unclonable Functions (PUFs):** PFUs have emerged as a hardware security technique that offers improved cryptography, anti-counterfeiting on integrated circuits (ICs), etc. It is a technique in hardware security that exploits inherent device variations to produce an unclonable, unique response for a given input. For a given "challenge"/input, a unique output is generated every time, which is unclonable. The unique identifier or key is not stored for a PUF. Instead, it is generated only when the response needs to be produced, giving it an edge over other security mechanisms.

3. **Random number generators:** There are two types of random number generators (ETAS, 2023): (1) Pseudo-random number generators are software-generated random numbers based on mathematical calculations and formulas (Rambus, 2023). The number is generated in a short period and is also efficient. These can be used in chipper algorithms for successful cryptographic key generation (Figure 14). (2) True random number generator: It is a sort of device based on a phenomenon called "entropy source"; being unpredictable, it generates indeterministic data and thus helps to seed security algorithms. These are being widely used nowadays in gaming, cryptography, key generation for various algorithms, chip manufacturing for devices, nonce generation, authentication of devices, and protection against physical attacks. This has emerged as a trustworthy option for security in embedded devices.

Figure 14. Working of a pseudo-random number generator

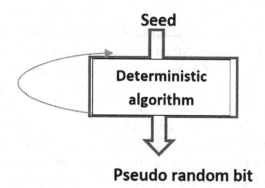

4. **Blockchain:** It is a chain of blocks that stores information. Lately, researchers and experts have started combining the features of blockchain and embedded systems to enhance device security. Blockchain as a service is widely used in health care management, supply chain, cryptocurrency wallets, secure generation of keys for smart cards, and physical and logical protection of physical keys.

5. **System and architectural protection techniques:** Creating a trusted execution environment using Trusted Platform Module (TPMs), cached side-channel mitigations, control flow integrity, checking for abnormal electromagnetic emissions, power outages, runtime monitoring of the devices, pre- and post-silicon manufacturing countermeasures etc., are considered in this method.

Table 4, indicated below, facilitates the research to use it to scope the research problem. Usually, in applied research, the challenge is to differentiate between functionality and novelty. Therefore, researchers can follow to scope of their research problem.

Table 4. Concept for scoping the research in embedded system security

Objective	Functionality	Novelty
PUF and Blockchain for IoT devices.	✓	
Lightweight CMOS implementation for Embedded devices.	✓	
Investigation of a new blockchain model to solve the problem of latency, complexity and scalability in embedded systems.		✓
Onboard intrusion detection system and attack resilient control techniques.		✓
Build the algorithm.		✓

Future Research Directions

This section deals with the possibility of exploring the areas that have the potential for the researcher to contribute in the area of cyber security in general and direction concerning the independent use case in particular. Cyber security in social media analytics concerning the detection of latent semantics to classify the content's orientation is a sought-after research domain. The use of deep learning methods are quite popular, e.g. LSTM and Bi -LSTM technique gives promising results in the field of natural language processing (NLP). Another potential domain is developing and optimizing multimodal systems for social media analytics from cyber security perceptive. The security of IoT devices is a paramount concern. The inherent problem with IoT devices is that they suffer from resource limitations. Therefore, the attacker aims to exploit the device's resources by using DDoS or DoS, e.g. the processing capabilities, the energy or even the device's power of receiving and transmitting the data. The transformer models have given good results in detecting the presence of attack with fewer features, which is computationally more feasible. Testing such methods and computational feasibility is a potential area of future research. Metamorphic malware continues to be a challenging area of research in cyber security intelligence. The use of virtualization techniques like sandboxing could be one potential area to delve into the problem and gain insight. Creating a morphing engine and using code obfuscation techniques are areas for future research.

CONCLUSION

The menace of disinformation has touched every individual in their day-to-day lives. Machine learning (ML) based supervised and unsupervised techniques are potential directions in this context. Researchers are working on the fusion of data to make it a multimodal system; however, data fusion increases a lot of noise and sparsity in the dataset. Therefore, preprocessing of the data and then feature extraction methods like TF-IDF are beneficial in applying natural language processing (NLP) in a given scenario. Research indicates that a random forest method is a good option. The assumption could be that in highly diverse data with high randomness, instead of harvesting feature vectors from the dataset, the classifier's performance will be good if the feature of randomness is calculated. This is precisely why the random forest is giving better results. In future, a new multimodal dataset with images, emoji, and text can be created using the dataset proposed in the research as a reference. Also, more work on different types of ML classifiers can be done to increase the accuracy achieved by this research.

DDoS detection in IoT devices is an important research topic because of the increasing prevalence of IoT devices, the growing threat of DDoS attacks, the unique challenges of IoT networks, and the potential of new technologies to improve DDoS detection. Researchers must continue to study this domain to develop effective DDoS detection techniques to help mitigate the risks of DDoS attacks in IoT networks. The lightweight approaches are potentially good because IoT devices suffer from the drawback of resource constraints. Nevertheless, advancements in hardware are trying to resolve the problem of resource constraints. Another potential track of research is the design and architecture of the IoT environment, especially for DDoS detection, which is categorized into centralized/localized or distributed/master-agent concepts. Both methods have their own merits and demerits.

Protection against malware-based attacks on networks is continued to be a top priority for the organization. ML/deep learning-based approaches are quite promising techniques. Research should focus on reducing the time window of detection of the attack as the malware is usually created to be elusive. They passively collect data for ex-filtration and hence compromise security control.

It has become common today to carry an embedded device with us wherever we go (like a smart card), as it is readily available and simple to operate. With accessibility, portability, and efficiency, there was also a concern for securing these daily-use devices. It has been observed that the devices are easily prone to hardware attacks like hardware trojans, IP counterfeiting, side-channel attacks, and timing attacks, to name a few. This chapter discussed the types of attacks occurring on the embedded devices, in particular, and methods that have been employed and used currently were elaborated. Research directions on enhancing the existing methods were proposed using some examples, and new techniques for improving the security of these devices have also been suggested.

REFERENCES

Aguinis, H., Gottfredson, R. K., & Wright, T. A. (2011). Best-practice recommendations for estimating interaction effects using meta-analysis. *Journal of Organizational Behavior*, *32*(8), 1033–1043. doi:10.1002/job.719

Aldwairi, M., & Alwahedi, A. (2018). Detecting fake news in social media networks. *Procedia Computer Science*, *141*, 215–222. doi:10.1016/j.procs.2018.10.171

Alkomah, F., & Ma, X. (2022). A Literature Review of Textual Hate Speech Detection Methods and Datasets. *Information (Basel)*, *13*(6), 273. doi:10.3390/info13060273

Aloseel, A., He, H., Shaw, C., & Khan, M. A. (2020). Analytical review of cybersecurity for embedded systems. *IEEE Access : Practical Innovations, Open Solutions*, *9*, 961–982. doi:10.1109/ACCESS.2020.3045972

Apriorit. (2023). *12 Common Attacks on Embedded Systems and How to Prevent Them*. Retrieved 15 Februrary, 2023 from https://www.apriorit.com/dev-blog/690-embedded-systems-attacks

Aqeel, M., Ali, F., Iqbal, M. W., Rana, T. A., Arif, M., & Auwul, R. (2022). A Review of Security and Privacy Concerns in the Internet of Things (IoT). *Journal of Sensors*, *2022*, 2022. doi:10.1155/2022/5724168

Blanco-Herrero, D., & Calderón, C. A. (2019, October). Spread and reception of fake news promoting hate speech against migrants and refugees in social media: Research Plan for the Doctoral Programme Education in the Knowledge Society. In *Proceedings of the Seventh International Conference on Technological Ecosystems for Enhancing Multiculturality* (pp. 949-955). 10.1145/3362789.3362842

Broadus, R. N. (1987). Toward a definition of »bibliometrics«. *Scientometrics*, *12*(5–6), 373–379. doi:10.1007/BF02016680

Burch, S. (2019). *YouTube Deletes 500 Million Comments in Fight Against Hate Speech*. Retrieved 15 Januar, 2023 from https://www.thewrap.com/youtube-deletes-500-million-comments-in-fight-against-hate-speech/

Cambridge Dictionary. (2023). *Hate speech*. Retrieved 12 February, 2023, from https://dictionary.cambridge.org/dictionary/english/hate-speech?q=Hate+speech

Chang, Y. W., Huang, M. H., & Lin, C. W. (2015). Evolution of research subjects in library and information science based on keyword, bibliographical coupling, and co-citation analyses. *Scientometrics*, *105*(3), 2071–2087. doi:10.100711192-015-1762-8

Chou, D. C., Yen, D. C., Lin, B., & Cheng, P. H.-L. (1999). Cyberspace security management. *Industrial Management & Data Systems, 99*(8), 353–361. doi:10.1108/02635579910301793

Donthu, N., Kumar, S., Mukherjee, D., Pandey, N., & Lim, W. M. (2021). How to conduct a bibliometric analysis: An overview and guidelines. *Journal of Business Research, 133,* 285–296. doi:10.1016/j.jbusres.2021.04.070

Donthu, N., Kumar, S., & Pattnaik, D. (2020). Forty-five years of Journal of Business Research: A bibliometric analysis. *Journal of Business Research, 109*(1), 1–14. doi:10.1016/j.jbusres.2019.10.039

Eriksson, J., & Giacomello, G. (2022). Cyberspace in space: Fragmentation, vulnerability, and uncertainty. In *Cyber Security Politics* (pp. 95–108). Routledge. doi:10.4324/9781003110224-8

ETAS. (2023). *Veränderungen in der ETAS Marken architektur.* Retrieved 15 Februrary, 2023 from https://www.escrypt.com/sites/default/files/flyer/Product_Flyer_KMS.pdf

Geldiyev, H., Churiyev, M., & Mahmudov, R. (2020). Issues regarding cybersecurity in modern world. *Digitalization and Industry 4.0: Economic and Societal Development: An International and Interdisciplinary Exchange of Views and Ideas,* 3-14.

He, C. (2020). *Transformer in CV: The increasing convergence of computer vision and NLP.* Retrieved 10 February, 2023 from https://towardsdatascience.com/transformer-in-cv-bbdb58bf335e

Hicks, D., & Wang, J. (2011). Coverage and overlap of the new social sciences and humanities journal lists. *Journal of the American Society for Information Science and Technology, 62*(2), 284–294. doi:10.1002/asi.21458

Junni, P., Sarala, R. M., Taras, V. A. S., & Tarba, S. Y. (2013). Organizational ambidexterity and performance: A meta-analysis. *The Academy of Management Perspectives, 27*(4), 299–312. doi:10.5465/amp.2012.0015

Khan, M. A., Pattnaik, D., Ashraf, R., Ali, I., Kumar, S., & Donthu, N. (2021). Value of special issues in the Journal of Business Research: A bibliometric analysis. *Journal of Business Research, 125,* 295–313. doi:10.1016/j.jbusres.2020.12.015

Kolias, C., Kambourakis, G., Stavrou, A., & Voas, J. (2017). DDoS in the IoT: Mirai and other botnets. *Computer, 50*(7), 80–84. doi:10.1109/MC.2017.201

Kshetri, N. (2017). Can Blockchain Strengthen the Internet of Things? *IT Professional, 19*(4), 68–72. doi:10.1109/MITP.2017.3051335

Lee, J. Y., & Lee, J. (2021). Current research trends in IoT security: A systematic mapping study. *Mobile Information Systems, 2021,* 1–25. doi:10.1155/2021/8847099

Li, Y., & Liu, Q. (2021). A comprehensive review study of cyber-attacks and cyber security; Emerging trends and recent developments. *Energy Reports, 7,* 8176–8186. doi:10.1016/j.egyr.2021.08.126

Lim, W. M., Yap, S. F., & Makkar, M. (2021). Home sharing in marketing and tourism at a tipping point: What do we know, how do we know, and where should we be heading? *Journal of Business Research, 122,* 534–566. doi:10.1016/j.jbusres.2020.08.051 PMID:33012896

Lohani, A. (2021). Countering Disinformation and Hate Speech Online: Regulation and User Behavioural Change. *ORF Occasional Paper, 296*, 1–36.

Lutkevich. (2023). *Definition: Natural language processing (NLP)*. Retrieved on 10 March 2023 from https://www.techtarget.com/searchenterpriseai/definition/natural-language-processing-NLP

Markets and Markets. (2023). Retrieved on 10 March 2023, from https://www.marketsandmarkets.com/Market-Reports/cyber-security-market-505.html

McGuinness, D. (2017). *How a cyber attack transformed Estonia*. Retrieved 15 January, 2023 from https://www.bbc.com/news/39655415

Mongeon, P., & Paul-Hus, A. (2016). The Journal Coverage of Web of Science and Scopus: A Comparative Analysis. *Scientometrics, 106*(1), 213–228. doi:10.100711192-015-1765-5

Moral-Munoz, J. A., Herrera-Viedma, E., Espejo, A. S., & Cobo, M. J. (2020). Software tools for conducting bibliometric analysis in science: An up-to-date review. *El Profesional de la Información, 29*(1). Advance online publication. doi:10.3145/epi.2020.ene.03

Palmatier, R. W., Houston, M. B., & Hulland, J. (2018). Review articles: Purpose, process, and structure. *Journal of the Academy of Marketing Science, 46*(1), 1–5. doi:10.100711747-017-0563-4

Papp, D., Ma, Z., & Buttyan, L. (2015, July). Embedded systems security: Threats, vulnerabilities, and attack taxonomy. In *2015 13th Annual Conference on Privacy, Security and Trust (PST)* (pp. 145-152). IEEE.

Pereira-Kohatsu, J., Quijano-Sánchez, L., Liberatore, F., & Camacho-Collados, M. (2019). Detecting and Monitoring Hate Speech in Twitter. *Sensors (Basel), 19*(21), 1–37. doi:10.339019214654 PMID:31717760

Pritchard, A. (1969). Statistical bibliography or bibliometrics? *The Journal of Documentation, 25*(4), 348–349.

Rajendran, G., & Nivash, R. (2019, July). Security in the Embedded System: Attacks and Countermeasures. *Proceedings of International Conference on Recent Trends in Computing, Communication & Networking Technologies (ICRTCCNT)*. 10.2139srn.3429857

Rajmohan, T., Nguyen, P. H., & Ferry, N. (2022). A decade of research on patterns and architectures for IoT security. *Cybersecurity, 5*(1), 1–29. doi:10.118642400-021-00104-7

Rambus. (2023). *Security: Provisioning and Key Management*. Retrieved 15 February, 2023 from https://www.rambus.com/security/provisioning-and-key-management/

Ranjan, P., & Vaish, A. (2021). Socio-technical attack approximation based on structural virality of information in social networks. *International Journal of Information Security and Privacy, 15*(1), 153–172. doi:10.4018/IJISP.2021010108

Rastogi, S., & Bansal, D. (2022). A review on fake news detection 3 T's: Typology, time of detection, taxonomies. *International Journal of Information Security*, 1–36. PMID:36406145

Reuters. (2022). *US Capitol riots: Six highlights from testimony released by the 6 January committee*. Retrieved on 15 March 2023 from https://indianexpress.com/article/explained/explained-global/us-capitol-riots-six-highlights-from-testimony-released-by-the-jan-6-committee-8352561/

Roman, S., & Bertolotti, F. (2022). A master equation for power laws. *Royal Society Open Science*, *9*(12), 1–11. doi:10.1098/rsos.220531 PMID:36483760

Searchlogistics. (2023). *Cyber Security Market Analysis*. Retrieved on 15 March 2023, from https://www.searchlogistics.com/grow/statistics/ransomware-statistics/

Security, I. B. M. (2022). *Cost of a Data Breach Report 2022*. Retrieved 15 Januar, 2023 from https://www.ibm.com/downloads/cas/3R8N1DZJ

Shetty, A. (n.d.). *WhatsApp messenger records 10bn messages in a day*. Retrieved on 10 March 2023 from https://www.firstpost.com/tech/news-analysis/whatsapp-messenger-records-10bn-messages-in-a-day-3606703.html#:~:text=WhatsApp%20Messenger%2C%20the%20popular%20U.S.,10B%20total%20messages%20a%20day!

Snyder, H. (2019). Literature review as a research methodology: An overview and guidelines. *Journal of Business Research*, *104*(July), 333–339. doi:10.1016/j.jbusres.2019.07.039

Spinellis, D. (2003). Reliable identification of bounded-length viruses is NP-complete. *IEEE Transactions on Information Theory*, *49*(1), 280–284. doi:10.1109/TIT.2002.806137

Sridhar, S., Hahn, A., & Govindarasu, M. (2012). Cyber-physical system security for the electric power grid. *Proceedings of the IEEE*, *100*(1), 210–224. doi:10.1109/JPROC.2011.2165269

Uchendu, B., Nurse, J. R., Bada, M., & Furnell, S. (2021). Developing a cyber security culture: Current practices and future needs. *Computers & Security*, *109*, 102387. doi:10.1016/j.cose.2021.102387

van Eck, N. J. (2011). *Methodological Advances in Bibliometric Mapping of Science*. Retrieved 10 March 2020 from https://repub.eur.nl/pub/26509/EPS2011247LIS9789058922915.pdf

Van Eck, N. J. & Waltman, L. (2014). Measuring scholarly impact. *Methods and Practice*, 285-320.

Van Eck, N. J., & Waltman, L. (2023). *VOSviewer Manual for VOSviewer version 1.6.19*. Univeristeit Leiden.

Van Eck, N. J., & Waltman, L. (2023). *VOSviewer v. 1.16.19*. Centre for Science and Technology Studies, Leiden University. Retrieved 14 February 2023, from https://www.vosviewer.com

Wallin, J. A. (2005). Bibliometric methods: Pitfalls and possibilities. *Basic & Clinical Pharmacology & Toxicology*, *97*(5), 261–275. doi:10.1111/j.1742-7843.2005.pto_139.x PMID:16236137

Wikipedia. (2020). *2020 Delhi riots*. Retrieved on 15 March 2023, from https://en.wikipedia.org/wiki/2020_Delhi_riots

Williams, P., Dutta, I. K., Daoud, H., & Bayoumi, M. (2022). A survey on security in internet of things with a focus on the impact of emerging technologies. *Internet of Things*, *19*, 100564. doi:10.1016/j.iot.2022.100564

Xin, Y., Kong, L., Liu, Z., Hou, H., & Wang, C. (2018). Machine Learning and Deep Learning Methods for Cybersecurity. *IEEE Access : Practical Innovations, Open Solutions*, *6*, 35365–35381. doi:10.1109/ACCESS.2018.2836950

Zhang, Z., Ning, H., Shi, F., Farha, F., Xu, Y., Xu, J., Zhang, F., & Choo, K. K. R. (2022). Artificial intelligence in cyber security: Research advances, challenges, and opportunities. *Artificial Intelligence Review*, *55*(2), 1–25. doi:10.100710462-021-09976-0

Zhang, Z., Ning, H., Shi, F., Farha, F., Xu, Y., Xu, J., Zhang, F., & Choo, K. K. R. (2022). Artificial intelligence in cyber security: Research advances, challenges, and opportunities. *Artificial Intelligence Review*, *55*(2), 1–25. doi:10.100710462-021-09976-0

Zhou, Y., & Feng, D. (2005). Side-channel attacks: Ten years after its publication and the impacts on cryptographic module security testing. *Cryptology ePrint Archive*.

ADDITIONAL READING

Ahmed, A. A. A., Aljabouh, A., Donepudi, P. K., & Choi, M. S. (2021). Detecting fake news using machine learning: A systematic literature review. *arXiv preprint arXiv*:2102.04458.

Ali, I., Ayub, M. N. B., Shivakumara, P., & Noor, N. F. B. M. (2022). Fake News Detection Techniques on Social Media: A Survey. *Wireless Communications and Mobile Computing*, *2022*, 2022. doi:10.1155/2022/6072084

Boutekkouk, F. (2022). A literature review on security-aware design space exploration approaches for embedded systems. *International Journal of Security and Networks*, *17*(4), 247–268. doi:10.1504/IJSN.2022.127153

Duru, C. C., Azubogu, A. C. O., & Aniedu, A. N. (2020). Review of embedded systems security. *UNIZIK Journal of Engineering and Applied Sciences*, *17*(1), 196–206.

Kilincer, I. F., Ertam, F., & Sengur, A. (2021). Machine learning methods for cyber security intrusion detection: Datasets and comparative study. *Computer Networks*, *188*, 107840. doi:10.1016/j.comnet.2021.107840

Liu, W., Niu, H., Luo, W., Deng, W., Wu, H., Dai, S., ... Feng, W. (2020, August). Research on technology of embedded system security protection component. In *2020 IEEE International Conference on Advances in Electrical Engineering and Computer Applications (AEECA)* (pp. 21-27). IEEE. 10.1109/AEECA49918.2020.9213603

Moghadasi, N., Luu, M., Adekunle, R. O., Polmateer, T. L., Manasco, M. C., Emmert, J. M., & Lambert, J. H. (2022). Research and Development Priorities for Security of Embedded Hardware Devices. *IEEE Transactions on Engineering Management*, 1–12. doi:10.1109/TEM.2022.3197240

KEY TERMS AND DEFINITIONS

Artificial Intelligence (AI): It refers to a system that has the capability of making inferences based on the learning of the system.

Cyber Crime: It refers to activities that can potentially cause harm to systems, applications, networks and other devices forming information and communication system.

Distributed Denial of Service Attack (DDoD): It refers to tools and techniques used to detect attacks on the network, systems, applications and others that can exhaust the system by flooding it with different methods, leaving the system unavailable for legitimate services and requests.

Fake News Detection: It refers to tools and techniques used in the detection of information which is not true, genuine or has any reality.

Hate Speech Detection: It refers to tools and techniques used in detecting hateful content being uploaded, circulated and used for malicious use in social media. Hate Speech refers to content with a negative orientation targeted to some group, individuals, society or government.

Internet of Things (IoT): It refers to a branch of ubiquitous computing that facilitates interconnected devices capable of sensing, processing and transmitting data.

Machine Learning (ML): It refers to the concept of training the machine with a given dataset to automate the system's decision-making and imitate the ways humans learn.

Malware Detection: It refers to tools and techniques used in the detection of malicious code that can potentially harm the systems.

Network Security: It refers to the tools and techniques used to protect the interconnected devices forming part of the information and communication system.

Social Media: It refers to an online platform that facilitates the network of individuals with some common interest, community building, interactions and sharing of information.

ENDNOTE

[1] We entered"cybersecurity" OR "cyber-security" OR "cyber security" in the search field. In the following, we will use the keyword"cybersecurity" for all three.

Chapter 11
Cyber Criminals and Data Privacy Measures

Karima Belmabrouk
iD https://orcid.org/0000-0003-1157-1274
Université des Sciences et de la Technologie d'Oran Mohamed Boudiaf, Algeria

ABSTRACT

Cyber criminals pose a significant threat to data privacy, seeking to exploit weaknesses in digital security systems to gain access to sensitive information. Data privacy measures, such as antivirus software, firewalls, and employee training, are implemented to protect against unauthorized access and theft of personal and sensitive data. However, cyber criminals continue to find ways to circumvent these measures, leading to an ongoing arms race in the world of cybersecurity. To stay ahead of evolving threats, ongoing investments in research and development, as well as partnerships between government agencies, private sector organizations, and cybersecurity experts, are crucial in strengthening data privacy measures and protecting against cyber criminals.

INTRODUCTION

Cybercrime is a growing concern in today's digital world, with cyber criminals using a variety of methods to steal information, commit fraud, and extort money from their victims. With the increasing amount of personal and sensitive information being shared online, the need for data privacy measures has become more important than ever.

Cyber criminals are individuals or groups who use computers, networks, and the internet to carry out criminal activities. They may use a variety of techniques to gain access to sensitive information, including phishing, malware, ransomware, and social engineering, among others. Once they have access to this information, they may use it for a variety of purposes, including identity theft, financial fraud, and espionage.

Data privacy measures are designed to protect sensitive information from unauthorized access or disclosure. These measures can include encryption, access controls, regular updates and patching, employee training and awareness, network security, backup and disaster recovery, and compliance with regulations and standards such as GDPR, HIPAA, and PCI DSS.

DOI: 10.4018/979-8-3693-1528-6.ch011

Encryption is the process of converting information into a coded form that can only be deciphered by authorized users. Access controls restrict access to information based on user credentials or other factors, such as time of day or location. Regular updates and patching are important for maintaining the security of software and systems, as they can help to close vulnerabilities that cyber criminals may use to gain access.

Employee training and awareness programs are critical for educating staff about the risks of cybercrime and how to prevent it. Network security measures such as firewalls and intrusion detection systems can help to detect and prevent unauthorized access to networks and systems. Backup and disaster recovery procedures ensure that critical data can be recovered in the event of a cyber-attack or other disaster.

Compliance with regulations and standards such as GDPR, HIPAA, and PCI DSS is important for ensuring that organizations are meeting legal and industry requirements for data privacy and security.

In summary, cyber criminals pose a significant threat to individuals and organizations, and data privacy measures are essential for protecting sensitive information from unauthorized access or disclosure. By implementing a range of measures such as encryption, access controls, regular updates and patching, employee training and awareness, network security, backup and disaster recovery, and compliance with regulations and standards, organizations can help to mitigate the risks of cybercrime and protect their data.

THE ORIGIN OF CYBER CRIMINALS AND DATA PRIVACY MEASURES

The origin of cyber criminals and data privacy measures can be traced back to the early days of computing and the internet. In the early days of computing, security was not a major concern, and the focus was on developing new technologies and improving computing performance.

However, as the internet and computer networks became more widespread, the potential for cybercrime became more apparent. The first computer virus, known as the "Creeper Virus," was created in the early 1970s, and the first known case of hacking occurred in 1971.

In the years that followed, the number and sophistication of cyber-attacks increased, and organizations began to take steps to protect their networks and data. In the 1990s, the need for data privacy measures became more apparent with the rise of e-commerce and the collection of personal information by companies.

As the internet and computing technology continued to evolve, so did cyber criminals and the methods they used to attack systems and steal data. Today, cybercrime is a multi-billion dollar industry that affects individuals, businesses, and governments around the world.

To combat cybercrime and protect data privacy, organizations and governments have implemented a range of measures, including encryption, access controls, regular updates and patching, employee training and awareness, network security, backup and disaster recovery, and compliance with regulations and standards such as GDPR, HIPAA, and PCI DSS. These measures are constantly evolving to keep pace with the changing threat landscape and the increasing value of data in the digital age.

Cyber criminals and data privacy measures is an important area of study in the field of cybersecurity. Cyber criminals use various techniques to steal or compromise sensitive data, such as personal information, financial data, or intellectual property. Data privacy measures are designed to protect this data from unauthorized access or use (University of York, 2023).

Key Findings From Recent Research on Cyber Criminals and Data Privacy Measures

There are various key findings from recent research on cyber criminals and data privacy measures like:

1. Cyber criminals use a range of tactics to steal or compromise data, including phishing, malware, social engineering, and ransomware. These attacks can be highly targeted or use broad-based methods to exploit vulnerabilities in computer systems.
2. The impact of cyber-attacks on businesses can be significant, including financial losses, reputational damage, and legal liabilities. Research suggests that small and medium-sized enterprises (SMEs) are particularly vulnerable to cyber-attacks due to limited resources and expertise in cybersecurity.
3. Effective data privacy measures can help prevent cyber-attacks and reduce the impact of any breaches that do occur. These measures can include data encryption, access controls, network segmentation, and regular security assessments.
4. Compliance with data privacy regulations, such as the General Data Protection Regulation (GDPR) and the California Consumer Privacy Act (CCPA), can help organizations meet their legal obligations and protect sensitive data. Research suggests that organizations that prioritize privacy compliance are more likely to have effective data privacy measures in place.
5. There is a growing demand for cybersecurity professionals with expertise in data privacy. According to recent research, the demand for cybersecurity professionals is expected to grow by 31% through 2029, and the average salary for cybersecurity professionals with data privacy expertise is significantly higher than for those without.

Overall, research on cyber criminals and data privacy measures highlights the importance of protecting sensitive data from unauthorized access or use. Effective data privacy measures can help prevent cyber-attacks and reduce their impact, and organizations that prioritize privacy compliance are more likely to have effective data privacy measures in place. The growing demand for cybersecurity professionals with data privacy expertise suggests that this is a critical area of focus for organizations looking to protect their sensitive data.

Different Tactics to Steal or Compromise Data

The most well-known tactics that cyber criminals use to steal or compromise data, include (University of York, 2023):

1. **Phishing:** This involves sending fraudulent emails, text messages or social media messages that appear to be from a legitimate source, with the aim of tricking the recipient into revealing sensitive information such as passwords or financial details. Here are some examples of phishing:
   a. **Spear Phishing:** Spear phishing is a targeted phishing attack that is customized to a specific individual or organization. The attackers research the victim's interests, job title, and other personal details to create a convincing message that is more likely to be clicked on or responded to.
   b. **Email Phishing:** Email phishing is a type of phishing attack that is delivered through email. The attackers create a message that appears to be from a legitimate source, such as a bank,

      social media platform, or online retailer, and ask the recipient to click on a link or provide personal information.

c. **Smishing:** Smishing is a type of phishing attack that is delivered through SMS text message. The attackers create a message that appears to be from a legitimate source, such as a bank or other financial institution, and ask the recipient to click on a link or provide personal information.

d. **Vishing:** Vishing is a type of phishing attack that is delivered through a phone call. The attackers pose as a legitimate representative of a company, such as a bank, and ask the recipient to provide personal information or to visit a website to complete a transaction.

e. **Social Media Phishing:** Social media phishing is a type of phishing attack that is delivered through social media platforms, such as Facebook or Twitter. The attackers create a fake profile or page that appears to be from a legitimate source and ask the recipient to click on a link or provide personal information.

Here are some numbers and statistics about phishing all over the world (Atlas VPN, 2020; Verizon, 2021; KnowBe4, 2021; Retruster, 2021; IBM Security, 2020; Hiscox, 2020; Symantec, 2020):

- The number of phishing attacks increased by 15% in 2020, with over 242 million attacks recorded, according to a report by Atlas VPN.
- In the first quarter of 2021, the most commonly used phishing lures included COVID-19-related scams, fake job offers, and fake login pages, according to a report by KnowBe4.
- According to a report by Verizon, 36% of data breaches involved phishing attacks in 2020, making it the most commonly used tactic for cybercriminals.
- The global average phishing attack rate was 1 in every 4,200 emails in 2020, according to a report by Retruster.
- The average cost of a successful phishing attack was $1.6 million in 2020, according to a report by IBM.
- In 2020, 22% of all reported cyber incidents were phishing attacks, according to a report by Hiscox.
- According to a report by Symantec, the top five countries with the highest phishing attack rates in 2020 were the United States, Canada, India, the United Kingdom, and Australia.

These statistics indicate the prevalence of phishing attacks all over the world, with COVID-19-related scams and fake job offers being commonly used lures. Phishing attacks are also a common tactic used in data breaches, with a high cost of successful attacks. The global average phishing attack rate is also significant, with over 20% of reported cyber incidents being phishing attacks. Countries with the highest phishing attack rates include the United States, Canada, India, the United Kingdom, and Australia. Organizations and individuals need to be vigilant and take steps to protect themselves against phishing attacks.

2. **Malware:** Malware is a type of software designed to harm or gain unauthorized access to computer systems. It can be introduced to a system through email attachments, infected websites or software downloads. Once installed, malware can give cyber criminals access to sensitive data or allow them to control the infected computer. Here are some examples of malware:

a. **Virus:** A virus is a type of malware that can replicate itself and spread from one computer to another. It can be transmitted through email attachments; software downloads, or infected websites. A virus can cause a range of damage to a computer system, from corrupting or destroying files to stealing personal information.

b. **Trojan:** A Trojan, or Trojan horse, is a type of malware that disguises itself as legitimate software to trick users into downloading it. Once installed, a Trojan can perform a range of malicious activities, such as stealing data, modifying system settings, or creating a backdoor for attackers to access the system.

c. **Worm:** A worm is a type of malware that can spread from one computer to another through a network or the internet. It can cause damage to a system by consuming network bandwidth, slowing down or crashing the system, or allowing attackers to gain access to the system.

d. **Ransomware:** Ransomware is a type of malware that encrypts a victim's files and demands payment in exchange for the decryption key. It can be delivered through a variety of means, including email attachments, infected websites, or software downloads.

e. **Adware:** Adware is a type of malware that displays unwanted advertisements on a victim's computer or mobile device. It can slow down the system and make it difficult to use, as well as potentially collect personal information about the user's browsing habits.

Here are some numbers and statistics about malware all over the world:

- In 2020, there were over 100 million new malware samples discovered, according to a report by AV-Test, an independent IT security institute.
- In the first quarter of 2021, the most commonly encountered malware families included Dridex, Emotet, and TrickBot, according to a report by Check Point Software Technologies.
- The number of ransomware attacks increased by 485% in 2020, with over 304 million attacks recorded, according to a report by SonicWall.
- According to a report by McAfee, the number of publicly disclosed security incidents increased by 100% from 2019 to 2020, with an average of 419 new threats per minute.
- The global cost of cybercrime is estimated to be $1 trillion in 2020, according to a report by Atlas VPN.
- In 2020, the average cost of a malware attack was $2.6 million, according to a report by Accenture.
- The financial sector is the most targeted industry for malware attacks, followed by the healthcare, manufacturing, and government sectors, according to a report by NTT Security.

These statistics indicate the growing threat of malware worldwide, with new samples being discovered on a regular basis. Ransomware attacks have seen a particularly significant increase, and the financial sector is the most targeted industry for attacks. The global cost of cybercrime is also substantial, reaching into the trillions of dollars. Organizations and individuals need to be aware of the risks and take steps to protect their systems and data against malware attacks.

3. **Social engineering:** This tactic involves using psychological manipulation to trick people into divulging sensitive information. For example, a cybercriminal may pose as a trusted authority figure to convince someone to reveal their login credentials. A cybercriminal might pose as a trusted authority figure, such as an IT support technician, and convince the victim to provide

sensitive information like login credentials or personal information. Here are some examples of social engineering:

a.   **Phishing:** Phishing is a type of social engineering attack in which an attacker sends a fraudulent email, text message, or other communication that appears to be from a legitimate source, such as a bank, a social media platform, or an e-commerce website. The message is designed to trick the recipient into providing sensitive information, such as login credentials or credit card details.

b.   **Baiting:** Baiting is a type of social engineering attack in which an attacker leaves a physical device, such as a USB drive or CD, in a public place where it is likely to be found. The device is infected with malware, and when a curious user plugs it into their computer, the malware is activated and the attacker gains access to the computer.

c.   **Pretexting:** Pretexting is a type of social engineering attack in which an attacker impersonates someone else in order to gain access to sensitive information or to convince the victim to take a particular action. For example, an attacker might impersonate a company employee in order to convince an IT help desk to reset a password or provide access to a system.

d.   **Tailgating:** Tailgating is a type of social engineering attack in which an attacker follows closely behind an authorized user to gain entry to a secure area. For example, an attacker might wait for an employee to swipe their access card to enter a building, and then follow closely behind them to gain entry.

e.   **Watering hole attacks:** A watering hole attack is a type of social engineering attack in which an attacker targets a website that is known to be frequented by a particular group of people, such as employees of a specific company or members of a particular industry. The attacker infects the website with malware, and when users visit the site, the malware is downloaded to their computers.

4.   **Ransomware:** Ransomware is a type of malicious software that infects a computer or network and encrypts files, demanding a ransom payment in exchange for the decryption key to restore access to the data. Here are some examples of ransomware:

a.   **WannaCry:** WannaCry is a ransomware attack that first appeared in 2017. The attack targeted computers running Microsoft Windows and encrypted users' files, demanding a ransom payment in Bitcoin to unlock them. The attack is estimated to have affected more than 200,000 computers in 150 countries.

b.   **Petya:** Petya is a type of ransomware that first appeared in 2016. The attack works by overwriting the Master Boot Record (MBR) of a computer, making it impossible to boot the system. The attackers then demand a ransom payment in Bitcoin to provide the decryption key.

c.   **Locky:** Locky is a ransomware attack that first appeared in 2016. The attack is delivered through a malicious email attachment, which, when opened, encrypts the user's files and demands a ransom payment in Bitcoin to unlock them.

d.   **CryptoLocker:** CryptoLocker is a type of ransomware that first appeared in 2013. The attack is delivered through a malicious email attachment or a drive-by download, and encrypts the user's files, demanding a ransom payment in Bitcoin to unlock them.

e.   **Ryuk:** Ryuk is a ransomware attack that first appeared in 2018. The attack targets large organizations and demands a high ransom payment in Bitcoin. The attackers use sophisticated techniques, including spear-phishing emails and exploiting vulnerabilities in remote access software, to gain access to the victim's network.

Here are some numbers and statistics about ransomware all over the world:

- Ransomware attacks increased by 485% in 2020, with over 304 million attacks recorded, according to a report by SonicWall.
- The average ransom demand increased by 43% in 2020, with an average demand of $170,404, according to a report by Coveware.
- In the first quarter of 2021, the most commonly used ransomware families included Ryuk, Sodinokibi, and Conti, according to a report by Check Point Software Technologies.
- The healthcare sector was the most targeted industry for ransomware attacks in 2020, followed by the manufacturing, professional services, and government sectors, according to a report by NTT Security.
- The global cost of ransomware attacks is estimated to be $20 billion in 2021, according to a report by Cybersecurity Ventures.
- The average cost of a ransomware attack was $4.44 million in 2020, according to a report by Sophos.
- In 2020, 54% of organizations hit by ransomware paid the ransom, according to a report by Emsisoft.

These statistics indicate the growing threat of ransomware all over the world, with a significant increase in attacks in 2020. The healthcare sector was particularly targeted, and the average ransom demand and cost of attacks are substantial. The cost of ransomware attacks is also significant, reaching into the billions of dollars. Over half of organizations hit by ransomware chose to pay the ransom. Organizations and individuals need to take steps to protect themselves against ransomware attacks, such as regularly backing up data and implementing strong security measures.

5. **Network intrusion:** Cyber criminals may attempt to gain unauthorized access to a network in order to steal sensitive data or cause damage to the system. This can be done through exploiting vulnerabilities in software or by brute-force attacks to guess login credentials. Cybercriminals might attempt to gain unauthorized access to a network by exploiting vulnerabilities in software or by guessing login credentials through brute-force attacks. Here are some examples of network intrusions:

    a. **Malware attacks:** Malware is malicious software that is designed to infiltrate computer systems and networks, with the intention of causing harm or stealing data. Malware attacks can take many forms, including viruses, worms, Trojans, ransomware, and spyware.

    b. **Denial-of-service (DoS) attacks:** A denial-of-service attack is designed to overwhelm a network or system with traffic, making it unavailable to legitimate users. DoS attacks can be launched from a single machine or from a network of computers that have been infected with malware.

    c. **Man-in-the-middle (MitM) attacks:** In a MitM attack, an attacker intercepts communication between two parties and has the ability to eavesdrop, modify or insert new messages into the conversation. This type of attack is often used to steal sensitive information such as passwords or financial data.

    d. **Password attacks:** Password attacks are a common form of network intrusion that involves guessing or cracking a user's password in order to gain unauthorized access to a system or network. These attacks can be carried out using various techniques such as brute-force attacks, dictionary attacks, or social engineering.

e. **Phishing attacks:** Phishing attacks are a type of social engineering attack that use fake emails, websites or other digital communication to trick users into providing sensitive information, such as passwords or credit card details. These attacks can be carried out via email, social media, or other messaging platforms.

f. **SQL injection attacks:** An SQL injection attack is a type of attack that targets a database-driven application by inserting malicious code into user input fields. The attacker can use this code to gain access to the database and steal or modify data.

Here are some numbers and statistics about network intrusion all over the world:

- The number of network intrusion attempts has been steadily increasing over the past few years, with over 2.7 billion intrusion attempts recorded in the first half of 2021, according to a report by SonicWall.
- In 2020, the top five industries targeted by network intrusion attempts were manufacturing, finance and insurance, government, healthcare, and retail, according to a report by NTT Security.
- The average time to detect a network intrusion is 207 days, according to a report by the Ponemon Institute.
- In 2020, the most common types of network intrusion attacks were brute force attacks, web application attacks, and malware, according to a report by Verizon.
- The average cost of a network intrusion attack was $4.27 million in 2020, according to a report by Accenture.
- According to a report by Symantec, the top five countries with the highest network intrusion attack rates in 2020 were the United States, China, India, the United Kingdom, and Germany.
- The average cost of a data breach caused by network intrusion was $4.27 million in 2020, according to a report by the Ponemon Institute.

These statistics indicate the increasing prevalence of network intrusion attempts all over the world, with a significant number of attempts recorded in the first half of 2021. Various industries are being targeted, and the average time to detect a network intrusion is considerable. The most common types of network intrusion attacks are brute force attacks, web application attacks, and malware. The cost of a network intrusion attack and resulting data breach is significant. Countries with the highest network intrusion attack rates include the United States, China, India, the United Kingdom, and Germany. Organizations need to implement strong security measures and continuously monitor their networks to prevent and detect network intrusion attempts.

As technology evolves, cyber criminals continue to develop new tactics and strategies to carry out their attacks. It is important to be vigilant and take appropriate measures to protect sensitive data.

Principle Measures to Protect Sensitive Data

Protecting sensitive data is a critical aspect of cybersecurity. Here are some measures that can be taken to safeguard sensitive data:

1. **Encryption:** Encrypting data is a way to protect it from unauthorized access by converting it into a code that can only be deciphered with the proper encryption key. This ensures that even if the data is intercepted, it will be unreadable and unusable without the key. Here are some examples of encryption:

a. **Secure Sockets Layer (SSL):** SSL is a commonly used encryption protocol that is used to secure online communication between a client and a server, such as during online banking or e-commerce transactions. It uses public key encryption to protect the data that is transmitted between the client and the server.

b. **File Encryption:** File encryption is a method of encrypting individual files or folders to protect their contents from unauthorized access. Many operating systems, such as Windows and macOS, offer built-in file encryption features.

c. **Virtual Private Network (VPN):** A VPN is a technology that allows for secure and encrypted communication between two devices or networks over the internet. It is commonly used to protect online privacy and to provide secure remote access to company networks.

d. **Pretty Good Privacy (PGP):** PGP is a popular encryption program that is used to encrypt and decrypt email messages. It uses public key encryption to protect the contents of the email message and the identity of the sender.

e. **Secure Shell (SSH):** SSH is a protocol used to secure remote access to servers and other networked devices. It provides encrypted communication between the client and the server, protecting sensitive data and preventing unauthorized access.

Here are some numbers and statistics about encryption all over the world:

- The global encryption software market is projected to reach $20.1 billion by 2025, growing at a compound annual growth rate (CAGR) of 16.1% from 2020 to 2025, according to a report by MarketsandMarkets.

- According to a survey by the Ponemon Institute, 54% of respondents said their organizations are increasing their use of encryption to protect sensitive and confidential information.

- In 2020, the most common type of data encrypted was personally identifiable information (PII), followed by financial data and intellectual property, according to a report by Thales.

- The average total cost of a data breach was $3.86 million for companies that did not use encryption, compared to $2.26 million for companies that did use encryption, according to a report by the Ponemon Institute.

- In 2020, the most commonly used encryption algorithms were Advanced Encryption Standard (AES), Secure Hash Algorithm (SHA), and Rivest-Shamir-Adleman (RSA), according to a report by Thales.

- The United States, China, and Germany are the top three countries with the highest number of patent filings related to encryption technologies, according to a report by the World Intellectual Property Organization.

- According to a survey by the European Union Agency for Cybersecurity, 63% of organizations in Europe use encryption for email and file sharing, while 50% use encryption for databases and 43% use encryption for applications.

These statistics indicate the growing use of encryption all over the world to protect sensitive and confidential information. The encryption software market is projected to reach a significant value by 2025, and many organizations are increasing their use of encryption to protect their data. The most commonly encrypted data is personally identifiable information, and the use of encryption can significantly reduce the total cost of a data breach. Advanced Encryption Standard (AES), Secure Hash Algorithm (SHA), and Rivest-Shamir-Adleman (RSA) are the most commonly used encryption algorithms. The United States, China, and Germany are leading in patent filings related to encryption technologies. A significant number of organizations in Europe use encryption for email, file sharing, databases, and applications.

2.   **Access control:** Limiting access to sensitive data is another important measure. Access should only be granted to those who need it and should be restricted based on job role and responsibilities. Here are some examples of access control:

   a.   **Physical access control:** Physical access control is the process of limiting access to physical spaces, such as buildings, rooms, or equipment. It can include measures such as locks, keys, access cards, and biometric controls, such as fingerprint or facial recognition.

   b.   **Network access control:** Network access control is the process of limiting access to computer networks, servers, and other networked devices. It can include measures such as firewalls, intrusion detection and prevention systems, and virtual private networks (VPNs).

   c.   **Role-based access control (RBAC):** RBAC is a method of access control that assigns access privileges based on the user's role within an organization. It can be used to limit access to sensitive information and resources to only those who need it to perform their job duties.

   d.   **Discretionary access control (DAC):** DAC is a type of access control that allows the owner of a resource, such as a file or folder, to determine who has access to it. It is commonly used in personal computers and file-sharing systems.

   e.   **Mandatory access control (MAC):** MAC is a type of access control that assigns access privileges based on security classifications and rules set by a system administrator. It is commonly used in government and military systems to protect classified information.

Here are some numbers and statistics about access control all over the world:

- The global access control market is projected to reach $12.8 billion by 2027, growing at a compound annual growth rate (CAGR) of 10.8% from 2020 to 2027, according to a report by Grand View Research.
- According to a survey by the Ponemon Institute, 63% of respondents said their organizations use role-based access control, while 51% use multifactor authentication.
- In 2020, the most common types of access control solutions were card-based systems, followed by biometric systems and keypad-based systems, according to a report by IHS Markit.
- The average cost of a data breach caused by a security incident related to access control was $4.77 million in 2020, according to a report by the Ponemon Institute.
- According to a survey by Microsoft, 91% of organizations say they have at least one access control issue, with the most common issues being weak passwords, excessive permissions, and shared accounts.
- In 2020, the healthcare industry had the highest average cost per record for a data breach caused by a security incident related to access control, at $499 per record, according to a report by IBM Security.
- According to a report by Gartner, the top five countries in terms of access control revenue in 2020 were the United States, China, Japan, the United Kingdom, and Germany.

These statistics indicate the growing importance of access control all over the world to protect sensitive and confidential information. The access control market is projected to reach a significant value by 2027. Many organizations use role-based access control and multifactor authentication to secure their data. The most common types of access control solutions are card-based systems, biometric systems, and keypad-based systems. A security incident related to access control can result in a significant cost for a data breach. Weak passwords, excessive permissions, and shared accounts are the most common access control issues faced by organizations. The healthcare industry has the highest average cost per record for a data breach caused by a security incident related to access control. The top five countries in terms of access control revenue are the United States, China, Japan, the United Kingdom, and Germany.

3.   **Regular updates and patching:** Keeping systems, software, and applications up-to-date with the latest security patches is essential to prevent vulnerabilities that can be exploited by attackers. Here are some examples of regular updates and patching:

    a.   **Operating system updates:** Operating system updates, such as Windows updates or macOS updates, are released regularly to address security vulnerabilities and improve the functionality of the operating system. It is important to install these updates regularly to ensure that your system is protected from the latest threats.

    b.   **Application updates:** Application updates, such as updates for web browsers or office software, are also released regularly to address security vulnerabilities and improve the performance of the application. It is important to install these updates as soon as they become available.

    c.   **Firmware updates:** Firmware updates are released for hardware devices, such as routers or printers, to address security vulnerabilities and improve the performance of the device. It is important to install these updates regularly to ensure that your devices are secure.

    d.   **Security patches:** Security patches are updates that are released to address specific security vulnerabilities in software or operating systems. These patches are usually released in response to new security threats, and it is important to install them as soon as possible to protect against these threats.

    e.   **Anti-virus and anti-malware updates:** Anti-virus and anti-malware software should be updated regularly to ensure that they could detect and protect against the latest threats. These updates may include new virus definitions, behavioral analysis, and other features to improve the effectiveness of the software.

Here are some numbers and statistics about regular updates and patching all over the world:

- In 2020, 60% of data breaches were caused by unpatched vulnerabilities, according to a report by the Ponemon Institute.
- According to a survey by the National Cyber Security Alliance, 60% of small businesses that experience a cyber attack are out of business within six months.
- A study by the University of Maryland found that an unpatched computer can be compromised within 3.5 minutes of being connected to the internet.
- In 2020, the most commonly exploited vulnerability in web applications was a flaw in the Apache Struts framework, according to a report by the Open Web Application Security Project (OWASP).
- A survey by SolarWinds found that 72% of IT professionals said their organization has experienced a security incident due to an unpatched vulnerability.
- According to a report by Secunia Research, the number of vulnerabilities discovered in software has increased by more than 150% over the past decade.
- A report by Verizon found that 99.9% of exploited vulnerabilities in 2020 were already known for at least a year.

These statistics highlight the critical importance of regular updates and patching to maintain the security of computer systems and prevent cyber attacks. A significant percentage of data breaches are caused by unpatched vulnerabilities, and small businesses are particularly vulnerable to the consequences of a cyber attack. Unpatched computers can be compromised within minutes of being connected to the internet, and the most commonly exploited vulnerability in web applications was a flaw in the Apache Struts framework in 2020. Many IT professionals have experienced a security incident due to an unpatched vulnerability. The number of vulnerabilities discovered in software is increasing, and the vast majority of exploited vulnerabilities are already known for at least a year. These statistics suggest that regular updates and patching are critical to maintaining the security of computer systems and avoiding costly security incidents.

4. **Employee training and awareness:** Training employees on how to identify and respond to security threats can help prevent data breaches caused by human error, such as phishing attacks. Here are some examples of employee training and awareness programs:

   a. **Cybersecurity training:** Employees are trained on how to identify and avoid cyber threats, such as phishing emails, malware, and social engineering attacks. They are also taught how to safeguard their own devices and data, as well as those of the company.

   b. **Diversity and inclusion training:** Employees are taught about different cultures, backgrounds, and perspectives to promote a more inclusive workplace. This can include training on topics such as unconscious bias, micro aggressions, and respect for differences.

   c. **Sexual harassment prevention training:** Employees are educated on what constitutes sexual harassment, how to prevent it, and how to report incidents. They are also made aware of the consequences of engaging in such behavior.

   d. **Sales and customer service training:** Employees are trained on how to communicate effectively with customers, handle objections, and close deals. They are also taught about the company's products and services, and how to provide exceptional customer service.

   e. **Safety training:** Employees are trained on how to stay safe on the job, including how to use equipment and machinery, handle hazardous materials, and prevent accidents. They are also taught about emergency procedures and first aid.

   f. **Compliance training:** Employees are trained on the laws and regulations that apply to their job, such as data privacy, anti-bribery, and anti-corruption laws. They are also taught about the consequences of non-compliance.

   g. **Leadership development training:** Managers and supervisors are trained on how to lead and motivate their teams, communicate effectively, and make strategic decisions. They are also taught about performance management and how to handle conflicts.

   h. **Mental health awareness training:** Employees are taught about mental health issues, such as stress, burnout, and depression. They are also educated on how to recognize the signs of mental health issues and how to seek help if needed.

Here are some numbers and statistics about employee training and awareness all over the world:

- In a survey by Wombat Security Technologies, 76% of organizations reported that they had experienced phishing attacks in 2018, but only 42% of organizations provided cybersecurity training to their employees.

- A report by Verizon found that 90% of data breaches were caused by human error.
- A survey by the Ponemon Institute found that the average cost of a data breach caused by human error was $3.5 million in 2020.
- In a study by CompTIA, 75% of companies reported that they had experienced at least one security breach caused by a phishing attack in 2019.
- A report by IBM found that the average cost of a data breach was $3.86 million in 2020, but organizations that had implemented security awareness training reduced the cost by an average of $270,000.
- According to a survey by Proofpoint, 88% of organizations worldwide experienced spear-phishing attacks in 2019, and 33% of those attacks resulted in a data breach.
- In a survey by the SANS Institute, 95% of respondents said that they believed security awareness training was important, but only 42% said that their organization provided training to all employees.

These statistics suggest that employee training and awareness are critical to maintaining the security of computer systems and preventing data breaches caused by human error. Phishing attacks are a common cause of security breaches, and organizations that provide cybersecurity training to their employees are more likely to avoid the costly consequences of a data breach. Spear-phishing attacks, which target specific individuals within an organization, are also on the rise. Although most respondents in a survey by the SANS Institute believed that security awareness training was important, many organizations do not provide training to all employees.

5. **Network security:** Securing networks through firewalls, intrusion detection and prevention systems, and other security measures can help prevent unauthorized access to sensitive data. Here are some examples of network security measures:

    a. **Firewalls:** Firewalls are hardware or software devices that control access to a network by examining and filtering incoming and outgoing traffic based on predefined security rules. They can prevent unauthorized access to the network and block malicious traffic.

    b. **Intrusion Detection and Prevention Systems (IDPS):** IDPS are software or hardware devices that monitor network traffic for signs of suspicious activity, such as malware or hacking attempts. They can alert network administrators of potential threats and take automated actions to prevent attacks.

    c. **Virtual Private Networks (VPNs):** VPNs are a type of network security that encrypts all data transmitted between remote devices and the corporate network, providing a secure connection that can't be intercepted or viewed by third parties.

    d. **Network Segmentation:** Network segmentation involves dividing a network into smaller subnetworks, known as segments, to isolate sensitive or critical data from the rest of the network. This can limit the impact of a potential breach or attack.

    e. **Access Control:** Access control mechanisms limit who can access the network, data, and resources. This can include authentication measures such as passwords, biometrics, and smart cards, as well as authorization measures that control what users can do on the network.

    f. **Antivirus and Antimalware Software:** These are programs that detect and remove viruses, malware, and other types of malicious software from network devices. They can prevent or minimize the impact of a cyber attack.

g. **Data Encryption:** Data encryption involves encoding data in a way that can only be read by authorized users who have the decryption key. This can prevent data theft, as even if the data is intercepted, it can't be read without the key.

Here are some numbers and statistics about network security all over the world:

- According to the 2021 Global Network Insights Report by Nokia, the number of distributed denial-of-service (DDoS) attacks increased by 20% in 2020, with a peak of 10.2 million attacks per month.
- In a survey by Juniper Networks, 63% of respondents reported that their organization had experienced at least one significant security breach related to network infrastructure in the past year.
- A report by Cisco found that 28% of data breaches in 2020 involved a compromise of the network.
- In a survey by Fortinet, 57% of organizations reported that they had experienced at least one network security incident in the past year.
- According to the 2020 Cyber Threat Intelligence Report by NTT Ltd., the healthcare and manufacturing sectors experienced the highest volume of cyberattacks targeting network infrastructure.
- A report by Akamai Technologies found that the average cost of a DDoS attack for organizations in 2020 was $2.5 million.
- In a survey by Dark Reading, 41% of respondents reported that their organization had increased their network security budget in 2020.

These statistics suggest that network security continues to be a critical concern for organizations around the world. DDoS attacks are a common threat, and the healthcare and manufacturing sectors have been particularly vulnerable. Data breaches often involve a compromise of the network, and organizations are increasing their investment in network security in response to the growing threat.

6. **Backup and disaster recovery:** Regularly backing up sensitive data and having a disaster recovery plan in place can help minimize the impact of a security breach and ensure that data can be quickly restored in the event of a cyber attack or natural disaster. Here are some examples of backup and disaster recovery:

a. **File backup:** This is the simplest form of backup, where you copy important files to another location, such as an external hard drive, cloud storage, or a network-attached storage (NAS) device. This ensures that you have a copy of your important data in case your primary storage device fails.

b. **Full system backup:** This involves creating a complete copy of your entire system, including the operating system, applications, and settings. This is useful if you need to quickly restore your entire system in case of a disaster.

c. **Incremental backup:** This type of backup only backs up the changes made since the last backup, which can save time and storage space. This is useful for frequently changing files, such as documents or database entries.

d. **Cloud backup:** This involves backing up your data to a remote server maintained by a cloud storage provider. This ensures that your data is stored offsite and can be accessed from anywhere with an internet connection.

e. **Disaster recovery plan:** This is a comprehensive strategy that outlines how your organization will respond to a major disruption, such as a natural disaster, cyber-attack, or equipment failure.

It typically includes procedures for backing up data, restoring systems, and communicating with stakeholders.

f. **High availability:** This involves implementing redundant systems to ensure that critical applications and services remain available in the event of a hardware or software failure. This can include using load balancing, clustering, and failover mechanisms to minimize downtime.

g. **Data replication:** This involves copying data to multiple locations in real-time to ensure that there is always a current copy available. This can be useful for organizations with geographically dispersed offices or for critical data that needs to be constantly available.

Here are some numbers and statistics about backup and disaster recovery all over the world:

- According to a survey by Unitrends, 30% of organizations experienced data loss in the past year, and 84% of those incidents resulted in downtime of at least one day.
- In a survey by Veeam, 58% of IT decision makers reported that their organization experienced an outage in the past 12 months, and the average cost of downtime was $67,651 per hour.
- A report by IBM found that the average cost of a data breach was $3.86 million in 2020, but organizations that had implemented a strong incident response plan and disaster recovery plan reduced the cost by an average of $2 million.
- In a survey by Acronis, 70% of organizations reported that they had experienced a significant data loss event in the past year, and the average cost of downtime for those incidents was $810,000.
- According to a report by the Disaster Recovery Preparedness Council, 74% of organizations worldwide are not adequately prepared for a disaster.
- In a survey by Datto, 46% of MSPs reported that their clients had suffered data loss or downtime due to a natural disaster, and the average cost of downtime for those incidents was $141,000.
- A report by the Ponemon Institute found that the average cost of a ransomware attack was $4.44 million in 2020, but organizations that had implemented a strong incident response plan and disaster recovery plan reduced the cost by an average of $2.2 million.

These statistics suggest that backup and disaster recovery are critical for organizations of all sizes to prevent data loss and minimize downtime. Data loss events are common, and the cost of downtime can be significant. Organizations that are well prepared for disasters can reduce the impact of a data breach, natural disaster, or ransomware attack. Despite the importance of disaster preparedness, many organizations are not adequately prepared, which puts them at risk for data loss and downtime.

Implementing these measures can help protect sensitive data and reduce the risk of a data breach.

The Impact of Cyber-Attacks on Businesses

Cyber-attacks can have a significant impact on businesses of all sizes and industries. Here are some potential effects of cyber-attacks on businesses:

1. **Financial loss:** Cyber-attacks can result in financial loss through theft of funds, ransom payments, or loss of revenue due to downtime and disruption of operations.
2. **Reputational damage:** A data breach can damage a company's reputation, erode customer trust, and lead to lost business.

3. **Legal consequences:** If sensitive data is compromised, businesses may be subject to legal consequences and regulatory fines, particularly if the attack involved the loss of personal or sensitive information.
4. **Business interruption:** Cyber-attacks can cause disruption to business operations, such as system downtime, which can result in lost productivity, revenue, and customer dissatisfaction.
5. **Intellectual property theft:** Cyber-attacks can lead to the theft of intellectual property, such as trade secrets, patents, and copyrights, which can impact a business's competitive advantage and future growth prospects.
6. **Supply chain disruption:** Cyber-attacks can also disrupt supply chains and impact a business's ability to deliver products or services, leading to lost business and reputational damage.

The impact of a cyber-attack can vary depending on the severity and nature of the attack, the size and type of business, and the effectiveness of the business's security measures. It is important for businesses to take proactive steps to protect their systems and data from cyber threats and have a plan in place to respond to a security breach if it occurs.

How Can Effective Data Privacy Measures Help Prevent Cyber-Attacks and Reduce the Impact of any Breaches That Do Occur?

Effective data privacy measures can help prevent cyber-attacks and reduce the impact of any breaches that do occur. Here are some ways data privacy measures can achieve this.

Reduce the Attack Surface

By limiting the amount of data that is collected, processed, and stored, businesses can reduce their attack surface, making it more difficult for attackers to find and exploit vulnerabilities.

How can we reduce the attack surface?

Reducing the attack surface refers to the process of minimizing the number of potential entry points that an attacker can use to compromise a system. Here are some ways to reduce the attack surface:

1. **Patch and update software:** Keeping software and systems up-to-date with the latest patches and security updates helps to address known vulnerabilities.
2. **Disable unnecessary services:** Disabling or removing unnecessary services or protocols reduces the number of potential entry points for an attacker.
3. **Use firewalls:** Configuring firewalls to restrict access to only necessary services and ports reduces the attack surface.
4. **Implement access controls:** Implementing access controls such as least privilege, separation of duties, and role-based access controls ensures that users only have access to what they need to perform their job functions.
5. **Use strong authentication:** Strong authentication mechanisms such as two-factor authentication and biometric authentication reduce the likelihood of successful attacks by ensuring that users are who they claim to be.

6. **Employ encryption:** Encrypting sensitive data and communications helps to prevent unauthorized access or interception of data.
7. **Regularly conduct vulnerability assessments and penetration testing:** Regularly testing systems for vulnerabilities and weaknesses helps to identify potential attack vectors and allows for proactive mitigation measures.

By implementing these measures, organizations can significantly reduce the attack surface and improve their overall security posture.

Implement Access Controls

Businesses can limit access to sensitive data by implementing access controls, such as multi-factor authentication, password policies, and role-based access. This can reduce the risk of insider threats and unauthorized access by external attackers.

How can we implement access controls?

Access controls are security measures that restrict access to sensitive data or system resources to only those users who have a legitimate need to access them. Here are some steps you can take to implement access controls:

1. **Identify the resources that require access controls:** Conduct an inventory of your data and systems to identify the resources that require access controls.
2. **Define roles and responsibilities:** Define roles and responsibilities for users within your organization, and assign access privileges based on job functions.
3. **Implement least privilege:** Implement the principle of least privilege, which means giving users only the minimum level of access they need to perform their job functions.
4. **Use multifactor authentication:** Require users to authenticate using more than one factor, such as a password and a fingerprint scan, to provide an additional layer of security.
5. **Implement access control policies:** Develop and implement policies that define the rules and procedures for access control, such as password complexity requirements, access request procedures, and user termination procedures.
6. **Regularly review and update access controls:** Regularly review and update access controls to ensure that they remain effective and appropriate.
7. **Use access control technologies:** Implement access control technologies such as access control lists, role-based access control, and attribute-based access control to help enforce access controls.

By following these steps, you can implement access controls that help to ensure the confidentiality, integrity, and availability of your data and systems.

Use Encryption

Encrypting sensitive data can help protect it from being read or stolen in the event of a breach. This can help minimize the impact of a breach and ensure that any stolen data remains secure.

How can we use encryption?

Encryption is the process of converting data into a code or cipher to prevent unauthorized access or interception. Here are some ways to use encryption:

1. **Secure data in transit:** Use encryption to secure data as it is transmitted over networks, such as email, web traffic, and messaging services. This can be achieved using transport layer security (TLS) and secure sockets layer (SSL) protocols.
2. **Secure data at rest:** Use encryption to secure data stored on devices such as hard drives, USB drives, and mobile devices. This can be achieved using encryption tools such as BitLocker, VeraCrypt, or FileVault.
3. **Use encrypted communication tools:** Use encrypted communication tools such as Signal, WhatsApp, or Telegram to encrypt voice, text, and video communications.
4. **Use encrypted cloud storage:** Use encrypted cloud storage services such as Dropbox, Google Drive, or OneDrive, which offer end-to-end encryption, to store data securely.
5. **Implement encrypted email:** Use encrypted email services such as ProtonMail, Tutanota, or Hushmail to send and receive encrypted email messages.
6. **Use encrypted messaging apps:** Use encrypted messaging apps such as Signal, WhatsApp, or Telegram to communicate securely with colleagues and clients.
7. **Implement full-disk encryption:** Use full-disk encryption to encrypt all data stored on a device, including the operating system and all files and folders.

By using encryption, organizations can protect sensitive data from unauthorized access, theft, or interception. However, it is important to note that encryption alone is not enough to guarantee security, and it should be used in combination with other security measures such as access controls, firewalls, and regular security audits.

Regularly Backup Data

Regularly backing up data can help ensure that important data is not lost in the event of a breach. This can help businesses recover more quickly and reduce the impact of a breach.

How can we regularly backup data?

Regular data backups are an essential part of any data protection strategy. Here are some steps you can take to regularly back up your data:

1. **Determine the frequency of backups:** Determine the frequency at which you need to back up your data. This will depend on the amount of data you generate and how critical it is to your operations.
2. **Choose a backup method:** Choose a backup method that suits your needs, such as full backups, incremental backups, or differential backups.
3. **Select backup media:** Choose a backup media that is appropriate for your needs, such as external hard drives, tape drives, or cloud storage services.

4. **Automate backups:** Automate the backup process as much as possible, using backup software or scripting tools to ensure that backups occur on a regular schedule.
5. **Test backups regularly:** Test backups regularly to ensure that they are working correctly and that data can be restored in the event of a disaster.
6. **Keep backups offsite:** Keep backups offsite to protect against loss from theft, fire, or other disasters.
7. **Retain backups for an appropriate period:** Retain backups for an appropriate period to ensure that you can restore data from an earlier point in time if necessary.

By regularly backing up your data, you can protect your organization against data loss due to hardware failure, natural disasters, cyber attacks, or other events. It is important to ensure that backups are performed regularly, and that the backup process is tested and validated to ensure that data can be restored when needed.

Train Employees

Educating employees on how to identify and respond to security threats can help prevent cyber-attacks caused by human error, such as phishing attacks.

How can we train employees?

Training employees is a crucial aspect of maintaining strong cybersecurity practices within an organization. Here are some steps you can take to train your employees in cybersecurity:

1. **Develop a cybersecurity policy:** Develop a clear and concise cybersecurity policy that outlines your organization's expectations for employee behavior and best practices for data protection.
2. **Provide regular training sessions:** Provide regular training sessions on cybersecurity best practices, such as how to identify and avoid phishing scams, how to create strong passwords, and how to secure personal devices used for work.
3. **Use real-world scenarios:** Use real-world scenarios to demonstrate the importance of cybersecurity practices and the potential consequences of a security breach.
4. **Encourage reporting:** Encourage employees to report suspicious activity or potential security incidents to the appropriate personnel.
5. **Conduct phishing simulations:** Conduct phishing simulations to test employee awareness and to help identify areas where additional training may be necessary.
6. **Provide ongoing education:** Provide ongoing education on emerging cybersecurity threats and trends to help employees stay informed and up to date on the latest risks and mitigation strategies.
7. **Reinforce good behavior:** Recognize and reward employees who demonstrate good cybersecurity practices and who report potential security incidents.

By implementing a comprehensive training program that is tailored to your organization's specific needs, you can help your employees understand the importance of cybersecurity and develop the skills and knowledge necessary to protect your organization's data and systems.

Incident Response Plan

Having a plan in place to respond to a security breach can help businesses minimize the impact of a breach and quickly recover from the attack.

What about incident response plan?

An incident response plan (IRP) is a structured approach for managing and responding to security incidents. Here are some steps you can take to create an effective incident response plan:

1. **Establish an incident response team:** Identify and train a team of individuals who will be responsible for managing security incidents.
2. **Define the scope and severity of incidents:** Establish criteria for identifying the severity and impact of different types of security incidents, and define the appropriate response for each level.
3. **Develop an incident response plan:** Create a step-by-step plan that outlines the actions to be taken in response to a security incident, including who will be responsible for each action and how to communicate with stakeholders.
4. **Test the incident response plan:** Test the incident response plan on a regular basis to ensure that it is effective and up to date.
5. **Monitor and detect incidents:** Implement a system for monitoring and detecting security incidents, such as intrusion detection and prevention systems, firewalls, and security information and event management (SIEM) solutions.
6. **Respond to incidents:** Once an incident is detected, follow the incident response plan to contain the incident, collect evidence, and restore systems and data.
7. **Review and improve the incident response plan:** Regularly review and update the incident response plan based on feedback from testing and real-world incidents, and adjust the plan as necessary to reflect changes in the threat landscape and organizational needs.

By creating an effective incident response plan, you can minimize the impact of security incidents and reduce the risk of data loss, downtime, and reputational damage. It is important to regularly test and update the plan to ensure that it remains effective in the face of evolving threats and changing business needs.

By implementing these data privacy measures, businesses can help prevent cyber-attacks and reduce the impact of any breaches that do occur. It is important for businesses to continually review and update their security measures to stay ahead of evolving cyber threats.

What About Compliance With Data Privacy Regulations?

Compliance with data privacy regulations is important for businesses to protect sensitive data and avoid legal consequences. Data privacy regulations are designed to ensure that businesses collect, process, store, and share data in a secure and transparent manner, and to protect the privacy rights of individuals.

Some of the key data privacy regulations that businesses may need to comply with include:

1. **General Data Protection Regulation (GDPR):** The GDPR is a European Union regulation that sets out rules for the processing of personal data by businesses operating within the EU or processing the data of EU residents.

The General Data Protection Regulation (GDPR) is a comprehensive data protection law that came into effect on May 25, 2018 in the European Union (EU). It replaced the previous EU data protection directive and is intended to strengthen and unify data protection for individuals within the EU.

The GDPR gives individuals greater control over their personal data and requires organizations to take steps to protect this data. It applies to all organizations, regardless of where they are located, that process the personal data of individuals within the EU.

Under the GDPR, personal data includes any information that can be used to identify an individual, such as name, address, email address, and IP address. The regulation requires organizations to obtain explicit consent from individuals for the processing of their personal data, and to provide clear and transparent information about how this data will be used.

The GDPR also requires organizations to implement appropriate technical and organizational measures to protect personal data from unauthorized access, loss, destruction, or alteration. It establishes strict requirements for data breach notification, including a requirement to report certain breaches to data protection authorities within 72 hours.

The GDPR imposes significant fines for non-compliance, including fines of up to €20 million or 4% of an organization's annual global revenue, whichever is greater.

In summary, the GDPR is a comprehensive data protection law that places significant requirements on organizations that process the personal data of individuals within the EU (Figure 1). Organizations must take steps to ensure compliance with the GDPR to avoid significant fines and reputational damage.

2. **California Consumer Privacy Act (CCPA):** The CCPA is a California state law that gives California residents the right to know what personal information is being collected about them and the right to have that information deleted (SPIRION, 2020).

The California Consumer Privacy Act (CCPA) is a comprehensive data privacy law that came into effect on January 1, 2020 in the state of California, USA. The law is intended to enhance the privacy rights and consumer protection for California residents.

Under the CCPA, consumers have the right to know what personal information is being collected about them, the right to request that this information be deleted, and the right to opt out of the sale of their personal information. The CCPA also requires organizations to provide certain disclosures and notices to consumers about their data collection and processing practices.

The CCPA applies to for-profit organizations that do business in California and meet certain criteria, such as having annual gross revenues over $25 million, or buying, selling, or sharing the personal information of 50,000 or more California consumers, households, or devices.

The CCPA also provides for a private right of action for consumers in the event of certain data breaches, and imposes significant fines for non-compliance, including fines of up to $7,500 per violation.

In summary, the CCPA is a significant data privacy law that places requirements on organizations that collect or process the personal information of California residents. Organizations must take steps to ensure compliance with the CCPA to avoid significant fines and reputational damage.

Figure 1. Infographic: Data protection regulation (European Council, 2022)

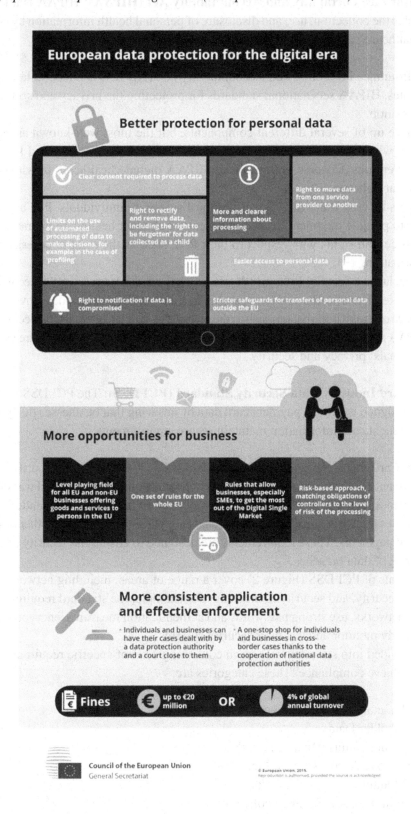

3. **Health Insurance Portability and Accountability Act (HIPAA):** HIPAA is a U.S. federal law that regulates the collection, use, and disclosure of personal health information by covered entities, such as healthcare providers and health insurance companies.

The Health Insurance Portability and Accountability Act (HIPAA) is a federal law enacted in 1996 in the United States. HIPAA sets national standards for protecting the privacy and security of individuals' health information.

HIPAA is made up of several different components, but the most well-known aspect of the law is the Privacy Rule, which governs the use and disclosure of individuals' protected health information (PHI) by covered entities. Covered entities under HIPAA include healthcare providers, health plans, and healthcare clearinghouses.

Under HIPAA's Privacy Rule, covered entities must safeguard individuals' PHI and disclose it only when necessary to provide treatment, receive payment, or conduct healthcare operations. HIPAA also gives individuals certain rights with respect to their PHI, such as the right to access and correct their own health information.

HIPAA also includes a Security Rule, which sets national standards for securing electronic PHI, as well as rules regarding breach notification and enforcement. In addition, HIPAA includes provisions related to the electronic exchange of health information, such as the creation of standard formats for electronic transactions.

Overall, HIPAA aims to improve the efficiency and effectiveness of the healthcare system while also protecting individuals' privacy and security.

4. **Payment Card Industry Data Security Standard (PCI DSS):** The PCI DSS is a set of security standards designed to protect payment card data by ensuring that businesses that process, store, or transmit payment card information maintain secure environments.

The Payment Card Industry Data Security Standard (PCI DSS) is a set of security standards established by the payment card industry to help prevent credit card fraud. The standard was created by major credit card companies including Visa, MasterCard, American Express, Discover, and JCB International.

PCI DSS outlines a set of requirements for merchants, service providers, and other organizations that handle credit card payments. These requirements are designed to ensure the security of cardholder data and reduce the risk of data breaches.

The requirements of PCI DSS (Figure 2) cover a range of areas, including network security, access control, physical security, and security monitoring. For example, the standard requires organizations to maintain secure networks, use strong passwords and authentication measures, encrypt data in transit and at rest, and regularly monitor and test their security systems.

PCI DSS is divided into six categories, each containing a set of specific requirements that must be met in order to achieve compliance. These categories are:

1. Build and Maintain a Secure Network
2. Protect Cardholder Data
3. Maintain a Vulnerability Management Program
4. Implement Strong Access Control Measures
5. Regularly Monitor and Test Networks
6. Maintain an Information Security Policy

Figure 2. PCI DSS requirements
Source: Levan (2023)

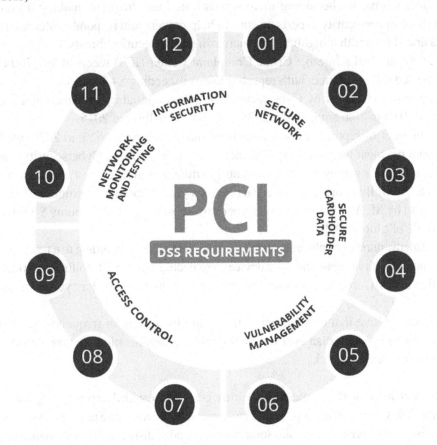

Organizations that handle credit card payments are required to comply with PCI DSS, and failure to comply can result in fines, restrictions on credit card processing, and damage to reputation. Achieving and maintaining compliance with PCI DSS can be a complex and ongoing process, requiring regular risk assessments, security testing, and monitoring.

Compliance with these regulations typically involves implementing appropriate data security measures, such as access controls, encryption, and incident response plans, as well as providing individuals with the right to access, correct, or delete their personal data.

Non-compliance with data privacy regulations can result in significant financial and reputational damage to a business, including fines, legal fees, and lost business. Therefore, it is important for businesses to understand their data privacy obligations and take steps to ensure compliance.

The Growing Demand for Cybersecurity Professionals With Expertise in Data Privacy

There is a growing demand for cybersecurity professionals with expertise in data privacy, due to the increasing importance of protecting sensitive data in the face of rising cyber threats and compliance with data privacy regulations. Here are some reasons why:

1. **Cybersecurity threats are increasing:** Cyber threats, such as data breaches, ransomware attacks, and phishing scams, are becoming more sophisticated and frequent, making it crucial for businesses to have cybersecurity experts on staff to help prevent and respond to attacks. Here are some numbers and statistics that highlight the increasing cybersecurity threats:

   a. In 2020, the FBI's Internet Crime Complaint Center (IC3) received 791,790 complaints of suspected internet crime, with reported losses exceeding $4.2 billion.

   b. According to a report by Cybersecurity Ventures, global cybercrime costs are expected to reach $10.5 trillion annually by 2025, up from $3 trillion in 2015.

   c. The number of reported ransomware incidents increased by 62% in 2020, with the average ransom payment increasing by 43%, according to a report by Cybersecurity Ventures.

   d. According to a survey by the Ponemon Institute, the average cost of a data breach in 2020 was $3.86 million, up 1.5% from the previous year (Ponemon Institute, 2020).

   e. A report by McAfee estimated that cybercrime cost the global economy $600 billion in 2017, or 0.8% of global GDP.

   f. In 2020, the number of phishing attacks increased by 220%, according to a report by Security.org.

   g. The number of internet-connected devices is expected to reach 30.9 billion by 2025, up from 13.8 billion in 2021, creating new attack surfaces and vulnerabilities for cybercriminals to exploit.

These statistics indicate that cybersecurity threats are increasing in frequency, sophistication, and cost, making it more important than ever for individuals and organizations to take steps to protect their data and systems from cyber attacks.

2. **Compliance requirements:** As mentioned earlier, compliance with data privacy regulations, such as the GDPR and CCPA, is a growing concern for businesses, and compliance requires specialized knowledge and expertise in data privacy. Here are some numbers and statistics about compliance requirements:

   a. In 2021, the number of compliance mandates increased to over 900 globally, up from around 800 in 2020, according to a report by SecurityScorecard.

   b. The cost of non-compliance can be significant. In a 2020 survey by Ponemon Institute, the average total cost of non-compliance was $14.8 million per year, up from $9.4 million in 2011 (Ponemon Institute, 2020).

   c. The financial sector is subject to the most regulations, with banks spending an average of $60 million per year on compliance, according to a report by Thomson Reuters (Thomson Reuters, 2019).

   d. In a 2021 survey by Egress, 63% of organizations said they had suffered a data breach caused by human error, highlighting the importance of compliance training and awareness programs (Egress, 2021).

   e. In 2021, the General Data Protection Regulation (GDPR) accounted for over half of all compliance citations globally, according to a report by Compliance Week (Compliance Week, 2021).

   f. In 2020, the global market for compliance software was valued at $2.4 billion, and it is projected to grow at a compound annual growth rate (CAGR) of 6.8% from 2021 to 2028, according to a report by Grand View Research (Grand View Research, 2021).

   g. The cost of compliance can be a burden for small businesses. According to a survey by the National Small Business Association, small businesses spend an average of $12,000 per year on compliance-related costs (National Small Business Association, 2017).

These statistics highlight the growing importance of compliance requirements for organizations in all industries, as well as the potential costs of non-compliance. As the number of regulations continues to grow, it is essential for organizations to stay up-to-date with the latest requirements and to invest in compliance training and software to ensure they remain in compliance with all relevant regulations.

3. **Privacy by design:** Data privacy is becoming a core part of the design and development of new products and services, and cybersecurity professionals with expertise in data privacy can help ensure that privacy is built into products and services from the outset. Here are some numbers and statistics about Privacy by Design:

    a. According to a survey by the International Association of Privacy Professionals (IAPP), 70% of organizations have implemented Privacy by Design (PbD) principles in at least one area of their business (Privacy governance, 2020).

    b. The European Union's General Data Protection Regulation (GDPR) explicitly requires organizations to implement PbD principles in their data processing activities (European Union, 2016).

    c. In a 2021 report, the Ponemon Institute found that organizations that implemented PbD saw a 22% reduction in the number of data breaches they experienced, compared to organizations that did not (Ponemon Institute, 2021).

    d. A report by the Information Commissioner's Office (ICO) found that embedding PbD in an organization can lead to cost savings and operational efficiencies, as well as improved customer trust and satisfaction (Information Commissioner's Office (ICO), 2018).

    e. In a 2021 survey by Cisco, 68% of respondents said they prioritize privacy as part of their overall business strategy (Cisco, 2021).

    f. The International Organization for Standardization (ISO) has developed a set of standards (ISO/IEC 29100) that provide guidance on implementing PbD principles in information and communication technology systems (International Organization for Standardization, 2011).

    g. The National Institute of Standards and Technology (NIST) has developed a framework for privacy risk management, which includes PbD as one of its core principles (National Institute of Standards and Technology, 2018).

These statistics indicate that Privacy by Design is becoming an increasingly important consideration for organizations across all industries, as data privacy concerns continue to grow. Implementing PbD principles can not only help organizations comply with privacy regulations, but it can also lead to cost savings, operational efficiencies, and improved customer trust and satisfaction. As a result, more organizations are prioritizing privacy as part of their overall business strategy, and standards bodies and regulators are developing guidelines and frameworks to help organizations implement PbD principles in their systems and processes.

4. **Business risk management:** As the risk of cyber-attacks and data breaches increases, businesses are looking to hire cybersecurity professionals to help manage that risk and prevent data loss and reputational damage. Here are some numbers and statistics about Business Risk Management (PwC, 2020), (IBM Security, 2020), (World Economic Forum, 2020), (Deloitte, 2019), (Grand View Research, 2021):

    a. A survey by the Disaster Recovery Institute found that 81% of organizations have experienced at least one significant operational disruption in the past five years, highlighting the importance of risk management.

b. According to a report by Allianz, the top three risks for businesses in 2021 are business interruption, pandemic outbreak, and cyber incidents.

c. A survey by PwC found that 49% of organizations have experienced fraud in the past two years, with the average cost of fraud being $42 million.

d. The cost of a cyberattack can be significant. In a 2020 report, IBM found that the average cost of a data breach was $3.86 million.

e. A report by the World Economic Forum found that climate-related risks, such as extreme weather events and natural disasters, are among the top risks facing businesses today.

f. In a survey by Deloitte, 60% of respondents said they have increased their focus on risk management in the past two years, with cybersecurity and data privacy being the top risk areas of concern.

g. The global enterprise risk management (ERM) software market is projected to grow at a compound annual growth rate (CAGR) of 10.5% from 2021 to 2028, reaching a market size of $8.15 billion by 2028, according to a report by Grand View Research.

These statistics indicate that managing business risk is becoming an increasingly important consideration for organizations in all industries, as the frequency and impact of risks continue to grow. While the specific risks facing businesses may vary, many organizations are focusing on risk areas such as cybersecurity, data privacy, and climate-related risks. To effectively manage risks, many organizations are investing in risk management software and increasing their focus on risk management overall.

As a result, there is a growing demand for cybersecurity professionals with expertise in data privacy, including privacy engineers, data protection officers, and privacy analysts, among others. These professionals typically have a deep understanding of data privacy regulations and best practices, as well as experience in implementing technical and organizational measures to protect sensitive data.

CONCLUSION

Cyber criminals pose a serious threat to data privacy and security. They use various tactics to steal or compromise sensitive data, such as phishing, malware, social engineering, and network intrusion. As technology evolves, cyber criminals continue to develop new and more sophisticated methods to carry out their attacks.

To protect against these threats, it is important to take appropriate data privacy measures. This might include implementing strong passwords, using two-factor authentication, keeping software up-to-date, regularly backing up data, and training employees on how to recognize and avoid common cyber threats.

In addition, regulatory measures like data protection laws and compliance standards can help ensure that organizations are taking appropriate steps to safeguard sensitive data. By taking a proactive approach to data privacy and security, we can help protect against the growing threat of cyber crime and help ensure that our data remains safe and secure.

REFERENCES

AtlasV. P. N. (2020). https://atlasvpn.com/blog/phishing-attacks-increased-by-15-in-2020

Cisco. (2021). *Consumer privacy survey*. Récupéré sur https://www.cisco.com/c/dam/en_us/about/doing_business/trust-center/docs/consumer-privacy-survey.pdf

Compliance Week. (2021). *Enforcement Tracker Q1 2021: GDPR fines lead the way*. Récupéré sur https://www.complianceweek.com/data-privacy/enforcement-tracker-q1-2021-gdpr-fines-lead-the-way/30391

Deloitte. (2019). *Global Risk Management Survey*. Récupéré sur https://www2.deloitte.com/: https://www2.deloitte.com/content/dam/Deloitte/us/Documents/risk/us-risk-2019-global-risk-management-survey.pdf

Egress. (2021). *Insider data breaches survey*. Récupéré sur https://pages.egress.com/rs/030-CPG-384/images/Egress-Insider-Data-Breaches-Survey-2021-Global-Report.pdf

European Council. (2022). Retrieved from Data protection in the EU: https://www.consilium.europa.eu/en/policies/data-protection/data-protection-regulation/#:~:text=The%20GDPR%20establishes%20the%20general,data%20processing%20operations%20they%20perform

European Union. (2016). *General Data Protection Regulation (GDPR)*. Récupéré sur Official Journal of the European Union: https://eur-lex.europa.eu/legal-content/EN/TXT/HTML/?uri=CELEX:32016R0679&from=EN

Grand View Research. (2021). *Enterprise Risk Management (ERM) Software Market Size, Share & Trends Analysis Report By Component, By Deployment, By Organization, By Vertical, By Region, And Segment Forecasts, 2021 - 2028*. Retrieved from https://www.grandviewresearch.com/industry-analysis/enterprise-risk-management-software-market

Hiscox. (2020). *Cyber readiness report 2020*. Récupéré sur https://www.hiscox.com/: https://www.hiscox.com/documents/2019-Hiscox-Cyber-Readiness-Report.pdf

impreva, Chris Levan. (2023). *PCI DSS Certification*. Récupéré sur impriva.com: https://www.imperva.com/learn/data-security/pci-dss-certification/

Information Commissioner's Office (ICO). (2018). *A framework for designing and managing GDPR compliance*. Récupéré sur Data protection by design and default: https://ico.org.uk/media/for-organisations/documents/2014223/gdpr-dpbd-201710.pdf

International Organization for Standardization. (2011). *ISO/IEC 29100:2011 Information technology—Security techniques—Privacy framework*. Récupéré sur https://www.iso.org/: https://www.iso.org/standard/45170.html

KnowBe4. (2021). *Data breach investigations report*. Récupéré sur https://enterprise.verizon.com/resources/reports/dbir/

National Institute of Standards and Technology. (2018). *A Tool for Improving Privacy through Enterprise Risk Management*. Récupéré sur NIST Privacy Framework: https://www.nist.gov/system/files/documents/2019/01/16/NIST-Privacy-Framework-1-16-19.pdf

National Small Business Association. (2017). *Small Business Taxation Survey*. Récupéré sur https://www.nsba.net/wp-content/uploads/2017/10/2017-Taxation-Survey.pdf

Ponemon Institute. (2020). *The true cost of compliance with data protection regulations*. Récupéré sur https://www.ponemon.org/local/upload/file/True%20Cost%20of%20Compliance%20Report%20FINAL%201.pdf

Ponemon Institute. (2021). *The state of data protection and management: An international study*. Récupéré sur https://www.ibm.com/downloads/cas/3OYPV7ED

Privacy governance. (2020). *International Association of Privacy Professionals (IAPP)*. Retrieved from https://iapp.org/resources/article/privacy-governance-report-2020/

PwC. (2020). *Global Economic Crime and Fraud Survey*. Retrieved from https://www.pwc.com/gx/en/services/advisory/forensics/economic-crime-survey.html

Retruster. (2021). *phishing and email security trends*. Récupéré sur https://www.retruster.com: https://www.retruster.com/blog/2021-phishing-and-email-security-trends

Security, I. B. M. (2020). *Cost of a data breach report 2020*. Récupéré sur https://www.ibm.com: https://www.ibm.com/security/data-breach

SPIRION. (2020). *The California Consumer Privacy Act of 2018*. Retrieved from https://www.spirion.com/wp-content/uploads/2020/07/Spirion_CCPA_v3.pdf

Symantec. (2020). *Internet Security Treat report, volume 25*. Symante/docs. Récupéré sur Internet security threat report, volume 25. https://www.symantec.com/content/dam/symantec/docs/reports/istr-25-2020-en.pdf

Thomson Reuters. (2019). *Cost of compliance 2019: Financial services at a tipping point*. Récupéré sur https://www.thomsonreuters.com/content/dam/ewp-m/documents/corporates/cost-of-compliance/cost-of-compliance-2019.pdf

University of York. (2023). *An introduction to cyber security and data protection*. Récupéré sur https://online.york.ac.uk/resources/introduction-to-cyber-security-data-protection/

Verizon. (2021). *Data Breach Investigations Report*. Author.

World Economic Forum. (2020). *The Global Risks Report*. Retrieved from https://www.weforum.org/reports/the-global-risks-report-2020

Chapter 12
Privacy Protection Challenges in Statistical Disclosure Control

Poonam Samir Jadhav

Department of Computer Engineering, SIES Graduate School of Technology, Nerul, India

Gautam M. Borkar

Department of Information Technology, Ramrao Adik Institute of Technology, D Y Patil (Deemed) University, Nerul, India

ABSTRACT

Due to privacy and confidentiality issues, a significant portion of the data collected by statistics agencies cannot be directly published. These issues span the legal and ethical spectrums. Statistical disclosure control (SDC) is an important tool to protect the privacy of individuals when releasing sensitive data for statistical analysis. However, there are several challenges that need to be addressed to ensure effective privacy preservation while also allowing for accurate statistical analysis. This chapter discusses the challenges faced by SDC in preserving privacy from a privacy preservation perspective. The challenges include the trade-off between privacy and data quality, increasing complexity of data, new data collection methods, and legal and ethical considerations. The rise of machine learning and artificial intelligence presents additional challenges. The chapter emphasizes the need for ongoing research and collaboration between statisticians, computer scientists, and policymakers to develop effective SDC techniques that balance privacy and data utility.

1. INTRODUCTION

Statistical agencies collect a vast amount of data, but not all of it can be published due to privacy and confidentiality concerns, which are both legal and ethical in nature. Even though all identifiers such as names and ID card numbers are removed, there may still be some occasions in which an individual can be re-identified via the demographic or particular information provided in the datasets (Chu et al., 2019).To address this issue, SDC seeks to modify the data to ensure that it can be released without disclosing confidential information, while still retaining its usefulness for analysis. This guide focuses

DOI: 10.4018/979-8-3693-1528-6.ch012

specifically on disclosure control for microdata, which refers to datasets that provide information on a set of variables for each individual respondent, including both natural persons and legal entities such as companies. The level of acceptable disclosure risk and the need for anonymization are determined by the data producer and guided by legislation, dissemination policies, and programs. SDC methods are used as part of anonymisation processes. They attempt to control/limit the risk of re-identification and attribute disclosure through manipulations of the data (Elliot et al., 2021). These factors are influenced by various considerations, such as the costs and expertise involved, data quality, potential misuse, legal and ethical matters, and maintaining the trust of respondents. Data producers have a moral, ethical, and legal responsibility to ensure that the data provided by respondents are only used for statistical purposes.

2. LITERATURE SURVEY

Following are various studies which worked on SDC.

Felix Ritchie et al. (2021) discusses the need to address the risks associated with releasing AI model specifications trained on sensitive data. It highlights the lack of clarity on how statistical disclosure control (SDC) procedures, designed for statistical outputs, relate to AI model specification. The authors bring together the fields of SDC and AI model risk to explore the conceptual and practical risks associated with releasing AI model specifications from a controlled environment. They suggest that technical and operational controls can be used to minimize the risks, but uncertainty remains on what exactly is "disclosive" in ML models.

Natalie Shlomo (2018) provides an overview of traditional methods of data dissemination and the need for statistical disclosure limitation (SDL) methods to protect confidentiality. It also discusses new forms of data dissemination, such as web-based applications and remote access, which present new challenges for statistical agencies. The main disclosure risk of concern is inferential disclosure, and the paper explores how differential privacy can be used to enhance the current SDL framework. Overall, the paper highlights the changing landscape of data dissemination and the need for statisticians to adapt to new challenges.

Matthias Templ et al. (2022) proposes a sequential noise addition approach to anonymize health surveillance event history data while maintaining data utility and reducing disclosure risk. Two proposals are made to handle time-varying variables. The approach was applied to a core residency data set from the Karonga health and demographic surveillance system, resulting in an anonymized data set with high data utility and acceptable disclosure risk. The proposed approach maintains the event order and time between events while limiting the number of response categories for time-varying variables. The results and methods presented in this study will be useful for anyone working on anonymizing longitudinal event history data with time-varying variables for sharing purposes.

Matthias Templ et al. (2015) discusses sdcMicro R package which provides an easy-to-use and object-oriented implementation of various methods for anonymizing and evaluating confidential micro-data sets. It includes popular disclosure risk and perturbation methods, and performs automated recalculation of risk and utility measures after each anonymization step. The package is optimized for working with large data sets and provides reporting facilities to summarize the anonymization process. A complex household survey test data set is used to demonstrate its functionality.

Jony et al. (2014) discusses about Double-phase micro aggregation. Double-phase micro aggregation is an improvement over classical micro aggregation for protecting privacy in distributed scenarios where there are no fully trusted parties. It enables the remote collection and sharing of biomedical data while keeping sensitive information confidential. The method achieves strong privacy protection while maintaining data quality and avoiding the limitations of centralized methods.

Amanda et al. (2022) proposes a new statistical disclosure control (SDC) method for mixed-type data using vine copulas. The method incorporates information from the marginal distributions of mixed-type variables and offers more flexibility in data perturbation compared to a previous SDC method using extended skew-t copula. The vine-SDC method allows for various forms of bivariate copulas in the vine decomposition, leading to a better fit for the joint distribution of the data. Additionally, the vine-SDC method demonstrates significant improvement in computational efficiency. The paper provides simulation and real healthcare survey data studies to compare the performance of the vine-SDC method with a common copula-based SDC method.

John M. Abowd et al. (2015) discusses the impact of statistical disclosure limitation methods used by data publishers to protect respondent privacy on economic research. The concept of statistical disclosure limitation is explained and the effects of its application on various research designs are considered. The paper also discusses scenarios where statistical disclosure limitation methods are discoverable and provides recommendations for researchers, journal editors, and statistical agencies.

Table 1. Literature survey

Sr.No.	Technique	Methodology	Limitations
Ritchie et.al.(2021)	Statistical disclosure control (SDC)	The paper introduces SDC methods for protecting sensitive information in machine learning models.	The author acknowledges the trade-off between privacy and model accuracy, as well as the challenges associated with applying SDC to machine learning models. The paper primarily focuses on introducing SDC methods for machine learning models and does not provide an empirical evaluation of their effectiveness.
Natalie Shlomo (2018)	Differential privacy added to SDC	Explores how differential privacy can be used to enhance the current SDL framework.	Possibility of reduction in data utility
Matthias Templ et al.(2022)	A hybrid approach that involves several techniques, including suppression, generalization, noise addition, and data swapping.	Anonymizing open-access health and demographic surveillance system (HDSS)	The proposed hybrid approach may not be suitable for all HDSS data sets, as the effectiveness of each anonymization technique depends on the specific data characteristics and context.
Matthias Templ et al.(2015)	SdcMicro R package for SDC	Focuses on statistical disclosure control (SDC) methods to the data in order to decrease the disclosure risk of data	The package may not be suitable for all types of data, especially if the data contains complex structures or dependencies.
Jony et al.(2014)	Double-phase micro aggregation	Focuses on SDC in distributed scenarios.	The architecture may face challenges in scaling up.
Amanda M.Y. et al.(2022)	SDC method using vine copulas	New statistical disclosure control (SDC) method for mixed-type data based on vine copulas.	Vine copulas assume that the variables in the data set are independent. However, this assumption may not hold in real-world scenarios where there may be complex relationships among the variables.
John M. Abowd et al.(2015)	SDC	This study investigates the impact of data publishers' techniques for preserving respondents' privacy on economic research.	Techniques are often ad hoc and may not be standardized or widely accepted. This can lead to inconsistencies in the way that different organizations handle confidential data, making it more difficult to compare and analyze data across different sources.

The findings from above literature survey are as given below:

- There is a trade-off between privacy and model accuracy when applying SDC methods to machine learning models.
- The effectiveness of each anonymization technique depends on the specific data characteristics and context, which means that the proposed hybrid approach may not be suitable for all data sets.
- The package may not be suitable for all types of data, especially if the data contains complex structures or dependencies.
- The architecture may face challenges in scaling up.
- Vine copulas, which are used in some SDC techniques, assume that the variables in the data set are independent, which may not hold in real-world scenarios where there may be complex relationships among the variables.
- SDC techniques are often ad hoc and may not be standardized or widely accepted, leading to inconsistencies in how different organizations handle confidential data and making it more difficult to compare and analyze data across different sources.

3. STATISTICAL DISCLOSURE CONTROL

The need for Statistical Disclosure Control (SDC) arises from the imperative to strike a harmonious balance between the growing demand for data-driven insights and the paramount importance of safeguarding individual privacy and sensitive information. In an era of pervasive data sharing and analysis, SDC techniques play a vital role in curtailing the risk of inadvertent disclosure of personal details while still enabling accurate statistical analysis and informed decision-making. By applying a suite of privacy-preserving methods, such as anonymization, aggregation, and noise addition, SDC ensures that data utility is maximized while minimizing the potential harm that could result from re-identification or unauthorized access, thereby fostering responsible data usage and engendering trust among data custodians, analysts, and the individuals whose information is being processed.

This section given below delves into the concept of data release, where the delicate balance between risk and utility in the anonymization process is contingent upon the intended users and the specific circumstances surrounding the release of a microdata file. Typically, three distinct data release methods are employed, catering to diverse target audiences and varying contextual requirements.

3.1 Release Types

Following are the various release types of microdata.

- Public Use File (PUF) is a type of anonymized dataset that is widely used in statistical disclosure control. PUFs are created by removing or modifying certain sensitive information in a dataset to protect individual privacy while preserving the utility of the data for research purposes.

For example, the National Center for Health Statistics (NCHS) in the United States creates PUFs from its National Health Interview Survey data. The PUFs are designed to be representative of the original data, but they have been modified to protect the privacy of survey participants. The modifications include suppressing certain values, adding noise to certain variables, and collapsing certain categories to reduce the risk of re-identification.

PUFs have been used in a wide range of research studies, including those on health, education, economics, and social science. However, there are still concerns about the effectiveness of PUFs in protecting privacy, especially with the increasing availability of sophisticated data mining techniques.In summary, PUFs are a useful tool for protecting individual privacy while preserving the utility of data for research purposes. However, additional techniques may be needed to ensure that PUFs provide sufficient privacy protection for sensitive data.

- A Scientific Use File (SUF) is a confidential dataset that is released to researchers for scientific research purposes while minimizing the risk of disclosure of sensitive information. The SUF is created by applying statistical disclosure control techniques to the original dataset, such as adding noise, suppression of values, or recoding variables. The SUF allows researchers to conduct analyses while protecting the confidentiality of individuals and organizations. An example of the use of SUF is in the field of health research, where researchers need access to individual-level data to analyze health outcomes but must protect the privacy of patients. A SUF could be created by modifying the original dataset, for example, by replacing exact values with ranges, recoding some variables, or adding noise to the data. The modified dataset would allow researchers to conduct their analyses while minimizing the risk of re-identification.

- Microdata available a controlled research data center are individual-level datasets that are released to researchers for scientific research purposes under strict controls to protect the confidentiality of individuals and organizations. The controlled access ensures that researchers adhere to strict protocols to maintain data confidentiality and privacy.An example of the use of microdata in a controlled research data center is in the field of labor economics, where researchers need access to individual-level data to analyze labor market outcomes, but must protect the privacy of workers and employers. A controlled research data center could provide researchers with access to a confidential dataset that includes information on workers' earnings, education, and demographics, as well as information on employers' characteristics. The researchers could conduct their analyses while minimizing the risk of re-identification of individuals or organizations.

3.2 Measuring Risk With Respect to Disclosure

- **Identity disclosure:** The process of revealing personal information about an individual, such as their name, address, or social security number, which can be used to identify them. In recent years, with the increasing amount of personal information being shared online, there has been a growing concern about identity disclosure and its potential impact on privacy and security. A common practice for protecting identity disclosure is to remove identity related attributes from released data (Dan Zhu, 2009).One area where identity disclosure has become particularly relevant is in the context of social media. Research has shown that social media users often reveal a significant amount of personal information online, which can make them vulnerable to identity theft and other forms of cybercrime .Suppose we have a dataset of 100 individuals, and we want to calculate the identity disclosure risk for this dataset. We have four quasi-identifiers (QIs) available: age, gender, occupation, and zip code.

To calculate the identity disclosure risk, the Average Re-identification Risk (ARR) metric can be used. The ARR measures the probability of re-identifying an individual using a set of QIs. It is calculated as given in following algorithm.

Algorithm:

1. Initialize a variable probability_sum to 0 and a variable count to 0.
2. For each individual i in the dataset, do the following:
   i. Randomly select an individual j from the dataset.
   ii. Find all individuals in the dataset who have the same age, gender, and occupation as i.
   iii. Calculate the proportion of those individuals who have the same zip code as i.
   iv. Add the proportion obtained in step 2iii to probability_sum.
   v. Increment the count by 1.
3. Calculate the average probability by dividing probability_sum by count.
4. Return the average probability as the output.

For example, suppose an individual i is chosen as a 35-year-old male accountant. It is found that there are 10 other individuals in the dataset who share the same age, gender, and occupation as i. Out of these 10 individuals, 2 have the same zip code as i. Therefore, the probability of correctly re-identifying i using the chosen subset of QIs is $2/10 = 0.2$.

This process is repeated for all individuals in the dataset, and the average of the probabilities obtained is taken. Let's say the average probability is 0.15. This means that the identity disclosure risk for this dataset using the chosen subset of QIs is 0.15. If the identity disclosure risk is deemed too high, SDC methods can be applied to the dataset to reduce the risk.

- **Attribute disclosure:** Refers to the process of revealing personal characteristics or traits of an individual, such as their age, gender, or interests. it was shown that it is possible to infer additional information about a user from data shared by other users,this type of information disclosure is called attribute disclosure (Athanasios Andreou, 2017). This type of disclosure can also have significant privacy and security implications, particularly in the context of online data sharing and analytics.

One area where attribute disclosure has become particularly relevant is in the context of targeted advertising. Research has shown that advertisers may use personal information, such as age, gender, and location, to target ads to specific individuals, while targeted advertising can provide benefits to both advertisers and consumers, it can also raise concerns about privacy and discrimination.

Suppose we have a dataset containing information about individuals' age, gender, and salary. We want to calculate the attribute disclosure risk of releasing the average salary of males aged 30-40.

To calculate the attribute disclosure risk, first, the sensitive attribute needs to be identified, which in this case is salary. Next, the quasi-identifiers, age and gender, need to be identified. After that, the number of individuals in the dataset who match the query (i.e., males aged 30-40) and have the same values for the quasi-identifiers should be counted. Let's assume that there are 100 such individuals. Then, the number of individuals in the dataset who match the query but have different values for the quasi-identifiers should be counted, which in this case is 500 individuals.

To calculate the attribute disclosure risk, we need to find the ratio of the number of individuals in the first group to the total number of individuals in the dataset. Therefore, the attribute disclosure risk can be calculated as $100 / (100 + 500) = 0.1667$ or 16.67%. This means that there is a 16.67% chance that an attacker who knows that a male aged 30-40 is in the dataset can correctly guess their salary based on the released average salary of males aged 30-40.

- **Inferential disclosure:** Refers to the risk of revealing sensitive information about an individual or a group of people by making inferences based on seemingly innocuous data. For example, a seemingly harmless data point such as a person's zip code can be used to make inferences about their income or ethnicity. This type of disclosure can pose a significant privacy risk, particularly when the inferred information is sensitive or personal. Inferential disclosure is most commonly considered when tabular data are released, but it is also appropriate for some microdata releases (George Duncan, 1989).

To estimate the inferential disclosure risk, the first step is to determine the probability that the released statistics can reveal sensitive information about individuals who are not in the dataset. In this scenario, we want to release the average salary of males aged 30-40 who work in the technology sector, but we do not know the exact number of individuals who meet these criteria. However, we do know that there are 1000 individuals in the dataset who work in the technology sector. One possible approach to estimate the inferential disclosure risk is to use a statistical model that considers the attacker's background knowledge and the released statistics. For example, a Bayesian network model can be used to represent the relationships between the sensitive attribute (salary), the quasi-identifiers (age, gender, sector), and the released statistics (average salary of males aged 30-40 in the technology sector).

3.3 Risk Measures

For many applications the measurement of disclosure risk is based on the idea of uniqueness and rareness (Matthias Temple, 2008). Following are categorization of risks.

- **Global risk:** Global risk refers to the risk of disclosing information that could potentially harm the population as a whole. Global risk is often associated with aggregate data or statistics that are derived from large datasets. For example, suppose a government agency collects data on the prevalence of a particular disease in a population. If the agency releases aggregate statistics that are too detailed, it could potentially disclose information that could lead to the identification of individuals with the disease. This could have serious consequences for the population as a whole, such as stigmatization, discrimination, or loss of trust in the government. In this case, the agency would need to apply statistical disclosure control techniques to ensure that the risk of disclosure is minimized while still maintaining the utility of the data for analysis.

Suppose we add a noise of +/- 5000 to the income of each individual in the dataset. The global risk can be calculated as the probability that an attacker can correctly identify the income of an individual, even after adding the noise. The global risk is calculated as shown in by formula given below:

Global Risk = (Number of individuals correctly re-identified) / (Total number of individuals in the dataset)

- **Household risk:** Household risk refers to the risk of disclosing information that could potentially harm a particular household or group of households. Household risk is often associated with microdata, which are individual-level data that are collected from surveys or administrative records. For example, suppose a research organization collects data on the income, education, and occupation of individuals in a particular neighborhood. If the organization releases microdata that are too detailed, it could potentially disclose information that could lead to the identification of individual households in the neighborhood. This could have serious consequences for those households, such as loss of privacy, targeted marketing, or even physical harm. In this case, the organization would need to apply statistical disclosure control techniques to ensure that the risk of disclosure is minimized while still maintaining the utility of the data for analysis. One common technique for protecting household-level data is to use data masking or perturbation techniques, which add noise or randomness to the data to prevent individual households from being identified.

Suppose we group the individuals in the dataset by their households, and add a noise of +/- 5000 to the total household income instead of individual incomes. The household risk can be calculated as the probability that an attacker can correctly identify the income of an individual in a household, given that they know the income of another individual in the same household. The household risk is calculated as shown in by formula given below:

Household Risk = (Number of individuals correctly re-identified in the same household) / (Total number of individuals in the same household)

3.4 Identifying Variables

SDC methods are often applied to identifying variables whose values might lead to re-identification. Identifying variables can be further classified into direct identifiers and key variables:

- A direct identifier is a variable in a dataset that directly reveals the identity of an individual, such as their name, social security number, or address. Direct identifiers pose a significant risk to confidentiality in statistical data analysis, as they can be used to re-identify individuals and violate their privacy.

One commonly used SDC technique for direct identifiers is anonymization, which involves removing or obfuscating direct identifiers from the dataset. For example, replacing a person's name with a unique identifier, or aggregating address information at a higher level of geographic resolution.

- Key variables in SDC include direct identifiers, quasi-identifiers, and sensitive attributes. Direct identifiers, as mentioned in the previous question, are variables that directly identify individuals, such as names, social security numbers, or addresses. Quasi-identifiers are variables that, in combination, may indirectly identify individuals, such as age, gender, and occupation. Sensitive attributes are variables that reveal sensitive information about individuals, such as income, health status, or criminal record.

Several SDC techniques are used to protect sensitive variables, such as data masking, aggregation, and perturbation. In some cases, data suppression may also be necessary to prevent disclosure of sensitive information.

- Categorical variables and continuous variables are two types of variables commonly encountered in statistical analysis. Categorical variables are variables that take on a limited number of values, typically representing a nominal or ordinal scale. Examples of categorical variables include gender (male/female), race (white/black/Asian/other), and education level (high school/college/postgraduate).On the other hand, continuous variables are variables that can take on any value within a certain range. Examples of continuous variables include age, weight, and height.

In statistical disclosure control, it is important to consider both categorical and continuous variables when protecting confidential data. Categorical variables may need to be grouped or recoded to reduce the risk of re-identification, while continuous variables may need to be randomized or perturbed to prevent disclosure. For example, in a study analyzing the relationship between income and education level, the income variable is continuous while the education level variable is categorical. The income variable may need to be perturbed to protect the confidentiality of the respondents, while the education level variable may need to be grouped into broader categories to prevent re-identification.

3.5 Common SDC Methods

Continuing from the previous answer, here are a few more common SDC methods for categorical variables:

- **Recoding:** Recoding involves collapsing categories of a categorical variable into larger categories or creating new categories to protect the confidentiality of sensitive information. For example, in a survey about political affiliation, categories such as "Democrat", "Republican", and "Independent" could be collapsed into "Major Parties" and "Minor Parties".
- **Local suppression:** Local suppression involves removing or masking certain cells of a contingency table that contain sensitive information. For example, in a contingency table of marital status and income, cells with small counts or high disclosure risk may be suppressed to protect the confidentiality of respondents.
- **Post-randomization method (PRAM):** PRAM involves adding random noise to categorical variables to protect the confidentiality of respondents. For example, in a survey about education level, a small amount of random noise could be added to each respondent's reported education level to make it more difficult to identify individual respondents

SDC methods are also used for continuous variables in order to protect the confidentiality of sensitive information while still allowing useful statistical analysis to be performed. Some common SDC methods for continuous variables, along with references to relevant literature, are:

- **Micro-aggregation:** Micro-aggregation involves grouping data into small clusters and then replacing the data within each cluster with a summary statistic, such as the mean or median. This method reduces the risk of disclosure by aggregating the data, while still preserving some of the original information.

- **Adding noise:** Adding noise involves adding random values to continuous variables to protect the confidentiality of respondents. For example, in a survey about income, a small amount of random noise could be added to each respondent's reported income to make it more difficult to identify individual respondents
- **Shuffling:** Shuffling involves randomly reordering the values of a continuous variable to protect the confidentiality of respondents. For example, in a survey about age, the values of the age variable could be randomly shuffled to make it more difficult to identify individual respondents.

3.6 Privacy Models

Privacy models play a crucial role in SDC, which is a set of techniques used to protect the confidentiality of sensitive data while still allowing data users to obtain useful statistical information. SDC is particularly important in the context of statistical agencies, which collect and disseminate data on a range of topics including demographics, health, economics, and more.

One of the main goals of SDC is to prevent the disclosure of sensitive information about individuals or organizations in a dataset. This can be achieved through various privacy models, which determine how data is anonymized or modified to protect the privacy of individuals in the dataset. For example, privacy models such as k-anonymity, l-diversity, and t-closeness are commonly used in SDC to anonymize data and ensure that individual records cannot be re-identified.

- K-anonymity is a data anonymization technique that aims to protect the privacy of individuals in a dataset by ensuring that each individual's record is indistinguishable from at least k-1 other individuals' records. In other words, it aims to prevent re-identification of individuals by ensuring that each record in the dataset cannot be linked to a unique individual (Latanya Sweeney, 2002).

For example, consider a dataset containing sensitive information about individuals, such as age, gender, and income. An attacker may be able to re-identify individuals in the dataset by linking their age, gender, and income together. To prevent this, we can use k-anonymity by generalizing or suppressing certain attributes in the dataset. Suppose we apply 2-anonymity to this dataset by generalizing the age attribute to age ranges and rounding the income attribute to the nearest 10,000. The resulting dataset is as shown in Table 2.

Table 2. K-anonymity outcome

Name	Gender	Age Range	Income
Alice	Female	20-29	60,000
Bob	Male	20-29	60,000
Carol	Female	30-39	50,000
Dave	Male	30-39	50,000
Eve	Female	40-49	70,000
Frank	Male	40-49	70,000
Grace	Female	20-29	90,000
Harry	Male	20-29	90,000

In this anonymized dataset, each record is indistinguishable from at least one other record, ensuring 2-anonymity. For example, Alice and Bob have the same age range, gender, and income, making them indistinguishable from each other. Similarly, Carol and Dave are indistinguishable, as are Eve and Frank, and Grace and Harry.

While k-anonymity can effectively protect privacy, it can also lead to loss of information and reduced data utility. For example, by generalizing the age attribute to age ranges, we lose the exact age of each individual in the dataset. Therefore, it is important to carefully consider the trade-off between privacy and data utility when applying k-anonymity to a dataset. The effectiveness of a microaggregation method is measured by calculating its information loss. A lower information loss implies that the anonymized dataset is less distorted from an original dataset, and thus provides better data quality for analysis.(Md Enamul Kabir,2015).

- L-diversity is another data anonymization technique that aims to enhance the privacy protection provided by k-anonymity by ensuring that each sensitive attribute in the dataset has at least L distinct values. This helps to prevent attribute disclosure attacks, where an attacker may be able to infer sensitive information about an individual by observing the values of a sensitive attribute in the dataset (A. Machanavajjhala, 2006).

Continuing with the same example as before, suppose we apply 2-anonymity and L-diversity with L=2 to the dataset containing sensitive information about individuals, such as age, gender, and income. In addition to generalizing or suppressing attributes to achieve 2-anonymity, we also ensure that each sensitive attribute has at least two distinct values in each group of records with the same quasi-identifier values. The resulting dataset is as shown in Table 3.

Table 3. L-diversity outcome

Name	Gender	Age Range	Income Range
Alice	Female	20-29	50,000-60,000
Bob	Male	20-29	50,000-60,000
Carol	Female	30-39	40,000-50,000
Dave	Male	30-39	40,000-50,000
Eve	Female	40-49	70,000-80,000
Frank	Male	40-49	70,000-80,000
Grace	Female	20-29	80,000-90,000
Harry	Male	20-29	80,000-90,000

In this anonymized dataset, each group of records with the same quasi-identifier values (i.e., gender and age range) has at least two distinct values for the sensitive attribute (i.e., income range), ensuring L-diversity. For example, Alice and Bob have the same gender and age range, but different income ranges, ensuring L-diversity. Similarly, Carol and Dave, Eve and Frank, and Grace and Harry each have at least two distinct values for the income range attribute.

While L-diversity can provide additional privacy protection compared to k-anonymity, it can also be more difficult to achieve, especially for datasets with many sensitive attributes. Additionally, L-diversity does not prevent attacks where an attacker may be able to link multiple quasi-identifiers together to re-identify individuals. Therefore, it is important to carefully consider the specific privacy risks and requirements of each dataset when choosing an appropriate anonymization technique.

- T-closeness is another data anonymization technique that aims to provide stronger privacy protection by ensuring that the distribution of the sensitive attribute in each group of records with the same quasi-identifier values is not significantly different from the distribution in the overall dataset. This helps to prevent attribute disclosure attacks where an attacker may be able to infer sensitive information about an individual by observing the values of a sensitive attribute in the dataset (Ninghui Li, 2007)

Continuing with the same example as before, suppose we apply 2-anonymity, L-diversity with L=2, and T-closeness with a distance measure of Euclidean distance to the dataset containing sensitive information about individuals, such as age, gender, and income. In addition to generalizing or suppressing attributes to achieve 2-anonymity and ensuring that each sensitive attribute has at least two distinct values in each group of records with the same quasi-identifier values to achieve L-diversity, we also ensure that the distribution of the income range attribute in each group is not significantly different from the distribution in the overall dataset to achieve T-closeness. The resulting dataset is as shown in Table 4.

Table 4. T-closeness outcome

Name	Gender	Age Range	Income Range
Alice	Female	20-29	50,000-60,000
Bob	Male	20-29	50,000-60,000
Carol	Female	30-39	40,000-50,000
Dave	Male	30-39	40,000-50,000
Eve	Female	40-49	70,000-80,000
Frank	Male	40-49	70,000-80,000
Grace	Female	20-29	80,000-90,000
Harry	Male	20-29	80,000-90,000

In this anonymized dataset, each group of records with the same quasi-identifier values (i.e., gender and age range) has at least two distinct values for the sensitive attribute (i.e., income range) and the distribution of the income range in each group is not significantly different from the distribution in the overall dataset, ensuring T-closeness.

While T-closeness can provide even stronger privacy protection than L-diversity, it can also be more computationally expensive to achieve. Additionally, T-closeness assumes that the sensitive attribute is continuous and can be modeled using a probability distribution, which may not always be the case for all datasets. Therefore, it is important to carefully consider the specific privacy risks and requirements of each dataset when choosing an appropriate anonymization technique.

3.7 SDC Application Workflow

SDC application workflow is shown in Figure 1.

Figure 1. SDC application workflow

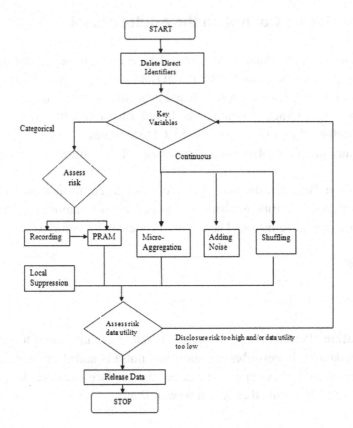

The stepwise working is as shown below:

Step 1: Identifying variables, those whose values might lead to re-identification, must be determined:

Direct identifiers precisely identify statistical units (company name, CIF, address, etc). Key variables (categorical or continuous), when considered together, can be used to identify individual units (region, activity, net turnover, total assets, total employment, etc).
Sensitive variables must not be discovered for any individual unit (insolvency status, etc).

Step 2: Deletion of direct identifiers, to guarantee primary confidentiality
Step 3: Key and sensitive variables identification, to address secondary confidentiality
Step 4: Individual disclosure risks measurement based on sample frequency counts (k-anonymity, l-diversity, etc)
Step 5: Application of SDC-methods to modify high-risk observations.

Step 6: Disclosure risk and information loss are recomputed comparing original and modified data.
Step 7: The goal is to release a safe data set with low (individual) risks and high data utility.

With continuation of above process this case study provides an illustration of a possible methodology for the anonymization process required in SDC.

3.8 Statistical Disclosure Control on the Adult Dataset

SDC process is applied on Adult Dataset. The adult dataset contains sensitive information about individuals including age, gender, education level, marital status, occupation, and income level. The dataset is commonly used for machine learning research and analysis. However, the release of this data could potentially compromise the privacy of individuals. In order to protect the privacy of individuals in the dataset, we will use statistical disclosure control (SDC) techniques.

The following is an example implementation of statistical disclosure control on the adult dataset:

1. **Data Preparation:** The adult dataset is pre-processed to ensure that no identifying information such as names or social security numbers are present. We will remove the "fnlwgt" column which contains identification information. The required code can be as follows:

```
import pandas as pd
adult_data = pd.read_csv('adult.csv')
adult_data = adult_data.drop(columns=['fnlwgt'])
```

2. **Data Perturbation:** Perturbation is a common SDC technique used to protect the privacy of individuals in a dataset. In perturbation, statistical noise is added to the data to make it difficult to identify individuals. For example, we can use the Laplace mechanism to add noise to the age variable as follows: The required code can be as follows:

```
import numpy as np
# Define the sensitivity of the age variable (how much the data can change
without compromising privacy)
sensitivity = 1
# Set the privacy parameter (epsilon) to control the amount of noise added
epsilon = 0.1
# Generate noise from the Laplace distribution
noise = np.random.laplace(loc=0, scale=sensitivity/epsilon, size=len(adult_
data))
# Perturb the age variable with noise
# Perturb the age variable with noise
```

Perturbation outcome is as shown in Table 5.

In this example, Laplace noise was added to the age variable using a sensitivity value of 1 and an epsilon value of 0.1.

Table 5. Perturbation outcome

Before Perturbation					
Age	Workclass	Education	Marital_Status	Occupation	Income_Level
39	State-gov	Bachelors	Never-married	Adm-clerical	<=50K
50	Self-emp-not-inc	Bachelors	Married-civ-spouse	Exec-managerial	>50K
After Perturbation					
Age	Workclass	Education	Marital_Status	Occupation	Income_Level
39.12	State-gov	Bachelors	Never-married	Adm-clerical	<=50K
50.03	Self-emp-not-inc	Bachelors	Married-civ-spouse	Exec-managerial	>50K

3. **Data Sampling:** Sampling is another SDC technique used to protect the privacy of individuals in a dataset. In sampling, a random subset of the data is selected and released instead of the entire dataset. For example, simple random sampling to select a subset of the adult dataset can be used as follows:

```
# Set the sample size (proportion of the data to be released)
sample_size = 0.5
# Randomly sample the adult data
sampled_data = adult_data.sample(frac=sample_size)
# Release the sampled data for research purposes
sampled_data.to_csv('adult_data_sampled.csv', index=False)
```

Sampling outcome is as shown in table 6.

In this example, simple random sampling was used to select a subset of the data with a sample size of 50%.

Table 6. Sampling outcome

Before Sampling					
Age	Workclass	Education	Marital_Status	Occupation	Income_Level
39	State-gov	Bachelors	Never-married	Adm-clerical	<=50K
50	Self-emp-not-inc	Bachelors	Married-civ-spouse	Exec-managerial	>50K
...	...	...	...	...	...
After Sampling					
Age	Workclass	Education	Marital_Status	Occupation	Income_Level
39	State-gov	Bachelors	Never-married	Adm-clerical	<=50K
41	Private	HS-grad	Married-civ-spouse	Craft-repair	<=50K
34	Private	7th-8th	Married-civ-spouse	Transport-moving	<=50K

4. **Data Aggregation:** Aggregation is another SDC technique used to protect the privacy of individuals in a dataset. In aggregation, individual-level data is aggregated to a higher-level summary statistic such as mean, median, or standard deviation. For example, we can aggregate the income level variable by computing the mean value as follows:

```
# Aggregate the income level variable by computing the mean
aggregated_data = adult_data.groupby(['education', 'occupation']).agg({'income_
level': 'mean'}).reset_index()
# Release the aggregated data for research purposes
aggregated_data.to_csv('adult_data_aggregated.csv', index=False)
```

Aggregation outcome is as shown in Table 7.

Table 7. Aggregation outcome

Before Aggregation					
Age	**Workclass**	**Education**	**Marital_Status**	**Occupation**	**Income_Level**
39	State-gov	Bachelors	Never-married	Adm-clerical	<=50K
50	Self-emp-not-inc	Bachelors	Married-civ-spouse	Exec-managerial	>50K
...	...	...	...	...	...
After Aggregation					
Education		**Occupation**		**Income_Level**	
Bachelors		Adm-clerical		<=50K	
Bachelors		Exec-managerial		>50K	
...		...		...	

4. CHALLENGES TO SDC

*   The risk-utility trade-off in the SDC process SDC is concerned with the protection of confidential data while releasing information for research or public policy purposes. One of the main challenges in SDC is finding a balance between disclosure risk and information loss.

Disclosure risk refers to the risk of a respondent being re-identified or their confidential information being disclosed. Information loss, on the other hand, refers to the loss of information that occurs when SDC techniques are applied to the data to reduce disclosure risk.

When implementing SDC techniques, it is important to find a balance between these two factors. If the techniques used are too stringent, then the risk of disclosure is low, but the resulting data may be of little use for research or policy purposes. Conversely, if the techniques used are too lenient, then the resulting data may be useful, but the risk of disclosure is high.

There are several SDC techniques available that can help balance disclosure risk and information loss, including cell suppression, perturbation, and aggregation. Cell suppression involves removing cells from a table or dataset that pose a high risk of disclosure. Perturbation involves introducing random

Figure 2. Risk vs. utility

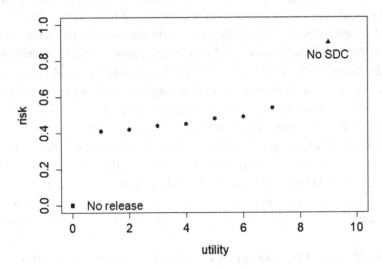

noise to the data to prevent re-identification. Aggregation involves grouping data into larger categories to reduce the risk of disclosure. One way to measure the trade-off between risk and utility is by using statistical measures such as the Gini coefficient or the entropy. These measures can be used to quantify the degree of inequality or diversity in the data, and can be used to evaluate the impact of different SDC methods on the risk-utility trade-off.

Another way to measure the trade-off is through the use of simulation or bootstrapping techniques. These methods involve generating multiple random samples from the original data and applying the SDC methods to each sample. The resulting sets of masked or perturbed data can be compared to the original data in terms of their statistical properties and their usefulness for analysis. This allows for a more comprehensive evaluation of the risk-utility trade-off and helps to identify the optimal SDC methods for a given dataset.

- **Methodological Challenges:** Methodological challenges to SDC refer to the theoretical and statistical aspects of privacy preservation. One of the main challenges is the trade-off between privacy and accuracy. This challenge arises because more aggressive methods of privacy preservation can lead to less accurate statistical analysis, while less aggressive methods can lead to privacy breaches. Another challenge is the need for differential privacy, which requires that the probability of an individual being identified remains the same regardless of whether or not their data is included in the analysis. Finally, another challenge is the need for robustness, which ensures that the methods used for SDC are resistant to attacks from external sources.
- **Practical Challenges:** Practical challenges to SDC refer to the implementation and use of SDC techniques in real-world scenarios. One challenge is the need for data holders to have sufficient knowledge and expertise to implement SDC techniques effectively. Another challenge is the need for secure data sharing mechanisms, such as secure multi-party computation or secure data linkage, which can enable effective collaboration between data holders without compromising privacy. Finally, another challenge is the need for transparency, which ensures that the methods used for SDC are understandable and explainable to stakeholders.

- **Legal and Ethical Challenges:** Legal and ethical challenges to SDC refer to the broader social, political, and ethical considerations surrounding the use of SDC techniques. One challenge is the need for legal frameworks and standards to regulate the use of SDC techniques, to ensure that privacy is protected while also enabling effective data analysis. Another challenge is the need for ethical considerations, such as the impact of SDC techniques on social justice and fairness, to be taken into account when designing and implementing SDC techniques. Finally, another challenge is the need for public awareness and engagement, to ensure that the wider public is aware of the implications of SDC techniques and can provide feedback and input.

- **Privacy-Preserving Techniques:** To address these challenges, researchers have developed privacy-preserving techniques for statistical analysis, such as differential privacy, k-anonymity, and l-diversity. Differential privacy adds noise to the data to protect individual privacy, while k-anonymity ensures that each record in the dataset is indistinguishable from at least k-1 other records. L-diversity adds diversity to the dataset by ensuring that each sensitive attribute has at least 1 distinct values.

- **Cross-Domain Privacy Preservation:** Cross-domain privacy preservation refers to the practice of safeguarding sensitive information when sharing data across different domains or entities, while still enabling meaningful analysis and collaboration. Statistical control disclosure is a crucial aspect of this approach, involving the application of statistical techniques to control and limit the potential disclosure of individual-level information when combining data from diverse sources. By carefully balancing the trade-off between data utility and privacy, cross-domain privacy preservation methods ensure that valuable insights can be extracted without compromising the confidentiality of personal data, fostering responsible data sharing and research across domains.

- **Ethical Use of SDC:** SDC encompasses the responsible application of privacy-preserving techniques to ensure that sensitive data is shared and analyzed in ways that respect individuals' privacy rights and uphold data stewardship principles. This involves employing robust anonymization, aggregation, and perturbation methods to prevent the inadvertent identification of individuals while maintaining data utility for legitimate research and analysis. By prioritizing ethical considerations and striving for a delicate equilibrium between data usability and privacy protection, the ethical use of SDC promotes trust, safeguards against potential harm, and facilitates valuable insights without compromising individual confidentiality.

- **Explainability and Accountability:** Explainability and accountability are integral to the implementation of Statistical Disclosure Control (SDC) methods, as they provide a means for comprehending and validating the effectiveness of privacy protection measures applied to data. In an era of increasing data sharing and analysis, it is imperative that decision-makers and stakeholders can grasp the mechanisms behind SDC techniques and their impact on data integrity and confidentiality. Clear explanations not only foster transparency but also enable an informed assessment of the trade-offs between privacy and data utility. By ensuring that SDC methods are accessible and understandable, organizations can build trust, facilitate meaningful collaboration, and uphold responsible data practices that prioritize both privacy concerns and the pursuit of valuable insights.

- **Synthetic Data and Re-Identification Attacks:** Within the realm of Statistical Disclosure Control (SDC), the emergence of advanced synthetic data generation techniques underscores the importance of rigorously evaluating the susceptibility of synthetic data to re-identification attacks. While synthetic data holds promise in preserving privacy during information sharing, its vulnerability to sophisticated re-identification strategies necessitates careful consideration. Effective countermeasures must be devised, employing a combination of techniques such as noise injection, targeted perturbation, and data augmentation. By proactively identifying potential risks and deploying robust safeguards, SDC ensures that the advantages of synthetic data are harnessed while minimizing the likelihood of re-identification, thus fortifying the privacy landscape and maintaining data confidentiality.

- **Recent Advances in SDC:** Recent advances in SDC include the use of machine learning and deep learning models to preserve privacy while still allowing accurate statistical analysis. These models are designed to learn the underlying data distribution and then use this knowledge to perturb the data in a way that preserves privacy. Other recent advances in SDC include the use of homomorphic encryption and secure multi-party computation.

- **Future Directions:** Future research in SDC and privacy preservation will likely focus on developing new methods and improving existing techniques. For example, researchers may focus on improving the efficiency of differential privacy, developing new models that are more resistant to re-identification attacks, and exploring the use of blockchain technology for privacy-preserving statistical analysis.

CONCLUSION

Statistical disclosure control (SDC) techniques such as perturbation, sampling, and aggregation can be used to protect the privacy of individuals in a dataset while releasing the data for research purposes. However, it is important to choose the appropriate SDC technique based on the data and privacy requirements. SDC faces new challenges in preserving privacy due to the increasing amount and complexity of data. The challenges include Big Data, privacy-utility trade-off, differential privacy, re-identification attacks, and privacy in machine learning. Addressing these challenges requires collaboration between researchers and practitioners from various domains, including statistics, computer science, and privacy law. Developing effective SDC methods that can handle large and complex datasets while preserving privacy is a key research direction for the future.

REFERENCES

Andreou, A., Goga, O., & Loiseau, P. (2017). Identity vs. Attribute Disclosure Risks for Users with Multiple Social Profiles. *IEEE/ACM International Conference on Advances in Social Networks Analysis and Mining,* 163–170. 10.1145/3110025.3110046

Chu, Ip, Lam, & K.P. (2022). Vine copula statistical disclosure control for mixed-type data. *Computational Statistics & Data Analysis*, 176.

Chu, A. M. Y., Lam, B. S. Y., Tiwari, A., & So, M. K. P. (2019). An Empirical Study of Applying Statistical Disclosure Control Methods to Public Health Research. *Journal of Empirical Research on Human Research Ethics*, *14*(5), 411–420. PMID:31731730

Dan, Li, & Wu. (2009). Identity disclosure protection: A data reconstruction approach for privacy-preserving data mining. Decision Support Systems, 48, 133-140.

Duncan, G., & Lambert, D. (1989). The Risk of Disclosure for Microdata. *Journal of Business & Economic Statistics*, 207–217.

Elliot, M., & Domingo-Ferrer, J. (2021). The future of statistical disclosure control. *The Journal of Privacy and Confidentiality*, *11*(1), 1–18.

Enamul Kabir, Mahmood, Mustafa, & Wang. (2015). Microaggregation Sorting Framework for K-Anonymity Statistical Disclosure Control in Cloud Computing. IEEE.

John & Schmutte. (2015). Economic Analysis and Statistical Disclosure Limitation. In Brookings Papers on Economic Activity. Springer.

Jony, N., & Anitha, M. (2014). Survey of Statistical Disclosure Control Technique. *International Journal of Research in Advent Technology*, *2*(5), 344–349.

Krueger, Mansouri-Benssassi, Ritchie, & Smith. (2021). Statistical disclosure controls for machine learning models. *Conference of European Statisticians*, 1-19.

Li, N. (2007). t-Closeness: Privacy Beyond k-Anonymity and L-Diversity. IEEE.

Machanavajjhala, A. (2006). L-diversity: Privacy beyond k-anonymity. IEEE.

Shlomo, N. (2018). Statistical Disclosure Limitation: New Directions And Challenges. *The Journal of Privacy and Confidentiality*, *8*(1). Advance online publication. doi:10.29012/jpc.684

Sweeney, L. (2002). k-Anonymity: A Model for Protecting Privacy. *International Journal of Uncertainty, Fuzziness and Knowledge-based Systems*, *10*(5), 557–570. doi:10.1142/S0218488502001648

Templ, M., Kanjala, C., & Siems, I. (2022). Privacy of Study Participants in Open-access Health and Demographic Surveillance System Data: Requirements Analysis for Data Anonymization. *JMIR Public Health and Surveillance*, *8*(9), 1–18. doi:10.2196/34472 PMID:36053573

Templ, M., Kowarik, A., & Meindl, B. (2015). Statistical Disclosure Control for Micro-Data Using the R Package sdcMicro. *Journal of Statistical Software*, *67*(4). Advance online publication. doi:10.18637/jss.v067.i04

Templ, M., & Meindl, B. (2008). Robust Statistics Meets SDC: New Disclosure Risk Measures for Continuous Microdata Masking. In Privacy in Statistical Databases. In *Lecture Notes in Computer Science* (Vol. 5262, pp. 177–189). Springer.

Chapter 13
Ransomware-as-a-Weapon (RaaW):
A Futuristic Approach for Understanding Malware as a Social Weapon

Kuldeep Mohanty
https://orcid.org/0009-0002-2117-2621
KIIT University, India

Sheryl Brahnam
https://orcid.org/0000-0001-7664-6930
Missouri State University, USA

Ghanshyam S. Bopche
National Institute of Technology, India

Satya Ranjan Dash
https://orcid.org/0000-0002-7902-1183
KIIT University, India

ABSTRACT

The use of information technology has widened in the past few years. With the evolving IT industries and infrastructure comes an ocean of development and opportunities and a series of new cyber threats. Ransomware is an inevitable threat that brings inconceivable devastation that one could hardly imagine. Essentially, ransomware is not a new threat. But it is evolving into a new and massive cyber threat that not only extorts money and sells user data into the darknet but has also started targeting users, forcing them to contribute to any existing social problems, for instance, poverty. Ransomware has mapped its journey from a weaker failure model to a highly evolving business model called ransomware-as-a-service (RaaS) model. This chapter discusses ransomware from its origin to an evolved cybercriminal business model. It also reveals all those hidden and unexplored consequences and threats that ransomware can bring with it, focusing on future technologies. Apart from looking into the future, the implications of ransomware as a weapon for social problems have been well discussed.

DOI: 10.4018/979-8-3693-1528-6.ch013

1. INTRODUCTION

Organizations and governments at all levels are increasingly using Information and Communication Technologies (ICT) to enhance productivity, improve efficiency in service delivery, speed-up development in all sectors of the economy, and improve governance. They use ICT to create, store, process, access, and transmit business or mission-critical information in electronic formats. This information could be strategic, demographical, historical, or legal, or may contain financial statements, procedural documents, data of citizens, industry or resources, etc. Essentially, the value associated with data collected by organizations or governments is increasing phenomenally, attracting the attention of adversaries and attackers. Cybercriminals can carry out identity theft to perform financial frauds, steal corporate information such as intellectual property, conduct Cyber espionage to steal state and military secrets, recruit criminals, and disrupt critical life-sustaining infrastructures such as power, banking and finance, transport, air traffic control, telecommunications, etc., by exploiting the vulnerabilities in any system connected to the Internet. Cyber threats are becoming more organized and targeted, reaping immense benefits from data compromises. Therefore, providing the desired level of security to the mission or business-critical data is the highest priority for economic prosperity, nation stability, and security.

Despite a million malware families in the bucket, ransomware (Ryan, 2021) is one of cyberspace's most notorious and inevitable threats. It is one of the most highly evolving malware of the time. Ransomware works by intruding into the system by bypassing firewalls and other traditional defense mechanisms like Demilitarized Zone (DMZ) and Intrusion Detection & Prevention System (IDPS), etc., and getting unauthorized access to the target system. Essentially, ransomware either locks the system or encrypts valuable files against a ransom that is supposed to be paid in the form of cryptocurrency, e.g., Bitcoins (Nakamoto, 2008). Ransomware can be classified into two types based on their attacking nature, i.e., Cryptographic Ransomware and Locker Ransomware (Oz et al., 2022). Cryptographic ransomware encrypts the valuable files of the target. It demands a ransom to get those decryption keys (which holds no guarantee) and is more prevalent in PCs, Workstations, Servers, and cloud storage.

In contrast, the Locker Ransomware locks the target system so that the user cannot access the system until the ransomware demand is fulfilled. It is more prevalent in Mobile (Android mainly) (Ko et al., 2019). Earlier, there was a time when the IT industry had not spread its tentacles worldwide. Ransom demands were still on. The difference was it was a phone call for your child or colleague, not your data or privacy. It's just the fact that things got digitized. The rapid growth of the IT industry has triggered an increase in the number of Cyber attacks. Cyber attackers have started making ransomware attacks as a primary weapon and a business model (RaaS) (Kshetri & Voas, 2022). From the failure of the first strain of ransomware, i.e., AIDS Trojan (KnowBe4, 2023a), to the successful attack stories of Wannacry ransomware (Da-Yu et al., 2019; Kumar et al., 2018) and the most recent Corona ransomware attacks (Cyberark, 2023), ransomware has become the biggest concern of the world! The damages caused by earlier ransomware strains were reversible. However, modern-age ransomware damages are irreversible without a proper backup (Oz et al., 2022). Ransomware is just like a silent killer but is a sharp killer, and to address this problem, we need an active detection mechanism that detects ransomware at the early stage of intrusion.

Every single day there are ransomware attacks that keep on happening. Figure 1 depicts the evolution of ransomware families from simple to more complex and unstoppable malware. However, Table 1 describes the target operating system, attack vector, encryption algorithms used, and behavior of the prominent ransomware families. Suppose we dive through the records of the past year. In that case, global

Figure 1. Evolution of ransomware in chronological order
Source: Oz et al. (2022)

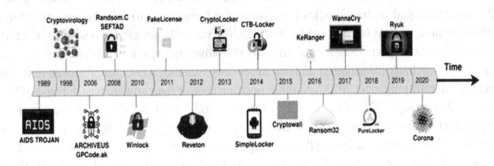

Table 1. Ransomware strains, their target operating system, attack vectors, encryption algorithm used, and behavior (Oz et al., 2022)

Year	1989	2004	2012	2013	2014	2015	2016	2017	2020
Strain Name	AIDS Trojan	GP Code	Revtone	Cryptolocker	Sypong	Encoder	KeRanger	WannaCry	Netwalker
Target Operating System	MS-DOS	Windows	Windows	Windows	Android	Linux	MAC	Windows	Windows
Spread Medium	Floppy Disk	Phishing email	Outdated plugins	Phishing email	Email attachment	A backdoor in Magneto CMS	Flaw in BitTorrent	Flaw in SMB Server	COVID-19 Advisory Email
Encryption algorithm used	Symmetric cryptography	Asymmetric cryptography	Symmetric cryptography	Asymmetric cryptography	Asymmetric cryptography	Symmetric cryptography	Asymmetric cryptography	Asymmetric cryptography	Asymmetric cryptography
Distinct features/ behaviors (if any)	Monitored boot time count	Encrypted 'My Documents' directory	Use of unstoppable DLL	Encrypted 'My Documents' directory	Payloads added themselves to the registry entries via bypassing	Payloads replicated itself in every directory with SUID permissions	Bypassed GateKeeper to infect the system with .RTF	Used a backdoor called Doublepulsar to lock registry	Used a VB script for UAC bypassing

giants such as NVIDIA, Optus, Toyota, and even Governments like Costa Rica and Bernalillo County, New Mexico, have faced massive losses as victims of ransomware attacks (Whiteblueocean, 2023). In April 2023, Costa Rica (SecurityIntelligence, 2023) declared a state of emergency right after almost 30 of its government organization suffered a ransomware attack by the Conti group of a Russian ransomware family resulting in unauthorized encryption of hundreds and gigabytes of sensitive data, which disrupted the country's foreign trade, tax, and customs system, civil servants' payroll, etc. All of the exfiltrated data was made public by the Cyber criminals as the victim failed to meet the ransom demands of $30 million. Soon After, NVIDIA (The Daily Swig, 2023) - the most prominent gaming chip company in the globe, was affected by the Lapsu$ ransomware family that demanded a ransom of $1 million, thus, resulting in the exfiltration of data over 1TB in size that contained client's data, source codes and login information. In September 2022, Optus (Cybersecuritydive, 2023) - an Australian telecommunications organization- was hit hard by an unknown ransomware group that demanded a ransom of about $1 million in exchange for 11.2 million customer information that also contained sensitive information like passport details, birthdates, etc. About 10,000 customers' stolen data was made online to prove its dominance over the system and pave a path to pressure the organization to pay the demanded lump sum as soon as possible. Even business organizations like Toyota, Kojjima Industries, Denso, and Bridgestone (Magazine, 2023) were wrapped in the tentacles of ransomware families. During February and March, these organizations became victims of the Lockbit and Pandora ransomware group, resulting in a 5% decline in productivity. The worst part was after an Internal cyber investigation. It was found that the customer's credentials, including bank information and social security number, were compromised and leaked into the darknet (SecurityIntelligence, 2023). Another peculiar case of ransomware was the case of Bernalillo, New Mexico (Statescoop, 2023). On the 5th of January, 2022, New Mexico's largest county - Bernalillo- was under a ransomware attack with several departments going offline. It impacted almost 675,000 residents in Bernalillo County, including those living in New Mexico's most populous city, Albuquerque. The worst scenario ransomware would have ever created was seen in this case. Essentially, the county's automatic door and surveillance camera were shut off. As a result, the jail inmates were confined to their for days - a violation of inmate confinement (Statescoop, 2023). The cases of ransomware attacks are massively rising, which makes it hard to count. Other dangerous ransomware attacks have impacted the global economy, like the WannaCry Ransomware in 2007 (Da-Yu et al., 2019; Kumar et al., 2018) and Coronavirus Ransomware (Cyberark, 2023) which emerged during the COVID-19 pandemic, thus hitting the healthcare management sectors badly. Today, ransomware has affected almost every sector of the globe, impacting the global economy and cyber peace.

The organization of the rest of the chapter is as follows: Section 2 discusses different attack phases common in a typical ransomware attack. The potential targets of the ransomware attack and real-time incidents that occurred worldwide are discussed in Section 3. The Ransomware-as-a-Service (RaaS) cybercriminals business model is discussed in Section 4. New trends in ransomware and its potential use as a social weapon, i.e., ransomware-as-a-weapon (RaaW), are discussed in Section 5. Finally, Section 6 concludes the chapter.

2. TYPICAL PHASES OF RANSOMWARE ATTACK

It does not matter whether the ransomware belongs to the cryptographic or locker family; it follows a five-fold action plan to intrude on the target system. Figure 2 illustrates a clear picture of the flow of the ransomware attack. The infection phase is a ransomware attack's first and foremost phase. It starts

Figure 2. Different phases in ransomware attacks

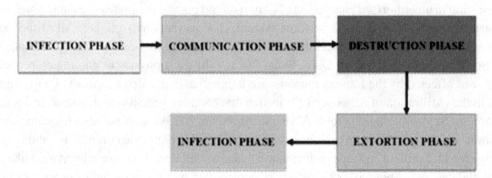

with choosing an attack vector. Typically, it is necessary to trap the target through a typical Cyber attack to inject the ransomware file into the target's system. There could be an ocean of attack vectors, but social engineering attacks (Heartfield & Loukas, 2015; Salahdine & Kaabouch, 2019) are the most common attack that traps the victim without getting noticed. One of the most common types of social engineering attacks is phishing. The phishing attack is one of a ransomware attacker's standard and most preferred attack vectors. These are one of the common attacks through which not only ransomware but a variety of malware gets access into the system. These are kinds of unauthorized mail that only appear to be legitimate but contain malicious links or attachments. Upon clicking or downloading, the related malware enters the system. Therefore, phishing has become one of the most preferred attack vectors since everything appears legitimate until scrutiny. Then the next phase of a ransomware attack includes communication with Control and Command (C&C) Server, a remote server on the attacker's side used by the ransomware families to send encryption keys to encrypt the target's system data. Essentially, this phase of the attack is carried out in either of two following ways i.e.

- Hard-coded IPs where the IP address or domain remains the same for every ransomware attack. It provides a sustainable and reliable connection during the attack process. Since this is a static IP address, the firewall can easily detect and block the attack. The use of hard-coded IPs makes the ransomware inoperable and thus leads to a lousy attack attempt.
- The attackers use Domain Generation Algorithms (DGA) (Salehi et al., 2018) to connect to C&C dynamically. It provides a unique domain name to the server for each communication by fast fluxing or shifting the domain names. The most significant advantage of using domain generation algorithms over hard-coded IP is that firewalls cannot easily detect it, which gives cybercriminals a suitable environment to carry out the attack successfully.

The third phase of the attack, commonly known as the destruction phase, is all about unauthorized exfiltration of data from the targeted system and encrypting the system with robust encryption algorithms (Abdullah, 2017; Tarcísio Marinho, 2023) that make the victim incapable of decrypting the system thus making the victim land in a tough spot to as whether go by paying ransom with no certainty of getting the decryption keys or losing the data anyway. It happens in the case of a cryptographic ransomware family, but what could be the flow in the case of locker ransomware families? In the case of locker ransomware families, the significant milestone of the ransomware in this phase is to lock the victim's system, thus preventing victims from accessing the system. There could be three types of locking i.e.:

- Screen Locking is where the system GUI is locked, and a ransom is demanded from the victim to access it. Mobile ransomware families do this to lock the mobile device, while some families like LockerPin set the specific parameters to Android System APIs to make the Android screen persistent.
- Browser Locking is where the Ransomware locks the victim's web browser and demands a ransom against it. The attacker locks the browsers of victims by redirecting victims to a web page that contains a malicious JavaScript code.
- Master Boot Record locking targets the MBR of the system that contains information to boot the OS. It prevents the system from loading the boot code by either replacing the original MBR with a bogus MBR or encrypting the original MBR. PETYA ransomware (KnowBe4, 2023b) is an example of a ransomware family that locks the master boot record.

The fourth phase of the attack is yet another critical phase where the attacker tries to justify the attack's actual purpose, i.e., to get the ransom from the victim. So let us understand the payment methodology in brief. An anonymous payment method or cryptocurrency is involved where the victim needs to transfer the demanded ransom in the form of Bitcoins (Paquet-Clouston et al., 2019) only. The apparent reason is that ransom in the form of Bitcoins preserves the attacker's identity; thus, no one can trace them. Cryptocurrency is decentralized and unregulated and not subject to local law authorities. But is the extortion phase consistently successful? Essentially, the victim may or may not pay the ransom because of the following:

- Victims lack familiarity with Bitcoin payment or cryptocurrency technology.
- The victim may not afford enormous ransom demands, so they prefer to accept losing data.
- The attacker may have exfiltrated the data before encryption and may sell in the darknet and earn money.

If the victim differs in fulfilling the ransom demands, it appears to be the loss of the attacker, but the ultimate control of victory is in the attacker's hands. There are four various approaches for data extortion i.e.:

- **Single extortion:** This is the most common type of extortion methodology followed by the attacker where the actual extortion happens with the involvement of a single party, i.e., a ransom is demanded from the victim against the decryption keys for his valuable encrypted file. This method may be more common and vulnerable to end users only. But still, this has been a constant wrath for an organizational attack.
- **Double extortion:** This is another type of extortion methodology where the attacker exfiltrates all the data and then starts encrypting files and data. In this type of attack, two parties are always involved, and it is more common in both end user and organizational attacks as this could be a potential reason for the downfall of a company from the business world. This can be well understood by an example. Suppose a company "X" has 'n' valuable customers. The company faces an attack where the attacker has stolen its data, including customer details or critical source codes and files, and then has encrypted it. Now the attacker is asking the victim company or organization for ransom against the security of the exfiltrated data. If the company refuses to pay, the attacker will release this data into the dark web. Although if, in the above scenario, the ransom is paid, there exists no guarantee of data not getting leaked. Some double extortion cases are Maze ransomware, Egregor, and Darkside.
- **Triple extortion:** This is the third type of extortion where the actual extortion happens in three stages, i.e., (1) Exfiltration, (2) Encryption, and (3) launching a DDoS attack. The attacker exfiltrated all the data, encrypted the file, and launched a DDoS attack. This type of attack is prone mainly to the organization as it holds the potential to bring the business down and eliminate the company from the market because of the following reasons that could hamper the company-client relationship: (1) Customer data could be made public and (2) DDoS attack brings the services down. Some cases of triple extortion in ransomware attacks are Suncrypt, RaagnarLocker, etc.
- **Quadruple extortion:** This is one of the worst types of extortion where not only the client's and company's data is exfiltrated, encrypted, and DDoS launched, but also the ransomware directly reaches out to the clients through some mails or textual media that their data is under seized and

could be published if the organization doesn't agree to ransom demands. Such an attack strategy not only affects business and cuts it down from the mainstream but also has some socio-psychological adverse effects on the victim: (1) It creates a trust issue among the victim, client, and market. Essentially, it creates a problem of coming up again and a permanent exit from the market. (2) This type of extortion also hampers the victim's psychological state since it not only takes the job but also smashes down the reputation in the market. Quadruple extortion could be one of the best methods for intentional ransomware attacks for business rivalries.

The attack's fifth and final phase is termed the concluding phase, where the attacker may or may not give the decryption keys against the ransom paid/not paid. In this phase, the attackers clean their digital footprints and move away.

3. POTENTIAL TARGETS OF RANSOMWARE ATTACK

PCs and workstations have been primary targets for ransomware attacks in the past few years. The reason is apparent. Nowadays, PCs are being used worldwide, and ransomware has made its way in the search for more ransom money. Mostly the cryptographic families of ransomware that use asymmetric encryption or hybrid encryption mechanisms target these systems, making data recovery impossible. Ultimately, the user has to pay the ransom. Starting from personal usage to computer systems in business and industrial sectors like healthcare, education, etc., is quite common nowadays. The use involves a lot of data handling activities like storing customers' bank credentials, demographic details, etc., which ultimately invokes the ransomware families to put their hands on it. Ransomware had already spread its tentacles over almost all the sectors of the globe's economy. Table 1. has already made us dive deep into the evolution of ransomware families. Reports suggest that about two-thirds, i.e., almost 66% of healthcare organizations, were hit by ransomware attacks in 2022 compared to a score of 34% in 2020 (Thomson Reuters, 2023). Emsisoft, a cybersecurity company, reported 25 ransomware attacks on healthcare institutions in 2022, affecting as many as 290 hospitals nationwide, including hospitals and multi-hospital health systems.

This figure had significantly increased compared to 2021, when Emsisoft counted 68 attacks on healthcare providers (TechTarget, 2023). Ransomware families have compromised healthcare sectors and Supervisory Control and Data Acquisition (SCADA) units (Butt et al., 2019; Ibarra et al., 2019). In one incident in March 2021, attackers targeted a water plant in Nevada using unknown ransomware. The SCADA system and backup systems were both impacted by the malware. However, the agencies pointed out that the SCADA system was not a full industrial control system because it offered monitoring and visibility capabilities. A facility in Maine was the subject of another incident in July 2021. Hackers infected the SCADA computer for wastewater management with the ransomware ZuCaNo. The agencies stated in their alert that "the treatment system was operated manually until the SCADA computer was restored utilizing local control and more frequent operator rounds." Ghost is a ransomware program that threat actors installed on the computers of a California water treatment facility. Around a month after the first breach, the business noticed three SCADA systems were showing a ransomware message. It led to the discovery of malware (Securityweek, 2023). Even ransomware didn't spare the Android and ios platforms (Alzahrani et al., 2020). In the United States, ScarePakage mobile ransomware initially came to the attention of Lookout, a San Francisco-based mobile security company, in late August 2014. People become infected by phoney Adobe Flash and popular antivirus programs that, when launched, purport to scan the device. The message to victims reads like this: "You are guilty of child porn, child maltreatment, zoophilia, or sending out mass spam. You are a bad person. The Federal Bureau of Investigation has locked your phone, and the only way to get back access to your data is to pay us. You cannot navigate away from the message; even if you restart your phone, the message reappears immediately. The cyber-criminals must be paid several hundred dollars in a MoneyPak voucher to give you back control of your device. Based on the language and terminology used in the code, the engineers at Lookout concluded that the authors are most likely from Russia or another country in Eastern Europe. Another group of attackers has discovered a way to pull off a similar scam on Apple devices after ransomware attacked Windows PCs and Android handsets. Many victims, primarily in Australia and the UK, reported being the target of an unknown attack in May 2014 that held their iPhones and iPads hostage and demanded they pay a $100 ransom. A Melbourne-based customer said: "My iPad abruptly shut up while I was using it. Oleg Pliss had hacked my device(s), and they requested 100 USD/EUR (paid by PayPal to lock404(at)hotmail.com) to return them to me, according to a message on the screen of my phone that is still visible today". This was just a trailer to the entire ransomware journey; the actual film counts a million hours to be documented. Technologies and areas like the Internet of Things (IoT), Industrial Internet of Things (IIoT), and Industrial Control Systems are evolving at a more incredible pace, thus attracting cyber attackers to put their hands on. Although the data available on ransomware attacks on future technologies like IoT is minimal, it still poses a greater risk in cyberspace.

However, the effects of a ransomware attack are not confined to a particular area or thing. It could completely disrupt the nation's economy in seconds, posing as a global social weapon. The ransomware attack cases mentioned demonstrate how detrimental they may be to society's socioeconomic, IT, and other well-adjusted sectors. The quadruple extortion previously discussed might restrict the closure of a successful company and increase the intensity of competitive relationships between companies. Not only would a company suffer financial losses, but a ransomware attack might also cause emotional stress and impair one's state of mind. Everything is getting the moniker "smart" before it, which denotes extensive use of Internet resources. Imagine a significant ransomware attack launched against an IoT-based smart city where virtually every component, from a home door to extensive administration systems, is automated.

The attack might cause an entire server to crash and IoT systems to fail, which would cause a nation's productivity to fall rapidly and interrupt services for the general public. If a ransomware attack on a significant business that houses mission-critical data is successful, it could result in the unauthorized exfiltration of such data. It might result in a worst-case scenario in which the country might even declare an emergency. Consider, for example, the possibility that nuclear weapon codes could be stolen and made accessible on the dark web. It might even result in a global upheaval of international relations.

Various solutions such as backup-based solutions (Baek et al., 2018; Lee et al., 2018; Min et al., 2018; Paik et al., 2018; Park et al., 2019), machine learning-based solutions (Alhawi et al., 2018; Chen et al., 2018; Chen & Bridges, 2017; Cohen & Nissim, 2018; Daku et al., 2018; Lee, Lee, & Yim, 2019; Vinayakumar et al., 2017), self-healing-based solutions (Al-Dwairi et al., 2022), whitelisting-based solutions (Kim & Lee, 2020; Kim et al., 2018), IoT-based solutions (Azmoodeh et al., 2018), Moving Target Defense-based solutions (Lee, Kim, & Kim, 2019; Monge et al., 2018), Cyber deception-based techniques (Chakkaravarthy et al., 2020; Gómez-Hernández et al., 2018; Gómez-Hernández et al., 2022; Keong Ng et al., 2020; Moore, 2016; Pascariu & Barbu, 2019; Rahim Saleh et al., 2021; Wang, Wu, Liu et al, 2018; Zscaler, 2023), backtracking-based solutions (Wang, Liu, Qiu et al, 2018), etc. proposed in the literature to deal with the problem of ransomware. Even though there are many approaches and methods for dealing with a ransomware assault, they are not entirely effective or successful models because ransomware is constantly evolving, making it an unpredictable behavioral pattern recognition malware. In addition to these technical fixes, raising public awareness is the most excellent strategy to stop ransomware attacks or cyberattacks and preserve online cyber peace. During the infection phase, ransomware targets users through social engineering techniques like phishing, malvertising, etc. Thus, the general public must know the different traps and tricks that could tempt them to fall victim to a cyberattack. Although there are many solutions in the literature, it is still unclear why ransomware assaults keep increasing and why the current solutions are insufficient.

The apparent cause is ransomware changing, making static and dynamic analysis challenging. The dynamics make it more difficult to predict ransomware behavior during the early phases of infection, rendering most machine learning-based detection systems ineffective. It necessitates the development of a more effective strategy for dealing with ransomware, which will significantly reduce the success rate of such attacks. Finally, it calls for thoroughly examining ransomware-as-a-weapon (RaaW) and how anti-social elements may use it as a social weapon.

4. RANSOMWARE-AS-A-SERVICE (RaaS): CYBERCRIMINAL BUSINESS MODEL

The demand and value of data have been increasing rapidly with IT Sectors' fast and evolutionary development. With technological advancement, different organizations have emerged, thus making society a data-driven society. The actual story begins here! Where there is a demand for data, there is a supply, and what if this is a malicious supply? Adversaries or cyber criminals are always running behind these data from different organizations, thus, leaking confidential information starting from passwords and bank details to even more data of international or global importance, such as missile codes, into the Darknet with a motto of contributing to the business that runs on the darker side of the Internet, i.e., Darknet and facilitates the Ransomware-as-a-Service (RaaS) model (Alwashali, Abd Rahman, & Ismail, 2021; CrowdStrike, 2023) which is entirely a business model for ransomware families.

Ransomware as a Service (RaaS) is a business model in which there is a deal between the operators and affiliates. The operators are the malware or ransomware developers who develop and supply ransomware development kits to the dark web, and affiliates are the ones who buy these ransomware kits and build their ransomware and carry out attacks smoothly with or without the skills and knowledge about it (Zscaler, 2023). Operators and affiliates make up the two main categories of the RaaS concept. Operators find companions on forums and set up a unique control and command dashboard so the affiliates can follow the shipment. In addition, they help affiliates with victim bargaining by setting up a victim payment site. Moreover, operators are in charge of overseeing a specific leak website (DLS).

The affiliates agree to a service fee for each ransom collected and pay the operators to use ransomware. Affiliates are the ones who have the decryption keys once they have targeted the victim, carried out a ransomware assault, and demanded payment. Figure 3 depicts the RaaS Model in operation. The affiliates agree to a service fee for each ransom collected and pay the operators to use ransomware. Affiliates are the ones who have the decryption keys once they have targeted the victim, carried out a ransomware attack, and demanded payment.

RaaS is now evolving as a big business of the dark web. The constant tie between the operators and the affiliates has made it a successful and more robust model for the business of malware developers. The well-distributed chain of the RaaS model allows for gathering more capital for malware develop-

Figure 3. Mechanism of RaaS business model

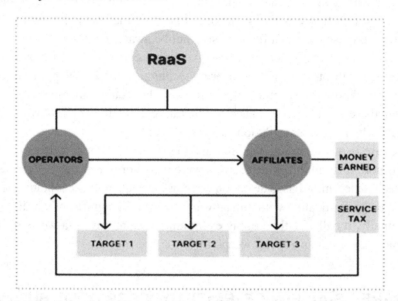

ers compared to that of a non-RaaS model. By implementing RaaS, anyone with or without technical knowledge can be a part of the chain and develop their ransomware by using the ransomware development kits and carrying out an attack easily. Increasing the team's efficiency reduces the time for massive attacks on multiple systems.

Well, there can be many revenue models implemented in RaaS. But some of the most common are:

- **Monthly subscriptions:** The affiliates are asked to pay a flat fee per month for the subscription.
- **Affiliate Program:** Just like a subscription model with a nominal change, i.e., the affiliates may require to pay a part of the income to the ransomware developers.
- **One-time license:** Where affiliates may require to pay a heavy amount but only once.
- **Pure profit sharing:** The affiliates may be charged little or nothing, but the whole profit goes to the developers.

5. DISCUSSION

The ransomware-as-a-service model proves that it has already stretched its tentacles widely and developed an incredibly successful business strategy on the dark web. But those times are long gone when ransomware could only be used to extort money to fund RaaS or expose a business rivalry by taking advantage of the rival's corporate resources and destroying them. There is more to ransomware than first meets the eye. Through the Ransomware-as-a-Service (RaaS) model, ransomware becomes a social weapon to combat socioeconomic or personal problems illegally. It eventually led to the emergence of another new model based on an entirely different concept, which could be referred to as the Ransomware-as-a-Weapon (RaaW) Model. Before studying the RaaW paradigm, it is crucial to be aware of recent developments in ransomware tactics.

5.1 New Days Ransomware Trends

When we talk about ransomware, the first thing we spell is 'ransom,' By ransom, we usually mean cash or currency in Bitcoins, as discussed earlier. But, nowadays, ransomware is way more than we think. Recently, a new kind of ransomware named 'Goodwill' (CloudSEK, 2023) was identified by CloudSEK researchers in March 2022. What makes goodwill ransomware different from others?

Unlike other ransomware families that demand currency in the form of Bitcoins in exchange for decryption keys, Goodwill ransomware demands social services for people in need in exchange for decryption keys. The ransomware demanded three things in exchange for decryption keys, i.e. (1) To donate goods and new clothes to the needy and homeless. Record the same action and post it on social media, (2) To take five poor, less fortunate, and underprivileged children and give them treats in cafes like Dominos, KFC, Pizza Hut, etc. Take pictures with them and upload them on social media platforms, and (3) Provide financial assistance to people in need in the hospital. Record the same and upload it on social media platforms. Once these three tasks are done, it instructs us to write a note on social media: "How have you transformed yourself into a good human being by becoming a victim of ransomware?" It releases the decryption keys after the demands are fulfilled.

If we consider all the circumstances, ransomware takes five children, feeds them at KFC, Pizza Hut, etc., and demands new clothes for the underprivileged and homeless. And provide financial support to those in need at the hospital. Why, though? Any of the following could serve as the cause: (1) The attacker might be trying to get notoriety by coercing others into performing social work illegally; (2) The attacker might have been a victim of poverty and understands what it's like to be homeless, starved, or lose a loved one due to lack of money during a medical emergency. (3) By decrypting the victim's files and demanding unexpected charitable donations as ransom, the attacker may be trying to raise awareness of the problem of poverty among people. (4) By manipulating the victim's psychology, the attacker may also try to force the victim to pay the ransom through donations. (5) Or the attacker may be a charitable trust or an NGO; today's lack of interest in charitable donations has caused these organizations' businesses to decline continuously. Hence, one might also go to such lengths to survive and make a living.

5.2 Ransomware-as-a-Weapon (RaaW) Model

The term "ransomware-as-a-weapon" (also known as "RaaW") model refers to an extension of the "ransomware-as-a-service" (or "RaaS") model that specifies how malware such as ransomware may be used to target and fulfill specific societal needs, address socio-economic issues, meet individual financial objectives, exact retribution for business rivalries, etc. through only unauthorized and illegal means. RaaW enables the attacker to visit RaaS providers on the dark web and take a RaaS Kit, which allows them to build their ransomware with or without technical expertise and install it to their target systems.

Figure 4 clearly distinguishes the working of the Ransomware-as-a-Weapon model, thus posing as a social weapon. In section 5.1, we covered the case of goodwill, which served as both a representative example and convincing proof of the development of ransomware into a model for using it as a weapon. The story continues, though! There are further repercussions and futuristic perspectives to comprehend ransomware as a societal weapon that could destroy stable and developed economies.

Figure 4. Ransomware-as-weapon model

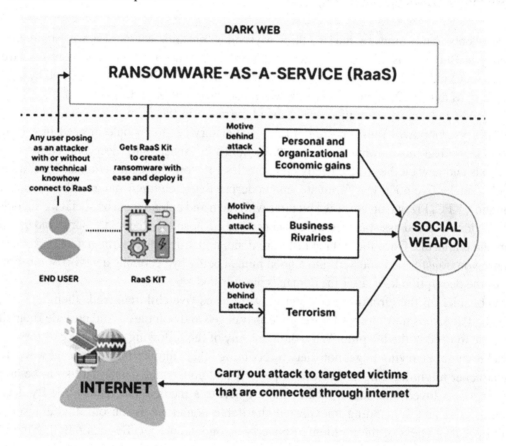

5.3 Using RaaW for Personal and Organizational Economic Goals

The COVID-19 epidemic recently caused a significant drop in the world economic index. This epidemic was the catalyst for the social service industries, such as Nonprofit Government Organizations (NGOs), which caused a financial crisis in NGOs as they needed it most. Future aid expenditures and donations are projected to decrease due to the economic slump. As a consequence, NGOs' staff members are in a position where they are likelier to lose their jobs and struggle to make ends meet daily. This could prompt NGOs to use RaaS to create ransomware and send malicious payloads to the targeted systems or users instead of making typical demands for ransomware strains. Instead, they could make business-centric demands, such as funding donations to 10 or more NGOs, and post proof of fulfillment on social media to get validated by the attacker that the demands are met well, which helps them in some way to operate their businesses successfully but illegally. Since the source of Goodwill remains untraced, it could be a higher probable scenario where the social service sector itself has carried out the attack.

The RaaW approach can be applied in more situations than only the hypothetical NGO scenario. Some more strategies and tactics could be used to apply this paradigm successfully. Nowadays, there are more startups. The demand for professionals in the sector of entrepreneurship is rising daily. The two main reasons most businesses fail as soon as they get started are ineffective planning and a need for a sound business strategy. This results in a significant loss on the investment they made for it, and they may be looking for ways to make up for the losses. The RaaW model gives them the key to the doors and might persuade them to use RaaS to launch a ransomware attack, asking them to pay the demanded ransom in Bitcoins or donate funds to the industry your startup intended for. This might prompt the startup agency to take advantage of the situation and turn the tables.

As security breaches and data theft incidents increase, so does the demand for data security. It is why reputable businesses/organizations and leading MNCs Cyber insure their data so that a capital payment would be made to cover their losses in the event of data loss. Imagine a corporation named "X" purchases cyber insurance (Alwashali, Abd Rahman, & Ismail, 2021) to protect its data. The data insurance firm is then forced to make the covered payment when it initiates a ransomware assault on itself (by colluding with a ransomware-as-service provider) to demonstrate that the data has been compromised. Such attacks may have been motivated by human greed or economic losses that must be made up some other way. This is a loss and a weakness for the data insurance companies.

As we explain in the instance of the Goodwill ransomware, in addition to these corporate objectives, there may be a million personal motives, which could end up being both an organizational and individual purpose. These days, more and more situations and issues, such as poverty, child labor, malnutrition, and corruption, need to be addressed and resolved as quickly as feasible. It is important to note that not everyone will fall victim to the same difficulties unless they try hard enough. This may make the person more determined to find a solution by whatever means necessary, motivating them to use RaaS to launch ransomware attacks against wealthy individuals and major corporations as the intended targets, making strange and unpredictable demands like goodwill ransomware. This could even provoke and coerce individuals through psychological games to disclose instances of corruption in exchange for some sensitive data.

5.4 Using RaaW for Business Rivalries

The level of rivalry in the corporate sector is increasing daily. The MNCs are actively competing with one another for market share. This fosters competition among organizations in the corporate world. Let's imagine a scenario where two reputable businesses offer telecom services, "X" and "Y." Always more people require company "X's" services than those of company "Y." This may prompt firm "Y" to use RaaS to launch a ransomware assault against company "X," in which quadruple extortion would be the most effective form of extortion. The attacker company exfiltrates all the sensitive data of the victim company, launches a DDoS attack to crash their servers, and may blackmail to send emails to the clients of the victim company informing them about the data leakage, which ultimately ruins the reputation and cut off the company from the business world. The customary ransom demand could be the case's twist now. Since both businesses are well established, the attacker company could demand the victim company leave the industry in exchange for the stolen private information and keep the stolen information only between the attacker and the victim company. This would preserve the reputation of both businesses. The attacker corporation could readily acquire the victim company's business.

5.5 Using RaaW for Terrorism

The worst-case scenario is if terrorists utilize Ransomware-as-a-Weapon (RaaW) to undermine international relations and national security. A terrorist can dodge a country's boundaries by avoiding numerous systems, such as the air defense system, surface-to-air missile controls, etc., thanks to advancements made in national defense systems, but it is still not impossible. It is important to remember that these are the technologies most susceptible to online threats. Even cutting-edge defensive technologies like the Internet of Military Things or the Internet of Battle Things (IoBT) lack a clear understanding of their safety when being penetrated by a cyber attack.

Consider a scenario in which a specific terrorist group is preparing an operation against a nation to launch terror attacks across national borders and spark an interstate conflict. What alternative to turning off the invading nation's cyber defensive systems could be best? Future terrorist attacks on the nation's defense system with RaaS assistance are possible, rendering the nation defenseless to attacks like air-strikes and large-scale bombs by the attacker's country. This might upset the tranquility of the country and weaken international ties, which would cause a wide range of issues, including an economic catastrophe.

Think about a different fictitious scenario where terrorist attacks go unnoticed, such as when a terrorist group uses RaaS to launch ransomware attacks against organizations that hold mission-critical data, such as intelligence and defense agencies. It might result in the exfiltration of information crucial to a mission, such as source codes for nuclear missiles or satellite navigation systems. This information might later be employed against the nation as a weapon.

5.6 Using RaaW Against Healthcare Industry

Since data is the foundation of the healthcare sector, the ransomware-as-a-weapon (RaaW) model might be effectively used against it. The healthcare sector creates enormous amounts of data daily, including data from Electronic Health Records (EHRs), remote monitoring systems that collect real-time data, and data from wearable health gadgets or IoMT devices that monitor our general vitals. Such data can draw in and entice anyone to emerge as an attacker who can utilize the RaaW paradigm to deliver malicious payloads to the server to exfiltrate data and then sell it on the dark web or use it for their benefit. Recall the period when the SARS-CoV-2 outbreak had the entire world in lockdown. At that point, the baseline for the data generated by hospitals and research institutes had been attained. Researchers and medical professionals worldwide vied to create a treatment or vaccine that could stop its spread. Any scientist might have utilized RaaW to take advantage of a different scientist taking a step closer to making history. Well, this isn't where the story comes to a complete halt. Suppose a scenario where RaaW may be used for interpersonal or professional rivalry via medical grounds. What if a government official of importance to the country is admitted for surgery that calls for the insertion of Internet of Medical Things (IoMT) equipment, such as a pacemaker, to manage the heart rhythm, which is prone to hacking? The opposing party could use the opportunity to send RaaW to complete the task. It is a typical example of medical grounds turning into battlefields.

5.7 Using RaaW to Hamper Critical Missions of National and International Importance

Several countries across the globe carry critical missions that hold national and international importance. These missions demand high security both physically and virtually. A very recent critical mission can be taken as an instance to understand the situation well. In recent years different space organizations launched satellites to orbit the moon and landers to conduct research operations in the lunar environment. Since satellites and ground stations are linked via specific communication interfaces, it is vulnerable to malicious activities. Although these ground stations have highly secured computing environments, the potentiality of ransomware can't be underestimated. The attacker can try to interfere with or break the communication links and take control of the satellite, which could result in the loss of thousands of millions. Other attacks like GPS spoofing could also be carried out to cause navigational errors. The hypothetical assumption of the lunar orbiter and lander marks the seriousness and shows the social and global negative impacts of the Ransomware-as-a-Weapon (RaaW) Model. The real catch is that even someone who doesn't have enough resources to carry out the attack can use the Ransomware-as-a-Service (RaaS) Model to extend it into Ransomware-as-a-Weapon (RaaW) Model to carry out the attack. Theoretically, in this situation, a former employee of the same company who had previously been dismissed could deploy RaaW as retaliation. Further, rival companies of the same company may use this situation and transmit malicious payloads at a minimal cost.

5.8 Using RaaW to Make Negative Impact on Global Supply Chain Management

Data is essential to Supply Chain Management (SCM) since it offers the required insights and optimization opportunities to improve and simplify different supply chain activities. Every company, whether a start-up or a multinational corporation, has a supply chain. RaaW deployment in a company's supply chain might negatively affect the economy and result in financial losses. It can cause operational interruptions by shutting down crucial supply chain processes, including procurement, production, shipping, etc., for an extended period or even permanently. In addition, if extortion techniques are used to a degree greater than simple extortion, this might result in the exfiltration of sensitive data, such as details about suppliers, partners, and even financial credentials. The whole enterprise may be destroyed by even double extortion. Suppose a scenario in which a competitor may use RaaW to directly target a company's supply chain to beat its rival company's operations and maximize profit. What if a significant MNC that is important to the market experiences this situation? The stock market will decline, and the stockholders will take substantial financial damage, ultimately leading to global economic tensions.

5.9 Using RaaW to Destroy International Relations and Diplomacy

International relations and diplomacy between nations are crucial to resolving conflicts and achieving interstate peace. What could be worse than a battle between friendly countries? This is precisely where the ransomware-as-a-weapon (RaaW) model is useful. A speculative assumption might make sense of this. For instance, there are two friendly nations, "X" and "Y," respectively, and another country, "Z," is a friend to both, but behind the back, country Z gains profit if X and Y engage in a war. Country "Z" can use RaaS secretly and extend it into RaaW to send malicious payloads to Country "Y" through Country "X" by spoofing. In simpler words, country X has no idea that its servers or computers have been compromised to send malicious payloads to country Y. Now if country Y uses some backtracking algorithms to track the face behind the attack, it will detect country X first. It will negatively impact the international relations and diplomacy between X and Y, thus turning them foes from friends. This hypothetical instance exemplifies how RaaW might be applied to deteriorate international relations between states. The integrity and reputation of a nation in the international community must be protected at all costs. Underestimating ransomware might have disastrous effects.

5.10 RaaS vs. RaaW

On the dark web, ransomware families operate under the Ransomware-as-a-Service (RaaS) model. Regardless of their technical expertise, anybody may use RaaS to buy ransomware kits, create their ransomware, and launch it against a specific system. A natural progression from the ransomware-as-a-service (RaaS) model is ransomware-as-a-weapon (RaaW). RaaW defines ransomware and suggests how it may be transformed into a social weapon that harms society or the entire world. This chapter introduces a new term called RaaW, demonstrating in stark terms how a regular person with no specific technical abilities may even harm society. Although RaaW is a new word in this book chapter, it has been used in every Ransomware attack through RaaS since it was first introduced.

6. CONCLUSION

When ransomware first entered the market in 1989 under the name AIDS trojan, it was a failure and a malware with which not to be bothered. The situation took little time to flip around and transform into one of the worst and most inevitable malware because of quick technology and infrastructure development. The Internet of Things (IoT), Cloud computing, cyber-physical systems (CPS), SCADA networks, and other emerging technologies necessitate a safer environment for computing. As ransomware is the most challenging type of malware to combat, it requires deploying an effective preventive model that considers the present situation and how to combat ransomware in various industries in the future. In this book chapter, we covered the history of ransomware, from its inception to the present, its potential for future development, and the fantastic opponents it may produce. We also talked about the ransomware-as-a-weapon (RaaW) model, which focuses on how a clearly defined business model, such as ransomware-as-a-service (RaaS), could be expanded to evolve itself as a social weapon and the unethical solution to all the issues.

REFERENCES

Abdullah, A. M. (2017). Advanced encryption standard (AES) algorithm to encrypt and decrypt data. *Cryptography and Network Security*, *16*(1), 11.

Al-Dwairi, M., Shatnawi, A. S., Al-Khaleel, O., & Al-Duwairi, B. (2022). Ransomware-Resilient Self-Healing XML Documents. *Future Internet*, *14*(4), 115. doi:10.3390/fi14040115

Alhawi, O. M., Baldwin, J., & Dehghantanha, A. (2018). Leveraging machine learning techniques for windows ransomware network traffic detection. *Cyber Threat Intelligence*, 93-106.

Alwashali, A. A. M. A., Abd Rahman, N. A., & Ismail, N. (2021, December). A survey of ransomware as a service (RaaS) and methods to mitigate the attack. In *2021 14th International Conference on Developments in eSystems Engineering (DeSE)* (pp. 92-96). IEEE.

Alzahrani, A., Alshehri, A., Alshahrani, H., & Fu, H. (2020). *Ransomware in Windows and Android Platforms*. arXiv preprint arXiv:2005.05571.

Azmoodeh, A., Dehghantanha, A., Conti, M., & Choo, K. K. R. (2018). Detecting crypto-ransomware in IoT networks based on energy consumption footprint. *Journal of Ambient Intelligence and Humanized Computing, 9*(4), 1141–1152. doi:10.100712652-017-0558-5

Baek, S., Jung, Y., Mohaisen, A., Lee, S., & Nyang, D. (2018, July). SSD-insider: Internal defense of solid-state drive against ransomware with perfect data recovery. In *2018 IEEE 38th International Conference on Distributed Computing Systems (ICDCS)* (pp. 875-884). IEEE.

Butt, U. J., Abbod, M., Lors, A., Jahankhani, H., Jamal, A., & Kumar, A. (2019, January). Ransomware Threat and its Impact on SCADA. In *2019 IEEE 12th international conference on global security, safety and sustainability (ICGS3)* (pp. 205-212). IEEE.

Chakkaravarthy, S. S., Sangeetha, D., Cruz, M. V., Vaidehi, V., & Raman, B. (2020). Design of intrusion detection honeypot using social leopard algorithm to detect IoT ransomware attacks. *IEEE Access : Practical Innovations, Open Solutions, 8*, 169944–169956. doi:10.1109/ACCESS.2020.3023764

Chen, L., Yang, C. Y., Paul, A., & Sahita, R. (2018). *Towards resilient machine learning for ransomware detection.* arXiv preprint arXiv:1812.09400.

Chen, Q., & Bridges, R. A. (2017, December). Automated behavioral analysis of malware: A case study of wannacry ransomware. In *2017 16th IEEE International Conference on machine learning and applications (ICMLA)* (pp. 454-460). IEEE. 10.1109/ICMLA.2017.0-119

CloudSEK. (2023). *GoodWill ransomware forces victims to donate to the poor and provides financial assistance to patients in need.* https://cloudsek.com/threatintelligence/goodwill-ransomware-forces-victims-to-donate-to-the-poor-and-provides-financial-assistance-to-patients-in-need

Cohen, A., & Nissim, N. (2018). Trusted detection of ransomware in a private cloud using machine learning methods leveraging meta-features from volatile memory. *Expert Systems with Applications, 102*, 158–178. doi:10.1016/j.eswa.2018.02.039

CrowdStrike. (2023). *Ransomware-as-a-Service Model.* https://www.crowdstrike.com/cybersecurity-101/ransomware/ransomware-as-a-service-raas/

Cyberark. (2023). *CoronaVirus Ransomware.* https://www.cyberark.com/resources/threat-research-blog/coronavirus-ransomware

Cybersecuritydive. (2023). *Australia's telecom giant Optus avoids ransom demand as attacker reverses course.* https://www.cybersecuritydive.com/news/optus-ransomware-retracted/632763/

Da-Yu, K. A. O., Hsiao, S. C., & Raylin, T. S. O. (2019, February). Analyzing WannaCry ransomware considering the weapons and exploits. In *2019 21st International Conference on Advanced Communication Technology (ICACT)* (pp. 1098-1107). IEEE

Daku, H., Zavarsky, P., & Malik, Y. (2018, August). Behavioral-based classification and identification of ransomware variants using machine learning. In *2018 17th IEEE international conference on trust, security and privacy in computing and communications/12th IEEE international conference on big data science and engineering (TrustCom/BigDataSE)* (pp. 1560-1564). IEEE. 10.1109/TrustCom/BigDataSE.2018.00224

Gómez-Hernández, J. A., Álvarez-González, L., & García-Teodoro, P. (2018). R-Locker: Thwarting ransomware action through a honeyfile-based approach. *Computers & Security*, *73*, 389–398. doi:10.1016/j.cose.2017.11.019

Gómez-Hernández, J. A., Sánchez-Fernández, R., & García-Teodoro, P. (2022). Inhibiting crypto-ransomware on windows platforms through a honeyfile-based approach with R-Locker. *IET Information Security*, *16*(1), 64–74. doi:10.1049/ise2.12042

Heartfield, R., & Loukas, G. (2015). A taxonomy of attacks and a survey of defence mechanisms for semantic social engineering attacks. *ACM Computing Surveys*, *48*(3), 1–39. doi:10.1145/2835375

Ibarra, J., Butt, U. J., Do, A., Jahankhani, H., & Jamal, A. (2019, January). Ransomware impact to SCADA systems and its scope to critical infrastructure. In *2019 IEEE 12th International Conference on Global Security, Safety and Sustainability (ICGS3)* (pp. 1-12). IEEE. 10.1109/ICGS3.2019.8688299

Keong Ng, C., Rajasegarar, S., Pan, L., Jiang, F., & Zhang, L. Y. (2020). VoterChoice: A ransomware detection honeypot with multiple voting framework. *Concurrency and Computation*, *32*(14), e5726. doi:10.1002/cpe.5726

Kim, D., & Lee, J. (2020). Blacklist vs. whitelist-based ransomware solutions. *IEEE Consumer Electronics Magazine*, *9*(3), 22–28. doi:10.1109/MCE.2019.2956192

Kim, D. Y., Choi, G. Y., & Lee, J. H. (2018, January). Whitelist-based ransomware real-time detection and prevention for user device protection. In *2018 IEEE International Conference on Consumer Electronics (ICCE)* (pp. 1-5). IEEE.

KnowBe4. (2023a). *AIDS Trojan or PC Cyborg Ransomware*. https://www.knowbe4.com/aids-trojan

KnowBe4. (2023b). *PETYA Pransomware Locks Users Out by Overwriting Master Boot Record*. https://blog.knowbe4.com/petya-ransomware-lock-users-out-by-overwriting-master-boot-record

Ko, J.-S., Jo, J.-S., Kim, D.-H., Choi, S.-K., & Kwak, J. (2019). Real Time Android Ransomware Detection by Analyzed Android Applications. *2019 International Conference on Electronics, Information, and Communication (ICEIC)*, 1-5. 10.23919/ELINFOCOM.2019.8706349

Kshetri, N., & Voas, J. (2022). Ransomware as a Business (RAAB). *IT Professional*, *24*(2), 83–87. doi:10.1109/MITP.2022.3157208

Kumar, M. S., Ben-Othman, J., & Srinivasagan, K. G. (2018, June). An investigation on wannacry ransomware and its detection. In *2018 IEEE Symposium on Computers and Communications (ISCC)* (pp. 1-6). IEEE.

Lee, K., Lee, S. Y., & Yim, K. (2019). Machine learning based file entropy analysis for ransomware detection in backup systems. *IEEE Access : Practical Innovations, Open Solutions*, *7*, 110205–110215. doi:10.1109/ACCESS.2019.2931136

Lee, K., Yim, K., & Seo, J. T. (2018). Ransomware prevention technique using key backup. *Concurrency and Computation*, *30*(3), e4337. doi:10.1002/cpe.4337

Lee, S., Kim, H. K., & Kim, K. (2019). Ransomware protection using the moving target defense perspective. *Computers & Electrical Engineering*, *78*, 288–299. doi:10.1016/j.compeleceng.2019.07.014

Magazine, C. P. O. (2023). *Toyota's Supply Chain Cyber Attack Stopped Production, Cutting Down a Third of Its Global Output.* https://www.cpomagazine.com/cyber-security/toyotas-supply-chain-cyber-attack-stopped-production-cutting-down-a-third-of-its-global-output/

Min, D., Park, D., Ahn, J., Walker, R., Lee, J., Park, S., & Kim, Y. (2018). Amoeba: An autonomous backup and recovery SSD for ransomware attack defense. *IEEE Computer Architecture Letters*, *17*(2), 245–248. doi:10.1109/LCA.2018.2883431

Monge, M. A. S., Vidal, J. M., & Villalba, L. J. G. (2018, August). A novel self-organizing network solution towards crypto-ransomware mitigation. In *Proceedings of the 13th International Conference on Availability, Reliability and Security* (pp. 1-10). 10.1145/3230833.3233249

Moore, C. (2016, August). Detecting ransomware with honeypot techniques. In *2016 Cybersecurity and Cyberforensics Conference (CCC)* (pp. 77-81). IEEE. 10.1109/CCC.2016.14

Nakamoto, S. (2008). *Bitcoin: A peer-to-peer electronic cash system. Decentralized business review.* Academic Press.

Oz, H., Aris, A., Levi, A., & Uluagac, A. S. (2022). A survey on Ransomware: Evolution, taxonomy, and defense solutions. *ACM Computing Surveys*, *54*(11s), 1–37. doi:10.1145/3514229

Paik, J. Y., Choi, J. H., Jin, R., Wang, J., & Cho, E. S. (2018, October). A storage-level detection mechanism against crypto-ransomware. In *Proceedings of the 2018 ACM SIGSAC Conference on Computer and Communications Security* (pp. 2258-2260). 10.1145/3243734.3278491

Paquet-Clouston, M., Haslhofer, B., & Dupont, B. (2019). Ransomware payments in the bitcoin ecosystem. *Journal of Cybersecurity*, *5*(1), tyz003. doi:10.1093/cybsec/tyz003

Park, J., Jung, Y., Won, J., Kang, M., Lee, S., & Kim, J. (2019, June). RansomBlocker: A low-overhead ransomware-proof SSD. In *Proceedings of the 56th Annual Design Automation Conference 2019* (pp. 1-6). Academic Press.

Pascariu, C., & Barbu, I. D. (2019, June). Ransomware Honeypot: Honeypot solution designed to detect a ransomware infection identify the ransomware family. In *2019 11th International Conference on Electronics, Computers and Artificial Intelligence (ECAI)* (pp. 1-4). IEEE.

Rahim Saleh, A., Al-Nemera, G., Al-Otaibi, S., Tahir, R., & Alkhatib, M. (2021). *Making Honey Files Sweeter: SentryFS--A Service-Oriented Smart Ransomware Solution.* arXiv e-prints, arXiv-2108.

Ryan, M. (2021). Ransomware Revolution: the rise of a prodigious cyber threat. In Advances in information security. Springer Nature. doi:10.1007/978-3-030-66583-8

Salahdine, F., & Kaabouch, N. (2019). Social engineering attacks: A survey. *Future Internet*, *11*(4), 89. doi:10.3390/fi11040089

Salehi, S., Shahriari, H., Ahmadian, M. M., & Tazik, L. (2018, August). A novel approach for detecting DGA-based ransomwares. In *2018 15th International ISC (Iranian Society of Cryptology) Conference on Information Security and Cryptology (ISCISC)* (pp. 1-7). IEEE

SecurityIntelligence. (2023). *Costa Rica State of Emergency Declared After Ransomware Attacks*. https://securityintelligence.com/news/costa-rica-state-emergency-ransomware/

Securityweek. (2023). *Ransomware Hit SCADA Systems at 3 Water Facilities in U.S*. https://www.securityweek.com/ransomware-hit-scada-systems-3-water-facilities-us/

Statescoop. (2023). *Months after ransomware attack, Bernalillo County, N.M., adopts cybersecurity policy*. https://statescoop.com/bernalillo-county-cybersecurity-policy-ransomware/

Tarcísio Marinho. (2023). *Ransomware encryption techniques*. https://medium.com/@tarcisioma/ransomware-encryption-techniques-696531d07bb9

TechTarget. (2023). *No relief in sight for ransomware attacks on hospitals*. https://www.techtarget.com/searchsecurity/feature/No-relief-in-sight-for-ransomware-attacks-on-hospitals#:~:text=Cybersecurity%20vendor%20Emsisoft%20recorded%2025,68%20attacks%20on%20healthcare%20providers

The Daily Swig. (2023). *Cyber-attack on Nvidia linked to Lapsus$ ransomware gang*. https://portswigger.net/daily-swig/cyber-attack-on-nvidia-linked-to-lapsus-ransomware-gang

Thomson Reuters. (2023). *Ransomware attacks against healthcare organizations nearly doubled in 2021*. https://www.thomsonreuters.com/en-us/posts/investigation-fraud-and-risk/ransomware-attacks-against-healthcare/

Vinayakumar, R., Soman, K. P., Velan, K. S., & Ganorkar, S. (2017, September). Evaluating shallow and deep networks for ransomware detection and classification. In *2017 international conference on advances in computing, communications and informatics (ICACCI)* (pp. 259-265). IEEE.

Wang, Z., Liu, C., Qiu, J., Tian, Z., Cui, X., & Su, S. (2018). Automatically traceback RDP-based targeted ransomware attacks. *Wireless Communications and Mobile Computing, 2018*, 1–13.

Wang, Z., Wu, X., Liu, C., Liu, Q., & Zhang, J. (2018, June). RansomTracer: exploiting cyber deception for ransomware tracing. In *2018 IEEE Third International Conference on Data Science in Cyberspace (DSC)* (pp. 227-234). IEEE. 10.1109/DSC.2018.00040

Whiteblueocean. (2023). *Top 5 Ransomware Attacks of 2022*. https://www.whiteblueocean.com/newsroom/top-5-ransomware-attacks-of-2022/

Zscaler. (2023). *Cyber-Deception Based Solution*. https://www.zscaler.com/resources/security-terms-glossary/what-is-deception-technology

Compilation of References

Abdel-Basset, M., Gamal, A., Sallam, K. M., Elgendi, I., Munasinghe, K., & Jamalipour, A. (2022). An Optimization Model for Appraising Intrusion-Detection Systems for Network Security Communications: Applications, Challenges, and Solutions. *Sensors (Basel)*, *22*(11), 4123. doi:10.339022114123 PMID:35684744

Abdullah, A. M. (2017). Advanced encryption standard (AES) algorithm to encrypt and decrypt data. *Cryptography and Network Security*, *16*(1), 11.

Abeoussi, J. M. D. (2019). *Black Hat and White Hat Hacking - The thin line of ethics*. EC-Council University.

Aboujaoude, E., Savage, M. W., Starcevic, V., & Salame, W. O. (2015). Cyberbullying: Review of an Old Problem Gone Viral. *The Journal of Adolescent Health*, *57*(1), 10–18. doi:10.1016/j.jadohealth.2015.04.011 PMID:26095405

Abu, M. S. (2018). Cyber threat intelligence–issue and challenges. *Indonesian Journal of Electrical Engineering and Computer Science*, *10*(1), 371–379. doi:10.11591/ijeecs.v10.i1.pp371-379

Addepalli, S. K., Karri, R., & Jyothi, V. (2020). U.S. Patent No. 10,735,438. Washington, DC: U.S. Patent and Trademark Office.

Advanced Persistent Threats and Nation-State Actors (n.d.). Cybersecurity and Infrastructure Security Agency CISA. https://www.cisa.gov/topics/cyber-threats-and-advisories/advanced-persistent-threats-and-nation-state-actors

Agnew, R. (1992). Foundation for a General Strain Theory of Crime and Delinquency. *Criminology*, *30*(1), 47–88. doi:10.1111/j.1745-9125.1992.tb01093.x

Aguinis, H., Gottfredson, R. K., & Wright, T. A. (2011). Best-practice recommendations for estimating interaction effects using meta-analysis. *Journal of Organizational Behavior*, *32*(8), 1033–1043. doi:10.1002/job.719

Ahmad, A., Desouza, K. C., Maynard, S. B., Naseer, H., & Baskerville, R. L. (2020). *How the integration of cyber security management and incident response enables organisational learning*.

Akers, R. (2009). *Social learning and social structure: A general theory of crime and deviance*. Routledge. doi:10.4324/9781315129587

Al Shuhaimi, F., Jose, M., & Singh, A. V. (2016). Software-defined network as a solution to overcome surveillance challenges in IoT. *Proceedings of the Reliability, Infocom Technologies and Optimization (Trends and Future Directions) (ICRITO), Noida, India, 7–9 September 2016*, 491–496.

Alam, M., Bhattacharya, S., Mukhopadhyay, D., & Bhattacharya, S. (2017). *Performance counters to rescue: A machine learning based safeguard against micro-architectural side-channel-attacks*. Cryptology ePrint Archive.

Alam, M., Sinha, S., Bhattacharya, S., Dutta, S., Mukhopadhyay, D., & Chattopadhyay, A. (2020). *Rapper: Ransomware prevention via performance counters*. arXiv preprint arXiv:2004.01712.

Alberts, C., & Dorofee, A. (2002). Introducing OCTAVE Allegro: Improving the Information Security Risk Assessment Process. *Managing Information Security Risks: The OCTAVESM Approach.* Addison Wesley. https://citeseerx.ist.psu.edu/viewdoc/download?doi=10.1.1.461.7807&rep=rep1&type=pdf

Aldwairi, M., & Alwahedi, A. (2018). Detecting fake news in social media networks. *Procedia Computer Science, 141,* 215–222. doi:10.1016/j.procs.2018.10.171

Al-Dwairi, M., Shatnawi, A. S., Al-Khaleel, O., & Al-Duwairi, B. (2022). Ransomware-Resilient Self-Healing XML Documents. *Future Internet, 14*(4), 115. doi:10.3390/fi14040115

Alex Hussar. (2022). www.cm-alliance.com/cybersurveillance-blog/iot-surveillance-5-cyber-attacks-caused-by-iot-surveillance-vulnerabilities

AlGhamdi, S., & Vlahu-Gjorgievska, W. K. T. E. (2020). Information security governance challenges and critical success factors. *Computers & Security, 99,* 102030. doi:10.1016/j.cose.2020.102030

Alhawi, O. M., Baldwin, J., & Dehghantanha, A. (2018). Leveraging machine learning techniques for windows ransomware network traffic detection. *Cyber Threat Intelligence,* 93-106.

Alkomah, F., & Ma, X. (2022). A Literature Review of Textual Hate Speech Detection Methods and Datasets. *Information (Basel), 13*(6), 273. doi:10.3390/info13060273

Allport, G. W. (1954). *The Nature of Prejudice.* Addison-Wesley.

Alnatheer, M. (2015). Information Security Culture Critical Success Factors. *Proceedings - 12th International Conference on Information Technology: New Generations, ITNG* (pp. 731-735). IEEE. 10.1109/ITNG.2015.124

Aloseel, A., He, H., Shaw, C., & Khan, M. A. (2020). Analytical review of cybersecurity for embedded systems. *IEEE Access : Practical Innovations, Open Solutions, 9,* 961–982. doi:10.1109/ACCESS.2020.3045972

Alves, F., Mateus-Coelho, N., & Cruz-Cunha, M. (2022). ChevroCrypto – Security & Cryptography Broker. *2022 10th International Symposium on Digital Forensics and Security (ISDFS),* (pp. 1-5). IEEE. 10.1109/ISDFS55398.2022.9800797

Alwashali, A. A. M. A., Abd Rahman, N. A., & Ismail, N. (2021, December). A survey of ransomware as a service (RaaS) and methods to mitigate the attack. In *2021 14th International Conference on Developments in eSystems Engineering (DeSE)* (pp. 92-96). IEEE.

Alzahrani, A., Alshehri, A., Alshahrani, H., & Fu, H. (2020). *Ransomware in Windows and Android Platforms.* arXiv preprint arXiv:2005.05571.

AMD. (2019). *AMD64 Architecture Programmer's Manual, Volume 3: General-Purpose and System Instructions.* AMD. https://www.amd.com/system/files/TechDocs/24594.pdf

American Psychiatric Association. (2013). *Diagnostic and statistical manual of mental disorders* (5th ed.).

Anderes, D., Baumel, E., Grier, C., Veun, R., & Wright, S. (n.d.). *The USe of Blockchain within Evidence Management Systems.* Alister, Inc.

Andreou, A., Goga, O., & Loiseau, P. (2017). Identity vs. Attribute Disclosure Risks for Users with Multiple Social Profiles. *IEEE/ACM International Conference on Advances in Social Networks Analysis and Mining,* 163–170. 10.1145/3110025.3110046

Anti-Defamation League. (2016). *Responding to Cyberhate: Progress and trends.* https://www.adl.org/sites/default/files/documents/assets/pdf/combating-hate/2016-ADL-Responding-to-Cyberhate-Progress-and-Trends-Report.pdf

Anti-Defamation League. (2022). *Hate Is No Game Hate and Harassment in Online Games 2022.* ADL Center for Technology & Society. https://www.adl.org/sites/default/files/documents/2022-12/Hate-and-Harassment-in-Online-Games-120622-v2.pdf

Anzueto-Ríos, A., Gómez-Castañeda, F., Flores-Nava, L. M., & Moreno-Cadenas, J. A. (2022, November). Metaheuristic Method for Dimensionality Reduction Tasks. In *2022 19th International Conference on Electrical Engineering, Computing Science and Automatic Control (CCE)* (pp. 1-5). IEEE. 10.1109/CCE56709.2022.9975991

Apostolaki, M., Zohar, A., & Vanbever, L. (2017). *Hijacking Bitcoin: Routing Attacks on Cryptocurrencies.* IEEE. doi:10.1109/SP.2017.29

Apple. (2022). *Performance Counters.* Apple. https://developer.apple.com/documentation/performance

Apriorit. (2023). *12 Common Attacks on Embedded Systems and How to Prevent Them.* Retrieved 15 Februrary, 2023 from https://www.apriorit.com/dev-blog/690-embedded-systems-attacks

Aqeel, M., Ali, F., Iqbal, M. W., Rana, T. A., Arif, M., & Auwul, R. (2022). A Review of Security and Privacy Concerns in the Internet of Things (IoT). *Journal of Sensors, 2022,* 2022. doi:10.1155/2022/5724168

ARM. (2019). *Armv8-A Architecture Reference Manual.* ARM. https://developer.arm.com/documentation/ddi0487/latest/

Ashley, C., & Preiksaitis, M. (2022). *Strategic Cybersecurity Risk Management Practices for Information in Small and Medium Enterprises.*

Associação Portuguesa de Apoio à Vítima [Portuguese Association for Victim Support]. (2022a). *Estatísticas APAV. Relatório Anual 2022* [APAV Statistics. Annual Report 2022]. https://apav.pt/apav_v3/images/pdf/Estatisticas-APAV_Relatorio-anual-2022.pdf

Associação Portuguesa de Apoio à Vítima [Portuguese Association for Victim Support]. (2022b). *Estatísticas 2022. Linha Internet Segura* [Statistics 2022. Safe Internet Line.]. https://internetsegura.pt/sites/default/files/2023-02/lis_2022_final-1.pdf

Atasever, S., Özçelık, İ., & Sağiroğlu, Ş. (2020, October). An Overview of Machine Learning Based Approaches in DDoS Detection. In *2020 28th Signal Processing and Communications Applications Conference (SIU)* (pp. 1-4). IEEE. 10.1109/SIU49456.2020.9302121

Atkins, S., & Lawson, C. (2020). *An Improvised Patchwork: Success and Failure in Cybersecurity Policy for Critical Infrastructure.*

AtlasV. P. N. (2020). https://atlasvpn.com/blog/phishing-attacks-increased-by-15-in-2020

Auxier, B., & Anderson, M. (2021). *Social Media Use in 2021.* Pew Research Center On Internet & Technology. https://www.pewresearch.org/internet/2021/04/07/social-media-use-in-2021/

Azmoodeh, A., Dehghantanha, A., Conti, M., & Choo, K. K. R. (2018). Detecting crypto-ransomware in IoT networks based on energy consumption footprint. *Journal of Ambient Intelligence and Humanized Computing, 9*(4), 1141–1152. doi:10.100712652-017-0558-5

Bachmann, M. (2008). *What makes them Click? Applying the Rational Choice Perspective to the Hacking Underground.* University of Central Florida.

Bachmann, M. (2010). The risk propensity and rationality of computer hackers. *International Journal of Cyber Criminology, 4*(1), 643–656.

Baek, S., Jung, Y., Mohaisen, A., Lee, S., & Nyang, D. (2018, July). SSD-insider: Internal defense of solid-state drive against ransomware with perfect data recovery. In *2018 IEEE 38th International Conference on Distributed Computing Systems (ICDCS)* (pp. 875-884). IEEE.

Baitha, A. K., & Vinod, S. (2018). Session hijacking and prevention technique. *Int. J. Eng. Technol, 7*(2.6), 193-198.

Bandyopadhyay, D., & Sen, J. (2011). Internet of things: Applications and challenges in technology and standardization. *Wireless Personal Communications, 58*(1), 49–69. doi:10.100711277-011-0288-5

Banerjee, S. S., Jha, S., Kalbarczyk, Z., & Iyer, R. K. (2021, April). BayesPerf: minimizing performance monitoring errors using Bayesian statistics. In *Proceedings of the 26th ACM International Conference on Architectural Support for Programming Languages and Operating Systems* (pp. 832-844). ACM. 10.1145/3445814.3446739

Bansal, D. (2022). *Double Spending and How It's prevented by Blockchain.* Retrieved March 15, 2023, from Topcoder: https://www.topcoder.com/thrive/articles/double-spending-and-how-its-prevetned-by-blockchain#:~:text=In conclusion%2C the blcokchain stops,quantitatively tied to the earlier ones.

Başkaya, D., & Samet, R. (2020, September). Ddos attacks detection by using machine learning methods on online systems. In *2020 5th International Conference on Computer Science and Engineering (UBMK)* (pp. 52-57). IEEE. 10.1109/UBMK50275.2020.9219476

Basu, K., Krishnamurthy, P., Khorrami, F., & Karri, R. (2019). A theoretical study of hardware performance counters-based malware detection. *IEEE Transactions on Information Forensics and Security, 15,* 512–525. doi:10.1109/TIFS.2019.2924549

Bauman, S., Perry, V. M., & Wachs, S. (2021). The rising threat of cyberhate for young people around the globe. In M. F. Wright & L. B. Schiamberg (Eds.), *Child and Adolescent Online Risk Exposure: An Ecological Perspective* (pp. 149–175). Academic Press. doi:10.1016/B978-0-12-817499-9.00008-9

Bawazeer, O., Helmy, T., & Al-hadhrami, S. (2021, July). Malware detection using machine learning algorithms based on hardware performance counters: Analysis and simulation. []. IOP Publishing.]. *Journal of Physics: Conference Series, 1962*(1), 012010. doi:10.1088/1742-6596/1962/1/012010

Bazm, M. M., Sautereau, T., Lacoste, M., Sudholt, M., & Menaud, J. M. (2018, April). Cache-based side-channel attacks detection through intel cache monitoring technology and hardware performance counters. In *2018 Third International Conference on Fog and Mobile Edge Computing (FMEC)* (pp. 7-12). IEEE. 10.1109/FMEC.2018.8364038

BBC News. (2022, January 26). *Crypto Money Laundering Rises 30%, Report finds.* BBC. https://www.bbc.com/news/technology-60072195#:~:text=Criminals%20laundered%20%248.6bn%20(£,to%20launder%20cryptocurrency%20by%20criminals.

Bedrosova, M., Machackova, H., Šerek, J., Smahel, D., & Blaya, C. (2022). The relation between the cyberhate and cyberbullying experiences of adolescents in the Czech Republic, Poland, and Slovakia. *Computers in Human Behavior, 126,* 107013. doi:10.1016/j.chb.2021.107013

Behl, A., & Behl, K. (2012). *An analysis of cloud computing security issues. Information and Communication Technologies (WICT).* IEEE.

Bennett, K., & Decker, C. (2019). *Certified Blockchain Business Foundations (CBBF), Official Exam Study Guide.* Blcokchain Training Alliance, Inc.

Bernatzky, C., Costello, M., & Hawdon, J. (2022). Who produces online hate? An examination of the effects of self-control, social structure, & social learning. *American Journal of Criminal Justice, 47*(3), 421–440. doi:10.100712103-020-09597-3

Bigelow, S. J. (2021). *Blockchain: An Immutable Ledeger to Replace the Database.* TechTarget - IT Operations. https://www.techtarget.com/searchitoperations/tip/Blockchain-An-immutable-ledger-to-replace-the-database

BitFlyer. (n.d.). *Checkpoint.* BitFlyer. https://bitflyer.com/en-eu/s/glossary/check-point#:~:text=Checkpoints%20are%20when%20block%20hash,to%20the%20checkpoint%20as%20irreversible

Blanco-Herrero, D., & Calderón, C. A. (2019, October). Spread and reception of fake news promoting hate speech against migrants and refugees in social media: Research Plan for the Doctoral Programme Education in the Knowledge Society. In *Proceedings of the Seventh International Conference on Technological Ecosystems for Enhancing Multiculturality* (pp. 949-955). 10.1145/3362789.3362842

Blaya, C., & Audrin, C. (2019). Toward an understanding of the characteristics of secondary school cyberhate perpetrators. *Frontiers in Education,* 4(46), 46. Advance online publication. doi:10.3389/feduc.2019.00046

Blaya, C., Audrin, C., & Skrzypiec, G. (2020). School bullying, perpetration, and cyberhate: Overlapping issues. *Contemporary School Psychology,* 26(3), 341–349. doi:10.100740688-020-00318-5

Bliuc, A. M., Faulkner, N., Jakubowicz, A., & McGarty, C. (2018). Online networks of racial hate: A systematic review of 10 years of research on cyber-racism. *Computers in Human Behavior,* 87, 75–86. doi:10.1016/j.chb.2018.05.026

Block O'Toole and Morphy (BOM). (2022). *Types of Negligence and How They Apply in Different Scenarios.* BOM. https://www.blockotoole.com/negligence/types-of-negligence.

Borba, E., Tavares, E., & Maciel, P. (2022). A modeling approach for estimating performance and energy consumption of storage systems. *Journal of Computer and System Sciences,* 128, 86–106. doi:10.1016/j.jcss.2022.04.001

Bossler, A. M., & Burruss, G. W. (2011). The general theory of crime and computer hacking: low self-control hackers. In T. J. Holt & B. H. Schell (Eds.), *Corporate Hacking and Technology-Driven Crime: Social Dynamics and Implications* (pp. 38–67). IGI Glob. doi:10.4018/978-1-61692-805-6.ch003

Botacin, M., & Grégio, A. (2022, December). Why We Need a Theory of Maliciousness: Hardware Performance Counters in Security. In *Information Security: 25th International Conference, ISC 2022, Bali, Indonesia,* (pp. 381-389). Cham: Springer International Publishing.

Bourdon, M., Alata, E., Kaâniche, M., Migliore, V., Nicomette, V., & Laarouchi, Y. (2020, January). Anomaly detection using hardware performance counters on a large-scale deployment. In *10th European Congress Embedded Real Time Systems (ERTS 2020).* IEEE.

Bowen, B. M., Devarajan, R., & Stolfo, S. (2011). Measuring the human factor of cyber security. Paper presented at *2011 IEEE International Conference on Technologies for Homeland Security (HST),* (pp. 230–235). IEEE. 10.1109/THS.2011.6107876

Breia, R. (2022). *What Is Blockchain Interoperability.* Sensorium. https://sensoriumxr.com/articles/what-is-blockchain-interoperability

Britz, M. T. (2013). Introduction and overview of computer forensics and cybercrime. In Computer Forensics and Cyber Crime: An Introduction (pp. 1 -20), South Carolina, Pearson (3).

Broadus, R. N. (1987). Toward a definition of »bibliometrics«. *Scientometrics,* 12(5–6), 373–379. doi:10.1007/BF02016680

Brown, C., & Hegarty, K. (2021). Development and validation of the TAR Scale: A measure of technology-facilitated abuse in relationships. *Computers in Human Behavior Reports,* 3, 100059. doi:10.1016/j.chbr.2021.100059

Brown, C., Sanci, L., & Hegarty, K. (2021). Technology-facilitated abuse in relationships: Victimisation patterns and impact in young people. *Computers in Human Behavior, 124*, 106897. doi:10.1016/j.chb.2021.106897

Brun, O., Yin, Y., Gelenbe, E., Kadioglu, Y. M., Augusto-Gonzalez, J., & Ramos, M. (2018). Deep learning with dense random neural networks for detecting attacks against IoT-connected home environments. *Proceedings of the 2018 ISCIS surveillance Workshop, Imperial College London. Recent Cybersurveillance Research in Europe. Lecture Notes CCIS, 821.* 10.1007/978-3-319-95189-8_8

Bugeja, J., Jacobsson, A., & Davidsson, P. (2016). On privacy and surveillance challenges in smart connected homes. *Proceedings of the European Intelligence and surveillance Informatics Conference (EISIC),* 172–175.

Bunker, G. (2020). Targeted cyber-attacks: How to mitigate the increasing risk. *Network Security, 2020*(1), 17–19. doi:10.1016/S1353-4858(20)30010-6

Burch, S. (2019). *YouTube Deletes 500 Million Comments in Fight Against Hate Speech.* Retrieved 15 Januar, 2023 from https://www.thewrap.com/youtube-deletes-500-million-comments-in-fight-against-hate-speech/

Business Australia. (2022). *Cybercriminals Becoming More Sophisticated: Report.* Business Australia. https://www.businessaustralia.com/resources/news/cybercriminals-becoming-more-sophisticated-report?utm_brand=BA&utm_prodcat=content&utm_p

Butt, U. J., Abbod, M., Lors, A., Jahankhani, H., Jamal, A., & Kumar, A. (2019, January). Ransomware Threat and its Impact on SCADA. In *2019 IEEE 12th international conference on global security, safety and sustainability (ICGS3)* (pp. 205-212). IEEE.

Cambridge Dictionary. (2023). *Hate speech.* Retrieved 12 February, 2023, from https://dictionary.cambridge.org/dictionary/english/hate-speech?q=Hate+speech

Caralli, R. A., Stevens, J. F., Young, L. R., & William, R. (2007). *TECHNICAL REPORT CMU/SEI-2007-TR-012 ESC-TR-2007-012 CERT Program.* CMU. https://resources.sei.cmu.edu/asset_files/TechnicalReport/2007_005_001_14885.pdf

Card, S., Mackinlay, J., & Shneiderman, B. (1999). *Readings in information visualisation: using vision to think.* Morgan Kaufmann.

Castaño-Pulgarín, S. A., Suárez-Betancur, N., Vega, L. M. T., & López, H. M. H. (2021). Internet, social media and online hate speech. Systematic review. *Aggression and Violent Behavior, 58*, 101608. doi:10.1016/j.avb.2021.101608

Celuch, M., Oksanen, A., Räsänen, P., Costello, M., Blaya, C., Zych, I., Llorent, V. J., Reichelmann, A., & Hawdon, J. (2022). Factors associated with online hate acceptance: A cross-national six-country study among young adults. *International Journal of Environmental Research and Public Health, 19*(1), 534. doi:10.3390/ijerph19010534 PMID:35010794

Chakkaravarthy, S. S., Sangeetha, D., Cruz, M. V., Vaidehi, V., & Raman, B. (2020). Design of intrusion detection honeypot using social leopard algorithm to detect IoT ransomware attacks. *IEEE Access : Practical Innovations, Open Solutions, 8*, 169944–169956. doi:10.1109/ACCESS.2020.3023764

Chang, Y. W., Huang, M. H., & Lin, C. W. (2015). Evolution of research subjects in library and information science based on keyword, bibliographical coupling, and co-citation analyses. *Scientometrics, 105*(3), 2071–2087. doi:10.100711192-015-1762-8

Chan, J. Y. L., Leow, S. M. H., Bea, K. T., Cheng, W. K., Phoong, S. W., Hong, Z. W., & Chen, Y. L. (2022). Mitigating the multicollinearity problem and its machine learning approach: A review. *Mathematics, 10*(8), 1283. doi:10.3390/math10081283

Chen, L., Yang, C. Y., Paul, A., & Sahita, R. (2018). *Towards resilient machine learning for ransomware detection.* arXiv preprint arXiv:1812.09400.

Chen, Q., & Bridges, R. A. (2017, December). Automated behavioral analysis of malware: A case study of wannacry ransomware. In *2017 16th IEEE International Conference on machine learning and applications (ICMLA)* (pp. 454-460). IEEE. 10.1109/ICMLA.2017.0-119

Chen, T. F., & Baer, J. L. (1995). Effective hardware-based data prefetching for high-performance processors. *IEEE Transactions on Computers*, *44*(5), 609–623. doi:10.1109/12.381947

Chen, Y., Li, Y., Cheng, X. Q., & Guo, L. (2006). Survey and taxonomy of feature selection algorithms in intrusion detection system. In Information Security and Cryptology: Second SKLOIS Conference, Inscrypt 2006, Beijing, China.

Cherdantseva, Y., Burnap, P., Blyth, A., Eden, P., Jones, K., Soulsby, H., & Stoddart, K. (2016). A review of cyber security risk assessment methods for SCADA systems. *Computers & Security*, *56*, 1–27. doi:10.1016/j.cose.2015.09.009

Chetty, N., & Alathur, S. (2018). Hate speech review in the context of online social networks. *Aggression and Violent Behavior*, *40*, 108–118. doi:10.1016/j.avb.2018.05.003

Chigada, J., & Madzinga, R. (2021). Cyberattacks and threats during COVID-19: A systematic literature review. *South African Journal of Information Management*, *23*(1), 1–11. doi:10.4102ajim.v23i1.1277

Choi, J., Park, G., & Nam, D. (2018, September). Efficient classification of application characteristics by using hardware performance counters with data mining. In *2018 IEEE 3rd International Workshops on Foundations and Applications of Self* Systems (FAS* W)* (pp. 24-29). IEEE.

Cho, J., Kim, T., Kim, S., Im, M., Kim, T., & Shin, Y. (2020). Real-time detection for cache side channel attack using performance counter monitor. *Applied Sciences (Basel, Switzerland)*, *10*(3), 984. doi:10.3390/app10030984

Chou, D. C., Yen, D. C., Lin, B., & Cheng, P. H.-L. (1999). Cyberspace security management. *Industrial Management & Data Systems*, *99*(8), 353–361. doi:10.1108/02635579910301793

Chowdhury, A. B., Mahapatra, A., Soni, D., & Karri, R. (2022). Fuzzing+ Hardware Performance Counters-Based Detection of Algorithm Subversion Attacks on Post-Quantum Signature Schemes. *IEEE Transactions on Computer-Aided Design of Integrated Circuits and Systems.*

Chu, Ip, Lam, & K.P. (2022). Vine copula statistical disclosure control for mixed-type data. *Computational Statistics & Data Analysis*, 176.

Chu, A. M. Y., Lam, B. S. Y., Tiwari, A., & So, M. K. P. (2019). An Empirical Study of Applying Statistical Disclosure Control Methods to Public Health Research. *Journal of Empirical Research on Human Research Ethics*, *14*(5), 411–420. PMID:31731730

Cibersurveillance, C. I., & Dataset, I. D. S. (2018). *CSE-CIC-IDS2018 on AWS.* https://www.unbca/cicdatas ets/ids-2018 html

Cinelli, M., De Francisci Morales, G., Galeazzi, A., Quattrociocchi, W., & Starnini, M. (2021). The echo chamber effect on social media. *Proceedings of the National Academy of Sciences of the United States of America*, *118*(9), 2023301118. doi:10.1073/pnas.2023301118 PMID:33622786

CIS. (2019). *CIS Controls® V7.1.* CIS. https://www.cisecurity.org/controls/

Cisco Networking Academy. (2020). *Enterprise Networking, Security, and Automation Companion Guide (CCNAv7)* (1st ed.). Cisco Press.

Cisco. (2021). *Consumer privacy survey.* Récupéré sur https://www.cisco.com/c/dam/en_us/about/doing_business/trust-center/docs/consumer-privacy-survey.pdf

Clark, L. A., & Watson, D. (1999). Temperament: A new paradigm for trait psychology. In L. A. Pervin & O. P. John (Eds.), *Handbook of personality: Theory and research* (pp. 399–423). Guilford Press.

CloudSEK. (2023). *GoodWill ransomware forces victims to donate to the poor and provides financial assistance to patients in need.* https://cloudsek.com/threatintelligence/goodwill-ransomware-forces-victims-to-donate-to-the-poor-and-provides-financial-assistance-to-patients-in-need

CMMI Institute LLC. (2020). *Over 1/2 of Cyber Professionals Expect a Cyber Attack within 12 Months.* CMMI Institute. https://cmmiinstitute.com/products/cybermaturity

Cohen, G. (2022). Throwback Attack: Operation Aurora signals a new era in industrial threat. *Industrial Cybersecurity Pulse.* https://www.industrialcybersecuritypulse.com/threats-vulnerabilities/throwback-attack-operation-aurora-signals-a-new-era-in-industrial-threat/

Cohen, A., & Nissim, N. (2018). Trusted detection of ransomware in a private cloud using machine learning methods leveraging meta-features from volatile memory. *Expert Systems with Applications, 102,* 158–178. doi:10.1016/j.eswa.2018.02.039

Cohen, L. E., & Felson, M. (1979). Social change and crime rate trends: A routine activity approach. *American Sociological Review, 44*(4), 588–608. doi:10.2307/2094589

Coleman, E. G., & Golub, A. (2008). Hacker practice: Moral genres and the cultural articulation of liberalism. *Anthropological Theory, 8*(3), 255–277. doi:10.1177/1463499608093814

Comissão para a Igualdade contra a Discriminação Racial [Portuguese Comission for Equality Against Racial Discrimination]. (2021). *Relatório Anual 2021: Igualdade e Não Discriminação em Razão da Origem Racial e Étnica, Cor, Nacionalidade, Ascendência e Território de Origem* [Annual Report 2021: Equality and Non-Discrimination on the grounds of Racial and Ethnic Origin, Color, Nationality, Ascendancy and Territory of Origin]. https://www.cicdr.pt/documents/57891/574449/20220809+-+Relat%C3%B3rio+Anual+CICDR+2021_.pdf/a7777160-f69a-48dd-8156-80d6bfcc93d0

Compliance Week. (2021). *Enforcement Tracker Q1 2021: GDPR fines lead the way.* Récupéré sur https://www.complianceweek.com/data-privacy/enforcement-tracker-q1-2021-gdpr-fines-lead-the-way/30391

Constantin, L. (2021). REvil ransomware explained: A widespread extortion operation. *CSO Online.* https://www.csoonline.com/article/570101/revil-ransomware-explained-a-widespread-extortion-operation.html

Conti, M., Dargahi, T., & Dehghantanha, A. (2018). *Cyber threat intelligence: challenges and opportunities. Cyber threat intelligence.* Springer.

Costa, P. T. Jr, & McCrae, R. R. (1992). The five-factor model of personality and its relevance to personality disorders. *Journal of Personality Disorders, 6*(4), 343–359. doi:10.1521/pedi.1992.6.4.343

Costello, M., & Hawdon, J. (2018). Who Are the Online Extremists Among Us? Sociodemographic Characteristics, Social Networking, and Online Experiences of Those Who Produce Online Hate Materials. *Violence and Gender, 5*(1), 55–60. doi:10.1089/vio.2017.0048

Costello, M., Hawdon, J., Bernatzky, C., & Mendes, K. (2019). Social Group Identity and Perceptions of Online Hate. *Sociological Inquiry, 89*(3), 1–26. doi:10.1111oin.12274

Council of Europe. (2016). *The European Commission against Racism and Intolerance (ECRI): Recommendation No. 15 on Combating Hate Speech*. https://rm.coe.int/ecri-general-policy-recommendation-no-15-on-combating-hate-speech/16808b5b01

Craigen, D., Diakun-Thibault, N., & Purse, R. (2014). Defining Cybersecurity. *Technology Innovation Management Review*, *4*(10), 13–21. doi:10.22215/timreview/835

CrowdStrike. (2023). *Ransomware-as-a-Service Model*. https://www.crowdstrike.com/cybersecurity-101/ransomware/ransomware-as-a-service-raas/

Cruz-Cunha, M. M., & Mateus-Coelho, N. R. (Eds.). (2021). *Handbook of Research on Cyber Crime and Information Privacy*. IGI Global.

Cuchta, T., Blackwood, B., Devine, T., Niichel, R., Daniels, K., Lutjens, C., Maibach, S., & Stephenson, R. (2019). *Human Risk Factors in Cybersecurity*. . doi:10.1145/3349266.3351407

Culbert, D. (2020). *Personal Data Breaches and Securing IoT Devices*. Available online: https://betanews.com/2019/08/13/securing-iot-devices/

Curtis, S. R., Rajivan, P., Jones, D. N., & Gonzalez, C. (2018). Phishing attempts among the dark triad: Patterns of attack and vulnerability. *Computers in Human Behavior*, *87*, 174–182. doi:10.1016/j.chb.2018.05.037

Cyberark. (2023). *CoronaVirus Ransomware*. https://www.cyberark.com/resources/threat-research-blog/coronavirus-ransomware

Cybersecurity and Infrastructure Security Agency. (2022). *2021 Trends Show Increased Globalized Threat of Ransomware*. CISA. https://www.cisa.gov/uscert/ncas/alerts/aa22-040a

Cybersecuritydive. (2023). *Australia's telecom giant Optus avoids ransom demand as attacker reverses course*. https://www.cybersecuritydive.com/news/optus-ransomware-retracted/632763/

Daku, H., Zavarsky, P., & Malik, Y. (2018, August). Behavioral-based classification and identification of ransomware variants using machine learning. In *2018 17th IEEE international conference on trust, security and privacy in computing and communications/12th IEEE international conference on big data science and engineering (TrustCom/BigDataSE)* (pp. 1560-1564). IEEE. 10.1109/TrustCom/BigDataSE.2018.00224

Daley, S. (2022). *20 Blockchain in Cybersecurity Examples*. Built In. https://builtin.com/blockchain/blockchain-cybersecurity-uses

Dan, Li, & Wu. (2009). Identity disclosure protection: A data reconstruction approach for privacy-preserving data mining. Decision Support Systems, 48, 133-140.

Das, S., Saha, S., Priyoti, A. T., Roy, E. K., Sheldon, F. T., Haque, A., & Shiva, S. (2021). Network intrusion detection and comparative analysis using ensemble machine learning and feature selection. *IEEE Transactions on Network and Service Management*.

Das, S., Werner, J., Antonakakis, M., Polychronakis, M., & Monrose, F. (2019, May). SoK: The challenges, pitfalls, and perils of using hardware performance counters for security. In *2019 IEEE Symposium on Security and Privacy (SP)* (pp. 20-38). IEEE. 10.1109/SP.2019.00021

Dastjerdi, A. V., & Buyya, R. (2016, August). Fog computing: Helping the Internet of Things realize its potential. *Computer*, *49*(8), 112–116. doi:10.1109/MC.2016.245

Da-Yu, K. A. O., Hsiao, S. C., & Raylin, T. S. O. (2019, February). Analyzing WannaCry ransomware considering the weapons and exploits. In *2019 21st International Conference on Advanced Communication Technology (ICACT)* (pp. 1098-1107). IEEE

Deloitte. (2018). *Secure IoT by Design*. Deloitte. https://www2.deloitte.com/us/en/pages/operations/articles/iot-platform-security.html

Deloitte. (2019). *Global Risk Management Survey*. Récupéré sur https://www2.deloitte.com/: https://www2.deloitte.com/content/dam/Deloitte/us/Documents/risk/us-risk-2019-global-risk-management-survey.pdf

Derasari, P., Koppineedi, S., & Venkataramani, G. (2020, August). Can Hardware Performance Counters Detect Adversarial Inputs? In *2020 IEEE 63rd International Midwest Symposium on Circuits and Systems (MWSCAS)* (pp. 945-948). IEEE.

Deuby, S. (2023). Timeline of a Hafnium attack. *Semperis*. https://www.semperis.com/blog/timeline-of-hafnium-attack/

Diesch, R., Pfaff, M., & Krcmar, H. (2020). A comprehensive model of information security factors for decision-makers. *Computers & Security*, *92*, 1–21. doi:10.1016/j.cose.2020.101747

Dimock, M. (2019, January 17). *Defining generations: Where Millennials end and Generation Z begins*. Pew Research Center. https://www.pewresearch.org/fact-tank/2019/01/17/where-millennials-end-and-generation-z-begins/

Do Nascimento, P. P., Colares, I. F., Maciel, R., Da Silva, H. C., & Maciel, P. (2021). Prediction, detection, and mitigation of DDOS attacks using hpcs: Design for a safer adaptive infrastructure. Handbook of Research on Cyber Crime and Information Privacy, 523-538.

Do, H.M., Gregory, M.A., & Li, S. (September 2021). SDN-based wireless mobile backhaul architecture: Review and challenges. *Journal of Network and Computer Applications, 189*. doi:10.1016/j.jnca.2021.103138

Donthu, N., Kumar, S., Mukherjee, D., Pandey, N., & Lim, W. M. (2021). How to conduct a bibliometric analysis: An overview and guidelines. *Journal of Business Research*, *133*, 285–296. doi:10.1016/j.jbusres.2021.04.070

Donthu, N., Kumar, S., & Pattnaik, D. (2020). Forty-five years of Journal of Business Research: A bibliometric analysis. *Journal of Business Research*, *109*(1), 1–14. doi:10.1016/j.jbusres.2019.10.039

Duncan, G., & Lambert, D. (1989). The Risk of Disclosure for Microdata. *Journal of Business & Economic Statistics*, 207–217.

Eck, J. E., & Clarke, R. V. (2003). Classifying common police problems: A routine activity theory approach. In M. J. Smith & D. B. Cornish (Eds.), Crime prevention studies: Vol. 16. Theory and practice in situational crime prevention (pp. 7-39). Monsey, NY: Criminal Justice Press.

Egress. (2021). *Insider data breaches survey*. Récupéré sur https://pages.egress.com/rs/030-CPG-384/images/Egress-Insider-Data-Breaches-Survey-2021-Global-Report.pdf

Eigner, W. (2013). Current Work Practice and Users' Perspectives on Visualization and Interactivity in Business Intelligence. In *17th International Conference on Information Visualization*. IEEE. 10.1109/IV.2013.38

Elamir, A. M., Jailani, N., & Bakar, M. A. (2013). Framework and Architecture for Programming Education Environment as a Cloud Computing Service. *ScienceDirect* [Elsevier.]. *Procedia Technology, 11*, 1299–1308. doi:10.1016/j.protcy.2013.12.328

Elliot, M., & Domingo-Ferrer, J. (2021). The future of statistical disclosure control. *The Journal of Privacy and Confidentiality*, *11*(1), 1–18.

Elnaggar, R., Servadei, L., Mathur, S., Wille, R., Ecker, W., & Chakrabarty, K. (2021). Accurate and Robust Malware Detection: Running XGBoost on Runtime Data From Performance Counters. *IEEE Transactions on Computer-Aided Design of Integrated Circuits and Systems, 41*(7), 2066–2079. doi:10.1109/TCAD.2021.3102007

Enamul Kabir, Mahmood, Mustafa, & Wang. (2015). Microaggregation Sorting Framework for K-Anonymity Statistical Disclosure Control in Cloud Computing. IEEE.

ENISA. (n.d.). *Compendium of risk management frameworks.* European Agency for Cybersecurity. https://www.enisa.europa.eu/publications/compendium-of-risk-management-frameworks

Eoin, Q. (2014). *Torts In Ireland.* Dublin., Gill education.

Erikson, E. H. (1963). *Childhood and society* (2nd ed.). Norton.

Eriksson, J., & Giacomello, G. (2022). Cyberspace in space: Fragmentation, vulnerability, and uncertainty. In *Cyber Security Politics* (pp. 95–108). Routledge. doi:10.4324/9781003110224-8

Estrada, D., Tawalbeh, L., & Vinaja, R. (2020). How Secure Having IoT Devices in Our Home. *J. Inf. Secur., 11.*

ETAS. (2023). *Veränderungen in der ETAS Marken architektur.* Retrieved 15 Februrary, 2023 from https://www.escrypt.com/sites/default/files/flyer/Product_Flyer_KMS.pdf

European Council. (2022). Retrieved from Data protection in the EU: https://www.consilium.europa.eu/en/policies/data-protection/data-protection-regulation/#:~:text=The%20GDPR%20establishes%20the%20general,data%20processing%20operations%20they%20perform

European Parliament. (2019). Access to legal remedies for victims of corporate human rights abuses in third countries. Policy Department for External Relations. *Directorate General for External Policies of the Union, PE, 603,* 47.

European Union. (2016). *General Data Protection Regulation (GDPR).* Récupéré sur Official Journal of the European Union: https://eur-lex.europa.eu/legal-content/EN/TXT/HTML/?uri=CELEX:32016R0679&from=EN

Eurostat. (2022). *Digital economy and society statistics - Households and individuals.* https://ec.europa.eu/eurostat/statistics-explained/index.php?title=Digital_economy_and_society_statistics_-_households_and_individuals

Fadhlillah, A., Karna, N., & Irawan, A. (2021, January). IDS performance analysis using anomaly-based detection method for DOS attack. In *2020 IEEE International Conference on Internet of Things and Intelligence System (IoTaIS)* (pp. 18-22). IEEE. 10.1109/IoTaIS50849.2021.9359719

Fáwolé, J., & Ciattaglia, L. (2023a). *Blockchain Secuirty: Common Vulnerabilities and How to Protect Against Them.* Hacken. https://hacken.io/insights/blockchain-security-vulnerabilities/

Fáwolé, J., & Ciattaglia, L. (2023b). *Sybil Attack in Blockchain: Examples & Prevention.* Hacken. https://hacken.io/insights/sybil-attacks/

Federal Bureau of Investigation's Uniform Crime Reporting. (2022, December 12). *FBI Releases 2021 Hate Crime Statistics.* FBI National Press Office. https://www.fbi.gov/news/press-releases/fbi-releases-2021-hate-crime-statistics

Fenten, N. (2018). *Risk Assessment and Decision Analysis with Bayesian Networks.* Taylor & Francis.

Ferrag, M. A., Maglaras, L., Moschoyiannis, S., & Janicke, H. (2020). Deep learning for cyber surveillance invasion detection: Approaches, datasets, and comparative study. *J. Inform. Secur. Appl., 50,* 102419. doi:10.1016/j.jisa2019.102419

Fischer, E. (2017, January). *Cybersecurity Issues and Challenges.* LIBRARY OF CONGRESS WASHINGTON DC.

Fitch, C. (2004). *Crime and Punishment: The Psychology of Hacking in the New Millennium.* SANS Institute.

Foreman, J. C. (2018). *A survey of cyber security countermeasures using hardware performance counters.* arXiv preprint arXiv:1807.10868.

Fortuna, P., & Nunes, S. (2018). A Survey on Automatic Detection of Hate Speech in Text. *ACM Computing Surveys*, *51*(4), 1–30. doi:10.1145/3232676

Fox, B., & Holt, T. J. (2021). Use of a Multitheoretic Model to Understand and Classify Juvenile Computer *Hacking* Behavior. *Criminal Justice and Behavior*, *48*(7), 943–963. doi:10.1177/0093854820969754

Fruhlinger, J. (2023). Equifax data breach FAQ: What happened, who was affected, what was the impact? *CSO Online*. https://www.csoonline.com/article/567833/equifax-data-breach-faq-what-happened-who-was-affected-what-was-the-impact.html

Furfaro, A., Pace, P., & Parise, A. (2020). Facing DDoS bandwidth flooding attacks. *Simulation Modelling Practice and Theory*, *98*, 101984. doi:10.1016/j.simpat.2019.101984

Furnell, S. M. (2001). Categorising cybercrime and cybercriminals: The problem and potential approaches. *Journal of Information Warfare*, *1*(2), 35–44.

Furnell, S. M., Dowland, P. S., & Sanders, P. W. (1999). Dissecting the "Hacker Manifesto". *Information Management & Computer Security*, *7*(2), 69–75. doi:10.1108/09685229910265493

Furnell, S., Emm, D., & Papadaki, M. (2015). The challenge of measuring cyber- dependent crimes. *Computer Fraud & Security*, *2015*(10), 5–12. doi:10.1016/S1361-3723(15)30093-2

Gaia, J., Sanders, G. L., Sanders, S. P., Upadhyaya, S., Wang, X., & Yoo, C. W. (2021). Dark Traits and Hacking Potential. *Journal of Organizational Psychology*, *21*(3), 23–46.

Ganfure, G. O., Wu, C. F., Chang, Y. H., & Shih, W. K. (2022). Deepware: Imaging performance counters with deep learning to detect ransomware. *IEEE Transactions on Computers*, *72*(3), 600–613.

Gao, Y., Makrani, H. M., Aliasgari, M., Rezaei, A., Lin, J., Homayoun, H., & Sayadi, H. (2021, June). Adaptive-hmd: Accurate and cost-efficient machine learning-driven malware detection using microarchitectural events. In *2021 IEEE 27th International Symposium on On-Line Testing and Robust System Design (IOLTS)* (pp. 1-7). IEEE.

Garcia-Serrano, A. (2015). *Anomaly detection for malware identification using hardware performance counters.* arXiv preprint arXiv:1508.07482.

Gaspar, T., Matos, G. M., Guedes, B. F., Cerqueira, A., Branquinho, C., Simões, C., Tomé, G., Reis, M., Ramiro, L., Marques, A., Camacho, I., Loureiro, N., Gaspar, S., Carvalho, M., Raimundo, M., Ramos, M., Moraes, B., Noronha, C., Sousa, B. S., . . . Costa, R. (2022). *A saúde dos adolescentes portugueses em contexto de pandemia*: Dados nacionais do estudo HBSC 2022 [The health of Portuguese adolescents in a pandemic context: HBSC 2022 national report]. https://aventurasocial.com/wp-content/uploads/2022/12/HBSC_Relato%CC%81rioNacional_2022.pdf

Geldiyev, H., Churiyev, M., & Mahmudov, R. (2020). Issues regarding cybersecurity in modern world. *Digitalization and Industry 4.0: Economic and Societal Development: An International and Interdisciplinary Exchange of Views and Ideas*, 3-14.

Gelenbe, E., & Yin, Y. (2017). Deep learning with dense random neural networks. In *Proceedings of the International Conference on Man–Machine Interactions.* Springer.

Gemalto. (2020). *Securing the IoT-Building Trust in IoT Devices and Data.* Available online: https://www.gemalto.com/:https://www.gemalto.com/iot/iot-surveillance

Gogoi, P., Bhattacharyya, D. K., Borah, B., & Kalita, J. K. (2011). A survey of outlier detection methods in network anomaly identification. *The Computer Journal*, *54*(4), 570–588. doi:10.1093/comjnl/bxr026

Gómez-Hernández, J. A., Álvarez-González, L., & García-Teodoro, P. (2018). R-Locker: Thwarting ransomware action through a honeyfile-based approach. *Computers & Security*, *73*, 389–398. doi:10.1016/j.cose.2017.11.019

Gómez-Hernández, J. A., Sánchez-Fernández, R., & García-Teodoro, P. (2022). Inhibiting crypto-ransomware on windows platforms through a honeyfile-based approach with R-Locker. *IET Information Security*, *16*(1), 64–74. doi:10.1049/ise2.12042

Gordon, L.A., Loeb, M.P, & Zhou, L. (2020). Integrating cost–benefit analysis into the NIST Cybersecurity Framework via the Gordon-Loeb Model. *J. Cybersecurity, 6.*

Görzig, A., Blaya, C., Bedrosova, M., Audrin, C., & Machackova, H. (2023). The amplification of cyberhate victimisation by discrimination and low life satisfaction: Can supportive environments mitigate the risks? *The Journal of Early Adolescence*, *43*(1), 5–36. doi:10.1177/02724316221078826

Gottfredson, M., & Hirschi, T. (1990). *A General Theory of Crime*. Stanford University Press., doi:10.1515/9781503621794

Grand View Research, Inc. (2022). *Blockchain Technology Market Size, Share & Trends Analysis Report By Type (Private Cloud, Public Cloud), By Application (Digital Identity, Payments), By Enterprise Size, By Component, By End Use, And Segment Forecasts, 2023 - 2030.* Grand View Research, Inc. https://www.grandviewresearch.com/industry-analysis/blockchain-technology-market

Grand View Research. (2021). *Enterprise Risk Management (ERM) Software Market Size, Share & Trends Analysis Report By Component, By Deployment, By Organization, By Vertical, By Region, And Segment Forecasts, 2021 - 2028.* Retrieved from https://www.grandviewresearch.com/industry-analysis/enterprise-risk-management-software-market

Gravelle, B. J., Nystrom, W. D., & Norris, B. (2022, November). Performance Analysis with Unified Hardware Counter Metrics. In *2022 IEEE/ACM International Workshop on Performance Modeling, Benchmarking and Simulation of High-Performance Computer Systems (PMBS)* (pp. 60-70). IEEE. 10.1109/PMBS56514.2022.00011

Gregg, B. (2019, October). Linux systems performance. In USENIX Association.

Gregg, B. (2021). *Computing Performance: On the Horizon.* USENIX Association, červen.

Gregg, B. (2019). *BPF Performance Tools.* Addison-Wesley Professional.

Gulmezoglu, B., Moghimi, A., Eisenbarth, T., & Sunar, B. (2019). *Fortuneteller: Predicting microarchitectural attacks via unsupervised deep learning.* arXiv preprint arXiv:1907.03651.

HackerOne. (2020). *The 2020 Hacker Report.* Available at: https://www.hackerone.com/resources/reporting/the-2020-hacker-report

HackerOne. (2021). *The 2021 Hacker Report.* Available at: https://www.hackerone.com/resources/reporting/the-2021-hacker-report

HackerOne. (2022). *The 2022 Hacker Report.* Available at: https://www.hackerone.com/resources/reporting/the-2022-hacker-report

Halima Ibrahim Kure. (2022). An integrated cyber security risk management framework and risk predication for the critical infrastructure protection. *Neural Computing & Applications.*

Han, C., Jornet, J. M., Fadel, E., & Akyildiz, I. F. (2013). A cross-layer communication module for the internet of things. *Computer Networks*, *57*(3), 622–633. doi:10.1016/j.comnet.2012.10.003

Handagama, S. (2022). *They Were Jailed for Hacking an Exchange. Blockchain Data Cleared Them*. CoinDesk. https://www.coindesk.com/policy/2022/03/01/they-were-jailed-for-hacking-an-exchange-blockchain-data-cleared-them/

Hardaker, C. (2013). "Uh....not to be nitpicky,but…the past tense of drag is dragged, not drug.": An overview of trolling strategies. *Journal of Language Aggression and Conflict, 1*(1), 58–86. doi:10.1075/jlac.1.1.04har

Hasan, M. K., Habib, A. A., Shukur, Z., Ibrahim, F., Islam, S., & Razzaque, M. A. (2023). Review of cyber-physical and cyber-security system in smart grid: Standards, protocols, constraints, and recommendations. *Journal of Network and Computer Applications, 209*, 103540. doi:10.1016/j.jnca.2022.103540

Hassan, A. M., & Awad, A. I. (2018). Urban transition in the era of the internet of things: Social implications and privacy challenges. *IEEE Access : Practical Innovations, Open Solutions, 6*, 36428–36440. doi:10.1109/ACCESS.2018.2838339

Hassan, A., Bhatti, S. H., Shujaat, S., & Hwang, Y. (2022). To adopt or not to adopt? The determinants of cloud computing adoption in information technology sector. [Elsevier.]. *Decision Analytics Journal, 5*, 100138. doi:10.1016/j.dajour.2022.100138

Hawdon, J., Oksanen, A., & Räsänen, P. (2014). Victims of online hate groups: American youth's exposure to online hate speech. In J. Hawdon, J. Ryan, & M. Lucht (Eds.), *The causes and consequences of group violence: From bullies to terrorists* (pp. 165–182). Lexington Books.

He, C. (2020). *Transformer in CV: The increasing convergence of computer vision and NLP*. Retrieved 10 February, 2023 from https://towardsdatascience.com/transformer-in-cv-bbdb58bf335e

He, Z., Miari, T., Makrani, H. M., Aliasgari, M., Homayoun, H., & Sayadi, H. (2021, April). When machine learning meets hardware cybersecurity: Delving into accurate zero-day malware detection. In *2021 22nd International Symposium on Quality Electronic Design (ISQED)* (pp. 85-90). IEEE.

Heartfield, R., & Loukas, G. (2015). A taxonomy of attacks and a survey of defence mechanisms for semantic social engineering attacks. *ACM Computing Surveys, 48*(3), 1–39. doi:10.1145/2835375

He, H., Maple, C., Watson, T., Tiwari, A., Mehnen, J., Jin, Y., & Gabrys, B. (2016). The surveillance challenges in the IoT enabled cyber-physical systems and opportunities for evolutionary computing & other computational intelligence. *Proceedings of the Evolutionary Computation (CEC), 1015–1021.*

Hevner, A. R., March, S. T., Park, J., & Ram, S. (2004). Design Science in Information Systems. *Management Information Systems Quarterly, 28*(1), 75–105. doi:10.2307/25148625

Hicks, D., & Wang, J. (2011). Coverage and overlap of the new social sciences and humanities journal lists. *Journal of the American Society for Information Science and Technology, 62*(2), 284–294. doi:10.1002/asi.21458

Hindelang, M. J., Gottfredson, M. R., & Garofalo, J. (1978). *Victims of personal crime: An empirical foundation for a theory of personal victimization*. Ballinger.

Hinduja, S., & Patchin, J. W. (2011). *Electronic dating violence: A brief guide for educators and parents*. US Cyberbullying Research Center. https://cyberbullying.org/electronic_dating_violence_fact_sheet.pdf

Hiscox. (2020). *Cyber readiness report 2020*. Récupéré sur https://www.hiscox.com/: https://www.hiscox.com/documents/2019-Hiscox-Cyber-Readiness-Report.pdf

Hiscox. (2022). *Cyber Readiness Report 2022*. Hiscox. https://www.hiscoxgroup.com/sites/group/files/documents/2022-05/22054%20-%20Hiscox%20Cyber%20Readiness%20Report%202022-EN_0.pdf

Hollinger, R. (1988). Computer hackers follow a Guttman-Like Progression. *Phrack Inc., 2*(22).

Hollinger, R. C. (1991). Hackers: Computer Heroes or Electronic Highwaymen? *Computers & Society, 21*(1), 6–17. doi:10.1145/122246.122248

Hollinger, R. C. (1992). Crime by Computer: Correlates of Software Piracy and Unauthorized Account Access. *Security Journal, 4*(1), 2–12.

Hollinger, R. C., & Lanza-Kaduce, L. O. N. N. (1988). The process of criminalization: The case of computer crime laws. *Criminology, 26*(1), 101–126. doi:10.1111/j.1745-9125.1988.tb00834.x

Holt, T. J. (2007). Subcultural Evolution? Examining the Influence of On and Offline Experiences on Deviant Subcultures. *Deviant Behavior, 28*(2), 171–198. doi:10.1080/01639620601131065

Holt, T. J. (2020). Computer Hacking and the Hacker Subculture. In T. J. Holt & A. M. Bossler (Eds.), *The Palgrave Handbook of International Cybercrime and Cyberdeviance* (pp. 725–742). Palgrave Macmillan. doi:10.1007/978-3-319-78440-3_31

Holt, T. J., Bossler, A. M., & Seigfried-Spellar, K. C. (2017). *Cybercrime and digital forensics: An introduction*. Routledge. doi:10.4324/9781315296975

Holt, T. J., Burruss, G. W., & Bossler, A. M. (2010). Social learning and cyber- deviance: Examining the importance of a full social learning model in the virtual world. *Journal of Crime and Justice, 33*(2), 31–61. doi:10.1080/073564 8X.2010.9721287

Holt, T. J., Navarro, J. N., & Clevenger, S. (2020). Exploring the moderating role of gender in juvenile hacking behaviors. *Crime and Delinquency, 66*(11), 1533–1555. doi:10.1177/0011128719875697

Hussain, A., Mohamed, A., & Razali, S. (2020). *A review on Cybersecurity: Challenges & emerging threats. NISS 2020 Proceedings*. ACM. doi:10.1145/3386723.3387847

Ibarra, J., Butt, U. J., Do, A., Jahankhani, H., & Jamal, A. (2019, January). Ransomware impact to SCADA systems and its scope to critical infrastructure. In *2019 IEEE 12th International Conference on Global Security, Safety and Sustainability (ICGS3)* (pp. 1-12). IEEE. 10.1109/ICGS3.2019.8688299

IBM Security and Ponemon *Institute* (2022). *Cost of a Data Breach Report 2022*. IBM. https://www.ibm.com/downloads/cas/3R8N1DZJ

IBM. (2021). *PowerPC Microprocessor Family: The Programming Environments for 64-bit Microprocessors*. IBM. https://www.ibm.com/docs/en/aix/7.2?topic=processors-powerpc-microprocessor-family

impreva, Chris Levan. (2023). *PCI DSS Certification*. Récupéré sur impriva.com: https://www.imperva.com/learn/data-security/pci-dss-certification/

Information Commissioner's Office (ICO). (2018). *A framework for designing and managing GDPR compliance*. Récupéré sur Data protection by design and default: https://ico.org.uk/media/for-organisations/documents/2014223/gdpr-dpbd-201710.pdf

Instituto Nacional de Estatística [Statistical National Institute]. (2022). *Sociedade da Informação e do Conhecimento. Inquérito à Utilização de Tecnologias da Informação e da Comunicação pelas Famílias 2022* [Information Society and Knowledge. Survey on the Use of Information and Communication Technologies by Families in 2022]. https://www.ine.pt/xportal/xmain?xpid=INE&xpgid=ine_destaques&DESTAQUESdest_boui=541053235&DESTAQUESmodo=2

Intel. (2020). *Intel 64 and IA-32 Architectures Software Developer's Manual: Volume 3A - System Programming Guide, Part 1*. Intel. https://software.intel.com/content/www/us/en/develop/articles/intel-sdm.html

International Organization for Standardization. (2011). *ISO/IEC 29100:2011 Information technology—Security techniques—Privacy framework*. Récupéré sur https://www.iso.org/: https://www.iso.org/standard/45170.html

Iredale, G. (2021). *Top 7 Benefits Of Blockchain Identity Management*. 101 Blockchains. https://101blockchains.com/blockchain-identity-management-benefits/

ISO/IEC. ISO/IEC 27005:2018(en) Information Technology—Security Techniques—Information Security Risk Management. (2018). Available online: https://www.iso.org/obp/ui/#iso:std:iso-iec:27005:ed-3:v1:en

ISO27005 Information security risk management

ISO31000 Risk Management.

Jabłońska, M. R., & Zajdel, R. (2020). The Dark triad Traits and Problematic Internet Use: Their Structure and Relations. *Polish Sociological Review*, *4*, 477–496.

Jackson, E. (2019). *What We Can Learn From Estonia's Real-World Use Case of Blockchain*. LinkedIn. https://www.linkedin.com/pulse/what-we-can-learn-from-estonias-real-world-use-case-eric-jackson/

Jacks, W., & Adler, J. R. (2015). A proposed typology of online hate crime. *Open Access Journal of Forensic Psychology*, *7*, 64–89.

Jaquet-Chiffelle, D. O., & Loi, M. (2020). Ethical and unethical hacking. In M. Christen, B. Gordjin, & M. Loi (Eds.), *The Ethics of Cybersecurity* (pp. 179–204). Springer Nature. doi:10.1007/978-3-030-29053-5_9

Jay, F. (2010). Law 101. Oxford University Press publisher.

Jennings, W. G., Piquero, A. R., & Reingle, J. M. (2012). On the overlap between victimization and offending: A review of the literature. *Aggression and Violent Behavior*, *17*(1), 16–26. doi:10.1016/j.avb.2011.09.003

Jinsheng, Z. (2018). Design of software architecture stability testing system in IoT framework. *Mod. Electron. Technique*, *41*(20), 118–121.

John & Schmutte. (2015). Economic Analysis and Statistical Disclosure Limitation. In Brookings Papers on Economic Activity. Springer.

Jonason, P. K., Strosser, G. L., Kroll, C. H., Duineveld, J. J., & Baruffi, S. A. (2015). Valuing myself over others: The *Dark triad* traits and moral and social values. *Personality and Individual Differences*, *81*, 102–106. doi:10.1016/j.paid.2014.10.045

Jones, D. N., Padilla, E., Curtis, S. R., & Kiekintveld, C. (2021). Network discovery and scanning strategies and the Dark Triad. *Computers in Human Behavior*, *122*, 1–10. doi:10.1016/j.chb.2021.106799

Jones, D. N., & Paulhus, D. L. (2014). Introducing the Short Dark triad (SD3): A brief measure of dark personality traits. *Assessment*, *21*(1), 28–41. doi:10.1177/1073191113514105 PMID:24322012

Jony, N., & Anitha, M. (2014). Survey of Statistical Disclosure Control Technique. *International Journal of Research in Advent Technology*, *2*(5), 344–349.

Jordan, T. (2017). A genealogy of hacking. *Convergence (London)*, *23*(5), 528–544. doi:10.1177/1354856516640710

Jordan, T., & Taylor, P. (1998). A sociology of hackers. *The Sociological Review*, *46*(4), 757–780. doi:10.1111/1467-954X.00139

Jung, T. J. (2019). *How Transparency through the Blockchain helps the Cybersecurity Community*. IBM Supply Chain and Blockchain Blog. https://www.ibm.com/blogs/blockchain/2019/04/how-transparency-through-blockchain-helps-the-cybersecurity-community/

Junni, P., Sarala, R. M., Taras, V. A. S., & Tarba, S. Y. (2013). Organizational ambidexterity and performance: A meta-analysis. *The Academy of Management Perspectives*, 27(4), 299–312. doi:10.5465/amp.2012.0015

Kadiyala, S. P., Jadhav, P., Lam, S. K., & Srikanthan, T. (2020). Hardware performance counter-based fine-grained malware detection. [TECS]. *ACM Transactions on Embedded Computing Systems*, 19(5), 1–17. doi:10.1145/3403943

Kagan, J. (2021). *Contributory Negligence*. Investiopedia. https://www.investopedia.com/terms/c/contributory-negligence.asp.

Kanimozhi, V., & Prem Jacob, T. (2019). Artificial Intelligence based Network Intrusion Detection with hyper-parameter optimization tuning on the realistic cyber dataset CSE-CIC-IDS2018 using cloud computing. *ICT Express*, 5(3), 211–214. doi:10.1016/j.icte.2019.03.003

Karim, N. S. A., Zamzuri, N. H. A., & Nor, Y. M. (2009). Exploring the relationship between Internet ethics in university students and the big five model of personality. *Computers & Education*, 53(1), 86–93. doi:10.1016/j.compedu.2009.01.001

Karuppiah, M., Das, A. K., Li, X., Kumari, S., Wu, F., Chaudhry, S. A., & Niranchana, R. (2019). Secure remote user mutual authentication scheme with key agreement for cloud environment. *Mobile Networks and Applications*, 24(3), 1046–1062. doi:10.100711036-018-1061-8

Ke, G., & Hong, Y. H. (2014, August). The research of network invasion detection technology based on genetic algorithm and bp neural network. *Applied Mechanics and Materials*, 599–601, 726–730. doi:10.4028/www.scientific.net/AMM.599-601.726

Keighley, R. (2022). Hate Hurts: Exploring the Impact of Online Hate on LGBTQ+ Young People. *Women & Criminal Justice*, 32(1), 29–48. doi:10.1080/08974454.2021.1988034

Keller, L. (2022). *Solana Loses Consensus after Bots flood Network, SOL takes Hit*. Forkast. https://forkast.news/headlines/solana-loses-consensus-bots-flood-sol/

Kemp, S. (2023). *Digital 2023: Global Overview Report*. DataReportal. https://www.slideshare.net/DataReportal/digital-2023-global-overview-report-summary-version-january-2023-v02

Keong Ng, C., Rajasegarar, S., Pan, L., Jiang, F., & Zhang, L. Y. (2020). VoterChoice: A ransomware detection honeypot with multiple voting framework. *Concurrency and Computation*, 32(14), e5726. doi:10.1002/cpe.5726

Kerner, S. O. S. M. (2023). SolarWinds hack explained: Everything you need to know. *WhatIs.com*. https://www.techtarget.com/whatis/feature/SolarWinds-hack-explained-Everything-you-need-to-know

Khan, N., Salleh, R. b., Koubaa, A., Khan., Z., Khan., M.K., & Ali, I. (2023). Data plane failure and its recovery techniques in SDN: A systematic literature review. *Journal of King Saud University - Computer and Information Sciences*, 35, 176-201.

Khan, R., Khan, S., & Zaheer, R. (2012) Future internet: The internet of things architecture, possible applications and key challenges. In *2012 10th International Conference on Frontiers of Information Technology*. IEEE.

Khan, S., Hussain, F.K., & Hussain, O.K. (2021). Guaranteeing end-to-end QoS provisioning in SOA based SDN architecture: A survey and Open Issues. *Future Generation Computer Systems, 119*, 176-187). doi:10.1016/j.future.2021.02.011

Khan, M. A., Pattnaik, D., Ashraf, R., Ali, I., Kumar, S., & Donthu, N. (2021). Value of special issues in the Journal of Business Research: A bibliometric analysis. *Journal of Business Research*, *125*, 295–313. doi:10.1016/j.jbusres.2020.12.015

Khasawneh, K. N., Ozsoy, M., Donovick, C., Abu-Ghazaleh, N., & Ponomarev, D. (2015, December). Ensemble learning for low-level hardware-supported malware detection. *In Research in Attacks, Intrusions, and Defenses: 18th International Symposium, RAID 2015*, (pp. 3-25). Cham: Springer International Publishing. 10.1007/978-3-319-26362-5_1

Khosravi-Farmad, M., & Ghaemi-Bafghi, A. (2020). Bayesian Decision Network-Based Security Risk Management Framework. *Journal of Network and Systems Management*, *28*(4), 1794–1819. doi:10.100710922-020-09558-5

Kim, D. Y., Choi, G. Y., & Lee, J. H. (2018, January). Whitelist-based ransomware real-time detection and prevention for user device protection. In *2018 IEEE International Conference on Consumer Electronics (ICCE)* (pp. 1-5). IEEE.

Kim, D., & Lee, J. (2020). Blacklist vs. whitelist-based ransomware solutions. *IEEE Consumer Electronics Magazine*, *9*(3), 22–28. doi:10.1109/MCE.2019.2956192

King, J. (2018). *Trustless Technology: The Core of the Blockchain. Blockchain Beach*. Blockchain Beach. https://www.blockchainbeach.com/trustless-technology-core-blockchain/

Kinkade, P. T., Bachmann, M., & Bachmann, B. S. (2013). Hacker Woodstock: Observations on an off-line Cyber Culture at the Chaos Communication Camp 2011. In T. J. Holt (Ed.), *Crime On-line: Correlates, Causes, and Context* (2nd ed., pp. 19–60). Carolina Academic Press.

Kirsch, C. (2014). The Grey Hat Hacker: Reconciling cyberspace reality and the law. *Northern Kentucky Law Review*, *41*(3), 383–403.

KnowBe4. (2021). *Data breach investigations report*. Récupéré sur https://enterprise.verizon.com/resources/reports/dbir/

KnowBe4. (2023a). *AIDS Trojan or PC Cyborg Ransomware*. https://www.knowbe4.com/aids-trojan

KnowBe4. (2023b). *PETYA Pransomware Locks Users Out by Overwriting Master Boot Record*. https://blog.knowbe4.com/petya-ransomware-lock-users-out-by-overwriting-master-boot-record

Ko, J.-S., Jo, J.-S., Kim, D.-H., Choi, S.-K., & Kwak, J. (2019). Real Time Android Ransomware Detection by Analyzed Android Applications. *2019 International Conference on Electronics, Information, and Communication (ICEIC)*, 1-5. 10.23919/ELINFOCOM.2019.8706349

Kolias, C., Kambourakis, G., Stavrou, A., & Voas, J. (2017). DDoS in the IoT: Mirai and other botnets. *Computer*, *50*(7), 80–84. doi:10.1109/MC.2017.201

Koroniotis, N., Moustafa, N., Sitnikova, E., & Turnbull, B. (2019). Towards the development of realistic botnet dataset in the Internet of Things for network forensic analytics: Bot-IoT dataset. *Future Generation Computer Systems*, *100*, 779–796. doi:10.1016/j.future.2019.05.041

Krishna, A. (2022). *Blockchain Security Issues – A Complete Guide*. Astra. https://www.getastra.com/blog/knowledge-base/blockchain-security-issues/

Krishnamurthy, P., Karri, R., & Khorrami, F. (2019). Anomaly detection in real-time multi-threaded processes using hardware performance counters. *IEEE Transactions on Information Forensics and Security*, *15*, 666–680. doi:10.1109/TIFS.2019.2923577

Krueger, Mansouri-Benssassi, Ritchie, & Smith. (2021). Statistical disclosure controls for machine learning models. *Conference of European Statisticians*, 1-19.

Kshetri, N. (2017). Can Blockchain Strengthen the Internet of Things? *IT Professional, 19*(4), 68–72. doi:10.1109/MITP.2017.3051335

Kshetri, N., & Voas, J. (2022). Ransomware as a Business (RAAB). *IT Professional, 24*(2), 83–87. doi:10.1109/MITP.2022.3157208

Kumar, M. S., Ben-Othman, J., & Srinivasagan, K. G. (2018, June). An investigation on wannacry ransomware and its detection. In *2018 IEEE Symposium on Computers and Communications (ISCC)* (pp. 1-6). IEEE.

Kure, H., & Islam, S. (2019). Cyber Threat Intelligence for Improving Cybersecurity and Risk Management in Critical Infrastructure. *Journal of Universal Computer Science, 25*(11), 1478–1502.

Kuruvila, A. P., Arunachalam, A., & Basu, K. (2020, December). Benefits and Challenges of Utilizing Hardware Performance Counters for COPPA Violation Detection. In *2020 IEEE Physical Assurance and Inspection of Electronics (PAINE)* (pp. 1-6). IEEE.

Kuruvila, A. P., Meng, X., Kundu, S., Pandey, G., & Basu, K. (2022). Explainable machine learning for intrusion detection via hardware performance counters. *IEEE Transactions on Computer-Aided Design of Integrated Circuits and Systems, 41*(11), 4952–4964. doi:10.1109/TCAD.2022.3149745

Landreth, B., & Rheingold, H. (1985). *Out of the inner circle: a hacker's guide to computer security*. Microsoft Press.

Lauritsen, J. L., Sampson, R. J., & Laub, J. H. (1991). The link between offending and victimization among adolescents. *Criminology, 29*(2), 265–292. doi:10.1111/j.1745-9125.1991.tb01067.x

Lawteacher.net. (2022). Principles of Criminal Liability: Intention and Recklessness. *Lawteacher.net.* https://www.lawteacher.net/free-law-essays/criminal-law/principles-of-criminal-liability.php.

Lee, G., Shim, S., Cho, B., Kim, T., & Kim, K. (2021). Fileless cyberattacks: Analysis and classification. *ETRI Journal, 43*(2), 332–343. doi:10.4218/etrij.2020-0086

Lee, J. Y., & Lee, J. (2021). Current research trends in IoT security: A systematic mapping study. *Mobile Information Systems, 2021*, 1–25. doi:10.1155/2021/8847099

Lee, K., Lee, S. Y., & Yim, K. (2019). Machine learning based file entropy analysis for ransomware detection in backup systems. *IEEE Access : Practical Innovations, Open Solutions, 7*, 110205–110215. doi:10.1109/ACCESS.2019.2931136

Lee, K., Yim, K., & Seo, J. T. (2018). Ransomware prevention technique using key backup. *Concurrency and Computation, 30*(3), e4337. doi:10.1002/cpe.4337

Lee, S., Kim, H. K., & Kim, K. (2019). Ransomware protection using the moving target defense perspective. *Computers & Electrical Engineering, 78*, 288–299. doi:10.1016/j.compeleceng.2019.07.014

Lei n.º 94/2017, de 23 de agosto [Law no. 94/2017, of 23 August]. *Diário da República – I Série*, N.º 162. Quarta alteração ao Código Penal, aprovado pelo Decreto-Lei n.º 48/95, de 15 de março [Fourth amendment to the Penal Code, approved by Decree-Law no. 48/95 of March 15]. https://dre.pt/dre/legislacao-consolidada/decreto-lei/1995-34437675-108044756?_ts=1680220800034

Leonard, M. (2018). *How Blockchain Helped bring down the Silk Road*. GCN. https://gcn.com/emerging-tech/2018/05/how-blockchain-helped-bring-down-the-silk-road/300085/

Leukfeldt, R., Kleemans, E. R., & Stol, W. (2017). Origin, growth, and criminal capabilities of cybercriminal networks. An international empirical analysis. *Crime, Law, and Social Change, 67*(1), 39–53. doi:10.100710611-016-9663-1

Levy, S. (1984). *Hackers: Heroes of the computer revolution* (Vol. 14). Anchor Press/Doubleday.

Li, C., & Gaudiot, J. L. (2018, September). Online detection of spectre attacks using microarchitectural traces from performance counters. In *2018 30th International Symposium on Computer Architecture and High-Performance Computing (SBAC-PAD)* (pp. 25-28). IEEE. 10.1109/CAHPC.2018.8645918

Li, N. (2007). t-Closeness: Privacy Beyond k-Anonymity and L-Diversity. IEEE.

Liao, W., Chen, P., & Kuai, S. (2017). A Resource Provision Strategy for Software-as-a-Service in Cloud Computing. The 14th International Conference on Mobile Systems and Pervasive Computing (Mobisc 2017). *ScienceDirect* [Elsevier.]. *Procedia Computer Science, 110*, 94–101. doi:10.1016/j.procs.2017.06.123

Li, C., & Gaudiot, J. L. (2021). Detecting spectre attacks using hardware performance counters. *IEEE Transactions on Computers, 71*(6), 1320–1331. doi:10.1109/TC.2021.3082471

Li, J., Zhang, L., Feng, X., Jia, K., & Kong, F. (2019). Feature extraction and area identification of wireless channel in mobile communication. *J. Internet Technol., 20*(2), 545–553.

Lim, W. M., Yap, S. F., & Makkar, M. (2021). Home sharing in marketing and tourism at a tipping point: What do we know, how do we know, and where should we be heading? *Journal of Business Research, 122*, 534–566. doi:10.1016/j.jbusres.2020.08.051 PMID:33012896

Ling, Y., Yang, C., Li, X., Xie, M., & Ming, S. (2022, September). WEB Attack Source Tracing Technology Based on Genetic Algorithm. In *2022 7th International Conference on Cyber Security and Information Engineering (ICCSIE)* (pp. 123-126). IEEE. 10.1109/ICCSIE56462.2022.00032

Linux kernel documentation. (2022). perf events. https://www.kernel.org/doc/html/latest/perf/index.html

Litan, A. (2021). *Hype Cycle for Blockchain 2021; More Action than Hype.* Gartner. https://blogs.gartner.com/avivah-litan/2021/07/14/hype-cycle-for-blockchain-2021-more-action-than-hype/

Liu, X., Zhao, M., Li, S., Zhang, F., & Trappe, W. (2017). *A surveillance framework for the internet of things in the future internet architecture.* Academic Press.

Li, Y., & Liu, Q. (2021). A comprehensive review study of cyber-attacks and cyber security; Emerging trends and recent developments. *Energy Reports, 7*, 8176–8186. doi:10.1016/j.egyr.2021.08.126

Loch, K. D., & Conger, S. (1996). Evaluating Ethical Decision Making and Computer Use. *Communications of the ACM, 39*(7), 74–83. doi:10.1145/233977.233999

Lockheed Martin. (2020). *Lockheed Martin And Guardtime Federal Join Forces To Thwart Software Cyber Threats.* Lock Heed Martin. https://news.lockheedmartin.com/2020-02-20-Lockheed-Martin-and-Guardtime-Federal-Join-Forces-to-Thwart-Software-Cyber-Threats

Lohani, A. (2021). Countering Disinformation and Hate Speech Online: Regulation and User Behavioural Change. *ORF Occasional Paper, 296*, 1–36.

Lohr, S. (2012). The age of big data. *New York Times, 11.*

Lopes, B., & Yu, H. (2017). Who do you troll and Why: An investigation into the relationship between the *Dark triad* Personalities and online trolling behaviours towards popular and less popular Facebook profiles. *Computers in Human Behavior, 77*, 69–76. doi:10.1016/j.chb.2017.08.036

Loukis, E., Janssen, M., & Mintchev, I. (February 2019). Determinants of software-as-a-service benefits and impact on firm performance. *Decision Support Systems, 117*, 38-47. doi:10.1016/j.dss.2018.12.005

Lutkevich. (2023). *Definition: Natural language processing (NLP)*. Retrieved on 10 March 2023 from https://www.techtarget.com/searchenterpriseai/definition/natural-language-processing-NLP

MachackovaH.BlayaC.BedrosovaM.SmahelD.StaksrudE. (2020). *Children's experiences with cyberhate*. EU Kids Online: The London School of Economics and Political Science. https://doi.org/ doi:10.21953/lse.zenkg9xw6pua

Machanavajjhala, A. (2006). L-diversity: Privacy beyond k-anonymity. IEEE.

Maciel, P. R. M. (2023). Performance, reliability, and availability evaluation of computational systems, Volume 1: Performance and Background. CRC Press.

Maciel, P. R. M. (2023). Performance, reliability, and availability evaluation of computational systems, Volume 2: Reliability, availability modeling, measuring, and data analysis. CRC Press.

Madarie, R. (2017). Hackers' Motivations: Testing Schwartz'S Theory Of Motivational Types Of Values In A Sample Of Hackers. *International Journal of Cyber Criminology*, *11*(1), 78–97.

Magazine, C. P. O. (2023). *Toyota's Supply Chain Cyber Attack Stopped Production, Cutting Down a Third of Its Global Output*. https://www.cpomagazine.com/cyber-security/toyotas-supply-chain-cyber-attack-stopped-production-cutting-down-a-third-of-its-global-output/

Malone, C., Zahran, M., & Karri, R. (2011, October). Are hardware performance counters a cost effective way for integrity checking of programs? In *Proceedings of the sixth ACM workshop on Scalable trusted computing* (pp. 71-76). ACM. 10.1145/2046582.2046596

Mani, V. (2017). Blockchain Technology from Information Security. *ISACA Journal*. https://www.isaca.org/resources/isaca-journal/issues/2017/volume-4/a-view-of-blockchain-technology-from-the-information-security-radar

Manoj, B., & Baker, A. (2007). Communication challenges in emergency response. *Communications of the ACM*, *50*(3), 51–53. doi:10.1145/1226736.1226765

Mantha, B. R., & de Soto, B. G. (2019). Cyber security challenges and vulnerability assessment in the construction industry. In *Creative Construction Conference 2019* (pp. 29-37). Budapest University of Technology and Economics. 10.3311/CCC2019-005

Marcum, C. D., Higgins, G. E., Ricketts, M. L., & Wolfe, S. E. (2014). Hacking in high school: Cybercrime perpetration by juveniles. *Deviant Behavior*, *35*(7), 581–591. doi:10.1080/01639625.2013.867721

Markets and Markets. (2023). Retrieved on 10 March 2023, from https://www.marketsandmarkets.com/Market-Reports/cyber-security-market-505.html

Martin, L. (2009). *Cyber Kill Chain®*. Lock Heed Martin. https://www.lockheedmartin.com/en-us/capabilities/cyber/cyber-kill-chain.html

Mateus-Coelho, N., & Cruz-Cunha, M. (2022). Serverless Service Architectures and Security Minimals. *2022 10th International Symposium on Digital Forensics and Security (ISDFS)*, (pp. 1-6). IEEE. 10.1109/ISDFS55398.2022.9800779

McCrae, R. R. (1996). Social consequences of experiential openness. *Psychological Bulletin*, *120*(3), 323–337. doi:10.1037/0033-2909.120.3.323 PMID:8900080

McCrae, R. R., & Costa, P. X. Jr. (1991). Conceptions and correlates of Openness to Experience. In R. Hogan, J. A. Johnson, & S. R. Briggs (Eds.), *Handbook of personality psychology*. Academic Press.

McGuinness, D. (2017). *How a cyber attack transformed Estonia*. Retrieved 15 January, 2023 from https://www.bbc.com/news/39655415

Merre, R. (2022). *Blockchain Interoperability: Challenges & Opportunities*. NGRAVE. https://www.ngrave.io/en/blog/blockchain-interoperability-challenges-opportunities

Microsoft. (2022). *Performance Counters*. Microsoft. https://docs.microsoft.com/en-us/windows/win32/perfctrs/performance-counters

Miethe, T. D., & Meier, R. F. (1990). Opportunity, choice, and criminal victimization: A test of a theoretical model. *Journal of Research in Crime and Delinquency, 27*(3), 243–266. doi:10.1177/0022427890027003003

Min, D., Park, D., Ahn, J., Walker, R., Lee, J., Park, S., & Kim, Y. (2018). Amoeba: An autonomous backup and recovery SSD for ransomware attack defense. *IEEE Computer Architecture Letters, 17*(2), 245–248. doi:10.1109/LCA.2018.2883431

Mirchev, M. J., & Mirtchev, S. T. (2020). System for DDoS attack mitigation by discovering the attack vectors through statistical traffic analysis. *International Journal of Information and Computer Security, 13*(3-4), 309–321. doi:10.1504/IJICS.2020.109479

Moeckel, C. (2019). Examining and constructing attacker categorisations: an experimental typology for digital banking. In *Proceedings of the 14th International Conference on Availability, Reliability and Security* (pp. 1-6). 10.1145/3339252.3340341

Monge, M. A. S., Vidal, J. M., & Villalba, L. J. G. (2018, August). A novel self-organizing network solution towards crypto-ransomware mitigation. In *Proceedings of the 13th International Conference on Availability, Reliability and Security* (pp. 1-10). 10.1145/3230833.3233249

Mongeon, P., & Paul-Hus, A. (2016). The Journal Coverage of Web of Science and Scopus: A Comparative Analysis. *Scientometrics, 106*(1), 213–228. doi:10.100711192-015-1765-5

Monther, A. A., & Tawalbeh, L. (2020). surveillance techniques for intelligent spam sensing and anomaly detection in online social platforms. *Iranian Journal of Electrical and Computer Engineering, 10*, 2088–8708.

Moore, C. (2016, August). Detecting ransomware with honeypot techniques. In *2016 Cybersecurity and Cyberforensics Conference (CCC)* (pp. 77-81). IEEE. 10.1109/CCC.2016.14

Moore, R. (2015). *Cybercrime: Investigating High-Technology Computer Crime*. Routledge.

Moral-Munoz, J. A., Herrera-Viedma, E., Espejo, A. S., & Cobo, M. J. (2020). Software tools for conducting bibliometric analysis in science: An up-to-date review. *El Profesional de la Información, 29*(1). Advance online publication. doi:10.3145/epi.2020.ene.03

Morris, R. G., & Blackburn, A. G. (2009). Cracking the code: An empirical exploration of social learning theory and computer crime. *Journal of Crime and Justice, 32*(1), 1–34. doi:10.1080/0735648X.2009.9721260

Moussa Dioubate, B. & Norhayate, W. (2022). *A Review of Cybersecurity Risk Management Framework in Malaysia Higher Education Institutions*.

Munther, M. N., Hashim, F., Latiff, N. A. A., Alezabi, K. A., & Liew, J. T. (2022). Scalable and secure SDN based ethernet architecture by suppressing broadcast traffic. *Egyptian Informatics Journal, 23*(1), 113–126. doi:10.1016/j.eij.2021.08.001

Munzner, T. (2014). *Visualisation analysis*.

Mushtaq, M., Akram, A., Bhatti, M. K., Chaudhry, M., Lapotre, V., & Gogniat, G. (2018, June). Night-watch: A cache-based side-channel intrusion detector using hardware performance counters. In *Proceedings of the 7th International Workshop on Hardware and Architectural Support for Security and Privacy* (pp. 1-8). ACM. 10.1145/3214292.3214293

Mushtaq, M., Benoit, P., & Farooq, U. (2020, October). Challenges of using performance counters in security against side-channel leakage. In *5th International Conference on Cyber-Technologies and Cyber-Systems (CYBER 2020)*. ACM.

Nakamoto, S. (2008). *Bitcoin: A peer-to-peer electronic cash system. Decentralized business review*. Academic Press.

National Institute of Standards and Technology. (2018). *A Tool for Improving Privacy through Enterprise Risk Management*. Récupéré sur NIST Privacy Framework: https://www.nist.gov/system/files/documents/2019/01/16/NIST-Privacy-Framework-1-16-19.pdf

National Small Business Association. (2017). *Small Business Taxation Survey*. Récupéré sur https://www.nsba.net/wp-content/uploads/2017/10/2017-Taxation-Survey.pdf

Nissenbaum, H. (2004). Hackers and the contested ontology of cyberspace. *New Media & Society*, *6*(2), 195–217. doi:10.1177/1461444804041445

NIST. (2018). Cybersecurity Framework. NIST. https://www.nist.gov/cyberframework

NIST. (n.d.a). *Cybersecurity Framework*. NIST.

NIST. (n.d.b). *800-53 Risk Management Framework*. NIST.

Nodeland, B., & Morris, R. (2020). A test of social learning theory and self-control on cyber offending. *Deviant Behavior*, *41*(1), 41–56. doi:10.1080/01639625.2018.1519135

Nolan, D. (2013). Varying the standard of care in Negligence. *The Cambridge Law Journal*, *72*(3), 651–688. doi:10.1017/S0008197313000731

Noor, M. A., Khanum, S., Anwar, T., & Ansari, M. (2021). A Holistic View on Blockchain and Its Issues. In H. Patel & G. S. Thakur (Eds.), *Blockchain Applications in IoT Security* (pp. 23–24). IGI Global. doi:10.4018/978-1-7998-2414-5.ch002

NVIDIA. (2021). *NVIDIA Tegra Linux Driver Package Development Guide*. NVIDIA. https://developer.nvidia.com/embedded/dlc/tegra-linux-driver-package-development-guide

Oltramari, A., & Kott, A. (2018). Towards a reconceptualisation of cyber risk: An empirical and ontological study. *Journal of Information Warfare*, *17*(1).

Omotosho, A., Welearegai, G. B., & Hammer, C. (2022, April). Detecting return-oriented programming on firmware-only embedded devices using hardware performance counters. In *Proceedings of the 37th ACM/SIGAPP Symposium on Applied Computing* (pp. 510-519). IEEE. 10.1145/3477314.3507108

Oracle. (2022). *Performance Analysis Guide*. Oracle Solaris 11.4 https://docs.oracle.com/en/operating-systems/solaris/solaris-11-4/perf-anal-guide/

Owen, D. G. (2007). The Five Elements of Negligence. *Hofstra Law Review*, *35*(4), 1–16.

Oyetunde, B. (2023). *7 GovTech trends to watch out for in 2023*. e-Estonia. https://e-estonia.com/7-govtech-trends-to-watch-out-for-in-2023/

Oz, H., Aris, A., Levi, A., & Uluagac, A. S. (2022). A survey on Ransomware: Evolution, taxonomy, and defense solutions. *ACM Computing Surveys*, *54*(11s), 1–37. doi:10.1145/3514229

Pabian, S., De Backer, C. J. S., & Vandebosch, H. (2015). *Dark triad* personality traits and adolescent cyber-aggression. *Personality and Individual Differences*, *75*, 41–46. doi:10.1016/j.paid.2014.11.015

Paik, J. Y., Choi, J. H., Jin, R., Wang, J., & Cho, E. S. (2018, October). A storage-level detection mechanism against crypto-ransomware. In *Proceedings of the 2018 ACM SIGSAC Conference on Computer and Communications Security* (pp. 2258-2260). 10.1145/3243734.3278491

Palmatier, R. W., Houston, M. B., & Hulland, J. (2018). Review articles: Purpose, process, and structure. *Journal of the Academy of Marketing Science*, *46*(1), 1–5. doi:10.100711747-017-0563-4

Pan, Z., Sheldon, J., & Mishra, P. (2022). Hardware-assisted malware detection and localization using explainable machine learning. *IEEE Transactions on Computers*, *71*(12), 3308–3321. doi:10.1109/TC.2022.3150573

Papp, D., Ma, Z., & Buttyan, L. (2015, July). Embedded systems security: Threats, vulnerabilities, and attack taxonomy. In *2015 13th Annual Conference on Privacy, Security and Trust (PST)* (pp. 145-152). IEEE.

Paquet-Clouston, M., Haslhofer, B., & Dupont, B. (2019). Ransomware payments in the bitcoin ecosystem. *Journal of Cybersecurity*, *5*(1), tyz003. doi:10.1093/cybsec/tyz003

Pariser, E. (2011). *The Filter Bubble: What the Internet Is Hiding From You*. Penguin Press.

Park, J., Jung, Y., Won, J., Kang, M., Lee, S., & Kim, J. (2019, June). RansomBlocker: A low-overhead ransomware-proof SSD. In *Proceedings of the 56th Annual Design Automation Conference 2019* (pp. 1-6). Academic Press.

Pascariu, C., & Barbu, I. D. (2019, June). Ransomware Honeypot: Honeypot solution designed to detect a ransomware infection identify the ransomware family. In *2019 11th International Conference on Electronics, Computers and Artificial Intelligence (ECAI)* (pp. 1-4). IEEE.

Paulhus, D. L., & Williams, K. M. (2002). The *Dark triad* of personality: Narcissism, Machiavellianism, and psychopathy. *Journal of Research in Personality*, *36*(6), 556–563. doi:10.1016/S0092-6566(02)00505-6

Payne, B. K. (2020). Defining Cybercrime. In T. J. Holt & A. M. Bossler (Eds.), *The Palgrave Handbook of International Cybercrime and Cyberdeviance* (pp. 1–25). Palgrave Macmillan. doi:10.1007/978-3-319-78440-3_1

Payne, B. K., Hawkins, B., & Xin, C. (2019). Using labeling theory as a guide to examine the patterns, characteristics, and sanctions given to cybercrimes. *American Journal of Criminal Justice*, *44*(2), 230–247. doi:10.100712103-018-9457-3

Peacock, D. (2013). *From underground hacking to ethical hacking*. University of Northumbria at Newcastle.

Peffers, K., Tuunanen, T., Rothenberger, A., & Chatterjee, S. (2007). A design science research methodology for information systems research. *Journal of Management Information Systems*, *24*(3), 45–77. doi:10.2753/MIS0742-1222240302

PEGA. (n.d.). *RMF -Risk Management Framework*. PEGA.

Peno, M. and Bogucki, O. (2021). Principles of Criminal Liability from the Semiotic Point of View. *International Journal for the Semiotics of Law - Revue internationale de Sémiotique juridique*, *34*(3). doi:10.1007/s11196-020-09691-z

Pereira, F., & Matos, M. (2015). Ciberstalking entre adolescentes: Uma nova forma de assédio e perseguição? [Cyber-stalking among adolescents: A new form of harassment and stalking?]. *Psicologia, Saúde & Doenças*, *16*(1), 57–69. doi:10.15309/15psd160207

Pereira, F., & Matos, M. (2016). Cyberstalking victimization: What predicts fear among Portuguese adolescents? *European Journal on Criminal Policy and Research*, *22*(2), 253–270. doi:10.100710610-015-9285-7

Pereira, F., Spitzberg, B., & Matos, M. (2016). Cyber-harassment victimization in Portugal: Prevalence, fear and help-seeking among adolescents. *Computers in Human Behavior*, *62*, 136–146. doi:10.1016/j.chb.2016.03.039

Pereira-Kohatsu, J., Quijano-Sánchez, L., Liberatore, F., & Camacho-Collados, M. (2019). Detecting and Monitoring Hate Speech in Twitter. *Sensors (Basel)*, *19*(21), 1–37. doi:10.339019214654 PMID:31717760

Perrin, A. (2021). *Mobile Technology and Home Broadband 2021*. Pew Research Center. https://www.pewresearch.org/internet/2021/06/03/mobile-technology-and-home-broadband-2021/

Perrin, A., & Atske, S. (2021, March 26). *About three-in-ten U.S. adults say they are 'almost constantly' online*. Pew Research Center. https://www.pewresearch.org/fact-tank/2021/03/26/about-three-in-ten-u-s-adults-say-they-are-almost-constantly-online/

Plunkett, J. (2018). *The Duty of Care in Negligence* (1st ed.). Oxford and Portland Publisher.

Ponemon Institute. (2020). *The true cost of compliance with data protection regulations*. Récupéré sur https://www.ponemon.org/local/upload/file/True%20Cost%20of%20Compliance%20Report%20FINAL%201.pdf

Ponemon Institute. (2021). *The state of data protection and management: An international study*. Récupéré sur https://www.ibm.com/downloads/cas/3OYPV7ED

Ponte, C., & Batista, S. (2019). *EU Kids Online Portugal. Usos, competências, riscos e mediações da internet reportados por crianças e jovens (9-17 anos)* [EU Kids Online Portugal. Internet uses, skills, risks, and mediations reported by children and youth (9-17-years-old)]. EU Kids Online. Lisboa: Faculdade de Ciências Sociais e Humanas da Universidade Nova de Lisboa. http://pnl2027.gov.pt/np4/%7B$clientServletPath%7D/?newsId=676&fileName=relatoriofinaleukidsonline.pdf

Posick, C. (2013). The Overlap Between Offending and Victimization Among Adolescents: Results From the Second International Self-Report Delinquency Study. *Journal of Contemporary Criminal Justice*, *29*(1), 106–124. doi:10.1177/1043986212471250

Poston, H., & Bennett, K. (2018). *Certified Blockchain Security Professional (CBSP), Official Exam Study Guide*. Blockchain Training Alliance, Inc.

Pritchard, A. (1969). Statistical bibliography or bibliometrics? *The Journal of Documentation*, *25*(4), 348–349.

Privacy governance. (2020). *International Association of Privacy Professionals (IAPP)*. Retrieved from https://iapp.org/resources/article/privacy-governance-report-2020/

Pruden, A. A. (2022, July 16). *The difference between pseudonymity and anonymity: When zero is more*. Venture Beat. https://venturebeat.com/datadecisionmakers/the-difference-between-pseudonymity-and-anonymity-when-zero-is-more/

PwC. (2020). *Global Economic Crime and Fraud Survey*. Retrieved from https://www.pwc.com/gx/en/services/advisory/forensics/economic-crime-survey.html

Quaranta, R. (2020). *Blockchain Framework and Guidance*. Shuamburg: ISACA.

Rahim Saleh, A., Al-Nemera, G., Al-Otaibi, S., Tahir, R., & Alkhatib, M. (2021). *Making Honey Files Sweeter: SentryFS--A Service-Oriented Smart Ransomware Solution*. arXiv e-prints, arXiv-2108.

Rahman, A., Islam, M. J., Band, S. S., Muhammad, G., Hasan, K., & Tiwari, P. (2023, April). Rahman., A., Islam, Md.J., Band, S., Muhammad, G., Hasan, & K., Tiwari, P. (2015). Towards a blockchain SDN-based secure architecture for cloud computing in smart industrial IoT. *Digital Communications and Networks*, *9*(2), 411–421. Advance online publication. doi:10.1016/j.dcan.2022.11.003

Rahmani, H., Sahli, N., & Kammoun, F. (2009, August). Joint entropy analysis model for DDoS attack detection. In *2009 Fifth International Conference on Information Assurance and Security* (Vol. 2, pp. 267-271). IEEE. 10.1109/IAS.2009.298

Rajendran, G., & Nivash, R. (2019, July). Security in the Embedded System: Attacks and Countermeasures. *Proceedings of International Conference on Recent Trends in Computing, Communication & Networking Technologies (ICRTCCNT)*. 10.2139srn.3429857

Rajmohan, T., Nguyen, P. H., & Ferry, N. (2022). A decade of research on patterns and architectures for IoT security. *Cybersecurity*, *5*(1), 1–29. doi:10.118642400-021-00104-7

Rambus. (2023). *Security: Provisioning and Key Management*. Retrieved 15 February, 2023 from https://www.rambus.com/security/provisioning-and-key-management/

Ramirez, R. B. (2017). *Making cyber security interdisciplinary: Recommendations for a novel curriculum and terminology harmonisation* [Thesis]. Massachusetts Institute of Technology.

Ramirez, R., & Choucri, N. (2016). Improving interdisciplinary communication with standardised cyber security terminology: A literature review. *IEEE Access : Practical Innovations, Open Solutions*, *4*, 2216–2243. doi:10.1109/ACCESS.2016.2544381

Ranjan, P., & Vaish, A. (2021). Socio-technical attack approximation based on structural virality of information in social networks. *International Journal of Information Security and Privacy*, *15*(1), 153–172. doi:10.4018/IJISP.2021010108

Rastogi, S., & Bansal, D. (2022). A review on fake news detection 3 T's: Typology, time of detection, taxonomies. *International Journal of Information Security*, 1–36. PMID:36406145

Rea-Guaman, A. M., Mejía, J., San Feliu, T., & Calvo-Manzano, J. A. (2020). *AVARCIBER: A framework for assessing cybersecurity risks*. Clust. Comput.

Reichelmann, A., Hawdon, J., Costello, M., Ryan, J., Blaya, C., Llorent, V., Oksanen, A., Räsänen, P., & Zych, I. (2020). Hate knows no boundaries: Online hate in six nations. *Deviant Behavior*, *42*(9), 1100–1111. doi:10.1080/01639625.2020.1722337

Reiger, D., Kümpel, A., Wich, M., Kiening, T., & Groh, G. (2021). Assessing the extent and types of hate speech in fringe communities: A case study of alt-right communities on 8chan, 4chan, and Reddit. *Social Media + Society*, *7*(4), 1–14. doi:10.1177/20563051211052906

Retruster. (2021). *phishing and email security trends*. Récupéré sur https://www.retruster.com: https://www.retruster.com/blog/2021-phishing-and-email-security-trends

Reuters. (2022). *US Capitol riots: Six highlights from testimony released by the 6 January committee*. Retrieved on 15 March 2023 from https://indianexpress.com/article/explained/explained-global/us-capitol-riots-six-highlights-from-testimony-released-by-the-jan-6-committee-8352561/

Reyns, B. W., Henson, B., & Fisher, B. S. (2011). Being pursued online: Applying cyber lifestyle routine activities theory to cyberstalking victimization. *Criminal Justice and Behavior*, *38*(11), 1149–1169. doi:10.1177/0093854811421448

Richet, J. L. (2013). From Young *Hackers* to Crackers. *International Journal of Technology and Human Interaction*, *9*(3), 53–62. doi:10.4018/jthi.2013070104

Rogers, M. (1999). *Psychology of hackers: Steps toward a new taxonomy*. InfoWar. http://www.infowar.com

Rogers, M. K. (2001). *A social learning theory and moral disengagement analysis of criminal computer behavior: An exploratory study* [Doctoral dissertation].

Rogers, M. K. (2006). A two-dimensional circumplex approach to the development of a hacker taxonomy. *Digital Investigation*, *3*(2), 97–102. doi:10.1016/j.diin.2006.03.001

Rogers, M. K. (2010). The psyche of cybercriminals: A psycho-social perspective. In S. Ghosh & E. Turrini (Eds.), *Cybercrimes: A multidisciplinary analysis* (pp. 217–235). Springer Berlin Heidelberg.

Rogers, M. K., Seigfried, K., & Tidke, K. (2006a). Self-Reported Computer Criminal Behavior: A Psychological Analysis. *Digital Investigation*, 3, 116–120. doi:10.1016/j.diin.2006.06.002

Rogers, M., Smoak, N. D., & Liu, J. (2006). Self-reported deviant computer behavior: A big-5, moral choice, and manipulative exploitive behavior analysis. *Deviant Behavior*, 27(3), 245–268. doi:10.1080/01639620600605333

Roman, S., & Bertolotti, F. (2022). A master equation for power laws. *Royal Society Open Science*, 9(12), 1–11. doi:10.1098/rsos.220531 PMID:36483760

Ryan, M. (2021). Ransomware Revolution: the rise of a prodigious cyber threat. In Advances in information security. Springer Nature. doi:10.1007/978-3-030-66583-8

Sabahi, F. (2011) Cloud computing security threats and responses. *Communication Sofware and Networks (ICCSN), IEEE 3rd International Conference,* (pp. 245–249). IEEE.

Sahoo, K. S., Tripathy, B. K., Naik, K., Ramasubbareddy, S., Balusamy, B., Khari, M., & Burgos, D. (2020). An evolutionary SVM model for DDOS attack detection in software defined networks. *IEEE Access : Practical Innovations, Open Solutions*, 8, 132502–132513. doi:10.1109/ACCESS.2020.3009733

Salahdine, F., & Kaabouch, N. (2019). Social engineering attacks: A survey. *Future Internet*, 11(4), 89. doi:10.3390/fi11040089

Salehi, S., Shahriari, H., Ahmadian, M. M., & Tazik, L. (2018, August). A novel approach for detecting DGA-based ransomwares. In *2018 15th International ISC (Iranian Society of Cryptology) Conference on Information Security and Cryptology (ISCISC)* (pp. 1-7). IEEE

Saraiva, M., & Coelho, N. (2022). CyberSoc Implementation Plan. *2022 10th International Symposium on Digital Forensics and Security (ISDFS)* (pp. 1-6). IEEE. 10.1109/ISDFS55398.2022.9800819

Saraiva, M., & Mateus-Coelho, N. (2022). CyberSoc Framework a Systematic Review of the State-of-Art. *Procedia Computer Science*, 204, 961–972. doi:10.1016/j.procs.2022.08.117

Sayadi, H., Wang, H., Miari, T., Makrani, H. M., Aliasgari, M., Rafatirad, S., & Homayoun, H. (2020, August). Recent advancements in microarchitectural security: Review of machine learning countermeasures. In *2020 IEEE 63rd International Midwest Symposium on Circuits and Systems (MWSCAS)* (pp. 949-952). IEEE.

Sayadi, H., Patel, N., Sasan, A., Rafatirad, S., & Homayoun, H. (2018, June). Ensemble learning for effective run-time hardware-based malware detection: A comprehensive analysis and classification. In *Proceedings of the 55th Annual Design Automation Conference* (pp. 1-6). IEEE. 10.1145/3195970.3196047

Sayegh, E. (2023, February 21). Spotlight On APT10. *Forbes*. https://www.forbes.com/sites/emilsayegh/2023/02/21/spotlight-on-apt10/?sh=29a3b73f491e

Schell, B. H., & Holt, T. J. (2010). A profile of the demographics, psychological predispositions, and social/behavioral patterns of computer hacker insiders and outsiders. In T. J. Holt & B. H. Schell (Eds.), *Corporate hacking and technology-driven crime: Social dynamics and implications* (pp. 144–168). IGI Global.

Searchlogistics. (2023). *Cyber Security Market Analysis*. Retrieved on 15 March 2023, from https://www.searchlogistics.com/grow/statistics/ransomware-statistics/

Security, I. B. M. (2020). *Cost of a data breach report 2020.* Récupéré sur https://www.ibm.com: https://www.ibm.com/security/data-breach

Security, I. B. M. (2022). *Cost of a Data Breach Report 2022.* Retrieved 15 Januar, 2023 from https://www.ibm.com/downloads/cas/3R8N1DZJ

SecurityIntelligence. (2023). *Costa Rica State of Emergency Declared After Ransomware Attacks.* https://securityintelligence.com/news/costa-rica-state-emergency-ransomware/

Securityweek. (2023). *Ransomware Hit SCADA Systems at 3 Water Facilities in U.S.* https://www.securityweek.com/ransomware-hit-scada-systems-3-water-facilities-us/

Seebruck, R. (2015). A typology of hackers: Classifying cyber malfeasance using a weighted arc circumplex model. *Digital Investigation*, *14*, 36–45. doi:10.1016/j.diin.2015.07.002

Seigfried-Spellar, K. C., & Treadway, K. N. (2014). Differentiating *Hackers*, Identity Thieves, Cyberbullies, and Virus Writers by College Major and Individual Differences. *Deviant Behavior*, *35*(10), 782–803. doi:10.1080/01639625.2014.884333

Seigfried-Spellar, K. C., Villacís-Vukadinović, N., & Lynam, D. R. (2017). Computer criminal behavior is related to psychopathy and other antisocial behavior. *Journal of Criminal Justice*, *51*, 67–73. doi:10.1016/j.jcrimjus.2017.06.003

Shafagh, H., Hithnawi, A., Burkhalter, L., Fischli, P., & Duquennoy, S. (2017). Secure Sharing of Partially Homomorphic Encrypted IoT Data. *Proceedings of the 15th ACM Conference on Embedded Network Sensor Systems ACM SenSys'17.*

Sharma, T. K. (2022). *What Is KYC & How KYC On Blockchain Can Help?* Blockchain Council. https://www.blockchain-council.org/blockchain/what-is-kyc-how-kyc-on-blockchain-can-help/

SharmaR. (2007). Peeping into a Hacker's Mind: Can Criminological Theories Explain Hacking? SSRN, 1-20. doi:10.2139/ssrn.1000446

Shetty, A. (n.d.). *WhatsApp messenger records 10bn messages in a day.* Retrieved on 10 March 2023 from https://www.firstpost.com/tech/news-analysis/whatsapp-messenger-records-10bn-messages-in-a-day-3606703.html#:~:text=WhatsApp%20Messenger%2C%20the%20popular%20U.S.,10B%20total%20messages%20a%20day!

Shlomo, N. (2018). Statistical Disclosure Limitation: New Directions And Challenges. *The Journal of Privacy and Confidentiality*, *8*(1). Advance online publication. doi:10.29012/jpc.684

Shumba, C. (2021). *Solana says It is Back Up and Running after a Surge in Transactions caused the Network to Crash the Day Before.* Insider. https://markets.businessinsider.com/news/currencies/solana-crash-network-transaction-volume-sol-crypto-back-running-system-2021-9

Singh, R., Kumar, H., & Singla, R. K. (2015). An invasion detection system using network traffic profiling and online sequential extreme learning machine. *Expert Systems with Applications*, *42*(22), 8609–8624. doi:10.1016/j.eswa.2015.07.015

Skinner, W. F., & Fream, A. M. (1997). A social learning theory analysis of computer crime among college students. *Journal of Research in Crime and Delinquency*, *34*(4), 495–518. doi:10.1177/0022427897034004005

SmahelD.MachackovaH.MascheroniG.DedkovaL.StaksrudE.ÓlafssonK.HasebrinkU. (2020). *EU Kids Online 2020: Survey results from 19 countries.* EU Kids Online: The London School of Economics and Political Science. doi:10.21953/lse.47fdeqj01ofo

Smith, P. K. (2012). Cyberbullying and cyber aggression. In. S. R. Jimerson, A. B. Nickerson, M. J. Mayer, M. J. Furlong (Eds.), Handbook of school violence and school safety: International research and practice (pp. 93-103). New York: Routledge.

Smith, P. K., Mahdavi, J., Carvalho, M., Fisher, S., Russell, S., & Tippett, N. (2008). Cyberbullying: Its nature and impact in secondary school pupils. *Journal of Child Psychology and Psychiatry, and Allied Disciplines, 49*(4), 376–385. doi:10.1111/j.1469-7610.2007.01846.x PMID:18363945

Snyder, H. (2019). Literature review as a research methodology: An overview and guidelines. *Journal of Business Research, 104*(July), 333–339. doi:10.1016/j.jbusres.2019.07.039

Sobb, T., Turnbull, B., & Moustafa, N. (2020). Supply chain 4.0: A survey of cyber security challenges, solutions and future directions. *Electronics (Basel), 9*(11), 1864. doi:10.3390/electronics9111864

Sobers, R. (2021). *134 Cybersecurity Statistics and Trends for 2021*. Varonis. https://www.varonis.com/blog/cybersecurity-statistics/

Southern Poverty Law Center. (2020). *The Year in Hate & Extremism 2020*. https://www.splcenter.org/sites/default/files/yih_2020-21_final.pdf

Southern Poverty Law Center. (2021). *The Year in Hate & Extremism 2021*. https://www.splcenter.org/sites/default/files/splc-2021-year-in-hate-extremism-report.pdf?utm_source=web

Southey, S. (2018). *Medicalchain — The Future of Healthcare*. Retrieved March 28, 2023, from Medium: https://medium.com/medicalchain/medicalchain-the-future-of-healthcare-5b130cbba439

Spinellis, D. (2003). Reliable identification of bounded-length viruses is NP-complete. *IEEE Transactions on Information Theory, 49*(1), 280–284. doi:10.1109/TIT.2002.806137

SPIRION. (2020). *The California Consumer Privacy Act of 2018*. Retrieved from https://www.spirion.com/wp-content/uploads/2020/07/Spirion_CCPA_v3.pdf

Spitzberg, B. H., & Cupach, W. R. (2014). *The dark side of relationships pursuit. From attraction to obsession and stalking* (2nd ed.). Routledge. doi:10.4324/9780203805916

Spitzberg, B. H., & Hoobler, G. (2002). Cyberstalking and the technologies of interpersonal terrorism. *New Media & Society, 4*(1), 71–92. doi:10.1177/14614440222226271

Sridhar, S., Hahn, A., & Govindarasu, M. (2012). Cyber-physical system security for the electric power grid. *Proceedings of the IEEE, 100*(1), 210–224. doi:10.1109/JPROC.2011.2165269

Srinivas, T. A. & Manivannan, S. S. (2020). Preventing Collaborative Black Hole Attack in IoT Construction Using a CBHA–AODV Routing Protocol. *International Journal of Grid and High Performance Computing, 12*(2), 25-46. http://doi.org/ . 2020040102 doi:10.4018/IJGHPC

Statescoop. (2023). *Months after ransomware attack, Bernalillo County, N.M., adopts cybersecurity policy*. https://statescoop.com/bernalillo-county-cybersecurity-policy-ransomware/

Statista Research Department. (2022). *Blockchain and Cryptocurrency: Global Investments, 2021*. Statista. https://www.statista.com/statistics/1260400/global-investments-in-blockchain-cryptocurrency/

Steinmetz, K. F. (2016). Hacked: A radical approach to hacker culture and crime. New York University Press.

Steinmetz, K. F., Holt, T. J., & Holt, K. M. (2020). Decoding the binary: Reconsidering the hacker subculture through a gendered lens. *Deviant Behavior, 41*(8), 936–948. doi:10.1080/01639625.2019.1596460

Stevens, R. (2022). *Bitcoin Mixers: How Do They Work and Why Are They Used?* Coindesk. https://www.coindesk.com/learn/bitcoin-mixers-how-do-they-work-and-why-are-they-used/

Suler, J. (2004). The online disinhibition effect. *Cyberpsychology & Behavior*, 7(3), 321–326. doi:10.1089/1094931041291295 PMID:15257832

Sun, Y., Song, H., Jara, A. J., & Bie, R. (2016). *Internet of Things and Big Data Analytics for Smart and Connected Communities*. Available online: https://ieeexplore.ieee.org/stamp/stamp. jsp?tp=&arnumber=7406686

Sweeney, L. (2002). k-Anonymity: A Model for Protecting Privacy. *International Journal of Uncertainty, Fuzziness and Knowledge-based Systems*, 10(5), 557–570. doi:10.1142/S0218488502001648

Symantec. (2020). *Internet Security Treat report, volume 25*. Symante/docs. Récupéré sur Internet security threat report, volume 25. https://www.symantec.com/content/dam/symantec/docs/reports/istr-25-2020-en.pdf

Szpor, G., & Gryszczyńska, A. (2022). Hacking in the (cyber)space. *GIS Odyssey Journal*, 2(1), 141–152.

Tajfel, H., & Turner, J. C. (1979). An integrative theory of intergroup conflict. In W. G. Austin & S. Worchel (Eds.), *The social psychology of intergroup relations* (pp. 33–47). Brooks-Cole.

Tan, B., & Karri, R. (2020, August). Challenges and new directions for ai and hardware security. In *2020 IEEE 63rd International Midwest Symposium on Circuits and Systems (MWSCAS)* (pp. 277-280). IEEE. 10.1109/MWSCAS48704.2020.9184612

Tarcísio Marinho. (2023). *Ransomware encryption techniques*. https://medium.com/@tarcisioma/ransomware-encryption-techniques-696531d07bb9

Taylor, P. A. (1999). *Hackers: Crime and the digital sublime*. Routledge.

Taylor, P. A. (2001). Hacktivism: in search of lost ethics? In D. S. Wall (Ed.), *Crime and the Internet* (pp. 59–74). Routledge.

TechCrunch is part of the Yahoo family of brands. (2022). TechCrunch. https://techcrunch.com/2022/07/06/marriott-breach-again/

TechTarget. (2023). *No relief in sight for ransomware attacks on hospitals*. https://www.techtarget.com/searchsecurity/feature/No-relief-in-sight-for-ransomware-attacks-on-hospitals#:~:text=Cybersecurity%20vendor%20Emsisoft%20recorded%2025,68%20attacks%20on%20healthcare%20providers

Templ, M., Kanjala, C., & Siems, I. (2022). Privacy of Study Participants in Open-access Health and Demographic Surveillance System Data: Requirements Analysis for Data Anonymization. *JMIR Public Health and Surveillance*, 8(9), 1–18. doi:10.2196/34472 PMID:36053573

Templ, M., Kowarik, A., & Meindl, B. (2015). Statistical Disclosure Control for Micro-Data Using the R Package sdcMicro. *Journal of Statistical Software*, 67(4). Advance online publication. doi:10.18637/jss.v067.i04

Templ, M., & Meindl, B. (2008). Robust Statistics Meets SDC: New Disclosure Risk Measures for Continuous Microdata Masking. In Privacy in Statistical Databases. In *Lecture Notes in Computer Science* (Vol. 5262, pp. 177–189). Springer.

Thackray, H., McAlaney, J., Dogan, H. Z., Taylor, J., & Richardson, C. N. (2016). *Social Psychology: An under-used tool in Cybersecurity*. Proceedings of the 30th International BCS Human Computer Interaction Conference. IEEE. 10.14236/ewic/HCI2016.64

The Daily Swig. (2023). *Cyber-attack on Nvidia linked to Lapsus$ ransomware gang*. https://portswigger.net/daily-swig/cyber-attack-on-nvidia-linked-to-lapsus-ransomware-gang

Thomas, M. (2019). *13 IOT security companies you should know*. Bulitin. https://builtin.com/internet-things/iot-security-companies-startups

Thomas, D. (2002). *Hacker culture*. U of Minnesota Press.

Thomson Reuters. (2019). *Cost of compliance 2019: Financial services at a tipping point*. Récupéré sur https://www.thomsonreuters.com/content/dam/ewp-m/documents/corporates/cost-of-compliance/cost-of-compliance-2019.pdf

Thomson Reuters. (2023). *Ransomware attacks against healthcare organizations nearly doubled in 2021*. https://www.thomsonreuters.com/en-us/posts/investigation-fraud-and-risk/ransomware-attacks-against-healthcare/

Tinetti, F. G., & Méndez, M. (2014, March). An automated approach to hardware performance monitoring counters. In *2014 International Conference on Computational Science and Computational Intelligence* (Vol. 1, pp. 71-76). IEEE. 10.1109/CSCI.2014.19

Trappe, W., Howard, R., & Moore, R. S. (2015). Low-energy surveillance: Limits and opportunities in the internet of things. *IEEE Security and Privacy*, *13*(1), 14–21. doi:10.1109/MSP.2015.7

Turgeman-Goldschmidt, O. (2005). Hackers' Accounts: Hacking as a Social Entertainment. *Social Science Computer Review*, *23*(1), 8–23. doi:10.1177/0894439304271529

Turkle, S. (1984). The Second Self: Computers and the Human Spirit. Granada.

U., P., & Rajagopalan, N. (2020). Concept of Blockchain Technology and Its Emergence. In H. Patel, & G. S. Thakur (Eds.), *Blockchain Applications in IoT Security* (pp. 1-20). IGI Global. doi:10.4018/978-1-7998-2414-5.ch001

Uchendu, B., Nurse, J. R., Bada, M., & Furnell, S. (2021). Developing a cyber security culture: Current practices and future needs. *Computers & Security*, *109*, 102387. doi:10.1016/j.cose.2021.102387

ul Hassan, S. Z., & Ahmad, S. Z. (2021). The Importance of Ethical Hacking Tools and Techniques in Software Development Life Cycle. *International Journal, 10*(3).

University of York. (2023). *An introduction to cyber security and data protection*. Récupéré sur https://online.york.ac.uk/resources/introduction-to-cyber-security-data-protection/

Uzoho, P. (2021). *Nigeria: Terrorists, Kidnappers Demanding Ransom in Cryptocurrency, Moghalu Says*. Arise News. https://www.arise.tv/nigeria-terrorists-kidnappers-demanding-ransom-in-cryptocurrency-moghalu-says/

Vale, A., Matos, M., & Pereira, F. (2021). Ciberabuso nas relações de intimidade dos adolescentes: Um diálogo entre a Psicologia e a Criminologia [Cyber dating abuse among adolescents: A dialogue between Psychology and Criminology]. In I. S. Guedes & M. A. Gomes (Eds.), *Cibercriminalidade: Novos Desafios, Ofensas e Soluções* (pp. 119–129). Pactor-Edições de Ciências Sociais, Forenses e da Educação.

Vale, A., Pereira, F., Gonçalves, M., & Matos, M. (2018). Cyber-aggression in adolescence and internet parenting styles: A study with victims, perpetrators and victims-perpetrators. *Children and Youth Services Review*, *93*, 88–99. doi:10.1016/j.childyouth.2018.06.021

Vale, A., Pereira, F., & Matos, M. (2020). Adolescents digital dating abuse and cyberbullying. In S. Caridade & A. Dinis (Eds.), *Adolescent Dating Violence: Outcomes, Challenges, and Digital Tools* (pp. 89–112). Nova Science Publishers.

Vale, M., Pereira, F., Spitzberg, B. H., & Matos, M. (2022). Cyber-harassment victimization of Portuguese adolescents: A lifestyle-routine activities approach. *Behavioral Sciences & the Law*, *40*(5), 604–618. doi:10.1002/bsl.2596 PMID:36102898

Van Eck, N. J. & Waltman, L. (2014). Measuring scholarly impact. *Methods and Practice*, 285-320.

van Eck, N. J. (2011). *Methodological Advances in Bibliometric Mapping of Science*. Retrieved 10 March 2020 from https://repub.eur.nl/pub/26509/EPS2011247LIS9789058922915.pdf

Van Eck, N. J., & Waltman, L. (2023). *VOSviewer v. 1.16.19*. Centre for Science and Technology Studies, Leiden University. Retrieved 14 February 2023, from https://www.vosviewer.com

Van Eck, N. J., & Waltman, L. (2023). *VOSviewer Manual for VOSviewer version 1.6.19*. Univeristeit Leiden.

Van Geit, W., De Schutter, E., & Achard, P. (2008). Automated neuron model optimization techniques: A review. *Biological Cybernetics*, *99*(4-5), 241–251. doi:10.100700422-008-0257-6 PMID:19011918

Varjas, K., Talley, J., Meyers, J., Parris, L., & Cutts, H. (2010). High school students' perceptions of motivations for cyberbullying: An exploratory study. *The Western Journal of Emergency Medicine*, *11*(3), 269–273. PMID:20882148

Verizon. (2021). *Data Breach Investigations Report*. Author.

Vijayan, J. (2019, June 4). Carbanak attack: Two hours to total compromise. *Dark Reading*. https://www.darkreading.com/attacks-breaches/carbanak-attack-two-hours-to-total-compromise

Vinayakumar, R., Soman, K. P., Velan, K. S., & Ganorkar, S. (2017, September). Evaluating shallow and deep networks for ransomware detection and classification. In *2017 international conference on advances in computing, communications and informatics (ICACCI)* (pp. 259-265). IEEE.

Vogels, A. E. (2019, September 9). *Millennials stand out for their technology use, but older generations also embrace digital life*. Pew Research Center. https://www.pewresearch.org/fact-tank/2019/09/09/us-generations-technology-use/

Vogels, A. E., Gelles-Watnick, R., & Massarat, N. (2022). *Teens, Social Media, and Technology 2022*. Pew Research Center. https://www.pewresearch.org/internet/2022/08/10/teens-social-media-and-technology-2022/

Vogels, E. (2021). *The State of Online Harassment*. Pew Research Center. https://www.pewresearch.org/internet/2021/01/13/the-state-of-online-harassment/

Von Solms, R., & Van Niekerk, J. (2013). From information security to cyber security. *Computers & Security*, *38*, 97–102. doi:10.1016/j.cose.2013.04.004

Wachs, S., Costello, M., Wright, M. F., Flora, K., Daskalou, V., Maziridou, E., Kwon, Y., Na, E. Y., Sittichai, R., Biswal, R., Singh, R., Almendros, C., Gámez-Guadix, M., Görzig, A., & Hong, J. S. (2021a). "DNT LET'EM H8 U!": Applying the routine activity framework to understand cyberhate victimization among adolescents across eight countries. *Computers & Education*, *160*, 104026. doi:10.1016/j.compedu.2020.104026

Wachs, S., Mazzone, A., Milosevic, T., Wright, M. F., O'Higgins Norman, J., & Blaya, C. (2021b). Online correlates of cyberhate involvement among young people from ten european countries: An application of the routine activity and problem behaviour theory. *Computers in Human Behavior*, *123*(3), 106872. doi:10.1016/j.chb.2021.106872

Wachs, S., & Wright, M. F. (2018). Associations between bystanders and perpetrators of online hate: The moderating role of toxic online disinhibition. *International Journal of Environmental Research and Public Health*, *15*(9), 2030. doi:10.3390/ijerph15092030 PMID:30227666

Wachs, S., Wright, M. F., Sittichai, R., Singh, R., Biswal, R., Kim, E. M., Yang, S., Gámez-Guadix, M., Almendros, C., Flora, K., Daskalou, V., & Maziridou, E. (2019). Associations between witnessing and perpetrating online hate in eight countries: The buffering effects of problem-focused coping. *International Journal of Environmental Research and Public Health*, *16*(20), 3992. doi:10.3390/ijerph16203992 PMID:31635408

Wall, D. S. (2001). *Cybercrime and the Internet*. Routledge. doi:10.4324/9780203164501_chapter_1

Wall, D. S. (2007). Policing cybercrimes: Situating the public police in networks of security within cyberspace. *Police Practice and Research, 8*(2), 183–205. doi:10.1080/15614260701377729

Wall, D. S., & Williams, M. (2007). Policing diversity in the digital age: Maintaining order in virtual communities. *Criminology & Criminal Justice, 7*(4), 391–415. doi:10.1177/1748895807082064

Wallin, J. A. (2005). Bibliometric methods: Pitfalls and possibilities. *Basic & Clinical Pharmacology & Toxicology, 97*(5), 261–275. doi:10.1111/j.1742-7843.2005.pto_139.x PMID:16236137

Wang, H., Sayadi, H., Rafatirad, S., Sasan, A., & Homayoun, H. (2020, July). Scarf: Detecting side-channel attacks in real-time using low-level hardware features. In *2020 IEEE 26th International Symposium on On-Line Testing and Robust System Design (IOLTS)* (pp. 1-6). IEEE.

Wang, M., Zheng, K., Yang, Y., & Wang, X. (2020). An explainable machine learning framework for intrusion detection systems. *IEEE Access : Practical Innovations, Open Solutions, 8*, 73127–73141. doi:10.1109/ACCESS.2020.2988359

Wang, X., Konstantinou, C., Maniatakos, M., & Karri, R. (2015, November). Confirm: Detecting firmware modifications in embedded systems using hardware performance counters. In *2015 IEEE/ACM International Conference on Computer-Aided Design (ICCAD)* (pp. 544-551). IEEE. 10.1109/ICCAD.2015.7372617

Wang, Z., Liu, C., Qiu, J., Tian, Z., Cui, X., & Su, S. (2018). Automatically traceback RDP-based targeted ransomware attacks. *Wireless Communications and Mobile Computing, 2018*, 1–13.

Wang, Z., Wu, X., Liu, C., Liu, Q., & Zhang, J. (2018, June). RansomTracer: exploiting cyber deception for ransomware tracing. In *2018 IEEE Third International Conference on Data Science in Cyberspace (DSC)* (pp. 227-234). IEEE. 10.1109/DSC.2018.00040

Wang, Z., Zhu, H., Liu, P., & Sun, L. (2021). Social engineering in cybersecurity: A domain ontology and knowledge graph application examples. *Cybersecurity, 4*(1), 31. doi:10.118642400-021-00094-6

Wardle, C. (2018). The Need for Smarter Definitions and Practical, Timely Empirical Research on Information Disorder. *Digital Journalism (Abingdon, England), 6*(8), 951–963. doi:10.1080/21670811.2018.1502047

Wardle, C., & Derakhshan, H. (2017). *Information disorder: Toward an interdisciplinary framework for research and policy making*. Council of Europe. https://rm.coe.int/information-disorder-toward-an-interdisciplinary-framework-for-researc/168076277c

Weaver, V. M. (2013, April). Linux perf_event features and overhead. In The 2nd international workshop on performance analysis of workload optimized systems. *FastPath, 13*(5).

What is Advanced Persistent Threat ? (n.d.). IGI Global. https://www.igi-global.com/dictionary/advanced-persistent-threat/69860

Whiteblueocean. (2023). *Top 5 Ransomware Attacks of 2022*. https://www.whiteblueocean.com/newsroom/top-5-ransomware-attacks-of-2022/

Whiters, K. L. (2019). *A Psychosocial Behavioral Attribution Model: Examining the Relationship Between the "Dark Triad" and Cyber-Criminal Behaviors Impacting Social Networking Sites* [Unpublished doctoral dissertation, College of Engineering and Computing, Nova Southeastern University].

Wikipedia. (2020). *2020 Delhi riots*. Retrieved on 15 March 2023, from https://en.wikipedia.org/wiki/2020_Delhi_riots

Williams, P., Dutta, I. K., Daoud, H., & Bayoumi, M. (2022). A survey on security in internet of things with a focus on the impact of emerging technologies. *Internet of Things, 19*, 100564. doi:10.1016/j.iot.2022.100564

Windisch, S., Wiedlitzka, S., Olaghere, A., & Jenaway, E. (2022). Online interventions for reducing hate speech and cyberhate: A systematic review. *Campbell Systematic Reviews*, *18*(2), e1243. doi:10.1002/cl2.1243 PMID:36913206

Wolfe, T. (2023, August 9). *What You Need To Know About the SolarWinds Supply-Chain Attack*. SANS Institute. https://www.sans.org/blog/what-you-need-to-know-about-the-solarwinds-supply-chain-attack/

Woo, L. L., Zwolinski, M., & Halak, B. (2018, March). Early detection of system-level anomalous behaviour using hardware performance counters. In *2018 Design, Automation & Test in Europe Conference & Exhibition (DATE)*, (pp. 485-490). IEEE.

World Economic Forum. (2020). *The Global Risks Report*. Retrieved from https://www.weforum.org/reports/the-global-risks-report-2020

Wright, M. F., Wachs, S., & Gámez-Guadix, M. (2021). Jóvenes ante el ciberodio: El rol de la mediación parental y el apoyo familiar [Youths' coping with cyberhate: Roles of parental mediation and family support]. *Comunicar*, *67*, 21–33. doi:10.3916/C67-2021-02

Xin, Y., Kong, L., Liu, Z., Chen, Y., Li, Y., Zhu, H., Gao, M., Hou, H., & Wang, C. (2018). Machine learning and deep learning methods for cybersecurity. *IEEE Access : Practical Innovations, Open Solutions*, *6*, 35365–35381. doi:10.1109/ACCESS.2018.2836950

Xue, Y., Tang, T., & Liu, A. X. (2019). Large-scale feedforward neural network optimization by a self-adaptive strategy and parameter-based particle swarm optimization. *IEEE Access : Practical Innovations, Open Solutions*, *7*, 52473–52483. doi:10.1109/ACCESS.2019.2911530

Xu, Z., Hu, Q., & Zhang, C. (2013). Why computer talents become computer hackers. *Communications of the ACM*, *56*(4), 64–74. doi:10.1145/2436256.2436272

Yar, M. (2016). Online crime. In Oxford Research Encyclopedia of Criminology and Criminal Justice. (pp. 1-27). doi:10.1093/acrefore/9780190264079.013.112

Yar, M. (2005). The Novelty of 'Cybercrime': An Assessment in Light of Routine Activity Theory. *European Journal of Criminology*, *2*(4), 407–427. doi:10.1177/147737080556056

Yar, M. (2006). *Cybercrime and society*. Sage Publications. doi:10.4135/9781446212196

Yeoh, W., Huang, H., Lee, W. S., Al Jafari, F., & Mansson, R. (2021). *Simulated phishing attack and embedded training campaign*.

Yeoh, W., Wang, S., Popovic, A., & Chowdhury, N. (2022). A Systematic Synthesis of Critical Success Factors for Cybersecurity. *JCOSE*. doi:10.1016/j.cose.2022.102724

Young, R., & Zhang, L. (2005). Factors affecting illegal hacking behavior. *AMCIS*, 3258-3264.

Yu, M., Halak, B., & Zwolinski, M. (2019, July). Using hardware performance counters to detect control hijacking attacks. In *2019 IEEE 4th International Verification and Security Workshop (IVSW)* (pp. 1-6). IEEE. 10.1109/IVSW.2019.8854399

Zamani, R., & Afsahi, A. (2012, June). A study of hardware performance monitoring counter selection in power modeling of computing systems. In *2012 International Green Computing Conference (IGCC)* (pp. 1-10). IEEE. 10.1109/IGCC.2012.6322289

ZebPay. (2022). *Crypto DDoS Attacks: What, Why and How?* ZebPay. https://zebpay.com/blog/what-is-crypto-ddos-attack-and-how-to-prevent-it#:~:text=Even%20if%20a%20node%20in,creating%20thousands%20of%20spam%20transactions

Zetter, K. (2016, May 17). That insane, $81M Bangladesh bank heist? Here's what we know. *WIRED*. https://www.wired.com/2016/05/insane-81m-bangladesh-bank-heist-heres-know/

Zetter, K. (2023, May 2). SolarWinds: The untold story of the boldest Supply-Chain hack. *WIRED*. https://www.wired.com/story/the-untold-story-of-solarwinds-the-boldest-supply-chain-hack-ever/

Zhang, X., Dwarkadas, S., Folkmanis, G., & Shen, K. (2007, May). Processor hardware counter statistics as a first-class system resource. In HotOS.

Zhang, Z., Ning, H., Shi, F., Farha, F., Xu, Y., Xu, J., Zhang, F., & Choo, K. K. R. (2022). Artificial intelligence in cyber security: Research advances, challenges, and opportunities. *Artificial Intelligence Review*, *55*(2), 1–25. doi:10.100710462-021-09976-0

Zhou, Y., & Feng, D. (2005). Side-channel attacks: Ten years after its publication and the impacts on cryptographic module security testing. *Cryptology ePrint Archive*.

Zhou, B., Gupta, A., Jahanshahi, R., Egele, M., & Joshi, A. (2018, May). Hardware performance counters can detect malware: Myth or fact? In *Proceedings of the 2018 on Asia conference on computer and communications security* (pp. 457-468). IEEE. 10.1145/3196494.3196515

Zhou, B., Gupta, A., Jahanshahi, R., Egele, M., & Joshi, A. (2021). A cautionary tale about detecting malware using hardware performance counters and machine learning. *IEEE Design & Test*, *38*(3), 39–50. doi:10.1109/MDAT.2021.3063338

Zhou, W., Jiang, X., Luo, Q., Guo, B., Sun, X., Sun, F., & Meng, L. (2022, December). AQROM: A quality of service aware routing optimization mechanism based on asynchronous advantage actor-critic in software-defined networks. *Digital Communications and Networks*. doi:10.1016/j.dcan.2022.11.016

Zhou, Y., Luo, Y., Obaidat, M. S., Vijayakumar, P., & Wang, X. (2021). PAMI-anonymous password authentication protocol for medical internet of things. *IEEE Global Communications Conference (GLOBECOM)*. IEEE. 10.1109/GLOBECOM46510.2021.9685900

Zscaler. (2023). *Cyber-Deception Based Solution*. https://www.zscaler.com/resources/security-terms-glossary/what-is-deception-technology

About the Contributors

Nuno Mateus-Coelho is a Professor of Information Security, Systems Intrusion, Cloud Security, and Data Privacy at Lusófona University, Porto, Portugal. He holds a BEng. in Information Systems Engineering, a MEng. in Computer Sciences Engineering from the Polytechnic of Porto - School of Engineering (ISEP) in the field and subject of cloud security and secure operating systems, and a DSc. Summa Cum Laude in Computer Sciences from the University of Trás-os-Montes and Alto Douro (UTAD) in the field and subject of information security and secure operating systems. He is an Expert Accredited by the European Commission on R&I projects in the Horizon 2020, COSME, and CEF programs in information technologies. He is a TED, IEEE, Websummit, and CNN Portugal Keynote Speaker, CEO & Founder of NRMC.PT. Since 2022, he has been the Chief-Editor of ARIS2 - Advanced Research on Information Systems Security, an International Journal, and Director of LAPI2S - Laboratory of Privacy and Information Systems Security.

Maria Manuela Cruz-Cunha is a Full Professor in the School of Technology at the Polytechnic Institute of Cavado and Ave, Portugal. She holds a Dipl. Eng. (5 years) in the field of Systems and Informatics Engineering, an M.Sci. in the field of Computer Integrated Manufacturing, a Dr.Sci in of Production Systems Engineering and Habilitation in Informatics Engineering. She teaches subjects related with Information Systems, Information Technologies and Organizational Models to undergraduate and post-graduate studies. She has authored and edited 28 books and her work appears in 200 papers published in journals, book chapters and conference proceedings. She is founder and conference chair of the "CENTERIS – Conference on ENTERprise Information Systems", "ViNOrg – Conference on Virtual and Networked Organizations Emergent Technologies and Tools" and "SeGAH – Serious Games and Applications for Health". She is the editor-in-chief of the "International Journal of Web Portals" and serves as associate editor of some journals.

* * *

Jude Ameh is currently undergoing PhD research in in Sheffield Hallam. He was previously a lecturer in the Cyber Security Department of Air Force Institute of Technology (AFIT), Kaduna. He is a cyber security professional with over 10 years' experience, he has worked within the financial services and information security audit and control space within leading-edge organizations. He is highly qualified and skilled in information systems security and controls, information systems audit, and computer security research.

Karima Belmabrouk received her engineering degree in 1998 and her magister degree in 2006 from the University of Science and Technology of Oran, USTO-MB. Since December 2006, she is an assistant professor and researcher in the computer science department of the USTO-MB. Her research interests are based on agent-based modeling and simulation, Web services composition, ontology and semantic Web as well as planning in artificial intelligence.

Akashdeep Bhardwaj achieved his PhD from University of Petroleum & Energy Studies (UPES), Post Graduate Diploma in Management (PGDM), Engineering graduate in Computer Science. He has worked as Head of Cyber Security Operations and currently is a Professor in a leading university in India. He has over 24 year experience working as an Enterprise Risk and Resilience and Information Security and Technology professional for various global multinationals.

Samo Bobek is a professor of E-business and Information Management at School of Economics and Business at University Maribor and a head of the E-business department. His research areas are E-business and Digitalization, IT/IS Governance and Information management, Business solutions implementation and business process reengineering, Digital transformation.

Sheryl Brahnam received her PhD in Computer Science at the Graduate Center of the City of New York in 2002. She is currently a professor at Missouri State University in the Department of Information Technology & Cybersecurity. She has approximately two hundred publications, with an h-index of 35 and an i10-index of 94. She is interested in many areas of computer science.

Maria Canudo is attending the Master's degree in Criminology at Faculty of Law, University of Porto, with a Bachelor's degree in Criminology from the same institution. Currently focused on cyber-crime, hacking, and personality theories.

Satya Ranjan Dash is an Associate Professor in School of Computer Applications, KIIT University, Bhubaneswar, India. He received his MCA degree from Jorhat Engineering College, Dibrugarh University, Assam and M.Tech. degree in Computer Science from Utkal University, Odisha. He received his Ph.D. in Computer Science from Utkal University, Bhubaneswar, Odisha in 2015. His research interest includes Machine Learning, Bioinformatics and Cloud Computing.

Michelangelo De Bonis has a Degree in Computer Engineering at the Polytechnic of Turin (2000); IEEE member; Cisco certified Instructor; Computer Science teacher in high-school; Consultant on networks and information security; Computer Science professor in Department of Agriculture, Food, Natural resources and Engineering at University of Foggia, Italy.

Baswaraj Gadgay is working as Department of Electronics and Communication Engineering, Visvesvaraya Technological University, Kalaburagi, Karnataka, India.

Crescenzio Gallo received his degree in Computer Science from the University of Bari, Italy, in 1978 and MSc in Information Science and Technology from the University of Milan, Italy, in 2007. During 1978-1980, he stayed at the Institute of Computer Science (ISI), University of Bari, Italy as a Research Assistant in Information Systems, and with Telespazio, Rome, Italy participating to Landsat satellite projects of European Space Agency (ESA). From 1993 to 2003 he has been a contract professor of Computer Science, and since January 2004 he is an Assistant Professor at the University of Foggia, Italy, Faculty of Medicine. His primary research interests include data analysis, artificial intelligence and bioinformatics.

Inês Guedes is graduated, Master and PhD in Criminology from the Faculty of Law of the University of Porto (FDUP). Assistant Professor at the same institution, teaching in the Bachelor's and Master's Degree in Criminology. She is a founding and integrated member of the The Interdisciplinary Research Centre on Crime, Justice and Security (CJS) of FDUP and a collaborating member of the Center for Legal, Economic and Environmental Studies (CEJEA) of University of Lusiada- Norte. She is part of the Board of Directors of the International Association of Portuguese Language of Criminology. She recently edited the book Cybercrime: new challenges, offenses and solutions, published by Editora Pactor, and, in recent years, has published and given national and international conferences in the fields of fear of crime and cybercrime.

Poonam Jadhav is an experienced educator in the field of computer engineering. With over 15 years of teaching experience, she has dedicated her career to guiding students towards academic and professional success. Poonam began her academic journey with a Bachelor's degree in Computer Engineering from University of Mumbai. She went on to pursue a Master's degree in Computer Engineering from University of Mumbai where she focused on Image Processing applications. In 2021Poonam joined the faculty at SIES Graduate School of Technology as an Assistant Professor in the Computer Engineering department. Over the past 15 years she has taught a wide range of courses, including Object Oriented Programming, Social media analytics, Computer Graphics, Linux and network configuration, Information Security, Python Programming, Software Engineering. She is known for interactive teaching style, innovative approaches. In addition to her teaching responsibilities, Poonam has started journey as researcher in the field of Bigdata Privacy. She has published one articles in top-tier academic journal. Overall, Poonam is a dedicated educator and researcher who has made significant contributions to the field of computer engineering. Her passion for teaching and learning is evident in her interactions with students and colleagues alike, and she continues to inspire and motivate those around her.

Paulo Maciel graduated in Electronic Engineering in 1987, and received his MSc and PhD degrees in Electronic Engineering and Computer Science from Univesidade Federal de Pernambuco, respectively. He was faculty member of the Electric Engineering Department of Universidade de Pernambuco from 1989 to 2003. Since 2001 he has been a member of the Informatics Center of Universidade Federal de Pernambuco, where he is currently Associate Professor. He is research member of the Brazilian research council (CNPq) and IEEE member. His research interests include Petri nets, formal models, performance and dependability evaluation, encompassing manufacturing, embedded, computational and communication systems as well as power consumption analysis.

Samuel Moreira, Ph.D. in Criminology, is an Invited Assistant Professor at the Faculty of Law, University of Porto, and at the Faculty of Law, University Lusíada – North (Porto), Portugal. He is a researcher affiliated with the research centers: CJS (Interdisciplinary Research Center on Crime, Justice, and Security), Faculty of Law, University of Porto; and CEJEA (Center for Juridical, Economic, and Environmental Studies), Faculty of Law, University Lusíada – North (Porto). His research interests include security, policing, and cybercrime, having authored/co-authored several national and international publications in these fields.

Joshua Ojo Nehinbe obtained Ph.D. in Computer Science from the University of Essex, UK in 2011 and M.Sc. in Computer Science (with research) from the University of Agriculture, Abeokuta in Nigeria in 2004. He has worked in the banking sector as a Software engineer; Globus support specialist, Head of IT and auditor of Information Systems. He also had cognate experience in IT consultancy with local and international firms. Joshua Nehinbe teaches Undergraduates and Post graduates students in the areas of Cyber security and forensics, database design and management, software engineering, Leading E-Strategy and data mining. He has published over 40 reputable journal papers, conference papers and co-authored book chapters with foreign experts in the areas of best industrial practices, security and forensics in Cyber Physical Systems. He is a professional member of the Institute of Electrical and Electronics Engineers (IEEE), British Computer Society (BCS), British Academy of Forensic Sciences (BAFS) and Nigeria Computer Society (NCS).

Michele Perilli has a Degree in Computer Science (1987); Degree in Information Technology (2005); Degree in TLC Technology (2006). Technical Manager in Telecom Italia S.p.A. (Italian TLC Carrier) from 1988 to 2001. Computer Science Engineering Consulting since 2001. Computer Science Professor at University of Foggia since 2006.

Pablo Pessoa graduated in Computer Network Technology from Faculdade Maurício de Nassau in 2014 and specialized in Computer Network Security from Faculdade Estácio (2017). He completed his Master's in Computer Science in 2021 and is currently a Ph.D. student at the Computer Science Center (CIn) of the Federal University of Pernambuco (UFPE) under the guidance of Professor Paulo Maciel. He completed his professional training in Digital Game Development at the Centro de Estudos e Sistemas Avançados do Recife (CESAR) in 2009. He has experience in information technology, network infrastructure management, and information security. He is interested in performance, reliability, availability, hardware performance counters, and system information security.

Carolina Roque has a Bachelor's degree in Criminology from Faculty of Law, University of Porto. Attending the Master's degree in Criminology at Faculty of Law, University of Porto. Currently conducting an quantitative study focused on the relationship between hacking, self-control and social learning components, which is the subject of the master thesis. Focused on topics like: cybercrime, cybersecurity, hacking and criminological theories.

Henrique S. Mamede is Assistant Professor with Habilitation Universidade Aberta Sciences and Technology Department.

Simona Sternad Zabukovšek is an associate professor of E-business and Information Management at the Faculty of Economics and Business at the University of Maribor. Her research areas include business process reengineering (BPR), business information solutions (ERP, CRM) with a focus on comparative analysis in different cultures, e-business with a focus on e-business models, concepts of e-learning vs. blended learning and implementation of them in organizations, user acceptance of IT/IS, digital transformation and information management.

Dauda Sule is currently a lecturer in the Cyber Security Department of Air Force Institute of Technology (AFIT), Kaduna. He was previously Marketing Executive of GGL Risk and Strategic Consulting - a training and consulting firm that is into organizing trainings and seminars pertaining to information and physical management, security, assurance and control; finance; fraud prevention and detection; and anti-money laundering. He is also an author and beta tester for eForensics Magazine and has written articles for the journal as well as the ISACA Journal and some cyber security blogs. He has delivered training workshops related to Digital Forensics and eDiscovery for eForensics Magazine among others.

Suleiman Usman is currently a lecturer with the Air Force institute of Technology, Kaduna, Nigeria and is running a PhD research with the Nigerian Defense Academy. He has published various articles in distinguished journals and has over five years experience lecturing in Computer Science and Cyber Security.

Abhishek Vaish is working at Indian Institute of Information Technology since 2007 and having rich experience in the field of Cyber Security. He started his career in the field of Cyber security after completing MS in Cyber Law and Information Security and then joined Wipro, Ltd as an Consultant in the field of Information Security. Presently, he is working as a faculty member in the department of IT of IIIT-Allahabad and actively teaching course in the field of Cyber security.

Maria Vale is a Master's and PhD student in Applied Psychology at the School of Psychology, University of Minho in Braga, Portugal, with a PhD grant funded by the Portuguese Foundation for Science and Technology under the POCH/FSE Program (Ref: 2021.07545.BD). Psychologist with prior experience in the Child and Youth Protection Commission. Her research interests include technology-facilitated violence and abuse (e.g., dating abuse, harassment, stalking, sexual abuse, bullying, and hate speech). She has been involved in research projects and has authored/co-authored national and international publications in these fields.

Marlene Matos has a PhD in Justice Psychology. Associate Professor and Coordinator of the Victimology and Justice Law Research Group, at the School of Psychology, University of Minho, Braga, Portugal. Psychotherapist, forensic expert, and supervisor at the university clinic (APSI), University of Minho, Braga, Portugal. Her research interest includes Psychology, Justice Psychology, Victimology (e.g., intimate partner violence, domestic violence, human trafficking, technology-facilitated abuse and violence), Criminology (e.g., intimate homicide, criminal proceedings), Psychotherapy (e.g., change efficacy and process), Forensic psychology evaluation (e.g., coparental conflict, post-divorce litigation, regulation of parental responsibility, parental dispute, resistance to parent visits). Principal researcher, scientific coordinator and consultant of several projects financed by Portuguese Foundation for Science and Technology, Portuguese government and also EEA Grants. She has authored/co-authored several national and international publications in these fields.

Index

A

Advanced Persistent Threats 17-18, 22
Anomalies 12, 111, 116, 118-119, 182
Anonymization 228, 230, 234, 238, 240
Application Programming Interface (API) 13, 15
Artificial Intelligence (AI) 1-2, 11-12, 15, 31, 46-47,
    114, 118, 120, 122, 156, 168, 196, 227

B

Bitcoins 248, 252, 257, 259
Blockchain 12, 51-58, 60-65, 68-69, 171, 176
Blockchain Bridge 68
Border Gateway Protocol (BGP) 61, 69

C

Central Bank Digital Currency (CBDC) 69
CIA Triad 55-56, 69
Cloud Computing 1-3, 5-6, 12-13, 15-16, 173, 175, 262
Collection 58, 110-111, 118, 120-121, 159, 169, 199,
    218, 227, 229
Community Cloud 6, 15
Contextual Aspects 83, 96
Countermeasures 40, 47, 111
Criminal Liability 70-71, 73, 75-76, 78-81
Criminal Prosecution 81
Cryptocurrency 52-53, 58, 62-63, 69, 248, 252
Cyber Criminals 52, 198-200, 205, 224, 249, 255
Cyberattacks 17-20, 22-25, 27, 29, 31, 39, 52, 64, 91,
    108-109, 112, 114, 116-118, 120, 122, 156-158,
    171, 173, 176, 181, 199-200, 212-213, 216-217,
    255
Cybercrime 22, 52, 71, 73-75, 84-86, 95, 97, 99, 173,
    175, 196, 198-199, 202, 224
Cyberhate 130, 132-142

D

Cybersecurity 12-13, 17-18, 22, 26-29, 31-46, 52, 94,
    99, 107-109, 112, 114-118, 120, 122, 166-178,
    181, 187, 198-200, 205, 210, 216, 221-222, 224,
    253

Data Privacy Measures 198-200, 213, 217, 224
Decentralized Finance (DeFi) 51, 64, 69
Disclosure 36, 198-199, 220, 227-233, 235-236, 240,
    242-243, 245
Distributed Denial of Service (DDoS) Attacks 13, 16,
    52, 56, 196
Distributed Ledger Technology (DLT) 51, 64, 68-69

F

Fake News Detection 197

G

Goodwill 57, 64, 257-259

H

Hack 25, 84-87, 100
Hate Speech Detection 197
Hybrid Cloud 5-6, 16

I

Immutability 51, 53-56, 58-59, 69
Infrastructure as a Service (IaaS) 1-2, 4, 16
Internet of Things (IoT) 114, 170-171, 173, 175, 181,
    197, 254, 262
Intrusion Detection 12-13, 16-18, 24, 35, 75-76, 109,
    119, 151, 171, 176, 181, 183-184, 199, 248

Intrusion Detection System (IDS) 16, 75
Intrusion Prevention System (IPS) 16

K

K-Anonymity 236-238
Know Your Customer (KYC) 58, 69

L

L-Diversity 236-238
Link Failure 153, 161-163

M

Machine Learning (ML) 12, 46, 114-115, 118, 120-
    121, 171-172, 176, 178-179, 181, 184, 191, 197,
    227, 240, 245
Malware 13, 18, 20-21, 23, 28, 35, 42, 52, 57, 61-62, 84,
    87, 89, 91, 94, 107, 115-118, 120-121, 151, 156,
    166-167, 173, 175-176, 184-186, 191, 197-198,
    202, 205, 224, 247-248, 251, 253, 255, 257, 262
Malware Detection 117, 121, 176, 184, 186, 197
Microdata 228, 230

N

Negligence 56, 70-73, 75, 78-81
Network Function Virtualization (NFV) 8, 16
Network Security 16, 40, 171, 173, 175, 181, 184, 188,
    197-199, 211, 220
Network Virtualization 7, 16

P

Performance Counters 108-112, 115-116, 119, 122
Perpetration 130, 132-133, 136-137, 139-140
Personality Traits 97, 99-100
Phishing 43, 62, 87, 89, 100, 107, 112, 116, 120, 198,
    201, 210, 216, 224, 251, 255
Platform as a Service (PaaS) 1-3, 16
Privacy Regulations 217, 221, 223-224
Private Cloud 5-6, 16
Pseudonymity 55, 69
Public Cloud 4, 16

Q

Quality of Service (QoS) 11, 16

R

RaaS 247-248, 250, 255-262
Ransomware 52, 56, 62, 112, 121, 158, 167, 175, 198,
    202, 204, 212, 247-251, 253-262
Re-Identification 228, 230-232, 234-235, 243, 245

S

Sensitive Attribute 232-233, 237-238
Session Hijacking 87, 107
Sinister 27, 95
Social Engineering 17-21, 35, 62, 85, 100, 107, 112,
    167, 175, 198, 224, 251, 255
Social Media 100, 112, 130-131, 138, 166, 177-179,
    190-191, 197, 257-258
Software as a Service (SaaS) 1-3, 16
Software Defined Network (SDN) 8, 16
Sophisticated 3, 12, 17-25, 27-29, 52, 54, 86-87, 89,
    92, 114, 117, 120, 167, 224, 231
SQL Injection 87, 107, 116
Stealth 184

T

Tactics 17, 19, 22, 24, 27, 52, 152, 200, 205, 224,
    256, 258
T-Closeness 236, 238
Trolling 99, 107
Typologies 83-84, 89-93, 101

V

Victimization 130, 132-133, 136-140, 142
Virtual Machine (VM) 13, 16
Virtualization 1-2, 6-8, 13, 16, 61, 191

W

Wireless Sensor Networks (WSNs) 70-76, 78-81

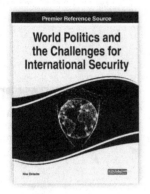

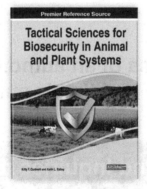

Ensure Quality Research is Introduced to the Academic Community

Become an Evaluator for IGI Global Authored Book Projects

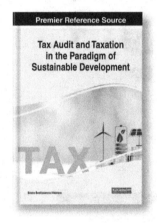

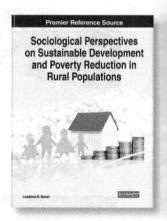

The overall success of an authored book project is dependent on quality and timely manuscript evaluations.

Applications and Inquiries may be sent to:
development@igi-global.com

Applicants must have a doctorate (or equivalent degree) as well as publishing, research, and reviewing experience. Authored Book Evaluators are appointed for one-year terms and are expected to complete at least three evaluations per term. Upon successful completion of this term, evaluators can be considered for an additional term.

If you have a colleague that may be interested in this opportunity, we encourage you to share this information with them.

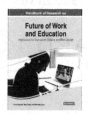

Printed in the United States
by Baker & Taylor Publisher Services